20

Lectures of the Arya

Albert Pike

FOREWORD.

This work as well as others from the pen of Albert Pike has been transcribed and prepared for the printer by Colonel M. W. Wood, 33°, Active Member of the Supreme Council, A. & A. S. Rite, S. J., U. S. A., a labor of love because of the close intimacy that existed between General Pike and Colonel Wood. It has been a very great task, and probably no one else could have done it so well. No words can adequately express the value of it. To Colonel Wood there must have come, through his unique labor, the satisfaction and the reward that he has made a contribution towards the Pike collection which is beyond price.

Of the present work, the *Lectures of the Arya*, Colonel Wood said:

"It is the grandest thing that he (Pike) ever wrote, being in a way a conspectus and resumé of all else that he had written on these topics."

Of the work, Pike himself said:

"Oldest literary monuments and records of human thought in the world and as the source and origin of the great philosophical doctrines of the world, but also, and far more, because they make known to us a sublime theosophy and purely philosophic faith believed in and understood by men of our own blood and lineage at a very remote period when they dwelt near the cradle of the race."

This work, occupying an unusual place, has long remained unpublished. In publishing it (and others) the Supreme Council has added to the literary wealth of the world. Pike knew that our language, philosophy, religions, are traceable to the Aryans, Indo and Irano, and he has presented to our view, through the *Lectures*, the emigration and last division of the race, their country, character and manners, their language, their deities and legends. That he was familiar with the work of scholars in many languages is shown by these books, which also show him to have been among the greatest of Orientalists; and that he literally sipped nectar with the gods, his poems will show.

As will be realized, this work, *Lectures of the Arya*, and the other two so far published (*Irano-Aryan Faith and Doctrine* as contained in the *Zend-Avesta* and *Indo-Aryan Deities and Worship* as contained in *Rig-Veda*) are not books to be read in a superficial or hasty manner.

As transcriber of these works, Colonel Wood referred to Pike's detestation of plagiarism, and how he, the transcriber, may have failed occasionally to give due credit for authorship in the multiplicity of quotations, extracts, paraphrases and commentaries; and that he had attempted to transcribe faithfully this great work, filled with reverence for the memory of his gifted friend, and desired that all sins in this category be ascribed to him, and not to Pike.

April, 1930.

H. W. WITCOVER, 33°,
Secretary General.

LECTURE ONE

THE ARYAN RACE

COUNTRY, CHARACTER AND MANNERS
OF THE INDO-ARYANS

Lepsius fixes the date of the reign of Menes, the great monarch of Egypt, at 3,893, and Bunsen at 3,643 years before Christ. The common chronology makes Nimrod or Belûs to have lived about 2,500, and Abraham to have been born about 2,000 years before our era.

The country formerly known as Sogdiana, and afterwards as Toorkhistan, between the rivers Oxus and Jaxartes, which flow into the Caspian Sea and the Sea of Aral, north of the great range of the Hindu Kush (formerly the Paropamisus or Indian Caucasus, and west of the Bolor Tagh), is a long way from Greece, Rome, England and Norway.

Yet, from 7,000 to 10,000 years before Christ, there lived a people in that region, which, as the bees send off in the spring their successive swarms, poured out its streams of emigration all over Europe, and into India, Bactria, Media and Persia; everywhere conquering the indigenous races, and becoming the Celts of Spain, Britain and Ireland, the Northmen of Sweden, Norway and Denmark, the ancient Goths and modern Germans, the Sclavic and Lithuanian races, the Greeks and Romans, the Hindûs and the Medians and Persians.

You hardly utter a sentence of our English tongue, without speaking some word which was spoken in the same sense by that ancient people, ten thousand years ago or more, in the mountain-valleys which they first inhabited. You have their idiosyncrasies of thought, the same indelible characteristics of race; for you are their descendants. From them you have your excellencies and your faults, your energy, your vigor of intellect, your philosophical cast of thought, your indomitable resolution, your persistent pursuit of the object you desire to attain; from them the religious leaning and inclination of your minds; from them your social institutions and relations, and the foundation-stones of your laws, customs and habits; from them all your philosophical and religious doctrines.

They were white men, as we are, the superior race in intellect, in manliness, the governing race of the world, the conquering race of all other races.

They called themselves Ârya, the Âryans, the Warlike, or, some think, the Noble. They were the ancestors of the Greek and Roman heroes, as well as of the northern Vikings, and especially prided themselves upon that which we call manliness, the *virtus* of the Romans, who in that word and in *vir*, a "man," perpetuated, as we yet do in the words *virile* and *virtue*, the old Âryan word *vîr*, to "be valiant," whence their *vîra*, "heroic, hero" and *vîraya*, "manliness, courage, heroism."

I hope to be able to interest you, in this opening lecture, by making you acquainted, so far as it is known, with the ancient history of your heroic ancestors, and their final separation into what I prefer to call the Indo-Aryans and the Irano-Aryans, of which two races Time has spared for us the ancient and Holy Scriptures, known ordinarily as the *Rig-Veda* and the *Zend-Avesta*.

In the other lectures of the course, I shall consider what our modern languages and the Greek and Latin have by descent from the old Aryan, the age and history of the *Rig-Veda*, and the meaning of the Vedic Deities and Vedic hymns; the age and history of the various parts of the *Zend-Avesta*, and the doctrines and meaning of the Deities of the Bactrian king and soldier, Zarathustra, familiarly known to us as Zoroaster.

In all else I shall, in a measure, only repeat to you, with comments of my own, what has been written by the scholars and professors, Max Müller, Muir, Wilson, Spiegel, Bunsen, Haug, Rawlinson and others; but in regard to the meaning of the Vedic Deities and the philosophical conceptions embodied in them, and to the nature of ancient Gâthâs or odes of Zarathustra himself, and the ideas and philosophic notions embodied in the Supreme Deity, Ahura Mazda, and the Amĕsha-Çpĕntas, his emanations, and in the other Irano-Aryan Deities, the views and opinions that I shall express are my own, for the most part wholly disagree with those of the commentators and translators, and have been the reason and supplied the motive, for writing the works that I propose to publish, and from which these lectures are extracted.

I think it cannot be without interest to you, to know what manner of men your remote ancestors were; and especially to find ample and indisputable proof that, at least seven thousand years ago, they were no more barbarians than you, but intellectually as well as in their social habits and daily life, the same men as yourselves. It is natural I should think so since no study has ever so deeply interested me. The single fact that we owe not one single truth, not one idea, in philosophy or religion to the Semitic race, is, of itself, ample reward for years of study, and it is a fact indisputable, if I read the *Veda* and *Zend-Avesta* aright.

By the Semitic race are meant the Phœnicians, Canaanites, Hebrews (or Abarim), Arabs (or Arabim) and Chaldeans, all of whom spoke one language, the roots of whose words were invariably of three letters. The Egyptians and Chinese were in no manner related to these, nor had their languages anything in common with theirs or with each other. Nor have the Aryan languages any manner of relationship with the Semitic. To impute to them a common origin is but to assert that of which there is not the least proof, and which cannot be true.

. The indigenous races of the countries conquered by the Aryans spoke none of these languages, but a vast variety of tongues, having no common origin, and, except within the narrow limits of small groups, no relationship with each other. It is the fashion to call them Turanian, and to designate them as a family. But the Turans were but one tribe of many, indigenous to Bactria and subjugated by the Irano-Aryans.

The *Zend-Avesta* consists of several parts, some of greater and some of less antiquity. One of these is the Vendidad, consisting of a number of Fargards or chapters, also of different ages. The first and second Fargards are historical, and older than the others, though not, by far, as ancient as the five Gâthâs.

The first Fargard was composed after the settlement of the Indus Country by the Indo-Aryans, after which, also, the *Rig-Veda* was composed, some of the hymns of which must be, as I shall show, conceded to have had their origin at least 5,000 years before Christ. That Hapta Hendu is one of the countries named in this Fargard, that being the country of the upper Indus, called in the *Veda*, Sapta Sindhu, this and the Zend word alike meaning the Country of the Seven Rivers, proves that when this Fargard was composed the Indo-Aryans had settled in that country. But also, as Persia is not named, it appears that it was composed after Media was conquered, but before the Irano-Aryans had subjugated Persia.

The first Fargard contains a recital of various countries created by Ahura Mazda. Dr. Haug and Baron Bunsen think it is a recital of the successive or various emigrations of the Aryans. Professor Spiegel thinks that it is only geographical.

But no countries are said to be *created* by Ahura Mazda, except those possessed by the Aryans. The countries named, therefore, had all been peopled and conquered by them; and the ancient traditions in the Fargard probably name the countries in the order of time in which they were conquered.

The first Fargard begins thus:

> Ahura Mazda said to the most noble Zarathustra, "I created, most noble Zarathustra, a place, a creation of delight, where before no pleasure was possible. If I had not, all the Aryan people would have emigrated to find a desirable Country. I created the first and best of Countries (*Airyana Vaêjô*), the desirable Country, creation of the Powers of Good. Then Aṅra-Mainyus, who is full of death, created an opposition to the same, a Mighty Serpent and Snow, the work of the Daevas. Ten winter months are there, two months of summer; and these are cold as to the water, cold as to the earth, cold as to the trees. After this, to the middle of the earth, then to the heart of the earth. Comes the winter. Then comes the most evil."

Baron Bunsen thinks that this means that by some great convulsion, the climate of the country named was suddenly changed, the region becoming an arctic instead of a temperate one.

I do not see any reason for believing that any legend or historical reminiscence like that is contained in this account. The second country created is Gau, in which Sughda is situated. This is evidently Sogdiana, the Fire-land, so called from the burning springs to be found in parts of it. It is the Steppe-Country, now Toorkhistan, stretching westward between the Oxus and Jaxartes, from the foot of the great mountain-range of the Bolor Tagh, to the Caspian Sea. In the second Fargard, Yima is represented as leading forth a large band of emigrants, to escape from the severe cold of the winter by seeking a region further south.

The Bolor Tagh range, composed of immense peaks, rising to an altitude of 20,000 feet, thirty or forty of which may, at some points, be seen at once, stretches north and south, sending down from its western ravines the headwaters of the Jaxartes and Oxus; and at its southern extremity forms a right angle with the huge chain of the Caucasus or Hindu Kush which stretches southwestwardly and westwardly, along the southern border of Bactria to the Caspian.

The third country created was "Mouru, the high, the holy," the present Merv, the Margiana of the ancients, southwest of Sogdiana, south of the Oxus and west of Bactria. The fourth was Bakhdi, the beautiful or fertile, with the tall banner, the ancient Bactria and modern Balkh, south of the upper Oxus and between that river and the Hindu Kush. The fifth is Nisa or Nisai, the position of which is in doubt, but which is said to be between Mouru and Bakhdi, touching, Burnouf thinks, on Hyrcania and Margiana.

The other countries named, lie to the southwest and southeast of these; and there is no doubt that this Fargard points to the region of country lying at the foot of the Bolor Tagh, and thence westward to and around the city of Samarkand, as the earliest home of the Aryan race. It had its origin, according to this account, in the high valleys of that range; and the ten months of winter and two only of summer are to be referred to the higher portions of these valleys. Dr. Haug thinks that Airyana-Vaêjô became altogether a mythical country, the seat of Gods and Heroes, where there is neither sickness nor death, frost nor heat. But the description of it in the Vendidad is that of an actual country, whose location, as we shall see, may be determined with certainty.

The twelfth country created was "Ragha of the three tribes," Raghu being the well-known town in Media mentioned by King Darius in the Achæmenian inscription at Bisutun in Persia, and the fifteenth is Hapta Hendu, the country now called the Pūnjâb, lying east of the Indus and south of the Himalayas, watered by the Indus itself and its affluents, anciently called the Hydaspes, the Hyphases or Bibasis, the Acesines, the Hydraotes, and the Hesidrus or Zaradrus, the last being the modern Sutlej.

This Fargard records only the last separation and latest emigrations of the great race; the advance to the southwest of one branch, and that to the southeast of the other; of the Irano-Aryans by Bactria, Parthia and Media towards the Persian Gulf, and of the Indo-Aryans across the Hindu Kush and by Kabul to the Indus country on its way to the region of the Ganges and the Indian Ocean. How long before the separation of these two races, even the latest of the earlier emigrations took place, we do not know. But the science of language proves to us, by the greater number of words owned in common by the Greek and Latin and the Sanskrit and Zend, and the identity of their grammatical forms, that the emigrations from the home of their fathers of those who colonized Greece and Italy were much later in time than those of the streams that flowed into Northern Europe and became the Celtic, Gothic, Germanic and Sclavonic races. The Celts were evidently the earliest outflow of the race: and there is good reason for Baron Bunsen's opinion that their departure from the cradle of the race took place at least 10,000 years before Christ.

After the vastly later separation of the two branches that which became Indians and Iranians, the ancient common language of the two changed, with the former into what is now known as the Sanskrit, and with the latter, into the Zend. Although these two ancient tongues are sisters and to a great extent dialects of the one original Aryan language, yet there are great differences between them and each has an individuality of its own, and is to a considerable extent a composite language, by the intermixture with it of the words of the indigenous tongues of the countries conquered. Each had become settled and fixed as a permanent language, when the most ancient existing compositions of each had their origin.

It must have required a long period of time, in which to change the ancient common language, with the Indian race into the Sanskrit of the *Veda*, and with the Iranian race into the Bactrian (miscalled the Zend) of the Gâthâs of Zarathustra. Philology cannot measure the periods required for effecting these changes, by years and centuries, any more than geology can tell us by ages the length of time of any one of its many epochs.

But there are other means, which I think will interest you, by which we can at least approximately ascertain the age of the earliest hymns of the two races.

For a very long time the hymns of the *Rig-Veda* were unwritten, handed down orally, from generation to generation, in the families of those wandering bands, who were found among all the subdivisions of the Aryan race. For the ancient Bards of the Gaels and Kymry were the legitimate brethren of the Rishis of the Land of the Seven Rivers, who were translated to the

skies and became stars. About 1,000 years before Christ, the hymns of the
Rig-Veda, written down, of course long before, were compiled. The Vedic
Sanskrit had then become a dead language, and the meaning of much of the
Veda was lost. A more modern dialect, also, had succeeded to the Bactrian
Zend, when Darius and other kings of the Achæmenian dynasty had the
rock inscriptions cut in arrow-headed characters, at Behistun and elsewhere.

There is evidence in the Bactrian tongue of the Gâthâs of Zarathustra,
that the so-called Zend contains in itself older forms of the original Aryan
tongue, than the Sanskrit does, as also the Latin contains more of the
ancient words than the Greek does; and I have no doubt that the antiquity
of the Gâthâs is very much greater than that of the oldest hymns of the *Veda*.

Yet there are in the *Veda* reminiscences of the ancient wandering life of
the Aryan herdsmen on the Steppes of Toorkhistan, when horses were
sacrificed to the Gods and eaten by the worshippers.

Now, we are curiously enough enabled, by the aid of astronomy, to
ascertain approximately, the date of the composition of the oldest Vedic
hymns. There are two Vedic Deities to whom many hymns are addressed,
called the Açvins. They are lauded and invoked as the heralds and precursors
of the dawn; are called the Twin Horsemen (*Açva* meaning a horse), and one
of them is said to be in the sky, while the other remains below the earth.

In the Hindū astronomy, which was reduced to a system about 600 years
after Christ, there are two stars still called the Açvini, two small stars in the
constellation Aries. Simply as stars, these, being of little size, are wholly
unimportant, and would never have attracted attention. But, 600 years
after Christ, the sun was in Aries at the vernal equinox, as it is now in
Pisces, or the Fishes, in consequence of the precession of the equinoxes;
and these two small stars then rose heliacally, that is, a little before the sun,
at the vernal equinox, and so announcing the coming of that season of
rains, of generation and of spring with her flowers and promises of genial
weather.

About 2,500 years before Christ, the sun was in the sign Taurus, the
Bull, at the spring equinox, and the great star, Aldebaran, in the Hyades,
rising at dawn "led up the opening year." The Bull, thus a symbol of the
power of the sun to make the Earth able to bear fruit, and of the generative
potency of the Deity, then became an object of adoration, as the Lamb did
afterwards, when the sun was in Aries (the Ram), at the vernal equinox.

Five thousand years or more, before Christ, the sun was in Gemini or
the Twins at that time of the year, and then the two Twins, the two great
and bright stars, Castor and Poludeukes, were at early dawn the heralds
of the coming spring. They became, therefore, to the Graeco-Aryans the
Dioskuroi, sons of Leda by Jupiter and Tyndarus, the Twin Horsemen,
called Anakes, or the benefactors, generally represented mounted on white

horses, armed with spears and riding side by side, the head of each covered with a bonnet, on whose top glitters a star. One, Castor, was said to have been mortal, and the other immortal; and Castor being killed, Pollux persuaded Zeus to restore him to life and shared his immortality with him, each alternately living and dying every day, or as some said, every six months.

This fraternal piety Zeus rewarded by placing them in the sky as the constellation Gemini, the Twins.

These were the Açvinau of the Vedic poets, and as they could only have been adored when they announced the coming of spring, we are enabled to say with certainty that the hymns in their honor were composed between 4,500 and 5,000 years before Christ.

HELIACAL RISING OF THE DIOSCURI IN GEMINI AT THE VERNAL EQUINOX
ASTRONOMICAL CORRESPONDENCE.

(A true copy of the original correspondence.)

Smithsonian Institution, Washington, August 25, 1873.

Times of rising of certain stars, reckoned in apparent solar time, at the epoch of the vernal equinoxes of the years B.C. 2500, and B.C. 5000.

	B.C. 2500			B.C. 5000		
	Lat. + 30°	Lat. + 35°	Lat. + 40°	Lat. + 30°	Lat. + 35°	Lat. + 40°
	A. M.	A. M.	A. M.	A. M.	A. M.	A. M.
Sun..........	6.00	6.00	6.00	6.00	6.00	6.00
Pleiades.......	5.40	5.39	5.37	4.05	4.10	4.16
Hyades........	6.44	6.45	6.46	5.09	5.17	5.27
Belt of Orion ..	8.33	8.40	8.48	7.03	7.19	7.38
Capella	5.21	5.04	4.46	3.54	3.44	3.38
Sirius	10.20	10.31	10.45	9.12	9.32	9.56
Castor	7.38	7.22	7.05	6.00	5.52	5.44
Pollux.........	8.04	7.51	7.36	6.24	6.18	6.11

The sun was within the limits of the constellation Gemini, at the vernal equinox, from the year B.C. 6800 till the year B.C. 4700.

Prepared by Prof. Wm. Harkness at the request of the Smithsonian Institution, for Albert Pike, Esq.

U. S. Naval Observatory,
Washington, Sept. 5, 1873.

Prof. Joseph Henry,
My dear Sir:

In reference to Mr. Pike's question "during what period of time the twin stars in Gemini rose heliacally at the vernal equinox—it was of course, during the time, i. e., during some part of the time while the sun was in Gemini, (6800 to 5000 B.C.)" allow me to make the following remarks.

By "the twin stars in Gemini" I understand Mr. P. to mean Castor and Pollux. If so, then, as those stars are *north* of the sun's path in the ecliptic, to all places in the northern hemisphere they will rise *before* the sun when their right ascension is the same as his. Hence Mr. P. is in error in supposing that their heliacal rising at the vernal equinox to places in latitude 30°, 35° and 40° north, must *necessarily* have occurred while the sun was in the constellation Gemini at the vernal equinox.

If Mr. P. will refer to the table which I sent you in answer to his former letter he will see that the state of affairs 5000 years before Christ was as follows: In latitude 30° north, Castor rose with the sun and Pollux 24 minutes later. In latitude 35° north, Castor rose 8 minutes before, and Pollux 18 minutes after, the sun. In latitude 40° north, Castor rose 16 minutes before, and Pollux 11 minutes after the sun.

These times of rising seem to fulfil the condition that "one star is in the heavens, while the other is in the earth," and it seems to me that Mr. P.'s question is now fully answered. If not, let me hear from you again.

Yours etc.
(Signed) WM. HARKNESS

(At this point in the manuscript of General Pike of this work, there are inserted two papers by the astronomer at the United States Naval Observatory, Professor Wm. Harkness. One of these is a table of the rising of certain stars, reckoned in apparent solar time, at the epoch of the vernal equinoxes of the years B.C. 2500 and B.C. 5000. This appears here *in extenso*. The other paper is a letter by the astronomer, Professor Harkness, to Professor Joseph Henry, secretary of the Smithsonian Institution from its organization in 1846, until his death in 1876. General Pike told the transcriber hereof in regard to these papers, and of their *raison d'etre*, years before his death. His statement in regard to the age of certain of the Vedic hymns was controverted by one who posed as well informed in such matters, and the General requested Professor Henry to furnish him with the astronomical data to corroborate his statement. The first of these, containing the table prepared by Professor Harkness, is on the Smithsonian stationery, and the other on ordinary note paper, both having been prepared before the days of typewriters. Professor Harkness was then an astronomer of note, and is quoted in the Britannica.)

Caius Plinius the Second, tells us, in the Thirtieth Book of his Natural History, that Eudoxus said that Zarathustra lived 6,000 years before Plato (who was born 429 years before Christ); and that so it is asserted also by Aristŏtĕlēs. Hermippus, Pliny informs us, who made a diligent study of the works of Zarathustra, explaining an immense number of his verses, stated that he lived 5,000 years before the Trojan War (which is supposed to have taken place about 1,190 years before Christ).

Zarathustra himself is expressly stated, more than once in the *Zend-Avesta* to have sacrificed in Airyana Vaêjô: and it is equally certain, I think, that he composed the five Gâthâs in Bactria, where he became king; and that these odes are much older than the oldest hymns of the *Rig-Veda*.

The second Fargard of the Vendidad contains the legend of Yima the son of Vivanhao; and it is by far the most interesting legend of the *Zend-Avesta*, because it contains a really historic account of the first Irano-Aryan emigration across the Oxus. Yima is the Yemshid of the later Persian legends or fables, and his father is said to have been the first teacher of the Ahurian faith.

This Fargard has been translated by Dr. Haug into English, and by Professor Spiegel into German, and from his German into English by Mr. Bleeck. These translations, especially of the Gâthâs, often differ very widely from each other, and we have to choose between them. Generally, I think, Mr. Bleeck's the less incorrect; but both, for reasons that I shall state in speaking of the Zend and Sanskrit books and languages, are exceedingly defective. Part of this second Fargard I read as follows:

> 1. Zarathustra asked Ahura Mazda: Ahura Mazda, Divine Spirit, Creator of the world of living beings, with whom, first among men, didst thou converse, Thou who art the Self-Existent Light? To whom besides me, Zarathustra, didst Thou teach the Ahurian faith, taught through Zarathustra?
>
> 2. Then replied Ahura Mazda: To Yima the Fortunate, the owner of great herds, O pious Zarathustra; with him, first of all men, I did converse, I who am Ahura Mazda, besides you, Zarathustra.
>
> 3. Then spake I unto him: O Zarathustra, I who am Ahura Mazda, saying: "O Yima the fair son of Vivanhâo, serve me in bearing abroad and expounding the true faith." Then answered me Yima the Fair, O Zarathustra, "I am not the Creator nor the Teacher [or, I am not fit or known to be], nor the Expounder, nor the Promulgator of the Law."
>
> 4. Then, O Zarathustra, I, who am Ahura Mazda said unto him: "If thou Yima, wilt not serve me as Expounder and Promulgator of the Law, then enlarge my domain, make my Aryan land fruitful, serve me as Protector, Defender and Ruler of my land [or, people]."
>
> 5. Then, O Zarathustra, Yima the Fair answered me: "I will enlarge thy domain, I will make thy land fruitful [or, a fruitful land thine], I will serve Thee as Protector, Defender and Ruler of Thy land [or, people]. During my rule there shall be no cold winds, nor heat, nor disease, nor death."

Ahura is represented here as proposing to Yima to serve him by committing to memory, promulgating, teaching, and bearing to a distance, as an apostle, the religious teachings of the Mazdayaçnian faith. This Yima declines, but assents to the request that he shall serve Ahura, by enlarging the Aryan country by colonization, and making it productive, or adding to it fertile provinces, and by being the protector, defender and ruler of the people. The object of the recital was not simply to state that Yima was not a teacher or apostle, but a leader of emigrants, extending the boundaries of the Aryan dominion, and a wise and beneficent sovereign; but its meaning is, that not teaching or religious ministration alone is the service of the Deity, but that it is also religious and acceptable service to enlarge the boundaries of the country, acquire new territory, protect and defend the people of Ahura and extend the rule of the true faith. And, perhaps, as Zarathustra himself was not a priest or teacher, but a soldier and king, it was a defense of his own title to be deemed to rule by divine right.

> 7. Then I, who am Ahura Mazda, created for him the instruments of conquest, a golden plough and a spear of gold. Yima is to be ruler there.

Then it is recited, not literally, but figuratively, in several verses, that Yima became possessed of many countries, more and more districts being annexed to the Aryan empire by continual increase and conquest; and that, as the country enlarged, the population increased and multiplied, until room was wanting. This Ahura is represented as declaring to him, to induce him to emigrate. And the account of his emigration and settlement thus proceeds:

> 10. Then Yima went forth to the stars, towards the south, towards the way of the Sun. He cleft the earth with his plow of gold, he pierced it with the spear, saying, "O Çpĕnta-Armaiti, beneficently go forth and go asunder [or, enlarge and expand], at my prayer, O thou sustainer of cattle, of beasts of burthen and of men."

Çpĕnta-Armaiti, one of the Amĕsha-Çpĕntas or divine emanations is the divine potency of production, acting through Nature: and the meaning of the passage is, that, keeping his course by the stars, Yima left the mother-land and journeyed southward, and in the country which he reached, ploughed and dug up the land and caused it to produce abundantly.

In the same figurative style it is recited that the Aryan settlement and cultivation extended in the region newly occupied, which finally became as large and extensive as the mother-country, the cattle, beasts of burden and men ever pressing onward, "according to their desire and will, as it is ever their will," and as it always has been from that day to this, to seek new homes and new regions to conquer and colonize.

With him, also, and with his assemblage, "of the best men, the renowned in Airyana Vaêjô, of the creation of Ahura, went to Ahura Mazda, and his assemblage of the Yazatas or adorable ones." Whether they crossed the

Oxus and settled first in eastern Bactria, in the valleys of the Bolor Tagh range of mountains, on the headwaters of the Amoo and Sirkhal rivers, and thence took a new departure, to settle in the great alluvial plain of Balkh, or whether the emigration was from the valleys further north, to the country around Samarkand, is uncertain. In the 22nd verse, the country inhabited by them is spoken of as cold and undesirable: but it is uncertain whether this is a continuation of the account of their emigration from their first halting-place, or whether it is a return to and further account of the reasons for the first movement westward. It represents Ahura as saying to Yima, that the evil of winter would come upon the country, destructive frosts, and heavy snows on the summits of the mountains and on the high table-lands. Wherefore he advises Yima to remove the cattle from the heights and the valleys, saying that before winter comes, there is pasturage, but during the winter there is none; that before winter the streams flow free; and in the spring the snows melt and they flow again; but during the winter they are frozen up.

> He says, "Clouds, O Yima, will come over the inhabited regions, which now behold the footsteps of the cattle and the flocks."

It is a picture of the ordinary condition in winter of a high region in a northern latitude among the mountains, as making emigration desirable. Every winter the pasturage disappeared, of course. The upper Oxus freezes every winter. Heavy snows fell in the valleys, and on the table-lands, from 10,000 to 15,000 feet above the level of the sea; and the waters of the upper streams and the lakes from which they flowed became solid ice.

Naturally, as the people became numerous and strong, they extended themselves southward and westward; and we come now to a poetic description of the home selected for his followers by Yima. It was a tract of country near a river, and alluvial, not capable of cultivation without irrigation. It was fertile; for food never failed there. The skies were bright and clear, the scenery glowed with golden hues, and it was populous with birds. There was neither excessive cold nor heat; and health and long lives blessed the inhabitants. There Yima caused permanent buildings to be erected, with floors, columns, courts and walled grounds; and great canals furnished the water for irrigation.

It extended a day's journey every way, and contained pasture-grounds for abundant cattle, and productions of every kind gave everything desirable for food.

There, it is said, there was neither strife nor vexation, nor enmities nor beggary, nor deceit, nor sickness, nor deformities,

no teeth exceeding the due proportion; no stature exceeding the due proportion of
the body; no other marks which are the tokens of Añra-Mainyus [the Evil Principle],
which he has made among men.

By which it appears that deformity was considered as a mark put on men
by the Evil One; and that Yima selected for his colonists only those in
whom there was no physical defect.

In the uppermost part of this region, it is said, there were nine bridges;
in the middle, six; in the lowermost part, three. It was therefore a region,
either of many streams or of many canals of irrigation.

I need not follow the description further here. And I shall quote but
two short passages, one that you may, by one example out of thousands,
see how difficult a book the *Zend-Avesta* is to understand; the other because
it gives valuable information in regard to Aryan thought and character.

In verse 31, Yima asked how he should establish the settlement directed
by Ahura. The answer is, according to Spiegel and Bleeck, "tread on this
earth with the heels; strike it with the hands so as to cause the man-inhabited
earth to cleave asunder." According to Haug, it is, "with thy heels extend
this earth; with thy hands make her asunder like as men now extend the
earth in cultivating." The real and certain meaning is, "travel, and by
emigration extend the Aryan dominion, and let the people with their hands
extend the production of the land, and enlarge the arable land, as here in the
mother-country men do, cultivating the soil."

The other passage is in verse 42. Zarathustra asks who spread abroad
the Mazdayaçnian Law (the tenets and doctrines or precepts of the true
religion), in the district which Yima made. And the answer is, the bird
Karshipta. And, in verse 43, where it is asked who is the ruler and director
of the people and the reply is, "Urvatât-Narô, and thou, Zarathustra." The
commentators attempt no explanation of this or the former phrase.
Karshipta is *husbandry, cultivation, agriculture;* and the extension of the
true faith is ascribed to it, because to it was owing the colonization of new
regions, and the support of the people, and of the troops that scourged
with defeat the unbelieving native tribes, and the invading Tâtars. The
word rendered by "bird" means "which advances, goes forward." *Urvatât-
Narô* means *magnanimity, great-mindedness,* and *heroism.* It and Zarathustra
are masters and directors; i. e., he and the greatness of soul which is of the
Deity, and abiding in him, govern the people.

Yima is spoken of in several other passages of the *Zend-Avesta;* and
from all, taken together, we learn that he was the son of Vivañhao who first
offered the Haôma to the Deities, and that he led the Irano-Aryans from a
mountainous and cold country, either into the country where Samarkand
afterward stood, or into that wide and fertile plain in Bactria, along the
River Bactra and along the Oxus, in which Balkh stands; and there subjected

to his rule the native tribes that occupied all the seven divisions of the country, formed by the streams that run northward from the Hindu Kush to fall into the Oxus. For many years, peace and abundance prevailed under his rule: but he at last fell away from the true faith, and in consequence was deposed. Repenting, he regained his power; relapsed, was again deposed, and Thraetaŏna succeeded him, at whose death he regained power, relapsed still again, and was succeeded by Kĕrĕçâçpa, another bold soldier, and so disappears from the scene.

The supreme chief was probably elected as the Germano-Aryans elected their kings—by the acclamations of the soldiery. No one knows how some of our Indian tribes elect their chiefs. But, in some way or other, they succeed in selecting their wisest and best men, which is very far from being certainly the result of popular elections by their descendants. Civilization seems to deprive men of that faculty.

Yima, therefore, is a genuine historical Irano-Aryan and, as will be seen, Indo-Aryan hero, entitled to be named "The First." His is the oldest historical name of our race. It is found, as we shall see, as well in the *Veda* as in the *Zend-Avesta;* and his reign cannot have been less than 6000 B.C. For when he emigrated, those whom he led southward, and those who remained, spoke the same language; and the Sanskrit and Zend were formed from it by the slow processes of change and development, before the Vedic hymns or even the Gâthâs were composed.

The heroes and sages of that period, with names changed by time, became immortal in tradition, and were as real men of our race, as Alfred the Saxon.

So much we find in regard to Yima in the Zend books; not in the Gâthâs, but in much later compositions, perhaps later than the conquest of Media, ages after the separation of the Irano- and Indo-Aryans.

We find him also celebrated in the Vedic hymns, composed in the Indus country, where he is called *Yama*, son of *Vivasvat*. Certain Sanskrit letters change regularly into certain other letters, in the same words in Zend; *s* becoming *h*, and *h* becoming *z; s* often becoming the nasal *nh;* and *çv* becoming *çp*. Thus, as *asu* becomes *anhu*, Vivasvat becomes *Vivañhao*.

A hymn found in the tenth book of the *Rig-Veda* and the eighteenth of the *Atharva-Veda*, is addressed to Yama (called *Vaivasvata*, or son of *Vivasvat*). It commences thus:

Worship with an oblation Yama the king, son of *Vivasvat* (*Vaivasvataṁ Yamaṁ Râjânaṁ*), the assembler of men, who departed to the mighty streams (*pravato mahú anu*), and explored the way for many. Yama was the first who found for us the way. This home is not to be taken from us. Those who are now born, go by their own routes to the land whither our ancient Fathers departed . . . . The Fathers have made for him this place. Yama gives him an abode distinguished by

days and waters and lights . . . . Then approach the benevolent Fathers, who
dwell in festivity with Yama.

Nothing can be clearer than that the first verses of this hymn represent
Yama as having gathered a body of Aryans together, and emigrated across
a great river, to another land, being the first to explore a route to it, by
which many afterwards followed, until the men of the poets' days could
find out new routes for themselves, the roads leading there having become
old ones, and the country so strongly populated that the Aryans were no
longer in danger of being expelled from it.

Afterwards, as appears by this very hymn, as well as by others, although
this language was retained, it came to have another meaning, and the emigration of Yama and the Fathers to be considered as their departure from this
life, and he as the first of mortals who died, and discovered a way to the
other world, where he feasts with the Gods.

The Irano-Aryans retained the original tradition, and never made Yima
a Deity. At a much later period, the myth grew up, that Yima brought
upon earth the golden age.

Through the hyperbolical and figurative expressions of the Zend books,
it is easy to read the simple historical facts of the legend. And thus these
books, in an unknown alphabet and an unknown language, and dead to the
world for ages, rescued at last, as if by a miracle, from the silent custody of
the dead past and of oblivion, unexpectedly explain to us the meaning of a
legend in the ancient books of the Indo-Aryans, the venerable *Vedas*, of that
separation of the two branches of the one race, which created two languages
out of the old mother-tongue, and caused the development and growth of
two great systems of religious faith; to one of which, far more than to the
teachings of Christ or Paul we owe our religious ideas; from which Paul
himself borrowed largely, and to which our philosophy and theosophy are
deeply indebted.

Whatever the origin of the Aryan race, I believe that all great streams
of emigration flowed forth from the country afterwards called Sogdiana,
lying between the Oxus and Jaxartes. Originally occupying the country
at the foot of the great range of the Bolor Tagh, and the valleys of the
affluents of these great streams in the lower regions of that range which is
called Harabĕrĕzaiti (a word afterwards changed into Alborj, the fabulous
mountain-peak of an unknown locality, of the Parsees), they had descended
at a very remote period, to which no history ascends, into the fertile valley
region of Samarkand, and had become in part, husbandmen, and in part
herdsmen, each tribe governed by its chief, and the herdsmen driving their
cattle to the steppes for pasturage.

From this region of vast fertility which I propose now to describe, went
the great bodies of Aryan emigrants that peopled Europe, and last of all the

ancestors of the Medes and Persians under Yima, and those who peopled the Indus country and conquered Hindustan. These, I think, went last, expelled, probably by a host of Tâtar, Toorkhish or Scythian invaders, and leaving to these the country that had been for so many centuries their home. All this I have endeavored to prove, in the works from which I compile these lectures. In these I can give you little more than my conclusions.

Sarasvati is a river and a River-Goddess, in the *Veda*, as Ardviçura is in the *Zend-Avesta*. The latter, I have concluded, was the Oxus, Amoo or Jiboon; and so, I think, originally was the Sarasvati. It is with reason that Ardviçura was said to be as great as all the rivers of the land together. The Bolor Tagh, at the angle of its junction with the immense Hindu Kush range, forms the space in which all the waters of the Oxus are collected, and from which they fall into Lake Aral, as formerly they fell into the Caspian, after uniting with the Jaxartes. The old channel still remains, to attest the ancient course of the river. The Hindu Kush or Indian Caucasus lying south of Bactria, as well as east of it, has summits that rise above 20,000 feet; and one eighty miles north of the city of Kabul is of much more considerable elevation. The sources of the Oxus fall from the passes that connect its valley with those of the Kabul and the Helmund, and the passes that connect these valleys have an elevation of from 8,000 to 10,000 feet.

One of the principal sources of the Oxus is in Lake Siricol, at an elevation of 15,600 feet above the level of the sea, in latitude 37° 27′ N., and longitude 73° 40′ E. The course of the river is estimated at 1,300 miles, and the fall of the upper course of it is, on an average, about 15 feet to the mile. Its waters are deep and turbid, and it has great rapidity. Near Balkh it is never fordable, has a depth of 12 to 15 feet, and is very wide, Mohun Lal being two hours and twenty-five minutes in crossing it, in a boat rowed by strong men.

Khanikoff (translated by the Baron de Bode) and Sir Alexander Burnes are the sources of our information in regard to the original seat of Aryan empire. Along the lower Oxus are many large bodies of fertile land, that once were irrigated from the river; and north of these extends a sandy desert, incapable of cultivation, no lands being arable except those along the rivers, susceptible of irrigation. This desert extends to the valleys of the Kurshī and the Zer Affshaun, Sir* Affshan or Zohik, on the latter of which lies Samarkand, and below it Bokhara. This river runs a little

---

Sir or *Zer*—The Jaxartes is now the *Sir Darya;* and the same word is found in the name of Lake *Siricol*, and of the *Sirkab*, an affluent of the Oxus. It is, no doubt, the Sanskrit *Saras*, a large pond, a piece of water in which the lotus grows, water; whence *Sarasvant*, the sea, a river, and the name of the river *Sarasvati*. The *apsaras* (*ap* meaning water), originally lotus ponds, became to the Indo-Aryans, female Deities or nymphs.

north of Samarkand and to the west of the city of Bokhara, and is the second
river of the Khaṇat. It heads in the mountains east of Samarkand, and
runs west, with many channels and canals, and beyond Bokhara bends and
runs south into Lake Denghiz, twenty-five miles long, near the Oxus; its
whole course being about 620 versts (or 460 miles). The headwaters of three
of the principal branches are in the Karatan Mountains. Along it, its whole
length, is a strip of cultivated country. There are a hundred canals, of
unknown age, along it, from above Samarkand, on both sides, deep, long,
with the water running swiftly in them, and like natural branches of the
river, which many of them, indeed, seem originally to have been. Anciently
this river was called Mazaf, and afterwards Sogd, and its whole valley is
very beautiful.

The great level tracts along the lower Oxus, on its northern side, are
also intersected in every direction by ancient canals; and so also is the
immense and fertile plain about Balkh, south of the Oxus, where Yima
established his colony.

At Samarkand there is a vast space of ruins. Three rivers from the
mountains run into the city, which formerly fed innumerable canals. The
whole valley in which the city lies, is covered with gardens and orchards.
In all the country from Samarkand to Bokhara (a little south of 40° N.
latitude), 2° 8' of longitude, wheat, rice, barley, millet and lucerne grow.
There are thirteen kinds of grapes. Apricots are produced in profusion, as
large as apples. Prunes, quinces, mulberries, almonds, apples, pears,
cherries, peaches, pomegranates and figs are abundant. Melons grow in
great profusion, and silk, cotton and tobacco are staple products.

The Kurshee runs parallel with the Zohik, and its valley is a sheet of
gardens and orchards, in places six miles in width on one side of the river,
and sixteen on the other, through the whole of which water is distributed by
canals.

Alexander, when he invaded India, led his Aryan troops back to this
cradle of their race; but no Grecian soldier imagined that the soldiers
of the Indian King Porus were of the same stock and strain as himself, and
that the languages spoken by him and them were but dialects of the same
ancient tongue. Maracanda or Samarkand was a great city in the time
of Alexander; and his Greeks named the Sir Affshan the Polymetis. To the
northeast, on a tributary of the Jaxartes, was Kureshata, which Kuros had
built, and which Alexander destroyed. Near the modern Bokhara stood
Tribactria, and Alexandria Ultima was founded by Alexander as a border
fortress.

The latitude of Samarkand is 39° 32', and that of Bokhara, 39° 25', the
river bending to the north between them. Naples, Pekin, Constantinople,
Rome, Bordeaux and Trebizond are all further north.

At the city of Bokhara, the thermometer is often at zero and below in winter; and in the summer the heat is very great, but at the city itself seldom higher than 90°, and the nights always cool, it being 1,200 feet above the sea. West of it the great plain of Toorkhistan spreads out, 2,000 feet above that level, declining westward to the Aral and Caspian.

The atmosphere is always serene, and the sky singularly clear. The heavens are brightly blue, without a cloud. The stars shine with uncommon luster, and the Milky Way with a glorious radiance. A star only three or four degrees above the horizon will be distinctly visible, although the moon is shining.

On either side of this original home of their race now stand fronting each other, to contend perhaps in arms for its ownership, two great Aryan nations. England and Russia, the Saxon, Norman, Dane and Celt commingled, on the south, and the Sclave on the north, each ignorant that the languages which their armies speak are but the off-shoots of that which was spoken in the valley of the Sogd ten thousand years ago. So it is that the exiles of a hundred centuries return again, to contend for the ancient home.

The emigrants under Yima probably entered Bactria by the way of the upper Oxus country. The present divisions of that region are Khūndūz, Khūlūm, Herlūk, Būdūkshan; and north of Khūndūz and Būdūkshan, and beyond the Oxus are the small states in the hill-country of Hissar, Khūlab, Dūrwaz, Shūgnan and Wūkhan. Those south of the Oxus have a pleasant climate and a prolific soil, and are well watered by rivulets flowing into the Oxus. Būdūkshan has beautiful vales, clear bright streams, romantic glens, beautiful landscapes, fruits, flowers and nightingales. Lake Siricol or Sūrikūl is in the center of the high plain of Pamir, an immense table-land, all level, and with short, rich pasture. The snow does not disappear from the hollows here in the summer, and the winters are severe. In this region below the table-land, are eight streams, north and south of the Oxus, running into it, between which may be the Seven Kareshvares or districts of the Aryan land, so often mentioned in the Zend-Avesta.

But I think that these Kareshvares are the seven divisions of Bactria, formed by the six considerable streams that flow northward from the Hindu Kush into the Oxus, across that country; and that Yima descended from the upper Oxus country to the great plain of Balkh. The great river Ardviçura flowing into the Sea Vouru-kasha, the wide extent of irrigated country, with canals as long as a man can ride in a day; and the large number of rivers flowing into the Ardviçura, suit no other country; and the description of the mountains is equally suited to it and unsuited to any other country. The height Haraiti, "which surrounds the region towards the east, flowed round by water," is unquestionably the Bolor Tagh, and the streams that flow from it do, making great bends, flow round a great extent of country.

Together with the Hindu Kush, it surrounds the eastern end of Bactria; and in these ranges tower up the great number of immense peaks that are named in the Zamyad Yasht of the *Zend-Avesta*.

Crossing the Hindu Kush by the principal pass that leads from Kabul, one emerges into a part of Bactria which is a mixture of villas, meadows, crystal canals, and gardens containing fruits of all kinds.

Balkh, anciently Zariaspa and afterwards Bactra, lies in a plain on the Bactras River. Coming from the south, the way to it for fifteen miles, is almost entirely the rough plains, bordered on both sides with beautiful gardens. It was formerly a very large and populous city. It is now a mass of ruins. It is said to have been the mother of cities, the buildings, in former days, extending as far as Mazar, fifteen miles. It is but a few miles from the Oxus, and as one follows the course of the river, downward from it, he passes through ancient ruins, alternating with deserts; the fertile plain continuing fifty-one miles from Mazar to Murdian, between the hills and the Oxus, and evidently alluvial. There are many villages set among fine gardens. Water runs everywhere, and everywhere the land in this plain is fit for cultivation. The water is divided into eighteen rivers, commonly called the eighteen streams of Balkh, and it is a striking coincidence that in the second Fargard of the Vendidad, it is said that Yima made eighteen bridges, above, midway, and below: and the size of the circle of Yima, a day's journey each way, corresponds with the size of this great plain.

Balkh is in latitude 36° 35'. Here, in this magnificent alluvial plain, abounding with water, eighteen aqueducts conducting it from the Oxus, was the first seat of Irano-Aryan Empire. There Yima established his capital, and there Zarathustra afterwards reigned, not the teacher of a new faith, but its soldier, and the liberator of his country from Tâtar or Toorkhish oppression.

Some scholars have concluded that the separation of the Irano-Aryan and Indo-Aryan branches took place in the Indus country. This has been largely discussed, and I have considered it fully. But the limits of a lecture will not permit even a summary of the reasons for and against the proposition. I am satisfied that it has no foundation in fact; and equally so that the separation was not in consequence of a schism, caused by the teachings of Zarathustra, which is the pet theory of Dr. Haug.

While the Irano-Aryans were extending themselves towards Media, the other branch of the race traversed the passes of the Hindu Kush, occupied Kabul, and at length crossed to the east side of the Indus, and after a long struggle with the native tribes, called by them Dasyus, made themselves masters of the land of the Seven Rivers; and here the Vedic hymns were composed by their bards.

These Vedic hymns, in part merely poetical, and in part devotional and composed for worship, embody a faith that was already ancient, at the time when the earliest of them were composed. When the mythological ideas of those who were the authors are better understood, there will undoubtedly be many additional data for determining the succession, and with some approximation to accuracy, the epochs, of the several Aryan emigrations. Already their order of succession has been in part settled by philological evidence, as I have stated it.

That the original seat of Aryan civilization was in Sogdiana, and that those remote ancestors of ours ranged as herdsmen, like the Tâtar tribes, over the Asian Steppes, except so far as a part of them cultivated the soil, is amply proven by both the *Veda* and *Zend-Avesta*. In one of the Vedic hymns the sacrifice of a horse and the eating of his meat by the worshippers are described, a kind of sacrifice which had evidently been long obsolete when the Indo-Aryans lived in the Punjab.

Everywhere in the hymns we find horses and cattle prayed for, as the chief wealth, while sheep are rarely mentioned. The same is the case in the *Zend-Avesta*. Milk was one of the chief articles of food; butter was the chief article of the sacrifices. The herdsman's life seems to have been more general than the husbandman's; and the former, mounted, armed and driving his herds over the wide pastures, liable at any time to be compelled to defend them against roving bands of Tâtars or Scyths, was probably considered to pursue a more honorable occupation than the other. Zarathustra encouraged and elevated agriculture, declaring it equivalent to worship and devotional exercises; and the nomadic life must have been in a great measure abandoned in Bactria and altogether so in India. Though much is said in the Gâthâs about driving the cattle to fresh pastures, yet when the great works for irrigation were carried forward on the Zer Affshan and Oxus, agriculture had become the principal interest of the state, which must then have become populous with a settled people, and have had a strong government, able to make itself respected and its will obeyed, and to concentrate the labor of multitudes of men on these extensive and still enduring works.

Moreover, while little is said about irrigation in the *Veda*, its hymns continually celebrate the exploits of Indra, Light, in shattering the heavy clouds with the thunderbolt, and so causing them to set free the rains, and make the earth produce.

That the Vedic faith and worship were very ancient, when the hymns were composed, will be more evident, I think, if my conclusions as to the nature and meaning of the Deities of the *Veda* are correct. It is enough to say here, that I think the conclusion justifiable, that the earliest Aryans had no other Deities than the sun, moon, and other luminaries of the sky;

and that after they had advanced beyond this, to the worship of Universals or Principles, Fire, Light, Heat and others, though they continued to adore the luminaries, they saw in them the limited manifestations, in place and form, of the Universals; and worshipped them both as such, and as luminous and independent bodies and orbs. For, while these orbs are much more rarely invoked than the Fire-Spirit and the Light-Spirit, and Sûrya (the Sun) is comparatively unnoticed, there are several Deities of which we have little more than the names; so that it is exceedingly uncertain what they were; and even their names disappear in the later mythologies; while of those that are preserved, the very identity is mistaken.

Even the earliest Hindū commentators, it may at once be said, were almost totally ignorant, as to the signification of the Vedic Gods. What these really were, is determinable only from the *Veda* itself. Indeed, it seems probable that when the latest hymns were composed, the specific individualities of many of the Deities at first worshipped had become obscured, by larger place filled by others, and by misunderstanding of the epithets applied and attributes ascribed, to these more ancient Gods. It is at least certain that some became what they were not at first, and that, as to some, the attributes ascribed to them at one period are inconsistent with those ascribed at another.

Few Deities or names of Deities are common to the *Veda* and *Zend-Avesta*. The significance of this fact to us, in connection with the history of the two branches of the race, is very great. Several stars and constellations are objects of adoration in the hymns of both, but not one of them has the same name in both. Of the Vedic Deities, Agni, the Fire, is Asha, the Fire, son of Ahura Mazda, and Asha-Vahista, the third Amĕsha-Çpĕnta or emanation. Indra is unknown to the *Zend-Avesta;* and so are Rudra, Vishnu, Aditi, and many others. The names, Mitra, of the *Veda* and Mithra of the *Zend-Avesta* are identical; and Mitra or Mithra was originally the Morning-Star, the Phosphor of the Greeks and Lucifer of the Latins, the planet Venus, originally, feminine, the name became masculine, at last, with both branches; but while Mitra continued to be Venus to the Indo-Aryans, it became the Light in the *Zend-Avesta*, and, at a later day, the Sun. In the *Veda*, Mitra is associated with Varuṇa and Aryaman, Jupiter and Mars; and these are not known in the Zend books.

Vayu, Flame, is invoked in terms of adoration, both in the *Veda* and *Zend-Avesta*. Pushan, the planet Mercury, adore'd in the *Veda*, is not mentioned in the Zend books, but Çraddha, worship or devotion, personified in the *Veda*, is Çraŏsha, meaning the same, in the *Zend-Avesta*. And this and the personifications of prayer, in the *Veda* as Brahmanaspati and Brihaspati, silent and uttered prayer, reveal to us a remarkable identity of thought in the Indo-Aryan and Irano-Aryan mind, in regard to the nature and efficacy of prayer and worship. In each creed they were powers and personified as Deities; and success, prosperity, wealth and victory in war were not their *rewards*, but *consequences* caused and *produced* by them—their fruit.

Each creed, therefore, was the development of an original creed, the worship, not of the latent and invisible potencies of Nature, but of the visible luminaries of the sky. Each retained, as the mythology of the Greeks and Romans did, somewhat of the original faith; but in each higher conceptions were attained, and the fundamental idea of each was the same.

In these divergencies to produce the results that appear in the *Veda* and *Zend-Avesta*, as for the formation of the two languages from the one original, a great space of time must have been required: and we are thus forced to assign to a very remote period the last great separation of the race. Long before this, also, the severance of the Greek and Latin branches had taken place. At a period largely still more remote, the Gothic and Sclavic branches emigrated, and still further back in the depths of antiquity, the Celtic branch commenced its long march—*how* long before, we cannot measure, or even conjecture.

Thousands of years afterwards, at any rate, and yet, I think, not less than four thousand years before our era, we find the ancestors of the Hindūs, a fair-skinned race, living and warring in the Punjab; and even earlier than that, the ancestors of the Medians and Persians conquering under Zarathustra the Scyths, Toorkhs or Tâtars from the north, and the indigenous tribes, in Bactria.

The Punjab (a Persian word meaning "five waters") is a plain, divided into five *Doabs* by the river, flowing into the Indus, that forms its western boundary, which intersect it, and extending from the Suleiman Mountains, or Himalayas, on the northeast, and the Hindu Kush Range, on the northwest, to the rivers Sutlej and Punjab; forming a delta; its extreme length and breadth being, from north to south 400, and from east to west 350 miles. It lies between the same parallels of latitude as the state of Mississippi, 30° and 35°. The soil is generally sandy; but grain and fruits of all kinds are cultivated; indigo, sugar and tobacco are largely produced; and the date, orange, fig, grape, apple, mulberry, banana and mango are among the fruits. Large trees are now scarce, extensive tracts having on them only mimosas, acacias and smaller shrubs. In summer, the climate is hot and dry; in winter cold, and often frosty. The large alluvial plains are fertile and are alluded to in the hymns to the River-Goddess Sarasvati; and the extensive pasture-grounds still support great herds of buffaloes (which also are named in the hymns), as well as cattle, horses and camels.

In the northeastern part is the valley of Cashmere, surrounded on all sides by mountains, and noted for its fertility and beauty. Here are produced fruits and flowers, especially roses unrivalled, of both tropical and temperate climates.

Owing to the cold, frosty climate of the winter, the people of the Punjab are vigorous and athletic. Below it is Scinde. West of it, beyond the Indus, Kabul; beyond the Sutlej, the Ganges country; and to the northwest, across the Hindu Kush, Toorkhistan.

There is nothing in the Vedic hymns to indicate that the country in which their authors lived was a tropical one. There are no references to the tropical fruits that grow in the Punjab; and it may well be doubted whether the earliest of the hymns were composed there. The name of the river and the Goddess Sarasvati may perhaps still be found in the name Ser Affshan, of the river of Samarkand and Bokhara.

If the "sea" spoken of is not the Indus, it is either the Indian Ocean or the Caspian. If the former, the hymns were not composed either in Sogdiana or the Punjab; for it was long after the settlement in the latter commenced, before the Ganges country was reached, and long after that, again, before the Indo-Aryans had reached the Indian Ocean. The area of the Caspian is 180,000 square miles; and it was of course known to the Aryans before they crossed the Oxus or the Hindu Kush; besides which it was then much larger.

The seven rivers of the Indus country are: the Sindhu (Indus), its eastern confluents, Vitastâ (anciently the Hydaspes), Asiknî (the Akesines), Purushnî (the Hydraortes), Vipâs (the Hyphasis), and Satadru (the Hesudrus); and the western, Kubhâ (the Kophen), which comes from Kabul.

The rainy season commences in the Punjab towards the end of June; but the rivers begin to swell with the first heats of spring and summer, by the melting of the snow on the mountains contiguous to their sources. It appears that Alexander the Great crossed the Indus and invaded the Punjab, some time in the beginning of May, and found the rivers swollen and constantly rising. Tamerlane passed the Indus in 1398, in October, nearly at the same spot where Alexander had crossed it 1,725 years before. On the Hydaspes, Alexander procured a fleet of two thousand vessels, and upon it carried his army down the Indus to the sea.

I have concluded that the earliest Vedic hymns were composed by the ancient Rishis (seven of whom, translated to the sky, were supposed to have become the Seven Stars of Ursa Major, which are called "the Seven Rishis"), in Sogdiana, after Yama or Yima had led the ancestors of the Irano-Aryans into Bactria; and only the later ones in the Punjab.

Of the social condition of the Indo-Aryans, Dr. Muir says, in the fifth volume of his "Sanskrit Texts," p. 473,

Although the hymns of the *Rig-Veda* exhibit a simpler, or less advanced, or less definitely fixed and developed stage of religious belief and conceptions than we meet with in the works of the earliest Greek poets, and a system of ideas widely diverse both from the mythological forms, and the theosophic opinions, of the later Indian Pantheon, and of subsequent speculations; and although some of the customs and practices of that early age were different from those which prevailed in later times, it would be a mistake to suppose that, in the former period the condition of society was of a very primitive description.

And he adds, that the inquiry with which these remarks conclude

has brought into view many signs of a considerable progress in civilization, and in even a certain sort of refinement, as then existing.

Of their religious worship I shall speak in the second lecture of this series. This I shall conclude with a brief statement of the information given us by the *Veda* as to their social condition, habits and institutions.

There is no doubt that the Indo-Aryans had, in the Vedic era, in the words of Professor Wilson (*Introduction, xvii., to vol. ii., of his translation of the Rig-Veda*),

attained to an advanced stage of civilization, little, if at all, differing from that in which they were found by the Greeks of Alexander's invasion.

And this advanced stage of civilization may be inferred also, as he remarks,

from the degree of perfection to which the grammatical construction of the language had been brought, and still more from the elaborate system of metrical composition of which so many examples occur, and of which the Sûktas attributed to the Rishi Poruchahepa afford such remarkable instances.

Both branches of the race had the manly and heroic nature and characteristics that were so finely displayed by the ancient Greeks, Romans, Gauls and Germans. They had villages, and were governed by chiefs, each independent of the other, many of whom are mentioned by name in the older books as well as the later of the *Zend-Avesta*, as residing on or beyond particular rivers. The *Veda* speaks frequently of the cities of the hostile natives of the country, Indra being said to have destroyed a hundred such, of Sambara, but I believe that no cities of the Aryans themselves are mentioned in the *Rig-Veda*. In the Vendidad, the "circle" built by Yima, was a large and well-built city, of the length on each side, of a riding-course, if Spiegel's translation is correct, as I think it is.

The word "king" is often found in the translations; but Râja, which is so rendered, means only a ruler or chief; and not a line in the *Veda* warrants the conclusion that there was an Indo-Aryan monarchy, governed by a single sovereign. Zarathustra became monarch over all the Irano-Aryan country; but until then, the people had lived in clans and confederacies, and each chief of a region was independent of all the others, and owned no superior. In *Rig-Veda i.*, 126, 1, a king or chief called Bhâvya is celebrated, who dwelt on the banks of the Sindhu. In *viii.*, 21, 18, Chitra and the chiefs are alluded to as living near the Sarasvati. Ten kings are alluded to as having fought against Sudâs, in *vii.*, 33, 3, and *vii.*, 83, 6, *ff.*

Numerous names of chiefs occur in the *Rig-Veda.* They were wealthy, for we have accounts given by the Ṛishis themselves, of vast numbers of cattle, of horses, chariots and gold, and elegantly-adorned female slaves, given by them to the priests and bards.

In the *Zend-Avesta*, the household comforts and luxuries of the chiefs and the wealthy, and the fine clothing and jewelry of their women and daughters are enlarged upon. The existence of the two classes, the rich and the poor, is distinctly referred to in the *Veda* and in the *Zend-Avesta.* And in the latter, in a Fargard of the Vendidad which declares the penalty of murder, that for killing a rich man is ten times greater than that prescribed for killing a poor man.

At first blush this seems an infamous law, but it is immediately and satisfactorily explained, "for," it is said, "he who kills a rich man may thereby unawares slay an hundred poor ones." For in that day, the prosperity of the employer was the good fortune of the laborer and the herdsmen, and men did not become rich by grinding the faces of the poor. There were no stocks or bonds, then, in which one could invest his profits, and live in luxurious laziness, as useless to man and God as a wolf or a vermin. Wealth consisted in lands, cattle, horses, camels, compelling the employment by every wealthy franklin of large numbers of laborers and dependents, who constituted his family, owed him military service, and were to him what the Scottish clansmen were to the Highland chieftains. Men did not then grow rich, one at the expense and by the spoliation of many; by means of stock-gambling and speculation and the spasmodic financial convulsions caused by irredeemable paper-money, a great public debt, huge monopolies and the vicious interferences of a national treasury, which, combining together, making it impossible for a laboring man even to buy his dinner without a speculation akin to gaming.

There was no standing army; there were no custom-houses, excises or duties, and articles of ordinary consumption for the poor did not pay toll to half a dozen dealers, by successive additions of profit doubling the cost, before they reached the mouths of the hungering consumers. Corn was not burned for fuel because it was not worth carrying from the producer to the consumer. Men worshipped the Deities in the open air, sacrificing on an altar built of stones or turf, when the rain-stars rose at early dawn, announcing the return of light, and Ushas, the Dawn, blushed in the east and paled the radiant glories of the Morning-Star; and the bards and priests looked to the generosity of the worshippers alone for their reward and sustenance.

All the legislation of either branch of the race during centuries would hardly have equalled in bulk the statutes of a single session of the legislature of the District of Columbia. There were no paper constitutions of government, to be violated by power or evaded by judicial knaveries of logic. The only law spoken of in the *Veda* or *Zend-Avesta*, is the divine law; and even in a later age the laws of Manu are not the statutes of a parliament or congress, but the corollaries of reason, justice and simple good sense. Among the Irano-Aryans, the most grievous of offenses was to lie or to violate a contract; and the next was to be in debt, because, it was explained, it causes men to lie.

In that day, the state and the true faith were everything, and the individual man, in comparison, nothing. To serve the state, and extend and by the sword defend the true religion, were the highest duties of life, and constituted its especial glory. Men pursued manly occupations, and did not do the work of women; and women were their counsellors and companions, honored and beloved, especially among the Irano-Aryans. The wisest and the best among the people became their rulers, the successful soldier being entitled to govern; and it had not been discovered that chicane and corruption were then to be in the management of public affairs.

There is no law, either in the *Veda* or *Zend-Avesta*, forbidding polygamy, nor any precept that disapproves it. It was not considered criminal or wrong, among any of the ancient nations, to have more than one wife. There are texts of the *Veda* that show that to some extent polygamy was indulged in. I remember none such in the *Zend-Avesta*, where the wife is always spoken of as the only wife; and it clearly appears from the *Veda* that monogamy was the rule and polygamy only the rare exception.

In *x.*, 85, 6, a later hymn, a wish is expressed, on the occasion of the marriage ceremonial, in the bride's favor, that she may be a queen (*Samrâ-juî*) over her father-in-law, her mother-in-law, her husband's sister and his brothers; and in the *Zend-Avesta* certain wives and daughters are spoken of in most exalted terms; but I must not conceal the discreditable fact that Indra is made to say, in *viii.*, 33, 17,

that the mind of a woman is ungovernable and her temper fickle.

The hymns of the *Veda* are so entirely poetic and devotional, that very few moral precepts are to be found in them. There are more in the *Zend-Avesta*, and there is nothing in either to sanction any other than a virtuous and upright life. In the *Atharva-Veda iii.*, 30, the poet says,

I impart to you concord, with unity of hearts and freedom from hatred. Delight one in another . . . . May the son be obedient to the father, and of one mind with his mother: may the wife, at peace with her husband, speak to him honied words. Let not brother hate brother, nor sister sister: concordant, and united in will, speak to one another with kind words. We perform in your house an incantation, to create concord among its inmates, whereby the Devas will not desert you, nor mutual hatred exist.

And the great duty of charity is thus inculcated in *Rig-Veda x.*, 117

The Devas have not ordained that hunger shall be our death. Even those who are amply fed are overtaken by diverse deaths. The prosperity of the liberal man never decays; while the illiberal finds no comforter. He who, himself well provided with sustenance, hardens his heart against the poor man who approaches him, starving, and who has long courted him, desirous of food, such a man meets with none to cheer him. He is the bountiful man who gives to the lean beggar who comes to him craving food. Success attends that man in the sacrifice, and he secures for himself a friend in the future. . . . . Let the powerful man be generous to the suppliant. Let him look down the long path. For riches revolve like the wheels of a chariot; they come now to one, now to another. . . . . He who keeps his food to himself, has sin to himself. A priest who speaks is more acceptable than one who is silent. A kinsman who is benevolent excels one who is stingy.

In *x.*, 107, liberality in giving to the sacrifice and the priests is thus lauded:

The givers of gifts dwell on high, in the sky; the bestowers of horses live with the sun; the givers of gold attain immortality; the bestowers of raiment prolong their lives. . . . . The wise man makes the giving of gifts his cuirass. Bountiful men neither die nor fall into calamity; they suffer neither wrong nor pain.

In the third Fargard of the Vendidad it is said that what is most acceptable to the Aryan land is, to sacrifice to and adore Mithra, and the next most acceptable thing is, that an Aryan should build himself a home there, provided with fire and cattle, a wife, children and good flocks; and the next, the production of food by cultivation, and the watering of dry land, or draining that which is too wet. What is the increase of the Mazdayaçnian Law? it is asked; and the answer is, given by Ahura Mazda,

when one diligently cultivates corn, O Holy Zarathustra. He who cultivates the fruits of the field cultivates piety, and promotes and extends the Mazdayaçnian Law.

In the fourth Fargard this law is enacted:

Who to a lending man does not pay back the debt, is a thief of the loan, a robber of what is lent to him.

And in the thirteenth,

> Whoso wounds a dog that guards the cattle, or cuts off his ears or his feet, if then a thief or a wolf comes and drives away the cattle without being detected, he who harmed the dog shall make good the loss;

a rule of the law of damages which one instinctively feels to be just.

References are made in various passages of the *Veda*, to well-dressed females, and well-made garments. Jewels and ornaments are spoken of, and were evidently prized as highly then as they are now; and we may gather from these passages, as we may more fully from some in the *Zend-Avesta*, that husbands and fathers indulged then, as they do now the taste of their wives and daughters for decoration. The materials and fashion of the garments are hardly spoken of.

In the *Zend-Avesta*, one who killed a priest was condemned to put off the loose-flowing garments of the civilian, and don the close-fitting dress of the soldier, and fight against the infidels all his life, in expiation of his crime. That seemed a better use to put a man to, than to hang him, and a means of restoration to the divine favor. It was not the clerical fashion then to send abandoned criminals from the scaffold to the arms of Jesus. Works meet for repentance seemed to these relatives of ours, to be essential to salvation.

There were professors of medicine, and of surgery among both branches of the race. Among the Irano-Aryans, one who desired a license to practice surgery, had to operate with the knife, first, upon an infidel prisoner. He was allowed three trials. If after each the subject died, the aspirant could never be permitted to operate upon an Aryan. If he did, either without such previous testing, or after failure, he was punishable as for homicide. And, in speaking of physicians, it is said that those who cure with medicinal herbs and plants, are not so successful or so excellent as those who cure by prayer. We have lost, long ago, that old faith in the efficacy of prayer, as we have lost many other things that we should have done more wisely to keep, and as we have got in their stead many other things that it would be profitable to throw away.

The principal vices seem to have been indulgence in wine or spirituous liquor of some kind, and gaming. It does not appear whether Surâ was really wine; but as grapes grow abundantly in the region which they inhabited, no doubt they had learned to make wine. Gaming seems to have been chiefly with dice; and it does not appear to have been a general habit, nor is any punishment denounced against it.

The Hymn x., 34, of the *Rig-Veda* is the lamentation of a ruined gamester. Its naïveness is amusing, but it also shows that there are many things in which the Aryan world has not changed. Of its fourteen verses, perhaps these may interest you:

> (2) She [his wife] never quarreled with or despised me. She was kind to me and to my friends [what more excellent and gracious quality than this could be ascribed to a wife? for are not one's friends generally odious to his wife?]. But I, for the sake of the unfriendly dice have neglected my devoted spouse.
>
> (3) My mother-in-law hates me; my wife will not remain with me. [In his need the gambler finds no one to console him. I cannot discover what enjoyment the gambler has any more than I can perceive what is the happiness of a worn-out hack-horse.]
>
> (4) Other men pay court to the wife of the man whose wealth is coveted by the impetuous dice. His father, mother, brothers, cry out, "We know nothing of him! Bind him and take him away."
>
> (7) Hooking, piercing, deceitful, vexatious, delighting to torment, the dice dispense transient gifts, and again ruin the winner.
>
> (8) The chief himself makes obeisance to them.
>
> (9) They roll downward, they bound upward . . . . These celestial coals, when flung on the dice board, scorch the heart, though cold themselves.
>
> (11) It tortures the gamester to see his own wife, and then to observe the wives and happy homes of others.
>
> (13) Never play with the dice; practice husbandry; rejoice in what thou hast, esteeming it sufficient. There, gamester, are thy cows, thy wife.
>
> (14) Be benignant, dice; be auspicious to us; do not bewitch us powerfully with your enchantment. Let your anger and ill-will abate. Let others than we be subject to the fetters of the brown ones.

Who will deliver *us* from the body of this death? Of this mania for gaming, legitimately inherited like a poisonous disease in the Aryan blood, and inflamed to a veritable insanity by the evil influences of fluctuating stocks, sharp practices and knavish devices, of a national debt represented by floating paper, by an irredeemable paper currency, expanded or contracted at the will and pleasure of a single man, for the benefit, if he pleases, of a particular interest, a particular manufacture, a particular section, or to enable a few to become rich by robbing others of the money—a passion fostered by lotteries that are the devil's devices, to serve the cause of the church or charity, or to aid particular institutions; by gift-concerts and raffles at fairs held in the temples of religion, by the very nature and hazards of much of the business of the day and the universal greed for fortune, to be obtained by some lucky chance or speculation, or some dishonest scheme that can be made to succeed only by legislative corruption?

It is a golden sentence of the old Aryan poets, a little modified: "Game not with the dice of any knavish or unsound venture or speculation! Practice thine honest vocation! With that which thou hast, be content, esteeming it sufficient."

In *Rig-Veda ix.*, 112, we have these amusing remarks, which give us a glimpse of some of the occupations of the Indo-Aryans:

(1) We different men all have our various imaginations and designs. The carpenter seeks something that is broken, the physician a patient, the priest some one who will offer libations.

(2) With dry sticks, feathers, metals and fire, the artisan continually seeks after a man with plenty of gold.

(3) I am a poet; my father is a physician; my mother is a grinder of corn. With our different aims, seeking to get gain, we run after them as after cattle.

(4) The draught-horse desires an easy-running carriage; merry companions a laugh; the maidens lovers, and frogs a pond.

The three Ribhus (deemed to have become stars) were celebrated for their skill as workers in wood and metal, and builders of chariots. The manufacture of weapons of war, spears, swords, knives, axes, was common. There were skilful workers in gold, makers of ornaments, and weavers of fine and delicate fabrics for the wealthy. The art of boat building was known, and working in leather was common. Tvashṭṛi, the softening and melting power of fire, was personified as a Deity, the artisan of the Gods, maker of the thunderbolts of Indra; and Asha-Vahista was the divine forger of human weapons, in the *Zend-Avesta*. In *x.*, 142, 4, Agni is said to shave the earth, as a barber shaves a beard.

In war, horsemen composed the principal part of the forces, at least of the Irano-Aryans; and foot soldiers are not especially mentioned, as such, in the *Rig-Veda*. War-chariots, drawn by two horses each, were used, proving that large bodies of men must have been engaged, and in open ground. Banners were borne in battle; and the bowmen are lauded as the most efficient part of the Aryan forces. From 30,000 to 60,000 Dasyus are said to have been slain in different battles.

In that, we find existing, as Professor Wilson says, in the Aryan towns or cities, the arts, sciences, institutions and vices of civilized life, golden ornaments, coats of mail, weapons of offense, the use of musical instruments, the employment of the needle, and also computation of the divisions of time to a minute extent, including repeated allusions to the seventh season or intercalary month.

Merchants are described in the *Veda* as earnestly pressing on board ship, for the sake of gain; and Professor Wilson believes that the Indian Ocean was known to the composers of the *Vedas*, and used at that period for purposes of commerce. But it is very uncertain whether any other sea than the Caspian is spoken of; and moreover, the word rendered by sea equally applied to the Indus. The ships spoken of were probably like those of which Alexander procured two thousand, to descend the Indus.

It is absolutely certain that at the time when the Vedic hymns, or at least all of them except the very latest, were composed, the Indo-Aryans had not extended into the Ganges country. They lived near and in sight of the mountains, where the rivers ran with great rapidity, and were engaged in hostilities with the Dasyus on the Sutlej. There are probably modern additions to many of the ancient hymns, and the allusions to the ocean may thus have been introduced. They certainly did not navigate in ships the Indian Ocean; and what they called the sea may have been a lake, like the Sea of Galilee.

It appears, though not very perspicuously described, that daughters shared the paternal inheritance. Women took part in sacrifices, and appeared abroad in public. The Irano-Aryans exchanged commodities with dealers from a distance, not only bartering the products of their farms, but gold obtained by mining operations carried on by them; for articles of luxury and dress for their women.

As it cost less then to carry on war, so it cost less to carry on the government of men, than it does now. It is odd that a race whom it costs so enormously to govern, and to carry on whose silly quarrels armies so enormous have to be kept on foot, should keep always in view another life, in which there is to be perfect peace, no armies, epaulets and glory, no profitable offices and no expenditures of public money.

In those ancient days, the machinery of government was very simple. Few laws were needed, and there were no paid legislators. The laws were simple and plain, and there was no costly judicial machinery to interpret them. Religion was a tax, because the priests and bards coveted largesses; but there were no temples or cathedrals, as, also, there were no idols and images, demanding gold and diamonds. For the most part, as among the ancient Greeks and Romans and the old Germanic tribes in their forests, men served the public in peace, and fought for it in war, without pay. Even when Rome had existed five hundred years or more, it could be truly said: *"jurisconsulti domus, oraculum civitatis"*: that the house of the lawyer was the oracle of the city; the wise and learned scorned to take fees for their opinions, and the prætors, as well as the consuls received no salary for serving the commonwealth. It cannot be otherwise now, than that men not able to serve the state without it, should be paid, that they may live while serving it; but it ought not to be the case, as it is, that there shall be a money value, and a demand for so much coin or currency, for *every* service, of *every* nature, rendered to the state; or that not to plunder it shall be deemed a singular excellence.

This sketch of those heroic men whose remote ancestors were also ours will only be complete when their religious and philosophical opinions are expounded. Nor will even this partial view give you an insight into their social condition, if you are left to suppose that their priests were always objects of reverence, and that satire and humor were alien to the Aryan mind. I hope you may have become sufficiently interested to desire to hear in other lectures an exposition of their intellectual idiosyncrasies, of their language and their religion; and I conclude this lecture with a part of the 103rd Hymn of the seventh Mandala, which is called a panegyric of the frogs, and, as Professor Müller says, is clearly a satire on the priests. We should hardly have the right to think highly of the shrewdness of any people, and especially of its poets, to whom the greed of the priests for gifts did not suggest hypocrisy and prove repulsive.

(1) These vow-fulfilling Brahmans, the frogs, after lying quiet for a year, have now uttered their voice, stimulated by Parjanya [the causer of rain].

(2) When the waters from the sky fall upon them as they lay like a dry skin in the pond, the voice of the frogs rose in concert, like the lowing of cows that have calves.

(3) When, at the coming of autumn, rain fell upon them, when they were ardently desiring it and parched with thirst, one, croaking, approaches, as a son to his father, another who is crying out.

(4) One of them seizes the other when they are delighted with the pouring down of the waters, when the speckled frog, soaked and up-leaping, joins his voice to that of the green one.

(5) When one repeats the sounds of the other, as a pupil does the words of his teacher, all your limbs seem in active exercise, as ye make a loud noise upon the waters.

(6) One lows like a cow, another bleats like a goat; one of these is speckled, another green. Called by one name, they are of diverse appearance, and modulate their voices diversely as they croak.

(7) Like Brahmans at the Atirâtra Soma-rite, like them talking round a full bowl, ye frogs surround the pond on this day of the year, which is the day of incoming autumn.

(8) The Soma-offering Brahmans raise their voices, performing their annual devotions; these Adhvaryus, sweating over their hot caldrons, issue forth like persons who have been hidden.

(9) They have observed the divine ordinances that fix the seasons of the year; these creatures do not forget the season; when autumn comes, these heated kettles obtain rest.

(10) The frog that lows, and the frog that bleats, the speckled one and the brown, have bestowed on us riches; giving us hundreds of cattle, the frogs prolong our lives, in the season of a thousand shouts.

In a much later poem, the Harivamça, the noise made by a frog, after his rest of sixteen half-months, among his wives, is compared by the poet to the recitation of the *Rig-Veda* by a Brahman surrounded by his pupils. On which verse Langlois naïvely says:

In our way of thinking nothing could equal the impertinence of a comparison in which a frog should be assimilated to a respectable ecclesiastic. But the Indians, as it seems, saw in such a comparison no tinge of impiety.

I am sorry to say, that if the Vedic or Bactrian bards were sensible to the charms of Aryan beauty, as their descendants have always been, they either thought love no proper subject for their songs (which can hardly be believed), or their amatory effusions are irretrievably lost. We owe to the devotional and patriotic instincts of the race, the preservation of all these ancient poems, and to time we must ascribe the loss of all that have not a religious character.

We find in the *Zend-Avesta* the Aryan women and their Fravashis spoken of with especial veneration: and the beneficent Deities Çpĕnta-Armaiti, Haurvaṭ, Amĕrĕtâṭ, Ardviçura and others are females. Some of them described as having the forms of youthful and beautiful maidens.

In the Farvardin Yasht, in which are lauded and invoked the Fravashis or immortal spirits of the living, the dead and the unborn, to whom extraordinary potencies and immense beneficence are ascribed, the especial aides of the Aryans against the infidel Turanians, the Drukhs and the Dævas, a section is devoted to those of women. That of the pure or pious Hvôvi, said to have been the wife of Zarathustra is first praised; then those of Freni, Thriti and Pouru-Chiçta, his daughters; and next, that of the pious Hutaôça. Many others are named, of whom nothing more than the names is known; but we have elsewhere a glimpse or two of Hutaôça.

When Zarathustra was striving to unite the Aryans for the purpose of endeavoring to expel from their country the Infidels, Drukhs, Toorkhs, Tâtars or Scyths, fierce horsemen, who had invaded it from the north, possessed themselves of the most fertile portion and there established themselves, with the aid of revolted native tribes, Turanians, Çarmanians, Cârians and Dâhians; and who harassed the Aryans, in the portions of the country which they still held, by constant raids and maraudings, it was all-important to gain over to the cause of the true faith, Vîstâçpa, the Gushtasp of the modern Persian legends, a powerful chief, at a distance from the residence of the patriot Zarathustra. Hutaôça, a noble Aryan maiden, was betrothed to him, and being enlisted in the cause by Zarathustra's teachings, he, by her influence, secured the active co-operation of Vîstâçpa, and was thus enabled to liberate the country.

To the Flame, it is said in one of the Yashts, offered Hutaôça with many brothers, for the clan of the Naôtaras, on a golden throne, a golden foot-stool, a golden covering, praying for this favor:

Grant me, O Flame, that ascendest heavenward, that I may be loved, may be received with love in the dwelling of Kavi Vîstâçpa.

And the Flame granted her this favor, as the creator Ahura Mazda approved it. And Zarathustra prayed to the Goddess Ashis-Vanuhi and Drvâçpa that he might secure the co-operation of the good and noble Hutaðça, for thinking the true doctrine and speaking and acting in accordance with it. She, he said, shall guard me the Mazdayaçnian Law in the heart, and worship Ahura, by her devotion aiding me in the good work.

And thus, in that ancient age of the world, when the continued existence of that great branch of the Aryan race, whence Kuros or Cyrus, the liberator of the enslaved children of Israel afterwards came, whose right hand the Lord God of Israel held, calling him His Shepherd, was dependent upon Aryan union, and the triumph of the Ahurian faith was doubtful and uncertain, it was a maiden who came to the aid of the liberator, won over to the cause the king by whom she was beloved, and earned a title to the veneration of all her race.

For the history of the world would have been very differently written, if the course of Aryan emigration to the southwest had been stopped, the Median Empire not established, if the Babylonian Empire had not been overthrown, and the captive Hebrews had not returned to Palestine. And it is at least certain that but for the influence of Hutaðça, Vîstâçpa would never have won what the world calls immortal honor, nor his name been gratefully remembered and sung by poets until our day. So true it is, as it always was and always will be, that a good and true woman is man's wisest adviser and the surest guardian of his honor.

LECTURE TWO

THE VEDA

THE ARYAN LANGUAGES

In this second lecture I hope to interest you in the *Veda* or Collection of Ancient Hymns of the Indo-Aryans, by making you acquainted with its nature, history and general character, with extracts from a few of the hymns; and to show you that the language in which it now exists, the Sanskrit, is one sister of several, among which is our common English tongue, all descended from one original Aryan language, spoken by our ancestors thousands of years ago, in the country afterwards known as Toorkhistan, lying between the Caspian Sea and Lake Aral on the west, and the Bolor Tagh range of mountains on the east, between the great rivers Oxus and Jaxartes.

The *Rich* (or, as commonly written, *Rig*) *Veda Sanhitâ*, which is called par excellence *"the Veda,"* is a collection of *Sûktas* (hymns), in ten *Mandalas* (circles), subdivided into rather more than a hundred *Anuvâkas*, or subsections. The *Sûktas* are divided into *vargas* (paragraphs or verses), of about five stanzas each. In quoting from the work, the reference commonly is to Mandala, Sûkta and Stanza.

There are, in all, something over a thousand *Sûktas*. Another division of these is into eight *Ashṭakas* (eighths), called also *Khandas* (portions), each subdivided into eight *Adhyâyas* or lectures.

Eight of the ten Mandalas (the ninth and tenth being much less ancient) were translated into English, principally in accordance with the notions of Sâyaṇa, Yaska and other Hindû commentators, by Professor H. H. Wilson, and published in four volumes. A very large number of the hymns of all the Mandalas, and an immense number of passages and single verses, have been translated by Dr. J. Muir, in Volumes *iv.* and *v.* of his *Original Sanskrit Texts:* and some have been translated by Professor Max Müller in his *Lectures on Languages* and *Chips from a German Workshop;* and he has also given to the world, in one volume (the first of a series, the rest of which are to follow), with copious and elaborate notes, the hymns addressed to the Maruts or Winds, of the first and second Mandalas.

I am under obligations, in this lecture, to all these, and to the criticisms contained in Professor Whitney's *Oriental and Linguistic Studies*, as well as to the *Oriental Religions* of Samuel Johnson. On the filiation and parallelism of the Aryan languages, I am, in common with Professor Müller and Dr. Muir, under immense obligations to that great work, the *Compara-*

tive Grammar of Professor Bopp, and I, at least, to Eichhoff's *Parallèle des Langues de l'Europe et de l'Inde.*

The hymns of the *Rich-Veda* and the five Gâthâs of Zarathustra are unquestionably the oldest literary compositions now extant in the world. The Vedic hymns contain the religious notions of the Indo-Aryan priests, poets and people, during that remote period when they inhabited the Punjab, and in part those of the race before its division into Indo- and Irano-Aryans.

The Exodus from Egypt, according to the approved chronology, occurred 1,648 years before Christ. The *Vedas* were compiled 1,200 years before Christ, being then of an unknown antiquity, and the language in which they had been composed and retained in memory having become a dead language. The Brahmans were then, as they have ever been since, unable to interpret them. Kingdoms and empires had been founded, risen to the heights of power and splendor, and grown gray with age, since these hymns were chanted at the sacrifices in the valleys of the Five Rivers, or of the Zer Affshan in Sogdiana, before they were so compiled.

And it is a curious and suggestive fact that it is to European scholars and philology the Brahmans of the present day owe the knowledge that their spoken-language is a branch of the Sanskrit, as the Portuguese is of the Latin, and their real understanding of their own sacred books. The five volumes of Dr. Muir's *Original Sanskrit Texts* have been written and published in English, for the instruction of the Brahmans and native scholars. It is even more singular that all real knowledge of the Zend language and books is due to French, German and Danish scholars, and that the translation by Dr. Bleeck of Professor Spiegel's German translation of the *Zend-Avesta* was made for and printed at the expense of a Parsee gentleman, for the use of the Parsees of Bombay.

The Book of Genesis records the ancient traditions and legends of the Semitic race, and makes known to us the ancient thought, the ancient feelings, joys, hopes and fears, of those who were the ancestors of the Chaldeans, Phœnicians, Kenanim or Canaanites, Hebrews, and the grand Arabian race. The *Veda* brings us face to face, if not with our ancestors, at least with the ancient descendants of our ancestors, in their tents and pastures, adoring the Fire, the Light and the Luminaries of Heaven, and sacrificing before the dawn, especially at the opening of the spring, to the Morning-Star, the Bright Twins, and to Ushas or Ushahina, the Dawn; nowhere else is there a sigh, a jest or a glimpse, save in the *Veda* or Gâthâs of the old Asiatic humanity.

Veda, from *vid*, to "know," meant "knowing" or "knowledge." It is the same word as the Greek οἶδα and ειδω, or ξοιδα and ξειδω, the Latin *video*, the Gothic *vait*, the Anglo-Saxon *wât*, the German *weiss*, and the English *wise, wot,* and to *wit.*   There are four collections of the hymns, the *Rich,* or *Rig-Veda;* the *Yajush,* or *Yajur-Veda;* the *Sâman,* or *Sâma-Veda,* and the *Atharvana* or *Atharva-Veda:* of which the *Rig-Veda* is the only real one for tracing the earliest growth of religious ideas in India, because it alone contains the most ancient hymns.   And it enables us to determine to some extent what the Aryan faith was prior to the Greek and Latin migrations; because we find in the Vedic hymns, their Deities and figurative expressions, the origin of much of the Grecian and Latin mythology.   For example, the Greek *Zeus* and *Dios* (the Jupiter of the Romans), and the Latin *Deus* are the same as the Sanskrit *Dyaus,* the Sky.   I shall hereafter bring to your notice many others, the influences attributed to the Pleiades, the peculiar attributes of Mercury, and others.

Rig-Veda means the *Veda* of *Praise, rich* being derived from a root that in Sanskrit means to "celebrate, shine, honor"; identical with *aich.*

Professor Müller ascribes the composition of the Vedic hymns to a later period than Bunsen does; and in his fear of shocking English prejudices, is exceedingly vague and unsatisfactory upon that point.   Even Bunsen is careful not to say that the *Veda* is older than the Hebrew books.   These sagacious and astute inquirers thoroughly satisfy and convince us that all the European languages are from the same ancient source as the Indian and Persian: but their attempts to show a relationship between them and the Semitic tongues are lamentable failures.

Müller well says that

> the real history of man is the history of religion, the ways by which the different families of the human race advanced towards a truer knowledge and a deeper love of God; . . . . this is the Light, the Soul and the Life of History.

He remarks that "the oldest, most primitive and simplest form of Aryan faith finds its expression in the *Veda.*"   To this it is impossible to assent. The notions embodied in the *Veda* are the fruit of a comparatively late intellectual development advancing from the worship of visible objects to that of universal potencies.   We do not know what the Aryan faith was when the Gothic and Sclavic migrations took place; and the Celtic was still earlier.   Nor do we know whether the northern mythology retains any-thing of the original Aryan faith, or of that which prevailed when the migra-tions occurred which peopled northern Europe; or whether it is wholly a growth of later ages in their new homes.   They certainly have no *names* of *Gods* in common with the Indo- or Irano-Aryans, and Thor, Odin and Frea have no parallels in the *Veda* or *Zend-Avesta.* The single exception is the *Aser.*

But Müller truly says that "No idols or animals are mentioned in the *Veda,* as objects of worship."   For, in fact, idols and images are not mentioned at all. They belong only to a faith which makes Gods after man's image. They do not represent the light and the heat, the flame, the winds and the dawn. The *Veda* invests few of its Deities with the human form, and if it represents Sarasvati, the River-Goddess as a maiden, as it does Ushas, the Dawn, and even Saraṇyû, the vaporous fleecy cloud, this is simply poetic personification. It does not represent any of them as actually coming down in human shape, and having commerce with men.

The same great scholar continues:

> We have in the *Veda*, ancient thought expressed in ancient language. [And this is true, even comparing its language with the Sanskrit of the later writings. For we find in it less regard for grammatical rules, more antique terminations, words not used in the later writings, and words with meanings not retained by them in later ages, but closer to the meanings of the original roots. He adds]: We see reflected in it a phase of the intellectual life of man, to which there is no parallel in any other part of the world. In its hymns we see man left to himself, to solve the enigma of this world, and life.

We see men of like natures, tempers, idiosyncrasies and intellects as ourselves, precisely such men as we should be if born under precisely the same circumstances, but with the simple desires of a simple life in the forests and on the plains, for almost all the hymns express the wants and wishes of the herdsman and the dweller in the woods only traversable by paths, or on the steppes where only the luminaries of the day and night could be his guides. Some show the occupation of the worshipper to be that of the husbandman. They are villagers, and not denizens of towns and cities. Continually the prayer is for wealth and treasure; but these seem always to mean only horses and cattle; and for food.

Professor Müller says,

> We study in the *Veda* a theogony of which that of Hesiod is but the last chapter. We can study therein man's natural growth, and the results to which it may lead, under the most favorable conditions.

That is true; and we can study the intellect and the intellectual development of the last created and the holiest race of men, whose history is that of the civilized world, and who owe nothing whatever of their intellectual wealth, their morals, their wisdom, their philosophy or their religious doctrines to any other race.

The vast reverence in which the *Veda* has been held for 2,500 years at least, by a very large and intellectual portion of the human race, certainly makes it an object of interest to us, the kinsmen of those who so have reverenced and yet do reverence it, and well worth the trouble of endeavor-

ing to understand it.   How it is regarded and reverenced, can best be told
in the language of Professor Max Müller:

> The highest authority for the religion of the Brahmans is the *Veda*.   All other works
> —the Laws of Manu, the six orthodox systems of philosophy, the Purânas, or legend-
> ary histories of India—all derive their authority from their agreement with the *Veda*.
> The *Veda* alone is called *Çruti*, or revelation.   Everything else, however sacred,
> can only claim the title of *Smṛiti*, or tradition.   The most elaborate arguments have
> been framed by the Brahmans to establish the divine origin and the absolute authority
> of the *Veda*.   They maintain that it existed before all time, that it was revealed
> by Brahman and *seen* by divine sages, who themselves were free from the taint of
> humanity . . . .   This *Veda*, then, as handed down through this wonderful chain
> [a series of sages, in succession becoming less divine and more human], is the supreme
> authority of all orthodox Brahmans.   To doubt the divine origin and absolute
> authority of the *Veda* is heresy.   Buddha, by denying the authority of the *Veda*,
> became a heretic.
>
> At the present day, there are but few Brahmans who can read and understand
> the *Veda*.   They learn portions of it by heart, these portions consisting of hymns
> and prayers, which have to be muttered at sacrifices, and which every priest must
> know . . . .   It may be doubted whether a copy of the entire *Vedas* is procurable
> in any part of Hindustan; it is more than probable that such a copy does not exist
> in Bengal . . . .   The author of the so-called Laws of Manu says, "The root of
> the Law is the whole *Veda* and the traditions and customs of those who knew the
> *Veda* . . . .   To the departed, to Gods and men the *Veda* is an imperishable eye.
> The *Veda* is beyond the power and beyond the reason of man.   Traditional codes
> of law, not founded on the *Veda*, and all the heterodox theories of man, produce
> no good fruit after death; they are all declared to rest on darkness . . . .   The
> imperishable *Veda* supports all creatures, and therefore I think it is the highest
> means of salvation for this creature, man."

Dr. Muir devotes a whole volume of his *Sanskrit Texts* (the third) to
the opinions regarding the origin, potencies, etc., of the *Vedas*, held by
Indian authors.   The *Rig-Veda* is the essence of Agni, drawn forth by
Prajapati and from its words Brahma in the beginning fashioned the several
names, functions and separate conditions of all creatures.   And the words
of the *Rig-Veda* and other *Vedas* are eternal, and have an eternal connection
with their meanings, and therefore the *Vedas* are eternal, and consequently
perfect and infallible.

That the hymns which compose the *Rig-Veda* must have existed for
ages before they were compiled, admits of no doubt.   On this subject
Müller says:

> In different songs the names of different kings occur, and we see several generations
> of royal families pass away before us, with different generations of poets.   Old
> songs are mentioned, and new songs are mentioned.   Poets whose compositions we
> possess are spoken of as the seers of olden times; their names in other hymns are
> surrounded by a legendary halo.   In some cases whole books or chapters can be
> pointed out, as more modern and secondary, in thought and language.   But, on

the whole, the *Rig-Veda* is a genuine document, not later even in its most modern portions, than the time of Lycurgus. It exhibits one of the earliest and rudest phases in the history of mankind; and brings us as near the beginnings, in language, thought and mythology, as literary documents can ever bring us, in the Aryan world.

To this I add, that seven of the ancient Rishis, sons of a Rishi, are spoken of in the *Veda* as having been translated to the sky, and as having become there the seven stars of Ursa Major or the Great Bear, which were ever after known as the seven Rishis. And it is to these, no doubt, and not to the Pleiades, which were but six in number, that the peculiar sanctity of the number seven was owing, afterwards believed to have been due to the seven luminaries, the Sun and Moon, Saturn, Jupiter, Mars, Venus and Mercury, of which Saturn and Mercury were not known in the pre-Vedic period as planets. These seven stars, always visible at night, never setting, and always circling round the North Star, were probably the origin of the seven Amĕsha-Çpĕntas of Zarathustra, and of the seven Hebraic archangels, afterwards assigned to the Sun, Moon, and five known planets.

The identity of the Açvins with the Twins, Castor and Poludeukēs of Greece, is proof positive that these stars were adored before the Grecian migration. The hymn that describes the sacrifice of the horse Dadhikra must be referred to the remote time when the ancestors of the Vedic poets drove their cattle to pasture over the wide steppes of Toorkhistan. One thing, also, that has an important bearing on the age of the Vedic hymns, has not, I think, as yet been noticed. The sea is sometimes mentioned in them, as the Sea Vouru-Kasha is in the *Zend-Avesta*. All the commentators agree that all the older hymns, at least, were composed before the Indo-Aryans possessed themselves of the Ganges country, after a long residence in the Punjab. The composers of the hymns, therefore, dwelling in the Punjab, on the upper Indus, in sight of the Himalayas, if not even further north, and with an immense unknown region, populous with hostile tribes, between them and the Indian Ocean, could have had no knowledge of that ocean; nor would the people have understood what they meant, in speaking of it. From this it inevitably results, either that the hymns were not composed in the Punjab, but at a much later day in lower India, and when the sea had become a familiar object needing only to be named to the people, and not needing to be described; or else those who composed the hymns and the people also, had seen and known, and were familiar with, some other sea. This latter hypothesis can only be satisfied by supposing them to have meant the Caspian, of which the Sea of Aral was then a part, its level being then much higher than it now is, and the extent of its waters much greater. And it would seem to follow that these hymns, in which the sea is spoken of, are of much older date and were composed in Sogdiana. For other reasons I believe this to be the true solution.　It is absolutely certain that most of the hymns were composed in the Punjab, and that none but the most modern, if even one of them, after the advance beyond the Sutlej.

We have some knowledge of times still more ancient than those of the Indo-Aryan occupancy of the Punjab—in the words of Müller,

> of the period during which the as yet undivided Aryan nation formed their myths. Comparative philology has this whole period within the pale of documentary history.　It has placed in our hands a telescope of such power, that, where formerly we could see but nebulous clouds, we now discover distinct forms and outlines; nay, it has given us what we may call contemporary evidence, exhibiting to us the state of thought, language, religion and civilization, at a period when Sanskrit was not yet Sanskrit, Greek not yet Greek, but when both, together with Latin, German and other Aryan dialects, existed as yet as one undivided language.

Of that which is the most important and interesting portion of the history of every race and nation, the history of the progress of its intellect, and of its religious and philosophical ideas, the *Vedas* contain the only authentic record.　And of this they contain, as I think and as I hope to be able, though necessarily with brevity, to show, very much more than any of the commentators have discovered, though in one direction they have imagined the Indo-Aryan ideas to have extended beyond their *real* intellectual horizon.

I do not speak of the Hindū commentators; making the *Vedas* the sacred books of a newer faith, they have utterly denaturalized them, and systematically misunderstood and misinterpreted them.

The language of the Indo-Aryans was, in the words of Pictet (*Origines Indo-Européennes*, pp. 1, 2),

> admirable by its richness, its force, its harmony, the perfection of its forms, in which were spontaneously reflected all the impressions of the race; not merely its mild affections and its simple admiration, but also its nascent aspirations towards a higher world; a language abounding in images and intuitive ideas; bearing within it, in germ, all the future affluence, both of the most sublime poetry, and of the most profound reflection.　At first one and homogeneous, that language, already perfected to a very high degree, served as a common instrument of 'expression to this primitive people, as long as it continued within the limits of its native country . . . . The radical affinity of all the Aryan languages, necessarily leads us to regard them as having sprung from one single primitive language. . . . . And as a language always presupposes a people to speak it, it further follows that all the Aryan nations have issued from one single source, though they may occasionally have become blended, at a later period, with some foreign elements.　Hence we may with certainty infer the existence, at a prehistoric period, of an Aryan people, free, originally, from all foreign intermixture, sufficiently numerous to have supplied those swarms of men which issued from its bosom, and sufficiently endowed by Nature to have created for itself the most beautiful, perhaps, of all languages.

And, Mr. Pictet might have added, sufficiently acute of intellect and thoughtful to have conceived the profoundest philosophical ideas, and to have furnished the germs of all the profoundest theological and religious truths. For Pythagoras and Plato, the Hebrew Kabbalah and Asiatic Gnosticism, Philo, the Alexandrian contemporary of Christ, and Saint John, or the writer of the Gospel that bears his name, and Paul, the Cilician Hebrew, reproduce the very ideas of the *Zend-Avesta*, which are only the more ample development of those contained in the *Veda*, and more ancient than any of these compositions.

"This people," Mr. Pictet says, "though unknown to tradition, is in a certain degree revealed to us by philological science." But it is also revealed to us by its thoughts and ideas, its Deities and its notions concerning them, its customs and manners, as partially disclosed by the *Veda* and *Zend-Avesta*, and the account of the struggles of the Indian and Bactrian branches for the supremacy of each and of its faith—of both against the native races of the countries which they flowed into—and also of the Bactrian branch against the hordes of northern horsemen that from beyond the Oxus invaded the land of the seven Kareshvares and made themselves masters of it.

Each stream of emigration encountered the opposition of aboriginal races, in every country into which it flowed, and everywhere they were conquerors, or the original language would have died out for each. Each intermingled with the indigenous races, one in greater, another in less proportion, and the language of each became a composite one, by greater or less accessions from the indigenous tongues. Hence the vast differences and also the striking identities between the Welsh tongue and the Sanskrit, the Sclavonic and Persian, the Gothic and Greek, the Old High German and the Latin; and hence also the great differences of physical and intellectual characteristics, and the peculiar and apparently permanent types of the Irish, Grecian, German, Roman and Hindū face. In fact, the language and the type and cast of features, and the intellectual character of some of the races, and their instinctive antipathies against each other, come chiefly from the conquered aborigines; while others have preserved infinitely more of the Aryan type, probably because the conquerors were, relatively to the conquered, more numerous; and these physical and intellectual differences are also, no doubt, greatly owing to immense original differences, of face, form and intellect, among the aboriginal races of Asia and Europe, whom the Aryans overcame and mingled with.

But among the Indo-Aryans of the Vedic period, this intermixture of races and languages had not begun to take place. The hymns of this people, composed during that period of several centuries, very distinctly reveal to us its character and habits, and give us very distinct indications of the locality in which they were composed—some of them, especially, speaking of the wide alluvial bottom lands upon fine, clear, bold-running rivers subject to overflow. The lands were fertilized by rains, and not by irrigation. The peaks of the mountains are not named, as a hundred of them are in the *Zend-Avesta*.

They show us this people, proud of their color and Aryan blood, pure and uncontaminated by barbarian intermixture, living in a state of warfare with, and conquering and dispossessing, the native tribes. They picture the people to us as more a people of herdsmen than of husbandmen, a brave, simple, sincere people, whose profound religious instincts are evidenced by the various prayers which the hymns contain, for protection and victory, and all the varied blessings which constitute the sum of human welfare.

Langlois, in the preface to his translation of the *Rig-Veda*, thus accurately and strikingly depicts their social and political condition and their worship:

> The Indo-Aryans were disposed to piety, both by their natural character, and the institutions of Manu. They were sustained in these sentiments by the chiefs of certain families, in which their religious traditions have been more especially preserved. In those primitive ages, the political system was precisely the same as that which Homer depicts; kings, the veritable shepherds of their people; cultivators or herdsmen united around their chiefs, and prepared, whenever necessity arose, to transform themselves into warriors; numerous flocks, and a profusion of rural wealth; towns, which were only large villages. Of these villages some served as retreats to renowned sages, who, while their dependents were tending their fields and herds, were themselves engaged in the cultivation of sacred science, in the company of their sons or their pupils, and fulfilled the functions of a Calchas or a Tiresias, to some Aryan Agamemnon or Œdipus in their neighborhood. Invited by the chiefs to perform sacrifice, they arrived with their sacred retinue; they ascended the mountain, to where an enclosure of lattice-work had been constructed; for temples were then unknown. There, beneath the vault of heaven, they recited their hereditary songs, or a newly composed hymn. They invoked the grand agents in Nature to grant success to the labors of the field, increase to the flocks, and a succession of brave and virtuous descendants. They implored, they threatened their Gods [this last statement is wholly an error]; and when the sacred rites had been scrupulously performed, they retired, loaded with gifts, carrying away cows, horses and cars filled with provisions, gold and precious stuffs. We see thus by what fortune these hymns have been preserved, forming, as they did, a patrimony to certain families, a species of productive capital, which it was their interest to turn to the very best account. Composed on certain recognized and venerable themes, and sometimes retouched and renovated by the imagination of a new bard, they grew old as they were transmitted from age to age, bearing on them, sometimes, the date of their composition, which was indicated by the name of their inspired author, or of some generous prince.

The Irano-Aryans ascended a mountain, to sacrifice, where they could have the earliest possible glimpse of the rising sun; and Garô-Nemâna, which afterwards became the heavenly abode of Ahura Mazda, originally meant "the mountain of worship." But it does not appear that the Indo-Aryans repaired to a mountain to sacrifice, but only that they did so in the open air, inviting the Devas to come down and sit upon the sacred grass.

The Rishis were simply sages or poets, and not necessarily priests; and most of the ministering priests were not Rishis, the latter being, in large part, itinerant bards, like Homer and those of the Welsh and Irish Celts. Some families of these were greatly distinguished, as, for example, the Angiras. Some of the hymns in the third Mandala are assigned to five successive generations of Rishis.

> The pious sages who lived of old [it is said in the first Mandala], and who conversed about sacred truths with the Devas. They [it is said in the seventh] were the associates of the Devas, those ancient, pious sages. The fathers found out the hidden light; with true hymns they generated the dawn.

This is the rendering of Dr. Muir, but it is not a correct reproduction of the original. The *Devas* are the denizens of *Dyu*, the Sky. They are simply the stars, and the ancient Rishis *became* their associates, by being translated to the sky as stars. Therefore it is said of the Devas, some were such from the beginning, and some became so afterwards. That these Rishis found out the hidden light, meant that, translated to the sky, they were where the light originates, and in the place whence it is manifested. And they *generated* the dawn, because, rising in advance of it, they seemed to lead it up into the sky, and were poetically said to *cause* or *produce* it. In the same manner, the sacrifice at dawn is said to cause the sun to ascend the sky. The Angirasas are said, sanctified by sacrifice and gifts, to have attained the companionship of Indra (the Light) and immortality; i. e., to have ascended to the sky, the abode of light, and as stars to have become immortal.

The value of the Hindū interpretations of the *Veda* may be judged of by this, which Müller says of the *Brahmanas*, the oldest of the Hindū works:

> Every page of the Brahmanas contains the clearest proof that the spirit of the ancient Vedic poetry and the purport of the original Vedic sacrifices were both beyond the comprehension of the authors of the Brahmanas.

There is throughout them, he says, a complete misunderstanding of the original intention of the Vedic hymns. And Professor Roth remarks that the *Vedā*, both as regards its language and its subject-matter, stood further removed from the Hindū of the sixth and seventh centuries before Christ, in which period the sacerdotal system reached its climax, than Homer did from the Greek of the era of Pericles. The Brahmanic notions in regard to the Deities, their origins and their functions were so totally different from those of the poets of the *Veda* as utterly to incapacitate them to understand the old text in any other senses than the false ones which suited their own preposterous mythology, and their refined and sublimated metaphysics.

Professor Wilson has stated part of the difficulties met with in translating the *Veda*. They are very great, so great that it will never be possible to translate the whole correctly. All grammar is disregarded in the original; one case or number of a noun substituted for another, one person and tense of a verb for another. The case is the same with the sister language of the Gâthâs of Zarathustra. The truth is that neither language had, in those early ages, a grammar. Many unusual words are employed in the *Veda*, Professor Wilson says, the meaning of which he thinks can only be arrived at by means of the Hindū interpretations. But these *unusual* words are simply old and obsolete ones, the Vedic language bearing somewhat the relation to the modern Sanskrit, that the language of Chaucer and the *Mirror for Magistrates* does to the English of today. And the Hindū interpretations are almost always so utterly unfounded, so evidently the result of preconceived notions, and so continually either perversions defiant of common sense and reason, or mere wild guesses, that I am quite sure they much more tend to obscure the meaning than to elucidate it.

Other great difficulties are, that for many Vedic words we have no equivalents in English, and that such of our words as are available do not convey the same ideas; and also, which is even more mischievous, that we have words to which ideas are now attached that were not possessed by the Vedic poets, and which, nevertheless, our commentators, in imitation of Sâyana and Yaska, insist on using, to represent Vedic words that meant nothing of the sort. Our words "heaven," "divine," "worlds," "spirit," "immortality," and many others, express ideas that were utterly unknown to the Vedic poets. Others of our words, such as "true," "holy," "wise," are constantly misapplied. The Vedic words *Kavi*, *Vipra*, *Vidvat*, *Medhâvin*, *Chikitvah*, and many others, mean, it is true, "wise, intelligent, knowing," but they do not have that meaning as and where they are employed, and so to translate them is to mistranslate.

Adjectives are also often used without substantives, and as substantives, and there are many other omissions of words, to be supplied by conjecture. In supplying these, the Hindū commentators rarely guess correctly. Often it does not appear what Deity is invoked, or to which one an epithet is applied. Sometimes whole sentences are to be supplied by conjecture and it is mere guessing whenever single words are omitted: as in

"The grandson of the waters has ascended above the crooked ———."
"The broad and golden——— spread around."
"Thou removest all ——— of men."
"Thou cuttest ——— to pieces."

The same phrase is often explained in utterly different senses by different commentators; while they continually disagree with each other, and each often with himself as to what a particular Deity means and is.

A curious helplessness manifests itself, in the writings of the English and German commentators, whenever they endeavor to define the meaning of one of several of the most important of the Vedic Deities, or any, indeed, of the very large number, except three or four. Agni, Ushas, the Maruts, Sûrya, Fire, the Dawn, the Winds, the Sun, are not to be mistaken. The meaning of all the others they either mistake or are uncertain about. The consequence is that a large part of what is said about these is misinterpreted. None of the Sanskrit sources of information are of the least value as aids in solving the enigmas which the *Veda* presents to us.

Professor Wilson followed these blind guides, and consequently much of his translation is incoherent nonsense; and still more of it, if it were correct, would make one wonder at the fatuity that so long preserved that which was so utterly worthless.

The words "truth" and "sin" often appear in his translation, as they do in those of Müller and Muir. But the reader will readily discover that these words do not reproduce the meanings of the original words. The former, in general, at least, means actuality or reality, and that particular reality of things which is produced by the light that makes them visible. It is in that sense that Light (Indra) is Truth, and that the celestial luminaries are "Lords of Truth." The word rendered by "sin" often means merely losing one's way; and where it actually means offending, and the God addressed is besought to forgive it, it means only the failure to perform the proper ceremonial of worship of such Deity, or the imperfect or careless performance of it.

It is constantly the case that Vedic words which in the lapse of ages had come to have in common acceptation derivative meanings quite other than their original ones, are rendered, in the translation into English, by words corresponding to and equivalents of these derivative and modern meanings. To understand this, we need only glance at many of our common English words. *Regard* originally meant the act of looking at; *respect*, the act of looking back; *respectable*, one to be looked back at; *umbrage*, a shadow; *extenuate*, to thin out, or make thinner, by flattening; *refrain*, to rein in; *precocious*, cooked too soon; *premature*, ripe too soon; *candor*, shining whiteness; *nervous*, sinewy; *obsequious* (a holy and obsequious tear), connected with obsequies, following one to the tomb; *libel*, a little book; *affront* ("may here affront Ophelia"), meet face to face; *nuisance* (from *nuire*, to "injure"), that which harms; *knave*, at first an innocent boy or youth, afterwards a servant ("Paul, a knave of Jesus Christ"—Duke of Lauderdale's Translation of the Bible); *vulgar*, of the common people; *idiot*, unlearned;

right, what is ordered; *just*, what is commanded; *animosity*, courage, high spirit; *usury*, interest; *traduce*, to promulgate; *sophist*, a lover of wisdom; *dogmatic*, doctrinal; *wits*, the bodily senses; *pragmatical*, businesslike; *speculation* ("no speculation in those eyes"), contemplation; *officious*, dutiful, attentive (as Dr. Johnson wrote of Levett, in praise, "officious, innocent, sincere"); *resentment*, feeling over again; *animadvert*, turn the mind to; *crafty*, skilful in any art; *cunning*, kenning, knowing; *sense*, feeling; *crude*, uncooked; *saucy*, salsus, salted; *moral*, customary; and hundreds of others.

If, now, there were an old book in our language, written centuries ago, using these words in their original meanings, and one now translating it into French were to take them in their present meanings, and translate accordingly, he would do precisely what some of the translators of the *Veda* and the *Zend-Avesta* have done, and make precisely such nonsense in French, as these do in English and German.

The *Atharva-Veda* is of comparatively recent date. The three others were collected together about 1,200 years before Christ, the Sanskrit having then ceased to be a spoken language. There evidently existed smaller collections before this, especially of the *Rig-Veda*. When the complete collection was made, Bunsen says,

> the compilers had completely lost sight of the original meaning of the old hymns. They treat them as made for the purposes of public worship, whereas it is clear that many of them, and in fact the very ancient ones, were not liturgies at all, but the outpourings of the free natural inspiration flowing out of the whole material life, and the great events, of the poet's own time, and the experience of the tribe and of the people.

Much of this is incorrect. Many of the hymns, no doubt, were not composed for use at the sacrifices; but almost all of them have a religious character, and *could* have been so used. And those that speak of wars and battles, of enemies slain and hostile cities demolished, do so in praise of the Deity whom they invoke and to whom they ascribe these victories.

Poems containing such "outpourings" would have dealt with human interests, emotions and relations, with the ordinary and home life, and the affections of the heart, and the charms and beauties of Nature. But there is hardly a word about love or women, or in praise of beauty, in the whole *Veda*. There are no martial strains, or songs of the chase, nothing that tells of home and household joys, no allusions to the beauties of Nature, no descriptions of scenery, no pictures of the trees in their garmenting of green, or of fruits and flowers; of all which every poetic soul loves to sing. That there were such songs, who can doubt; but all these the tide of time has swept away; and the religious spirit of the race, the only sure preserver of the ancient records, has preserved only those poems that were of a devotional character, with but a few insignificant exceptions.

But this is truly said:

> not only is the scene of these songs, the Indus country, unknown to the compilers, but likewise the religion. [And it is by far more completely unknown than even this learned scholar knew, for he knew not what most of the Vedic Gods meant, nor the profound conceptions which they embodied.] Brahma and Brahmanism had dispelled the old religious ideas. The highest Vedic Gods, Agni, Varuṇa, Indra, had [disappeared, or] degenerated into Gods of the second order, into mere guardians of the world. [The character of Vishṇu had entirely changed, and his original individuality as heat had disappeared.] The form of the language, lastly, is not only different, and far more ancient, but the language of the Vedas is a living language; that of the compiler is more modern, but one already become petrified, and obsolete among the people . . . . a learned language. In the time of Buddha [the post-Vedic], Sanskrit, in its turn, had become a dead language. He lived in the Sanskrit country, but he preached in Pali. When the Aryans crossed the Sutlej, they took with them the language of the country of the Five Rivers. Then the Brahmanical system sprung up, the old language gradually died away, and the Sanskrit, "the perfect language," took the place of the language of the seers.

It is time that I should speak, somewhat in detail, of the relationship of the Sanskrit, Zend, Greek, Latin and various European languages; for it is by means of the words and grammatical forms common to all or to part of these, that the original identity of all the races that speak these languages, is established; and nothing is more curious and interesting than the recent discoveries of philology, or historically so important as the facts that they conclusively and irrefutably demonstrate.

Recent discoveries have proven beyond possibility of dispute the existence all over Europe, long before any immigration of the Aryans, of successive races of men, each enduring an unknown but immense length of time, the oldest coëval with ancient geological formations. These most ancient races were savages, using weapons and implements of stone, the Troglodytes who were of diminutive stature and dwelt in caves, and whose bones are found mingled with those of animals of species hundreds of thousands of years ago extinct; the lacustrine dwellers in huts upon causeways built out into lakes, and other primitive races, whose arrow-heads and other weapons of flint alone testify that they lived. Another period of time came, when weapons of bronze were used; and then another in which they were of iron. When the Aryan race first reached Greece and Italy, at least, other and much higher races had succeeded these, at least in parts of Europe, all of which, with very rare exceptions, were in the end fused with the conquerors, and as separate peoples disappeared. Two of the exceptions, one of which survives to our day, were the Etrurians who maintained a separate existence long after Rome was founded, of whose language no man can read a sentence, and who, long believed to have come from Asia into Italy, are now proven, by monuments on the road, to have descended into it from the Rhætian Alps. The other is the Basques, whose origin and that of their language are unknown, but who are believed by one who knew the language thoroughly, to be of Tâtar (not Mongol) descent.

Whether the degree of civilization of the native tribes and peoples conquered by the successive waves of Aryan emigration was greater or less, and whatever was the condition of civilization of each particular body of Aryans, there is no doubt that, everywhere in greater or less degree, the language of the victors was itself victor, and its most important words, as well as its most common ones, were everywhere retained. The vitality of words is wonderful. We hear, every day, a word not of the highest estate now, that has today the same meaning, to "seize," that it had seven thousand years ago in the Punjab, the verb *grabh*.

The case was the same in Asia as in Europe. The Aryans found an indigenous and powerful population everywhere, and fragments of those native races still exist, and speak their old languages, in the north and in the south of India. There were a multitude of tribes speaking many different tongues, like the American Indians, none of them in the least connected with or resembling that of the Aryans; and having no relationship among themselves. From these aboriginal inhabitants of Asia and Europe came the differences in type of the existing Aryan races, and in a great measure the differences in language. How else are we to account for the difference in features between the Irishman and the high-caste Hindū, and for the fact that some of these races do not have and cannot pronounce certain letters?

That all the languages which we have mentioned are, to the extent stated, outflowings from the original tongue, and that, indeed, much of the difference between them has been owing, not to the intermixture of foreign elements, but to natural changes, modifications and decay, has been too conclusively proven, for doubt to be possible. Professor Max Müller, than whom there is no higher authority, says, in his work on *The Languages of the Seat of War in the East:*

> That the Sanskrit, the ancient language of India, the very existence of which was unknown to Greeks and Romans before Alexander, and the sound of which had never reached a European ear till the close of the last century, that this language should be a scion of the same stem, whose branches overshadow the civilized world of Europe, no one would have ventured to affirm before the rise of comparative philology. It was the generally received opinion, that if Greek, Latin and German

came from the East, they must be derived from Hebrew, ... an opinion for which at the present day not a single advocate could be found, while, formerly, to disbelieve it would have been tantamount to heresy. No authority could have been strong enough to persuade the Grecian army that their Gods and their hero-ancestors were the same as those of King Porus, or to convince the English soldier that the same blood was running in his veins as in the veins of the dark Bengalese. And yet there is not an English jury nowadays which, after examining the hoary documents of language, would repel the claim of a common descent and a legitimate relationship between Hindû, Greek and Teuton. Many words still live in India and in England that witnessed the first separation of the northern and the southern Aryans, and these are not to be shaken by any cross-examination. The terms for *God*, for *house*, for *father, mother, son, daughter*, for *dog* and *cow*, for *heart* and *tears*, for *axe* and *tree*, identical in all the Indo-European idioms, are like the watchwords of an army. We challenge the seeming stranger, and whether he answer with the lips of a Greek, a German or an Indian, we recognize him as one of ourselves. Though the historian may shake his head, though the physiologist may doubt, and the poet scorn the idea, all must yield before the facts furnished by language. There was a time when the ancestors of the Celts, the Germans, the Sclaves, the Greeks and Italians, the Persians and Hindûs, were living together beneath the same roof.

The same scholar thus classes the various Aryan languages:

The *Indic*, consisting of various dialects spoken in India, and the classical and Vedic Sanskrit.

The *Iranic*, of the Persian and those of Afghanistan, Kurdistan, Bokhara, Armenia and the Os or Sron, a Circassian Tribe, and the ancient Zend or Bactrian.

The *Celtic*, of Wales and Brittany, Scotland, Ireland, Cornwall and the Isle of Man.

The *Italic*, of Portugal, Spain, Provence, France, Italy and Wallachia, the old Provençal, and the ancient Oscan, Latin and Umbrian, in Italy.

The *Illyric*, probably; or Albanian.

The *Hellenic*, of Greece.

The *Wendic*, of Lithuania, Kürland and Livonia (or the Lettish), Bulgaria, Russia, Illyria (Slovenian, Croatian and Servian), Poland, Bohemia (the Slovakian), Lusatia, the old Prussian, and the Ecclesiastical Sclavonic.

The *Teutonic* of the High German, Low German and Scandinavian, which include:

The *High German*—the Old High German and present language of Germany.

The *Low German*—the Old Gothic, Anglo-Saxon, Old Dutch, Old Frisic, Old Saxon, and the present tongues of England, Holland, Friesland, and north of Germany (Platt-Deutsch).

And the *Scandinavian*—the Old Norse, and the present languages of Denmark, Sweden, Norway and Iceland.

The names that express the family relations, coming from one source, prove that, at that early day those relations of family, marriage, etc., existed; and many other words demonstrate the existence at the same time, of particular customs, manners and habits of life. By means of these, language has been made to tell much of the history of those ancient times and of the daily life of men of whom, not long ago, nothing was known. We thus obtain a character of historical reality, for a period the very existence of which had been doubted.

No one can now discuss this subject without making large use of the labors of Professor Max Müller, who has done more to make the subject attractive and interesting than any other person. But he has by no means exhausted the subject, and I owe very much to Eichhoff and Muir; and the great work on *Comparative Grammar* of Franz Bopp removes all doubt which mere identity of words might leave, by an exhaustive demonstration, not only of that identity, but of the sameness of grammatical forms in all the languages known as Aryan.

Let us look first at the words that express the family relations—

The Sanskrit word for "father" is *pitar;* Zend, *patar;* Greek, πατήρ; Latin, *pater;* French, *père;* Gothic, *fadar;* German, *vater;* English, *father;* Russian, *batia;* Irish, *athair.*

The first remark to be made on this word is, that as the vowel in the first syllable is *a,* in every one of these languages except the Sanskrit, it must have been so in the original Aryan word, and Zend is an older dialect of that original language, than Sanskrit, and this will be found to be confirmed by many other words.

And the second is, that the word is derived from a verbal root, *pa,* which means, not to "beget," but to "protect, support, nourish." As "begetter," the father was called in Sanskrit *janitar,* from the verb *jan,* to "beget, produce," whence the Greek γενος, and γενεσις; Latin, *genus* (kind), and *gens* (people, race); French, *genre* and *gent;* Gothic, *kuni* and *knods;* English, *kin* and *kind, generation, gender,* etc.; and Lithuanian, *gymis* and *gimtis.*

From the same root *pa* come the Sanskrit *papus;* the Greek, παππος; Latin, *pappus;* French and English, *papa,* and *pape, pope.*

"Mother" is, in Sanskrit and Zend, *matar;* Greek, μητηρ; Latin, *mater;* German, *mutter;* Lithuanian, *mote, motina;* Russian, *matere; mati;* Gaelic, *mathair.* It is from the root *ma,* to "fashion," whence, among the earliest Aryans, *mâtar* had the meaning of "maker."

"Brother" was, in Sanskrit, *bhratar;* Zend, *bratar;* Greek, φρατηρ; Latin, *frater;* Gothic, *brothar;* German, *bruder;* Lithuanian, *brolis;* Russian, *brat;* Gaelic, *brathair;* and Celtic, *brawd.*

"Sister": Sanskrit, *svasar;* Zend, *gañhar;* Latin, *soror;* Gothic, *swistar;* German, *schwester;* Lithuanian, *sessir;* Russian, *sestra;* Celtic, *chwaer.*

"Daughter": Sanskrit, *duhitar;* Zend, *dughdar;* Greek, θυγατηρ; Gothic, *dauhtar;* German, *tochter;* Lithuanian, *dukté;* Russian, *dszczer, docz.* Of this word, Müller remarks that we learn from it something of the habits of our remote ancestors; for that *duhitar* is derived from *duh,* a root which in

Sanskrit means to "milk"; and the name of "milk-maid," given to the daughter of the house discloses to us how poetical and pastoral the life of the early Aryans was. It shows, he says, a kind of delicacy and humor, if we imagine a father calling his daughter "his little milk-maid," rather than *suta*, "his begotten," or *filia*, "the suckling." This meaning had long been forgotten, before the Aryans separated, and *duhitar* had ceased to be a nickname, and had become the proper name of daughter.

That is pretty, fanciful and taking, in a popular lecture; but it cannot be accepted as a substantial result of comparative philology. *Duḥ*, in Sanskrit had the original meaning of "draw, pull, draw out," as it has in the Latin *duco*, "I draw, lead, etc.," and in our English, *tug;* and its meaning to "milk" is not only derivative, but expressed the act of sucking by an infant, as well as that of milking cattle, precisely as we say, "tugging at the breast."

The ordinary words for son and daughter in Sanskrit are *putras* and *putic*, probably from *puç*, to "nourish, bring up, rear"; whence the Latin *puer* and *puella*, "boy" and "girl" and the Greek παις, "boy, son."

In the *Veda*, the two names for "father" are used together as if to express the full idea of that relationship. Thus (*i.*, 164, 33):

Dyaûs me pitâ janitâ,

which in Latin and Greek becomes

Jovis (or Deus) mei patēr genitor,

Ζεὺς ἐμοῦ πατὴρ γενετήρ.

We still retain in English, meaning "father," the Sanskrit word *tâta* from *tât*, to "protect, honor," in Greek, τεττα, from τιω, to "honor"; Latin, *tata*, used in each language as an appellation of one's father or senior. The Spanish *tio*, "uncle," and our English word *daddy*, applied equally to one's father or to an old man, are from the Sanskrit.

So from the Sanskrit *nanâ*, "mother" or "aunt," came the Greek ναννη, "aunt"; and that word in English was formerly spelled *naunt*, so disclosing its parentage.

"Grandson" was, in Sanskrit, *naptar, napat;* Zend, *napa;* Greek, ανηπσιος; Latin, *nepos;* and "granddaughter," in Sanskrit, *naptrî;* Zend, *napti;* Latin, *neptis.*

Devar, devara, "husband's brother," in Sanskrit, became δαηρ, with the same meaning in Greek; *levir,* in Latin; *dēwēris,* in Lithuanian, and *dewer* in Russian. Also, *çvaçuryas,* "brother-in-law," in Sanskrit, became *schwager* in German; and in Lithuanian, *szwogeris.* That this particular relationship should be expressed by the same word in Hindūstan, Poland and Germany, strikingly exemplifies the truth whose immense value was not until lately realized, that the duration of monuments erected by the hands is nothing in comparison to that of words, which traverse so many ages and countries without losing anything of their original meaning.

"Son-in-law" is in Sanskrit, *jâmâtar;* in Zend, *zâmâtar;* in Greek, γαμβρος; in Latin, *gener;* in French, *gendre.* Father-in-law, Sanskrit, *çvaçura;* Zend, *qasura;* Greek, ἑκυρος; Latin, *socer.* "Father's brother," Sanskrit, *pitṛivya;* Greek, πατρος; Latin, *patruus.*

Our word "widow" is the Sanskrit, *vidhavâ;* and Latin *vidua,* meaning the same. "Son" is the Sanskrit, *sûnu;* Zend, *hunu;* Greek, "υιος.

"Daughter-in-law" was, in Sanskrit, *snushâ;* Greek, νυος; Latin, *nurus.*

"Nephew" and "niece" are the Sanskrit *naptar* and *naptrî.* The former became, in Greek, ἀνεχιος; Latin, *nepos;* French, *neveu;* Gothic, *nithiis;* German, *neffe;* Russian, *netu;* and the latter, in Latin, *neptis;* Gothic, *nithio;* German, *nichte;* Greek, ανεχια; Celtic, *nith.*

Our word "sun" is the Sanskrit *sûnas,* "the sun," from *sur* to "blaze, shine"; the Greek σειρ, σειριος, and Latin *Sirius,* "the dog-star," are from the same; as are the Gothic *sunna, sunno,* and Russian *soluce.* From the same root is, in Sanskrit, *sûrya,* "the sun"; Latin *sol;* French, *soleil;* Gothic, *sauil;* Lithuanian, *saule;* Zend, *hvare;* Celtic, *haûl.*

Mâs, in Sanskrit, is the "moon"; *mâsas,* "a month"; *mâna,* "measure"; all from *mâ,* to "measure, divide out." Hence the Greek, μηνη, μεις, μην; Latin, *mensis;* Gothic, *mena, menotho;* German, *mond, monath;* English, *month;* Lithuanian, *menû;* Russian, *miesiac;* Gaelic, *mios;* Celtic, *mis.*

"Star" is the Sanskrit *târâ,* "a star"; Latin, *stella;* Gothic, *stairno;* German, *stern;* and from the Sanskrit *âstron,* "ether, light," from *as, ash, ush,* to "burn, blaze," are the Greek αστηρ, αστρον, "a star"; Latin, *astrum;* French, *astre;* and our *astral, asteroid,* etc.

From the Sanskrit *Agni,* "fire," are the Greek αιγλη, "splendor"; Latin, *ignis,* "fire"; Gothic, *auhus;* Lithuanian, *ugnis;* and Russian, *ogn.* Our word "fire" is from the Sanskrit, *pranças,* "burning"; Greek, πυρ; German, *feuer.*

From the Sanskrit *laukas,* are the Greek λυχη; Latin, *lux;* Russian, *lucz;* Celtic, *llug;* Gothic, *liuhath;* German, *licht* and English, *light.*

"Day" is from the Sanskrit *divas,* "day"; Latin, *dies;* Gothic, *dags;* German, *tag;* Celtic, *dydd.*

"Night," Sanskrit *niç, niça;* Greek, νυξ; Latin, *nox;* Gothic, *nahts;* German, *nacht;* Lithuanian, *naktis;* Russian, *nocz;* Gaelic, *noiche;* Celtic, *nos.*

"Winter" is, in Sanskrit, *himan, haiman;* whence, Greek, Χειμα; Latin, *heims;* Lithuanian, *ziema;* Russian, *zima.*

"Man" is from *manas,* "thought, intellect"; while the Latin *vir,* "a man," Gothic *wair,* German *wer,* Lithuanian *wyras,* Gaelic *fear,* and Celtic *gwz,* all are the Sanskrit *vîra, varas,* "a hero," from *vîr,* to "defend, protect."

From *açva*, "a horse," are the Greek, 'ιππος; Zend, *açpa;* Latin, *equus*, and Gaelic, *each.*

From *sthuras, sthiras*, "a bull," are the Greek and Latin ταυρος and *taurus*, and the Gothic *stiurs*, German *stier*, and English *steer.*

"Buck" is from the Sanskrit *bukka*, "a goat"; "sow," from Sanskrit *sûs*, Greek and Latin, συς and *sus;* and our word "swine" from the same is found in the Russian *swinia.*

Çva, "a dog," is, in Zend, *çpa;* Greek, κυων; Latin, *canis;* Gothic, *hunds;* English, *hound;* Lithuanian, *szû;* Russian, *szczenia.*

"Tooth" is, in Sanskrit, *dantas;* Latin, *dens;* Gothic, *tunthus;* Lithuanian, *dantis;* Celtic, *dant;* and we have the same root in our word "dentist."·

From the Sanskrit *Dyaus, Dyu*, "the sky," are the various names of God, *Zeus*, Δις, Διος, in Greek; *Deus, Divus*, in Latin; Θεος, in Greek; *Dieu*, in French; *Dia*, in Gaelic; *Duw*, in Kymric; *Drewas*, in Lithuanian; . and we have the same root, *div*, to "shine," in our words, "divine" and "divinity."

The Latin words *rex*, "king," and *regina*, "queen," are the Sanskrit *râja*, "ruler" or "chief," *rajni*, "queen."

From the Sanskrit *pati*, Zend *paiti*, "master, lord," are the Greek ποσις, "husband," and the Latin *potens, potio*, "potent, able."

From the Sanskrit *jambha*, "tooth," are the Greek, γομφος, and our English word "gums."

Pad, pada, "foot," in Zend *pâdha*, is the Greek πους, ποδος, Latin, *pes, pedis*, and we have it still in "pedal and foot-pad." "Knee" is the Sanskrit *jânu;* Zend, *zhenu;* Greek, γόνυ; and Latin, *genu.*

"Bone," Sanskrit *asthi;* Zend, *açti;* Greek, ὀστέον; Latin, *ôs.* "Navel" is the Sanskrit *nabhi;* "entrails," the Sanskrit *antra;* Greek "εντερον; Latin *venter.* "Mouse" is Sanskrit *mûsh*, Greek μυς, Latin *mus.*

From *madhu*, Sanskrit and Zend, "honey," are μεθυ, in Greek, and our *mead* and *metheglin.*

"House" is in Sanskrit *dama;* Zend, *demana;* Greek, δομος; Latin, *domus.* "Door" is the Sanskrit *dvâr;* Greek, θυρα; Latin, *fores. Svapna*, "sleep," in Sanskrit, became *gafna* in Zend, 'υπνος, in Greek, *sopor* and *somnus* in Latin. "Oar" is from the Sanskrit *aritra;* Greek, ἐρετμός; and "rower" is *aritar*, ερετης, in the same.

"Path" is the Sanskrit *pathin*, Zend *pathan*,·and Greek πατος, "roadway." "Murmur" is the Sanskrit *marmara*, Greek μορμορω, Latin *murmuro.* "Light" (in weight) is the Sanskrit *laghu*, Greek ἐλαχυς "little," Latin *levis.* "Same," Sanskrit, *sama;* Zend, *hama;* Greek, 'ομος; Latin, *similis.* "New," Sanskrit, *nava;* Zend, *nava;* Greek, νεος; Latin, *novus.* "Middle"; Sanskrit, *madhya;* Zend, *maidhya;* Greek, μεσος; Latin, *medius.* "Sweet" is the Sanskrit *svadu;* Latin, *suavis.* "Name" is the Sanskrit *nâman;* name;

Latin, *nomen;* Persian, *nam.* "Warm" is Sanskrit *gharma;* Zend, *gărĕma.* "Spy" is Sanskrit *spaç,* Zend *spoç.*

The number of words that have been thus traced from the Sanskrit and Zend into the modern Aryan tongues by Bopp, Eichhoff, Müller, Muir and other scholars, is very large, and may yet be greatly added to. One is surprised to find a larger number of Latin words identical with the Sanskrit words, than of Greek; and that Greek agrees more with Zend than with Sanskrit.

Whether *duhitar* originally meant a "milk-maid," or not, many Aryan words were formed in that spirit, as new words originating in California and Australia have found their way into general use. Such words literally applicable only during a nomadic mode of life, when our forefathers tended their herds on the wide steppes of Toorkhistan, with the heavenly luminaries for their guides and to enable them to count the passing of the hours, came by degrees to have quite other meanings.

The equivalent word of "ox" and "cow," in Sanskrit was *go,* though "ox," "oxen," are from the Sanskrit *ukshan.* The plural of *go* is *gâvas.* The Old High German *chuo, chuowi* were the same words. *Go-pah* meant originally, a "herder or keeper of cattle"; but it at last came to mean a "king"; and *goshu-yûdh,* "fighting among or for the cows," is used in the *Veda* as the name of a "warrior" in general; while one of the most frequent words for battle is *gâv-ishti,* literally, "striving for cows"; whence, in the later Sanskrit, *gâveshana* means simple "research, inquiry, etc.," i. e., a striving to attain the truth, physical or philosophical. All these words compounded with *go,* "cattle," prove that the people who formed them led a life half nomadic and pastoral.

But the *Vedas* and Gâthâs show clearly enough this character of the people. I do not dwell on that. The far more interesting question is as to the identity of languages; and as to that, time and space will not permit me to do more than indicate the nature of the proof.

The name for a wife left husbandless, in the later languages, comes from the same ancient source, and is ante-Vedic. In the Sanskrit, *dhava* is a "man," or a "husband," and this with the negative or primitive preposition *vi,* "without," prefixed, makes *vi-dhava,* "without a husband, husbandless, a widow." This compound has been preserved in languages that have lost the simple word, *dhava,* and we have the Celtic *feadbh,* the Gothic *viduvo,* the Sclavonic *vdova,* the old Prussian *widdewû,* and the Latin *vidua,* as well as the English *widow.*

Professor Müller, to whom I owe what I have just stated, traces the descent of many other words, and says:

The evidence which we have gone through, must be sufficient to show that the race of men which could coin these words—words that have been carried down the stream of time, and washed upon the shores of so many nations, could not have been a race of savages, of mere nomads and hunters.

And this will much more clearly appear when we come to understand their philosophical notions, and what was meant by their Deities and the enigmatic language of their poets.

They had homes, marriage and family relations, and names for relatives by marriage, which are yet preserved in the European languages. *Dama*, a "house" or "home" is the Greek δομος, the Latin *domus*, the Sclavonic *domii* and the Celtic *daimh* as it is the Gothic *timrjan* to "build," from which came the English word "timber." And our word "door," in ancient times, at least, the most essential part of the house, is preserved in the Sanskrit *dvar*, *dvâras*, the Gothic *daur*, the Lithuanian *durrys*, the Celtic *dôr*, the Greek θυρα, and the Latin *fores*. The builder or architect has the same name in Sanskrit and Greek, *takshan*, being the Greek τεκτων. In the Greek αστυ, "house," we find the Sanskrit *vâstu*, "house"; in the Sanskrit *puri*, "town," the Greek πολις, "town or city"; and that roads were not unknown, appears from the Sanskrit *path*, *pathi*, *panthan* and *pâthas*, all of them names for roads; the Greek πἄτος, and the Gothic *fad*.

Most of the names connected with the chase and war differ in the different Aryan dialects, while those connected with more peaceful occupations are generally common to all. This shows that the Aryans had led a long life of peace, before they separated; and this is equally demonstrated by the vast works for irrigation made by them on the Sarasvati or Zer Affshan and Oxus. They warred only when their increased numbers compelled them to spread into new regions. It was the new generations that formed new terms, connected with the warlike and adventurous life of their onward migrations. Hence it is, that not only the Greek and Latin, but all Aryan languages, have the peaceful words in common, and that they all differ so strangely in their warlike expressions. Thus, too, the domestic animals are generally known by the same names in England and in India, while the wild beasts have different names even in Greek and Latin. Thus the words for "cattle, ox, steer, heifer, horse, foal, dog, sheep, calf, she-goat, sow, hog, mouse, fly and goose" are common, some to a larger and some to a smaller number of the derivative languages. Our English word "steer," meaning an ox, is, in Sanskrit, *sthûra;* in Zend, *staora;* in Greek, ταυρος; in Latin, *taurus;* in Spanish, *toro;* in Teutonic, *stiur;* in Lithuanian, *taura-s;* in Sclavonic, *tour;* and in Irish, *tôr.*

The oldest term for ploughing is *ar*, which we find in the Latin *arare;* Greek, αρουν to "ear"; Old Sclavonic, *orati;* Gothic, *arjan;* Lithuanian, *arti;* and Gothic, *ar.* Hence the common name of the "plough" αροτρον;

aratrum; Old Saxon, *erida;* Old Norse, *ardhr;* Old Sclavonic, *oralo* and *oradlo;* Lithuanian, *arkla-s;* Welsh, *aradyr* and *arad;* Cornish, *aradur.*

So, in the Sanskrit *pada* and *agra* each was a "field"; Greek, πεδον; Umbrian, *perum;* Latin, *pedum,* in *oppidum;* Polish, *pote;* Saxon, *folda;* Old High German, *feld;* English, *field;* Greek, αγρος; Latin, *ager,* and Gothic, *akr-s.*

In Sanskrit, *sveta* meant "white," and corresponds to the Gothic, *hveit;* Old High German, *huiz* and *wiz;* Anglo-Saxon, *hvit;* and our *wheat;* Gothic, *hvaitei;* and Lithuanian, *kwety-s.* "Corn" meant, originally, "what is crushed or ground"; Sanskrit, *kûrna;* Russian, *zerno;* Gothic, *kaurn;* Lithuanian, *girna* (a "mill-stone," and the plural *girnos,* a "hand mill"). The Russian word for "mill-stone" is *zernov;* and the Gothic name for "mill," *qvairnus,* the later *quirn.*

The name for "clothes" is the same among all the Aryan nations, being *vastra* in Sanskrit, *vasti* in Gothic, *vestis* in Latin, εσθης in Greek, *fassradh* in Irish, *gwisk* in Welsh. To "weave" is *ve,* in Sanskrit, and in a causative form, *vap.* With *ve* coincide the Latin *vieo* ("weave or twist together"), and the Greek radical of ϝητριον; with *vap,* the Old High German *wob,* the English *weave* and *web,* the Greek ϝφαινω. To "sew" is in Sanskrit *siv,* whence *sûtra,* a "thread." The same root is preserved in the Latin *suo,* the Gothic *siuja,* the Old High German *siwu,* the English *sew,* Lithuanian *siuv-u,* the Greek κασσυω, for κατα-συω.

When we speak of a "hymn" that is sung, we use a word identical with the Sanskrit *sumna* and Zend *humna,* a "hymn"; Greek ϋμνος; Latin *hymnus.*

"Eat" is the Sanskrit *ad,* to "eat"; Greek, εδω, εσθω; Latin, *edo;* Lithuanian, *ĕdmi;* Russian, *iem;* Gothic, *ita, itan;* German, *esse;* Anglo-Saxon, *etan;* Gaelic, *itham;* Kymric, *esu.*

From the Sanskrit *vah* and *vâh,* Zend *vaz,* to "draw, carry," whence *vâhika,* a "car or chariot," Latin, *veho,* "I carry," *vehiculum,* a "carriage," we have our word "vehicle."

The Sanskrit *lup,* to "cut," *lopa,* "cut off," we have in our word "lop." "Venerate, veneration" are from the Sanskrit *van,* to "honor," to "reverence." From *svan,* the Latin *sonare,* is our verb to "sound."

The Gothic *svietan,* Anglo-Saxon *swaetan,* and our "sweat," are the Sanskrit *svid,* to "sweat."

From the Sanskrit *jna, jnâ,* to "know"; *jnata,* "known," come the Greek γνωσις, and our words "know" and "knowledge."

Is our word "attic" from the Sanskrit *atta,* a "room on the top of the house"?

The Sanskrit *anta,* "end," in the Gothic *ande* and Anglo-Saxon *ende.*

"Thin" is the Sanskrit *tanu*, Latin *tenuis*. "Nest," the Sanskrit *nîda;* Latin, *nidus*. "Drop" is the Sanskrit *drapsa*, a "drop"; and "stand" is the Sanskrit *stha*, Latin *stare*.

From the Sanskrit *luṇṭ*, to "plunder," comes the English word, adopted from the Hindustani, *loot*, "booty, plunder"; and the cant word *lush*, meaning the gains of theft, is probably the Sanskrit *lush*, to "rob," and may have been carried from India by the gipsies or zingari.

Iron is in Zend *ayanha*: "bring, bear," Sanskrit and Zend, *bar:* from the Zend *fri*, to "love, be kind to," *fryô*, "friend," our word "friend" may come: the Zend *ga* means to "go": and the Zend *mithah*, "lies" is the Greek μυθος, "myth."

My friend, Doctor Mackey, has found in some book on the *Veda*, that "The Vedic Hymns," referring to the continual renovation of the flame, as it was fed by fuel, called Agni, *Yavioshtha*, the "ever young," and that from this the Greeks got their *Hephaistos*, the Vulcan of the Romans. But *yavishṭha* does not mean "ever young." *Yuvan*, for *yavan*, in Sanskrit, means "young," and from it are the Latin *juvenis*, "youth," *junior*, the Anglo-Saxon, *iong, iung, geong*, and our words "juvenile" and "young." *Yavishṭha* is the superlative of this, and means "youngest"; and, applied to Agni, the latest born or kindled fire. *Hephaistos* is probably from the Sanskrit *havyâça*, "fire."

The value and usefulness of some of the metals were known before the separation of the Aryan race, as is proven by a few words; but the names of most of the metals differ in different countries. Iron was known, and its value appreciated, and we find traces of the old names for silver and gold.

It is clear, therefore, that ages before even the composition of the Vedic hymns in the Punjab, the arts of sewing and spinning and weaving were known to our ancestors, and that of extracting from the ores and working some of the metals. Gold is found in the sands of the Oxus. *Khani*, in Sanskrit, meant to "mine"; and *khnenta*, the ninth country named in the first Fargard of the Vendidad as created by Ahura Mazda, meant, probably, the mining region.

Remember that all these are proofs of what language was spoken, before the last stream of the great Aryan emigrations took its course towards India, to halt on its way in the land of the Seven Rivers; before even the earliest wave of emigration flowed forth, which was to reach Spain, Gaul, Germany, and the British Isles—the great Celtic emigration.

If at that remote period the original people had a decimal system of numeration, from *one* to a *hundred*, the names of the numbers whereof, with the changes of letters found in other words, are still possessed and used by the existing races that we consider Aryan, their original unity will be completely demonstrated.

The fact that the race should have had such a system is not "marvelous," though Professor Müller thinks it so, and is eloquent upon it.   In what is known as the "Creek Nation" of American Indians (who were neither a Nation nor Creeks, when they became known to us, but a confederation of fragments of tribes) originally not related to each other, there are spoken six distinct languages, in which are five wholly different decimal systems of numeration, from one to ten thousand.   The Nachïs, as far as I could learn, count only from one to ten; but I found only two persons who remembered that language.

Professor Müller thinks that such system could have been settled upon by only a small community, and that the Aryan system must have been adopted when the whole race numbered but a few souls.   Might that not be said to be the meaning of any word?

The decimal system is as follows, in Sanskrit, Zend, Greek, Latin, Lithuanian, Gothic, Old High German, Old Sclavonic, Welsh or Kymric, and Irish or Gaelic, in the order named:

"One," *ekas, aêva,* εἷς (οὒνη), *unus, wienas, ains,* ——, ——, *yedin, un, aon;* Russian, *odin* (ἴδιος, ισολε); German, *ein;* Anglo-Saxon, *án.*

"Two," *dvau, dva,* δυω, *duo, du, tvai, zui, dva, deu (dwi), da;* Russian, *dwa;* German, *zwei;* Anglo-Saxon, *twégen, twá.*

"Three," *trayas, thri,* τρεῖς, *tres, trys, threis, tri, tri (tra), tri;* Russian, *tri;* German, *drei;* Anglo-Saxon, *thrý, threó.*

"Four," *chatvaras, chathwârô,* τεσσαρες, Æolian, πισσυοες, *quatuor, keturi, fidvôr, fiorir, chetyri, pedwar (pedeir), ceithar;* Russian, *czetyre;* German, *vier;* Anglo-Saxon, *feower.*

"Five," *pancha, panchan,* πεντε, Æolian, πεμπε, *quinque, penki, fimf, finf, pyaty, pumm, coig;* Russian, *piat;* German, *fünf;* Anglo-Saxon, *fíf.*

"Six," *shash, csvas,* ἓξ, *sex, szeszi, saihs, shesty, chwech, sia;* Russian, *szest;* German, *sechs;* Anglo-Saxon, *six, seox, siex.*

"Seven," *saptan, haptan,* ἑπτα, *septem, septyni, sibun,* ——, *sedmy, seith, seachd;* Russian, *sedm;* German, *sieben;* Anglo-Saxon, *seofon.*

"Eight," *ashtan, astan,* ὀκτω, *octo, asztûni, ahtau, ahtowi, osmy, wyth, ochd;* Russian, *osm;* German, *acht;* Anglo-Saxon, *eahta.*

"Nine," *navan, navan,* ἐννεα, *novem, dewyni, niun,* ——, *devyaty, naw, noi;* Russian, *dewiat;* German, *neun;* Anglo-Saxon, *nigon.*

"Ten," *daçan, daçan,* δεκα, *decem, deszint, taihun, desyaty, deng (deg), deich;* Russian, *desiat;* German, *zehn;* Anglo-Saxon, *tyn.*

The great differences in the designation of the number *one,* spring from this, that this number is expressed by pronouns of the third person, whose original abundance affords satisfactory explanation regarding the multiplicity of these expressions.

One hundred is, in Sanskrit, *çatan;* Zend, *çatem;* Greek, ἑκατον; Latin, *centum;* Lithuanian, *szimtas;* Gothic, *hund;* German, *hundert;* Russian, *sto;* Kymric, *cant;* Gaelic, *ciad;* Anglo-Saxon, *hund-teontig.*

Have the derivative races retained the ancient pronouns of the first and second person?

"I" and "me" are, in Sanskrit, *aham* and *mâm, mâ;* Zend, *azĕm* and *manm, mâ;* Greek, ἐγων and *mé;* Latin, *ego* and *mĕ;* Gothic, *ik* and *mik;* Lithuanian, *asz, manen;* Old Sclavonic, *az, mya;* Gaelic, *mi* and *me, mem;* Kymric, *mi* and *fi, fif;* Romance, *ieu* and *me, mi;* Spanish, *yo* and *me, mi;* Portuguese, *eu* and *me, mim;* Italian, *io* and *me, mi;* French, *je* and *me, moi;* Tudesco, *ih, mih;* German, *ich, mich;* Dutch, *ik, mij;* Swedish, *jag, mig;* Danish, *jeg, mig;* Prussian, *as, mien;* Russian, *ia, menia;* Servian, *ja, mene, me;* Bohemian, *ga* and *mne, mĕ;* Polish, *ia* and *mnie, mie;* Persian, *men, merâ;* Anglo-Saxon, *ic* and *min.*

"We" and "us": Sanskrit, *vayam* and *asmê, asmân* and *nas;* Zend, *vaêm, nô;* Greek, αμμες, αμμε (also, ἡμεις, νωι and ἡμας, νωι); Latin, *nos, nos;* Gothic, *veis, unsis;* Lithuanian, *més, mùs;* Old Sclavonic, *my, ny;* Romance, Spanish and Portuguese, *nos, nos;* Italian, *noi, noi* and *ci;* French, *nous, nous;* Tudesque, *wir, unsih;* German, *wir, uns;* Dutch, *wij, ons;* Swedish, *wi, oss;* Danish, *wi, os;* Prussian, *mes, mans;* Russian, *my, nas;* Servian, *mi, nas;* Bohemian, *my, nas;* Polish, *my, nas;* Persian, *mâ, mârâ;* Gaelic, *sinu, sinu* and *sinnin;* Kymric, *ni, ni* and *nin;* Anglo-Saxon, *we* and *us.*

"Thou," "thee": Sanskrit, *twam, twâm, twâ;* Zend, *tûm* and *thaňm, thwâ;* Greek, τοίν, τέ (also, σν, σε); Latin, *tu, te;* Gothic, *thu, thuk;* Lithuanian, *tù, taweň;* Old Sclavonic, *ty, tya;* Gaelic, *tù* and *thu, thut;* Kymric, *ti, thi* and *thit;* Romance, Spanish, Portuguese, Italian, *tu, te* and *ti;* French, *tu, te* and *toi;* Tudesque, *du, dih;* German, *du, dich;* Dutch, *du, dij;* Swedish and Danish, *du, dig;* Prussian, *tu, tien;* Russian, *ty, tebia;* Servian, *ti, tebe* and *te;* Bohemian, *ty, tebe* and *tĕ;* Polish, *ty, ciebie, cie;* Persian, *tû, turâ;* Anglo-Saxon, *thù* and *thé.*

"Ye," "you" (nominative and accusative): Sanskrit, *yûyam* and *yushmê, yushmân* and *vas;* Zend, *yûshĕm* and *yûs, vô;* Greek, "υμμες, "υμμε (also, ὑμεισ, σφωι, ὑμας, σφωι); Latin, *vos, vos;* Gothic, *yus, izvis;* Lithuanian, *yûs, yùs;* Old Sclavonic, *wy, wy;* Gaelic, *sibh, sibh* and *sibhibh;* Kymric, *chwi, chwi* and *chwich;* Romance, *vos, vos;* Spanish, *vos, vos* and *òs;* Portuguese, *vos, vos;* Italian, *voi, voi* and *vi;* French, *vous, vous;* Tudesque, *ir, iwih;* German, *ihr, euch;* Dutch, *gij, u;* Swedish, *i, eder* and *er;* Danish, *i, eder* and *ier;* Prussian, *jous, waus;* Russian, *wy, was;* Servian, *wi, was;* Bohemian and Polish, *wy, was;* Persian, *shumâ, shumârâ;* Anglo-Saxon, *ge* and *eow.*

The pronoun of the third person, in the accusative, singular and plural, also deserves notice. It is substantially the same in all the languages except the Celtic.

"Him," "them": Sanskrit, *svayam* (*sva*, "self"); Zend, *hvaêm*, *qaêm* (dative and genitive, *hê*, *hoi*); Prâkrit (dative and genitive), *sê;* Greek, *ˀε*, *σφέ* (dative and genitive, *οιˀ*, *ουˀ*); Latin, *se* (dative and genitive, *sibi*, *sui*); Gothic, *sik* (dative and genitive, *sio*, *seina*); Lithuanian, *sawen* (instrumental, *sawimi;* dative, *saw;* genitive, *sawens;* locative, *sawiye*); Old Sclavonic, *sya* (instrumental, *soboyû;* dative, *sebye*, *si;* genitive, *sebe;* locative, *sebye*); Romance, Spanish, Portuguese, Italian, *se*, *si;* French, *se*, *soi;* Tudesque, *sih;* German, *sich;* Dutch, *zich;* Swedish and Danish, *sig;* Prussian, *sien;* Russian, *sebia*, *s;* Servian, *sebe*, *se;* Bohemian, *sebe*, *sê;* Polish, *siebie*, *sie;* Persian, *khûd;* Anglo-Saxon, *hine* and *he*.

To show you the identities of grammatical forms would far exceed the due limits of a lecture. They are striking and entirely conclusive, as even those will show that I shall refer to.

In Sanskrit, Zend, Greek, Latin, German, Lithuanian and Old Sclavonic, these forms of verbs, in the first person singular and plural, present tense, indicative mood:

"I stand": *tishthâmi; histâmi;* ˀιστημι; *sto; stâm; stowmi; stoyun.*
"I give": *dadâmi; dadhâmi; didomi; do;* ——; *dûmy; damy.*
"I am": *asmi; ahmi;* ἐμμι; *sum; im; esmi; yesmy.*
"I carry": *vahâmi; vazâmi;* εχω (ϝεχω); *veho; viga; wezû; vezun.*
"We stand": *tishthâmas; histâmahi;* ˀισταμες; *stâmus; stâmês; stowemê; stoim.*

In the second person singular:
"Thou art": *asi, ahi;* ἐσσι; *es; is; essi; yesi.*
"Thou standest": *tishthasi; histahi;* ˀιστης; *stas; stâs; stowi; stoishi.*

Third person singular:
"He is": *asti; açti;* εστι; *est; ist; esti; yesty.*
"He stands": *tishtati; histati;* ˀισταтι; *stat; stât; stow; stoity.*

When we find in Sanskrit, Greek and Latin, among many others, the verbs and participles, which, hoping not to weary you, I will repeat in that order of the languages, it becomes impossible to doubt that the three have descended from an older tongue to which these words or their roots belonged.

Sanskrit	Greek	Latin	
Dâ, *dadâmi*	*didomi*	*do*	to give
Dâtar	*dotor*	*dator*	giver
Dâna	*doron*	*donum*	gift
Sthâ, *tishthâmi*	*histēmi*	*sto*	to stand, place

Sanskrit	Greek	Latin	
Star, stṛiṇ̃ōmi	*stornumi*	*sterno*	to spread
Bhar	*phero*	*fero*	to bear
Bhu	*phuo*	*fui*	to be, I was
Lih, lehmi	*leikho*	*lingo*	to lick
Tan, tanōmi	*tanuo, teino*	*tendo*	to stretch
Jan, jananmi	*gennao*	*gigno*	to beget
Janus	*genos*	*genus*	birth, kind
Jna, janami	*gignosco*	*gnosco*	to know
Jnata	*gnotos*	*notus*	known
Ajnata	*agnotos*	*ignotus*	unknown
Ad	*edō*	*edo*	to eat
Vah, vahami	*ocheomai*	*veho*	to carry
Sarp	*herpo*	*serpo*	to creep
Sarpa	*herpeton*	*serpens*	serpent
Pat, patāmi	*petomai*	*peto*	to fall, fly, seek
Sadas	*hĕdos*	*sedes*	seat
Chhid	*schīzo*	*scindo*	to cut
Dam	*damaō*	*domo*	to subdue
Manas	*Menos*	*mens*	mind
Kar, karōmi	*kraino*	*creo*	to do, fulfil, create
Vam	*emeō*	*vomo*	to vomit
Stan	*stenō*	*tono*	to groan, sound, thunder
Lu	*luō*	*luo*	to cut, loose, pay
Vid, vedmi	*ϝειδω*	*video*	to know, see
Tras	*treo*	*terreo*	to frighten
Taksh	*tiktō*	*texo*	to make, beget
Adiksham	*edeixa*	*dixi*	I showed, told
Adikshata	*edeixate*	*dixistis*	ye showed
Mātra	*metron*	*metrum*	a measure

Sanskrit and Latin words are:

Sanskrit	Latin	
Mard	*madeo*	to rub, crush, bite
Diç	*dico*	I show, tell
Nah	*necto*	I bind
Pish	*pinso*	I pound
Siv	*suo*	I sew
Syuta	*sutus*	sewn
Pishta	*pistus*	pounded
Pā	*poto*	I drink
Chi	*scio*	to perceive, know
Tap	*tepeo*	to be hot
Vach	*vocò*	to speak, call
Kup	*cupio*	to be excited, angry, desirous
Kṛip	*carpo*	to cut, pluck
Sparç	*spargo*	to touch, scatter
Prachh	*precor*	to ask, pray

Sanskrit	Latin	
Mar	*morior*	to die
Mṛita	*mortuus*	dead
Svan	*sono*	to sound
Vart	*verto*	to be, turn
Ard	*ardeo*	to afflict, to be on fire
Avākshīt	*vexit*	he carried
Vāta	*ventus*	wind
Skand	*scando*	to go, ascend
Tudāmi	*tundo*	to wound, beat
Tutôda	*tutudi*	I have beaten
Tatâna	*tetendi*	I stretched
Praja	*progenies*	progeny
Sthâman	*stamen*	strength, thread
Hyastana	*hesternus*	of yesterday
Makshu	*mox*	quickly, shortly
Kad?	*quid?*	what?
Nanu	*nonne?*	is not?
Çushka	*siccus*	dry
Tanu	*tenuis*	slender
Açu	*ocior*	swift, swifter
Rasa	*ros*	liquid, dew
Phulla	*folium*	flower, leaf
Vanas, van (to love)	*venus, venustas*	beauty

So again in Sanskrit, Greek and Latin:

Sanskrit	Greek	Latin	
Nau	*naus*	*navis*	a ship .
Dhuma	*thumos*	*fumus*	smoke, spirit
Kalama	*kalamos*	*calamus*	a reed

I have laid before you these portions of the great mass of evidence recently supplied by comparative philology in regard to the identity of the races of which I have spoken, at the risk of being tedious and wearisome, that you might be able yourselves to speak with knowledge and positively upon the question. It is the proper business of a lecturer to communicate knowledge; and on such subjects as this to convince by proof and argument. What is considered fine writing is becoming the vice of the commentators, and in some of them has proved fatal to accuracy of views and conclusions. To perpetuate an error or beget one, in order to turn a period well and utter pretty sentences, is a mischievous practice, not fit to be indulged in, where the simple truth is the only object to be attained, the only desirable result.

I am now ready to discuss the meaning of the Vedic Deities. That the subject should be of interest to you, it was necessary, not merely to say, but to prove, that the men whose faiths were embodied in the *Veda* and

Zend-Avesta were of our own blood; for if they had not been, what they believed would be of as little interest to us as the religious belief of the Scythians and Huns. What they believed will to some extent teach us what those believed who were their common ancestors and ours. The study of ancient thought is always fascinating; and it will be much more so when the thought is that of men of our own race, and we can find in their creeds and conceptions the origins of much of our own philosophy and religion; and when, as we shall find in the figurative expressions of the *Veda* the source of much of the Greek and Roman mythology, we *may* also find the original meaning of much, in our own doctrines, that, by change of the primitive meanings of words and transformation of ideas, has become unintelligible and undecipherable to us.

In endeavoring to explain to you, as I understand them, the conceptions embodied in the Vedic Deities and in the doctrines of Zarathustra, I shall express opinions that have not been advanced by the commentators, and of the soundness of which I must attempt to satisfy you; for I cannot expect you to take them upon trust; and upon them consists in great measure, I think, the value and importance of these ancient books. Permit me to repeat, on the subject of this lecture, these remarks of Eichhoff:

> Everywhere, in the course of this work, we have found, in the principal languages distributed among the peoples of Europe, the traces of their Indian origin, traces certain and ineffaceable, although modified by times and places. The Celts, the first colonists that came from Central Asia, and were forced by successive emigrations to the very ends of the Occident, have preserved of their ancient idiom, then doubtless only in the rough, a vague and indecisive remembrance, almost confined to the elementary sounds. Among the Germans, the roots are complete, their connexion logical, their forms fixed, but still impressed with a certain rudeness, that attests the infancy of the language. Among the Sclaves, the forms are harmonized, their separation from the mother country having been later. They are developed and enriched among the Latins, and gain in elevation and nobleness, until the genius of Greece issuing last from ancient Asia, to illuminate a new continent, charms us by the graces of a language carried to its highest perfection. Thus the Indian tongue becomes a comparative scale, that determines the places of the different peoples in the great migrations of the human race. It fills the gaps of history, by marking the progress of each epoch, less by its literary traditions in which the imagination riots, clad in a thousand colors, than by the aggregate of its vocabulary, the faithful interpreter of our European languages. In our days, too, every nation shares in this as intimately as the Greek and Latin days.

The great scholar Ernest Renan, in his work *"De l'Origine du Langage,"* after speaking of the original Aryan land and the great mountain range of the Bolor Tagh, says:

> Let us salute these sacred summits, where the great races which bore in their bosom the Future of Humanity, for the first time contemplated the Infinite, and inaugurated the two facts which have changed the face of the world, morality and reason.

When the Aryan race shall have become, after thousands of years of efforts, mistress of the planet which it inhabits, its first duty will be to explore this mysterious region of Bokhara and Little Thibet, which perhaps conceals from science revelations so precious. With what lights will not the origin of language be illuminated on the day when we shall find ourselves face to face with those places where were uttered for the first time the sounds that we still use, and where were created the intellectual categories which govern the exercise of our faculties! Even as the years of complete maturity do not equal in fruitful curiosity the first months during which the consciousness of the child awakes, so no place in the world has played a part comparable to that of the mountain or valley without a name, where man awoke to a knowledge of himself. Let us pride ourselves as much as we please, upon the progress of our reflection; but let us never forget that all this progress does not free us from the necessity of recurring, in order to express our thought, to those sounds and grammatical forms that were spontaneously selected by the ancient patriarchs who, at the base of the Swaiis laid the foundations of that which we are and of that which we shall become.

Renan does not assign to the Aryan languages an antiquity so great as has been claimed for them. "There were in the world," he says, "brilliant material civilizations, kings, organized empires, when our ancestors were still dull creatures, like the German or Bas-Breton peasant." His reasons need not engage our attention, for they are entirely inconclusive. But this, which he adds, is superbly true; "and it was, notwithstanding, these austere patriarchs who, in the bosoms of their chaste and submissive families, thanks to their pride of character, to their worship of the right, to their attachment to their customs, to their modesty, laid the foundations of the future. Their ideas, their words, were to become the law of the moral and intellectual world. They created these eternal words, which after many changing shades, were to become *honor, goodness, virtue* and *duty*."

When you come to comprehend the profound ideas of the Vedic poets and of Zarathustra, and reflect that what they composed and sung the people must have understood, you will be far from agreeing that, at that early day, at least, our ancestors or relatives were either a dull or an unimaginative people; and you will agree with scholars and thinkers equal to Rénan, that no race had then appeared on the earth, except our own, that could have produced such compositions.

Professor Müller, in an article entitled "Manners and Customs," in the second volume of his "*Chips from a German Workshop*," gives what is to me a very curious, striking and interesting proof of the identity of Sanskrit, Greek, Gothic, German and Saxon. I think it will interest you. He says, speaking of the closeness of the bond that unites nations so distant from each other as the inhabitants of Ceylon and Iceland:

Let us consider but one instance. "I know," in modern German, is *ich weiss;* "we know," in the plural, *wir wissen*. Why this change of vowel in the singular and plural? Modern German can give us no answer, nor ancient German, not even the most ancient German of the fourth century, the Gothic of Ulphilas. Here too, we find *vait*, "I know," with the diphthong in the singular, but *vitum*, "we know," with the simple vowel. A similar change meets us in the ancient language of England, and King Alfred would have said *ic wât*, "I know," but *we witon*, "we know." If then we turn to Greek, we see here the same anomalous transition from *Foida*, "I know," to *Fismen*, "we know"; but we look in vain for any intelligible explanation of so capricious a change. At last we turn to Sanskrit, and there not only do we meet with the change from *veda*, "I know," to *vidma*, "we know"; but we also discover the key to it. In Sanskrit, the accent of the perfect falls throughout on the first syllable in the singular, in the plural on the last; and it was this change of accent which produced the analogous change in the length of the radical vowel. So small and apparently insignificant a fact as this, the change of *i* into *â* (*ai*) whenever the accent falls on it, teaches us lessons more important than all the traditions put together, which the inhabitants of India, Greece and Germany have preserved of their earliest migrations and of the foundations of their empires, ascribed to their Gods, or to the sons of their Gods and heroines. This one fact proves that before the Hindûs migrated to the southern peninsula of Asia, and before the Greeks and Germans had trodden the soil of Europe, the common ancestors of these three races spoke one and the same language, a language so well regulated and so firmly settled that we can discover the same definite outlines in the grammar of the ancient songs of the *Veda*, the poems of Homer and the Gothic Bible of Ulphilas. What does it mean, then, that in each of these three languages, "I know" is expressed by a perfect, originally meaning, "I have perceived"? It means that this fashion or idiom had become permanent, before the Greeks separated from the Hindûs, before the Hindûs became unintelligible to the Germans. And what is the import of the shortening of the vowel in the plural, or rather of its strengthening in the singular? Its import is, that at an early period in the growth of the most ancient Aryan language, the terminations of the first, second and third persons singular had ceased to be felt as independent personal pronouns; that hence they had lost the accent, which fell back on the radical vowel; while in the plural, the terminations, continuing to be felt as modificatory pronominal suffixes, retained the accent and left the radical vowel unchanged.

The facts of language, Professor Müller adds, however small, are historical facts, and no explanation of this fact, which is one out of thousands, "has yet been started, except that long before the earliest literary documents of Sanskrit, which go back to 1500 B.C., long before Homer, long before the first appearance of Latin, Celtic, German and Sclavonic speech, there must have been an earlier and more primitive language, the fountain-head of all."

I must not close this lecture, necessarily very rudimentary without a few words in regard to what is now called "folk-lore." In an article in the same volume of his "*Chips*," entitled "Popular Tales from the Norse," on the subject of a collection of Scandinavian *Folkeeventyr*, translated by Dr. Dasent, Professor Müller says:

But we have not done with Dr. Dasent's book yet. There is one part of it, the introduction, which in reality tells the most wonderful of all wonderful stories— the migration of these tales from Asia to the north of Europe . . . . Like the blue and green and rosy sands, which children play with in the Isle of Wight, these tales of the people, which Grimm was the first to discover and collect, are the detritus of many an ancient stratum of thought and language, buried deep in the past. They have a scientific interest. The results of the science of language are by this time known to every educated man, and boys learn at school—what fifty years ago would have been scouted as absurd—that English, together with all the Teutonic dialects of the Continent, belongs to that large family of speech, which comprises, besides the Teutonic, Latin, Greek, Sclavonic and Celtic, the Oriental languages of Persia and India . . . It has also been proved that the various tribes who started from this central home to discover Europe in the north and India in the south, carried away with them, not only a common language, but a common faith and a common mythology.

[He quotes from Dr. Dasent] This is now the first article of a literary creed, and the man who denies it puts himself as much beyond the pale of argument, as he who, in a religious discussion, should meet a grave divine of the Church of England, with the strict contradictory of her first article, and loudly declare his conviction that there was no God.

And he says:

These very stories, these Mährchen, which nurses still tell, with almost the same words, in the Thuringian Forest and in the Norwegian villages, and to which crowds of children listen under the pipal trees of India. These stories, too, belonged to the common heirloom of the Indo-European race, and their origin carries us back to the same distant past, when no Greek had set foot in Europe, no Hindū had bathed in the sacred waters of the Ganges . . . . The memory of a nation clings to its popular stories with a marvelous tenacity. For more than a thousand years the Scandinavian inhabitants of Norway have been separated in language from their Teutonic brethren on the Continent, and yet both have not only preserved the same stock of popular stories, but they tell them in several instances in almost the same words . . . . There are stories, common to the different branches of the Aryan stock, which could not have traveled from India to Europe at so late a time as that of Nushirvan. They are ancient Aryan stories, older than the Pañchatantra, older than the Odyssey, older than the dispersion of the Aryan race.

Among other instances given by him of this, he says:

The story of the donkey in the lion's skin was known as a proverb to Plato. It exists as a fable in the Hitopadesa, "The Donkey in the Tiger's Skin." Many of the most striking traits of animal life, which are familiar to us from Phædros, are used for similar purposes in the Hitopadesa. The mouse delivering her friends by gnawing the net, the turtle flying and dying, the tiger or fox as pious hermits, the serpent as king, a friend of the frogs, all these are elements common to the early fabulists of Greece and India. One of the earliest Roman apologues, the dispute between the belly and the other members of the body, was told in India long before it was told by Menenius Agrippa, at Rome.

Professor Müller admits, however, that he does not mean to say

that the old nurse who rocked on her mighty knees the two ancestors of the Indian and German races, told each of them the story of Snow-white and Rose-red, exactly as we read it in the tales from the Norse, and that these told it to their children, and thus it was handed down to our own times. [All that he desires to prove is] that the elements or the seeds of these fairy tales belong to the period that preceded the dispersion of the Aryan race; that the same people, who, in their migrations to the north and the south, carried along with them the names of the Sun and the Dawn, and their belief in the bright Gods of heaven, possessed in their very language, in their mythological and proverbial phraseology, the more or less developed germs that were sure to grow up into the same or very similar plants, on every soil and under every sky.

And his conclusion is, that many of our fairy tales were not invented at all,

but are the detritus of ancient mythology, half-forgotten, misunderstood, and reconstructed [and that] the loves and feuds of the powers of Nature, after they had been told, first of Gods, then of heroes, appear in the tales of the people as the flirting and teasing of fairies and imps.

It is a fact, not a supposition, he remarks, far more startling than the supposition of the ancient origin of these nursery tales,

that those Aryan boys, the ancestors of the Hindūs, Romans, Greeks and Germans, should have preserved the ancient words from *one* to *ten*, and that these dry words should have been handed down to our own school-boy days, in several instances, without the change of a single letter.

Dr. Mantell calls the shells and other fossil remains found in the rocks formed during countless ages, "the medals of creation"; and the expression is a felicitous one. They reveal to us the material history of our planet, of its varied and successive forms of life and the immense changes which its outer strata have undergone, during the countless ages of the past. But we feel even a profounder interest in the intellectual history of man, of our own or other races—of our own especially, to whom we are united by those invisible bonds that make the successive generations of each race, if not all humanity, in a large sense a unit. For we, and our fates and fortunes, our disputes and revolutions, our faiths and our philosophies, our acquired truths and clinging errors, our hopes and fears for what lies beyond this life, all are the legacies devised to us by the ancestors of our race, the sequel and consequences of what was thought and said and done by those who live again in us, and whose natures, intellects and idiosyncrasies we inherit.

It even interests us to inspect a copper coin of Antoninus, and more still, and in proportion not at all to the intrinsic value of the metal, but to its age, a golden one of Antiochus or of some old Parthian or Bactrian king. They are purchased at fabulous prices, royally kept in costly cabinets, exhibited with pride, and studied with intense interest, and art reproduces them in facsimiles, for the instruction and delight of thousands. Even the old pine-tree shillings of Massachusetts, which our own fathers used as cheap and current coin, have an ever-increasing value, and are eagerly sought for and jealously preserved.

Our daily language has its far more curious coins and medals of the past, which still pass current and are the counters of thought, their age and origin for the most part unknown and unsuspected.

Mr. Swinton, in his *Rambles among Words* has recorded, with many interesting philological facts, some thoughts worthy to be remembered. I can hardly do more than allude to them. The book is accessible and curiously interesting. He says,

> The conception of language that has arisen prophetic in the thought of modern times, is a high and great one. Speech is no more the dead mechanism it used to be conceived. Each language is a living organism . . . . Language is indeed alive. Primordial creation and manifestation of the mind, language throbs with the pulses of our life. This is the wondrous babe, begotten of the blended love of spirit and of matter—physical, mystical, the Sphynx. Through speech man realizes and incarnates himself; and Oken has an oracular utterance, that without speech there is no world.

And he well says,

> In the *Vedas* of the Indians, especially the hymns of the *Rig-Veda*, and in the *Zend-Avesta* of the Persians, primæval documents of the Iranic World, we see the germs of all we call Europe. Here were the beginnings of the cultures of the Occidental World. Science was born in that mind, the intuition of Nature, the instinct for political organization, and that direct, practical normal conduct of life and affairs. From this mind, too, flowered out the grandest and most spiritual of languages. The Japhetic or Iranic tongues are termed by the master philologers the organic group, to distinguish them from the agglutinative and inorganic speech—floors that underlie them in the geology of language. They alone have reached the altitude of free intellectual individuality and organism. To them belongs the splendid plasticity of Sanskrit, Greek, German, English. Such are the primæval lines in the genesis of the English language. And so it is that sounds and structures, words and forms, that were heard along the Ganges five thousand years ago, words heard in Benares and Delhi, in Persia and Greece, are now scaling the Rocky Mountains of the Western World.

And he thus eloquently and truly concludes his work:

> The flower and aroma of a nation is its language. The conditions of a grand language are a grand life. For words are metaphysical beings, and draw of the life of the mind. Not in these wondrous hieroglyphs of words, not in these mystic runes is the power; in the mind which loads these airy messengers with burdens of meaning is the vis and vivification of speech. Over the transformations of a language, the genius of a nation unconsciously presides; the issues of words represent issues in the national thought. And in the vernal seasons of a nation's life, the formative energy puts forth verbal growths opulent as flowers in spring.

As the ancient Semitic language, which was developed into the Babylonian, Arabic, Canaanitish, Hebrew and Phœnician, has contributed only
here and there an isolated and alien word or name to our English tongue,
and these have taken upon themselves, for the most part, Aryan significations, so the influence of the Semitic mind is neither seen nor felt in our
religion or philosophy, in our laws, organizations or institutions. There
is hardly a tinge of Judaism in our Christianity. All the doctrine of the
Word and Holy Spirit, however diverse, Arian, Athanasian, or Sabellian, is
Aryan, as all our conceptions of the Deity are, and had their origin, as I
shall hope to prove to you, in the teachings of the *Veda* and *Zend-Avesta.*

Until the beginning of the present century the history of the Aryan
race was, for the most part, a history of separation and dispersion. Portions
of the race came together and coalesced occasionally here and there; but
the general progress was one of divergence, of the formation of new races,
new languages, that each forgot the common origin and looked upon the
others as aliens. Spread over the world, from the high plain of Pamir, from
India, Persia, and the Caucasus, to the snowy wastes of Russia, to Germany,
and all Southern Europe, and to the English Isles and Scandinavia, the
hearts of the various nations nowhere beat in concert, nor were any bonds
of brotherhood acknowledged among them.

Perhaps destiny has decreed that here the old Aryan race shall be
reproduced, by the confluence of streams of emigration from all the Aryan
lands. For here the work of fusion of many races has well begun.

Permit me to conclude this lecture with a few sentences, uttered, among
others, publicly by me, in the City of Washington, on the occasion of a
Masonic ceremonial, in March, in the year 1860.

> Our hermetic Brethren termed the alchemical operation, itself only a symbol
> by which they were supposed to hope to produce the philosophical Stone, or the
> universal Alkahest, that was to turn all the baser metals to gold, The "Great
> Work." This latest of the republics, this great country, in which, fortunately, there
> is ample scope and verge enough for the experiment, is, as it were, an immense
> crucible, wherein is now being carried onward to successful or unsuccessful issue,
> the grandest work of alchemy that a wondering world has ever fixed its gaze upon.*
>
> For here are flung together thirty-one millions of people, native and foreign-
> born, of many races, and speaking many tongues, of every creed and faith, of every
> phase of opinion, of many habits of thought, total strangers to each other; a vast
> mass of apparently discordant elements, hostile, heterogeneous, incongruous; to be,
> if possible by any chemistry, made in process of time to combine into one homogen-
> eous whole.
>
> The antipathies that inflame and exasperate, and make our sky moody and
> threatening, are those of race and its instincts, and of opinions growing unconsciously
> out of ancient faiths and unfaiths.

*This was four years before Zangwill was born.—*Transcriber.*

Out of this apparently chaotic mass and aggregate of seeming irreconcilables, let us not doubt, the provident and benign Wisdom of the Almighty means to produce a great and harmonious unity; and to make this nation one, in heart and impulses, as it has one mission and one destiny.

In this, as it were, chemical operation, there must needs occur much effervescence and uproar, explosions of anger, evolvings of new, crude, gaseous theories, and all the discrepant jarrings, which superficial observers, not looking beyond the mere outer and temporary phenomena, mistake for irreconcilable antagonisms and conflicts never to be terminated.

The differences of race will never cease to produce their habitual effects. Opinions and faiths will never be moulded into one monotonous sameness. But a wise Providence will use and is using these differences as the very means of producing true unity and real harmony, by causing them to become like the instrumental divisions of an orchestra, which balance each other, and completely accord, without assimilation. It is some grand law of Heaven's enacting, that the universal harmony should flow grandly forth, from the clashing elements in all the worlds. . . . . Differences of race may become the indispensable means of harmony of action and of interests. Harmony consists in equilibrium, and equilibrium subsists by the analogy of contraries; and our very differences of race and temper, in the North and South, may, if wisely dealt with, and not mistaken for hostile antagonisms, be profitably used as the means of knitting us more closely together.

The solid unity of England is the result of the long-continued conflicts, and *ultimate harmonized* and partial *intermingling*, of Britons, Saxons, Danes and Normans; and the compact nationality of France has come from the original antagonism of Gaul and Frank, and the subsequent and long-continued dissonance of Burgundy, Picardy, Normandy, Brittany, and its other incoherent provinces.

Differences of opinion and apparent antipathies, often offensively expressed, and embodied in aggressive political action, and even culminating in war, are yet manifestly seen to be, in God's providence, blessings, if wisely availed of and profited by, and the means which it suits His wisdom to use, in order finally to establish a new, distinct and grand nationality, a unit of force, power and action, ruled by the same great ideas of popular liberty and order, of brotherhood, and equality, in the eye of the law, with a national character, one, original, with no prototype; in which nationality and character all the varying shades of race, temperament and peculiarity are not to be obliterated or tamed down into one monotonous sameness, but blended, mingled and combined into one admirably harmonious whole.

. So I believed then, and now that I know that the various white races of Europe are of one blood, I see with the eye of faith, by means of the intermingling and fusion here of the races so long separated, the regeneration of the ancient Aryan people, with all its old and noble characteristics; and I know, at least, that it is not impossible.

LECTURE THREE

DEITIES OF THE VEDA

AGNI—INDRA

As I have said in the preface to the work from which I have extracted what I shall read to you this evening, I wrote it as a study, and not as a teaching; for myself, and not for others.

It is not at all the fruit of a meditated purpose, and was not begun as a diagnosis of the Deities of the *Veda*, an attempt to discover the distinctive personality and individuality of each; which it afterwards became, or even of any one of them. The fruits of it to myself have been sufficient to reward me abundantly for all the labor it has cost. Nothing in the field of study has ever so much interested me, as this endeavor to penetrate into the adyta of the ancient Aryan thought, to discover what things, orbs, principles or phenomena, or potencies of Nature our remote ancestors worshipped as Gods; and what their Deities really *were*, in the conception of the composers of the Vedic hymns. It has had a singular charm for me, this inquiry into the true meaning of names, epithets and phrases, often, in appearance, indiscriminately applied to different Deities, often seemingly inappropriate and the expressions of a wild and riotous imagination; and which had become, literally accepted and misunderstood, the sources, seeds or germs of the legendary myths and many of the Deities of the Grecian mythology, and the Brahmanic fables and pantheon.

I have felt the most intense satisfaction in deciphering, as it seemed to me I did, these hieroglyphics of the ancient Aryan thought, infinitely better worth the labor than all that are engraved on the monuments of Egypt and Assyria; in identifying myself in some measure with them, understanding them by degrees, and thinking with them, without preconceived ideas to prevent this, and having long led a life akin to theirs, and become familiar, in the forest and on the plains and mountains, with the bright denizens of the sky and the other pages of the great Book of Nature.

I have endeavored to solve, one by one, the enigmas contained in their figurative and seemingly extravagant language, whose meaning was only to be discovered by beginning with their simplest notions and conceptions, and making the curious processes of their thought my own, trying, as it were, to *be* them intellectually, and to think their thoughts.

Thus I have satisfied myself that every one of their Deities had for them a perfectly distinct and clear personality and individuality; that their ideas were not in the least vague, incoherent or confused; that their imagination was perfectly well-regulated, and that every epithet and phrase was logically appropriate and correct; and so also I found it to be in the most ancient and difficult parts of the *Zend-Avesta*, the five Gâthâs or Odes of Zarathustra.

I found in both the most profound philosophical and metaphysical ideas, which those of every ancient and modern philosophy and religion have but developed; I found none of the absurdities and silly conceits and extravagant fictions of Brahmanism, nor any legitimate foundation for any of them, although the *Veda* is beyond measure reverenced by the Brahmans, and held by them as the supreme and divine authority, whose texts settle all disputed questions. I found that the Vedic poets were men of singularly clear and acute intellects, profound thought, and an infinite reverence for the beings that they worshipped.

This inquiry has opened to me an entirely new chapter of the history of human thought, and given me a far higher conception of the Aryan intellect and a profound conviction of the superiority of the race over every other, at its origin, and of the immutability of its characteristics, which are now what they were in its infancy and in the vigor of its young manhood. The Greek and the Roman were great, because they were Aryans.

And I now see, and shall endeavor to show to you, how, out of the primitive simplicity of a natural and reasonable religion, and of ideas simple and yet profoundly philosophical, there grew the most monstrous and debasing faiths, the most absurd and delirious fables, and the most abominable and degrading superstitions—the worship of animals, legends of the amours and adulteries of the Gods, conceptions of monstrous idols, the most irrational mysticism, and the incoherent nonsense of the Kabbalah and lunacies of Gnosticism.

But I also see, growing out of or developing the same ancient ideas, the doctrines of Plato and Philo Judæus, of which were born the modern philosophies of religion, the doctrine of emanation, and of creation by the Word, the self-revealing and manifestation of the inconceivable Deity.

I was at first led to look into such portions of the *Veda* as were accessible to me, to ascertain the origin of a Hindū word, whose letters I found to be the initials of the names of certain Vedic Gods. Until then, these Deities were wholly unknown to me. I knew only of Brahm and Maya, and Brahma, Vishṇu and Siva, and the other Gods treated of in the works on Hindū mythology, of which I had read more than enough.

I found the *names* of the Deities required; but the meaning of the word depended, I thought, on what was *meant* by the Deities, on what it was that was adored and worshipped as one and the other of these Deities. And I discovered, to my surprise, that the commentators could, as to this, give me no satisfactory information, except as to the character of one of them, Agni. I found myself utterly at a loss to determine what any of the

Deities, except four or five, named in the *Veda* really were. The commentators had no clear and definite ideas as to most of them, and did not even attempt to conjecture what they were, and where they did conjecture, the case was no better. Some were sometimes one thing, and sometimes another, to the same commentator. The personality assigned to some was clearly contradicted by the plain letter of texts translated by themselves. In a kind of despairing helplessness, they said that the poets had no fixed, settled, definite ideas as to the functions, potencies or personality of most of the Deities; but ascribed the same functions, attributes, character and powers, sometimes to one and sometimes to another, making each in turn supreme, superior and inferior.

Agni plainly was Fire, domestic, sacrificial and celestial; but also he was wise, intelligent, bestower of benefits, and invested with a multitude of attributes and characteristics seemingly incoherent, confused and extravagant, which the commentators made no effort to explain, in any manner, philosophic or otherwise. Sometimes he was found performing the exploits of Indra, sometimes they performed them jointly; sometimes Indra seemed to have become Agni, and sometimes Agni was declared to be half a dozen Gods together. At all this they simply stared in dismayed astonishment.

Ushas was unmistakably the Dawn, mysteriously connected with Indra; cherished by him, beloved by him; but suddenly he appears on the scene, angry with her, smashing her car with his thunderbolt, and compelling her, alarmed for her life, to take to flight.

> It means the too ardent love of the Sun, consuming the fading splendors of the Dawn, a maiden to whom her lover's fiery embraces are fatal,

one commentator said; and the passage was choicely worded and sounded prettily fanciful; but unfortunately the text stubbornly represents her as in fault, and Indra as enraged, and lauds him for his heroism in shattering her chariot.

Sûrya was undoubtedly the sun; the Maruts, the winds; and Soma, the juice of a plant or weed, the *Asclepias Acida* or *Sarcostoma Viminalis*. And this juice of a pounded weed (the Haŏma of the *Zend-Avesta*) was also a Deity, invested with the most extraordinary powers, exhilarating the Gods, and even enabling Indra to do great deeds, prayed to for favors, wealth and good fortune; and also said to sometimes be the moon. Pitu, food, and the wooden posts planted near the altars were also Gods. Indra was said to be the firmament but this made many of the texts which spoke of him to be utter nonsense; and many expressly contradicted that theory. As to Varuṇa, Mitra, Aryaman, the Açvins, Vishṇu, Vayu, Yama, Rudra, Tvashṭri, Pushan, Aditi, Brahmanaspati and Brihaspati, there was not even a conjecture, as to some; as to the last two, a guess partly correct; and as to the rest nothing more than contradictory conjectures or feeble and helpless suggestions.

It seemed as though the most of the Deities were mere names, without intellectual reality; and as though the Vedic bards had no fixed, definite, consistent ideas as to any of their Gods. What Varuṇa was, no one knew; but the prayers to him were made to beseech him to pardon sins, and to address him as supreme; though elsewhere he clearly occupies a subordinate position. The *Veda* seemed hardly to have been worth the trouble of translating; and the Brahmanic commentaries only made confusion worse confounded. Of philosophical ideas and doctrine, none of the commentators had discovered even a trace; and more than half the book, as translated, was arrant nonsense, of which it was hard to say which portion was worse and most worthless; but those relating to Vishṇu would probably have secured a majority of votes.

At first I proposed to myself only to ascertain, if I could, what three of the Deities were. Indra was not one. I commenced with Agni. I first copied the principal texts addressed to him or speaking of him: then I summed up the significant portions of these, and from the whole endeavored to attain to an understanding of the Vedic conceptions in regard to him. His close connection with Indra led, in fact compelled, me to do the same as to the latter; and thus diverted from my first purpose, and becoming deeply interested, I continued to inquire in the same manner, as to each Deity in succession, until what I wrote grew into a book, and led me to an undertaking that seemed even more hopeless, the interpretation of the *Zend-Avesta*.

As to the *Veda*, when I once had the key, the discovery of the meaning of each successive Deity made the task easier as to the next, and gave me new assurance that I was not misled.

I state these things, in part, to give you the assurance that I set out with no theory as to the nature of any of the Gods of the *Veda*. I did not think, at first, of looking for meanings and interpretations of the texts outside of the translations; or of learning more, in regard to the Deities, than the learned scholars whose works I had could tell me.

In the words of Professor Müller,

> We can watch, in the *Veda*, ideas and their names growing, which we meet with in Persia, Greece and Rome only as full-grown or fast decaying. . . . . We get nearer to that distant source of religious thought and language, which has fed the different national streams of Persia, Greece, Rome and Germany.

And we can clearly see that the human mind had made a great advance, when it had come to worship, not the visible fire itself, but the Universal

Fire, conceived of as a person, and invested with reason, intelligence and beneficence, in addition to power. For this made it veritably God, though not God the Creator.

Müller remarks that none of the Aryan Gods are represented as inferior to or limited by others, and that this is the keynote of the ancient Aryan worship. But he does not explain it. He could not, as he understands the *Veda*. It is indeed the key, I think, by which we may unlock the hidden meanings. All the powers and names of all the Devas are distinctly ascribed to Agni; but nothing is said in disparagement of the others. Indra is said to be greater than them all; and Varuṇa is invested with the attributes of supremacy. For it is Indra, the *Light*, that shines by and as every luminary, and Indra is a manifestation of Agni.

There is nothing slavish or brutal, sensual or groveling, in these old hymns, nothing of the barbarian or savage. A spirit of grave thoughtfulness pervades them; they are highly devotional and reverential; of philosophy there is little or nothing in the language of philosophy; but the idea that there was a Being, of whom no cognition could be had, in fire, an entity or spirit, wise, powerful, provident, beneficent, was of the same profound nature as that of the immortal soul of man united with the body, or of the Divine Soul in Nature. The savage attributes *intelligence* to his idol and the star, and the child to her doll; but the conception of the one Universal Fire manifested and revealed in every particular fire, was not the idea of a savage or a child, but of a philosopher and metaphysician; and I think that as these hymns are better understood, and as we penetrate more deeply into the thought of the poets who composed them we shall find ideas there of emanation and manifestation, of the Principle, Essence or Substance itself beyond reach of the senses or our cognition, and only attainable unto by the intellect, limiting itself by form and positing itself in place, its manifestation of itself and yet not all itself or its Very Self, which have reappeared in all the great philosophies of the world, and been essentials in all the great religions.

It is true, as Professor Müller has said, even truer than he thought it, that

> There are hymns in the *Vedas*, so full of thought and speculation, that, at that early period, no poet in any other nation could have conceived them.

But let us not find more in the *Veda* than it contains—in which, commentary too much consists. Müller says:

> We find in the *Veda* that which is really the very essence of *all* religion, and without which there can be *no* religion, a belief in personal immortality.

I do not find that belief in the *Veda;* and I do not agree that without it there is no religion. There is a total absence in the Hebrew writings, of any teaching or any evidence of a belief that the soul lives on when the body dies, and even in the time of the Apostles, the Sadducees who sat in the same council with the high priest, openly denied the resurrection; and yet, certainly, the ancient Hebrews had a religion, and were not without one altogether, until they learned the doctrine of the immortality of the soul from the Medo-Aryans at Babylon. The man who believes in a God, or Gods, who rewards the good and punishes the bad in this life and may be propitiated by adoration or sacrifice, has a religion.

Moreover, the soul may exist after this life, in one or more states of existence, and yet not be immortal. It is doubtful if any of the ancients believed in an existence absolutely without end. We have assurance of another life; but not of an eternal life. As God alone is infinite, so he alone is by his nature eternal; for eternity of existence is self-existence. Food gives the "immortality" of the *Veda* and *Zend-Avesta,* and the original word, in general, evidently means only continuance, and not even great length, of life. Not even Agni was conceived of as without beginning. The resurrection of the dead is not hinted at. The body, burned, becomes light, and, as light, ascends to feed the Devas, which are the stars. Only a few of the sages are translated to the sky and become Devas, immortal as the stars are immortal. There is, in the *Veda,* absolutely no other future life.

The old Aryan poet of the herdsmen and husbandmen sees that fire and its manifestations, light and heat, are human existence, and the generative causes of reproduction, and that light alone, the fire revealing itself *as* light, alone, reveals to man the existence of the material universe. What they reveal, they seem to create. He is awakened by the Dawn or the Sun, and it seems to restore him to life. Or, watching before the Dawn for its beautiful coming on the expectant hills, he sees the light-bearer, the beautiful and brilliant Morning-Star, rise calmly in the sky, cast long lines of silver light upon the grassy openings of the woods, and look upon him from the bosom of the lake or river, as it smiles kindly upon him from the sky; and he adores the Morning-Star, the Dawn, the Sun, as manifestations of the one great universal Light, "the Light which is the life of men"; but I do not find, that, as Müller says he does,

> he calls him whom his eyes cannot behold, and who seems to grant him the daily pittance of his existence, his life, his breath, his brilliant lord and protector,

in the sense that he invokes the favor of a God who is not fire nor light, nor any force or power or essence or principle of Nature; but a being invisible and incomprehensible, *above* Nature and its forces. I think I can most positively assert that there is no such conception in the *Veda*. There is in the *Zend-Avesta*. Ahura Mazda, the Very Light, contains in himself the Infinite Wisdom, and utters it as the Word, and is veritably God.

The Vedic poet makes the Fire a *person*, and invests it, as Unity and a Universal, with the characteristic of immaterial being. He adores the Fire-Spirit, the universal Light-Principle, the Heat-Principle, and various other potencies and manifestations as causes of particular effects, of the fire, as Gods; and they become to him not merely powers, but persons, protectors and benefactors. Every idol is that to the savage; but the fire is far more than that to the Aryan poet. It *is* the light which it *manifests* by self-revealing; and it *is* the sun, moon, planets, stars, by which also it reveals *itself* in light. These also have their distinct existence as persons; and these and the light and fire and heat and flame hear his prayers and are intelligent and wise.

Even prayer, adoration silent or uttered, food, fuel, the Soma juice, become Deities, by a strictly logical process of thought, and not by mere vagary of the fancy or imagination. They feed the fire, become of its substance, and ascend as light to the sky. He adores the fire and light in the Aurora and the lightning, as he does in the domestic and sacrificial fire. The winds are Gods for him, and that potency of the fire that rarefies the air and causes it to ascend, and so is the father of wind. Even the rivers and lakes become Goddesses; and though Agni is himself all the Devas, yet, manifested by self-limitation as the sacrificial fire, he is the messenger of the Devas, bearing upward to them the oblations transformed into part of his own being, and mediates with them for the worshipper. He is the son of strength, and exists in the fuel, because the fire for every sacrifice was produced by strength, applied to one piece of wood whose pointed end, revolving in another produced heat and finally combustion, and so begot Agni anew, to consume his parents.

It was but a step, and one that was inevitable, to ascend from the Vedic conception of fire and its manifestations to the conception of a being distinct from the fire, and of which being, both fire and light were the revealings. It did not need to invent new attributes for him; but only to transfer to him those of Agni. The next step was to conceive of this being as cause and Creator. These steps Zarathustra took, attaining to the conception of Ahura Mazda, whose two names, both nouns, mean light and splendor, whose son the fire was, as flowing forth from him. The Brahmans took them also, conceiving of Brahm as sexless, moved by love to create Maya within himself by division of himself, and thence creating the universe. And the manifestation or revealing of the very self of fire, as light, which, revealing the universe of things *created* it, contained in itself the doctrine of the emanation of the Logos, "the Word, that was in the beginning with God, and that was God," the thought of God, manifesting God, as the thought of man reveals the soul of man, and *is* the soul of man partially and limited by revealing itself—the doctrine of Plato, Philo and St. John and Paul, long ages before either of them lived, found in the creed of Zarathustra, in Çpĕnta-Mainyu, the Divine Intellect immanent in the Deity Ahura Mazda, and Vohu-Manô, the same Intellect uttering itself in partial revealings in every human intellect, and in the prayers and manthras that were the very words of Ahura, spoken through mortal lips, inspired in mortal intellects, by Vohu-Manô.

But for the immense antiquity which it would compel us to ascribe to them, one reading the simpler and therefore older hymns of the *Veda* would as unhesitatingly ascribe them to the bards of a people who led a nomadic and pastoral life on the steppes of Toorkhistan, as he would ascribe the poetry of the Bedouins to a people leading a like life in the Arabian deserts.

They smell of the free air of the plains. They tell us of a simple people whose wealth consisted chiefly in their herds of cattle, and to whom horses, mares and camels were of especial value. Milk was their ordinary and favorite beverage. Their dogs were held in the highest estimation, and among the Irano-Aryans were almost sacred, to kill or injure one being a crime, punished almost as severely as the murder of a man; and one of the hymns of the *Veda*, which has been strangely misunderstood to mean by the cattle of the Angirasas the golden clouds of the dawn, celebrates a bitch, Saramâ, which, when the cattle of these ancient sages were driven off in the night by a band of the Panis, a tribe of mountaineers, trailed or tracked the cattle to the mountain fastness into which they had driven them conducting the owners thither before dawn, who when daylight came, recovered them. The recovery is ascribed to Indra, the daylight which enabled them to find the cattle; and a curious conversation is detailed in the legend, between Saramâ and the Panis. The Angirasas, returning, rejoiced and sacrificed, for that they now had milk again. Their herds were their wealth, and butter the principal oblation to the Devas. Undoubtedly, at any rate, they had in the Punjab the old original worship, largely developed, and more spiritualized, which they long before had, when wandering on the steppes and tending their herds, guided in traversing these and the forests, by the stars. Some of the older hymns, it is probable, were composed and sung there. In the Gâthâs of Zarathustra, although he urged the people to agriculture, as equivalent to worship, it was recounted as a grievous hardship that the Tâtar marauders prevented the driving of the Aryan cattle to distant pastures, when those near at hand were exhausted.

To understand these hymns, it is necessary, also, to bear in mind what visible Nature was to these ancient poets. Let us at once dismiss all the current nonsense about the Aryan herdsmen being "startled" at the ordinary phenomena of peaceable Nature, "amazed" and "entranced" by the glories of the dawn and sunrise, "alarmed" when the sun set, lest he should not rise again, and "watching anxiously" at the dawn, to see if he would do so. All that is merely imaginary. It never occurred to them that the sun might not rise again. They never doubted of the permanence of the visible universe, or of the entire regularity of its movements. Thunderstorms, earthquakes and tornadoes "startled" them, *because* they were unusual and violent. I never knew an American Indian express any wonder at the skies and their circling luminaries, at the dawn or the sunrise. An eclipse alarmed them, because it broke the regular continuity of things to which they were accustomed. It is only here and there a man among any people, old or young, that speculates or thinks at all about the phenomena of the universe. Not one man in a thousand *cares* to see the sunrise, or ever looks up, except casually to the stars, nor does one in a hundred of *civilized* men ever see the dawn. I never have known an Indian display the least curiosity in regard to the heavenly hosts, or ask a question in regard to any of them or their revolutions.

The ancient Aryans no more "wondered" at the earth on which they trod being where it was, than at themselves who were on it. To them it was not an object of speculation. It was there, and they cared to know no more. It was a solid plane surface to them, of which they never conceived as a globe or orb, nor speculated as to its boundaries. The question how the sun managed to reappear in the east, every morning, after setting in the west, and where he went during the night, never occurred to the herdsmen. If it occurred even to the poet, we find no hint of such speculation in the *Veda*.

The sky was a solid vault, to poet and herdsmen alike. They had no idea of any space above it, or of any other "heavens" or "worlds" than what their eyes beheld. The luminaries were not *bodies* to them, like our earth, but merely light, invested with form, whether they regarded them as fixed in the sky and revolving with it, or as revolving in the expanse between earth and sky, they deemed them there for the service of the earth and men. The poets must have considered that they revolved in the expanse (Prithivi) below the sky and above the cloud-region; and thus the expanse was considered as consisting of three divisions, which the translators persist in calling the "three worlds."

Our modern faith need not smile contemptuously at the ideas of these ancients, in regard either to Nature or the Deity. As to all that, we are more knowing, but very little wiser, than they were. It may be that they were wiser than we are. We have, at least, perverted and corrupted their ideas. We know more than they did about the extent, arrangement and movements of the universe, the qualities and attributes of matter; the formulas of the mathematical, chemical and physical laws, that apply to matter and regulate movement, and the action and effect of the forces of Nature: we have larger and higher ideas of the attributes that we impute to the Source, Father or Creator, the Regulator and Sustainer of the Universe; and we venerate him less in proportion as we remove him from us, and find in his infinity no loving sympathy for our little wants and wishes and feeble wailings. Our world was very large to them, engaging the whole attention of the Deities. To us, it is smaller than a grain of sand, compared to the whole universe; and God is not exclusively engaged with our affairs. But we are as ignorant as they were, of what God and matter, and light and heat, and the other forces of Nature are. Of electricity, light and heat, in their essence, we know nothing at all; and, after all, in God we only worship either an infinite human intellect, or a force, of a nature utterly unknown to us, to which we ascribe two human faculties, will and intelligence, as our ancestors ascribed them to the fire.

These ancient men were alone in the world, with Nature, and its manifestations of force, motion and life. Stability or permanency, movement and life, were the three great facts, patent and palpable to them, about which they could not doubt, and as to the causes whereof it did not occur to them to inquire. Whatever was apparent to their senses, visible, tangible or audible, was real, and nothing else was so. The conception of invisible powers and forces was of later growth. In everything that was real, they saw life, and knew no difference between their own life, and that of all Nature around them.

The old Aryan herdsman or priest or poet had no conception of his self as a soul or spirit, distinct from his body, dwelling in it, or clothed by it as by a garment, or using it as an instrument. He no more imagined that of himself than of his horse. Nor did he conceive of any God whatever, as a Spirit, in our sense of the word, i. e., a somewhat that is no-thing, not matter, and wholly separate from all that is appreciable by the senses.

In these respects, as we shall see hereafter, the creed of Zarathustra made a long leap in advance. And it is possible that there may have been thoughtful men among the Indo-Aryans, to whom the possibility of a God above the powers of Nature had suggested itself, and whose vague hopes extended beyond this life; but the faith of the author of Ecclesiastes or The Preacher was undeniably that of the Vedic bards, and the immortality hoped for by them was to be translated to the sky, to shine there as stars.

Bearing all this in mind we may hope to understand their ideas of the Devas and other Gods. By far the larger number of the hymns of the *Rig-Veda* are addressed to *Agni* and *Indra*.

Most of the apparently contradictory texts that speak of Agni are readily explained. He was the actual Fire produced by attrition, of which flame, light and heat were manifestations; the animal heat that was vitality; the Celestial Fire, manifested in the lightning, the Aurora, the comets; in the light and heat emitted from the sun, and in the light alone emitted from the luminaries of the night; and all the luminaries were but embodied forms of Agni.

But as each and all of these are but partial manifestations of the universal fire, Agni is also that universal, conceived of as one, the invisible Fire-Spirit, and as such is invested with personality and intelligence, with will, power, wisdom and beneficence. In a single hymn, he is besought to accept a log as an offering. As the earthly fire, of the house or the sacrifice, he is the youngest of the Devas; for he is conceived of as born, whenever reproduced by attrition. As the fire of the sacrifice, he is the messenger of the Gods and mediator. He is also called the son of strength, the meaning of which I have already stated, conqueror of horses, high-born, loving hymns, delighting in riches, lord and giver of wealth, wise and powerful, giving rain, invincible strength and food; the sage, who goes *wisely* between heaven and earth, like a friendly messenger between two hamlets. He is asked to prepare the sacrifice, and to sit down on the consecrated grass. Such is Müller's translation. But only a paraphrase or commentary can express the real meaning of the text, and be indeed a translation. "High-born" evidently means originating above the earth, and passing to and fro between the earth and sky. He grants riches, because his light and heat, and the vital warmth cause production of food and animals. That he delights in riches may mean that he eagerly consumes the offerings cast into the flames; or that he delights to produce riches. Manifested as lightning, he shatters the clouds and produces rain. His warmth, and the food whose production he causes, and which he cooks, give strength; and as the material fire he performs or makes effectual the sacrifice, and becomes manifest and visible on the grass. That he is conqueror of horses means, perhaps, that he surpasses them in the speed with which he extends and darts through the woods.

He is called the child of the sky, because his light flows forth, or is produced or born there; and the dawn is called his mother, as producing the light of morning.

We are all familiar with the philosophical doctrine that God *is* all his manifestations. Properly translated, the Gospel according to St. John says,

In the beginning was the Word, and the Word was with God, and God *was the Word* [and in verse 18, of the same chapter], No man hath at any time seen God; the only-begotten Son, who is in the bosom of the Father, he hath manifested God. [Christ said, *viii.*, 42] I proceeded forth and came from God; [in *x.*, 30] I and the Father are one; [38] The Father is in me, and I in Him; [*xii.*, 45] He that sees me, sees him that sent me; [*xiv.* 9., 10] He that hath seen me hath seen the Father; I am in the Father and the Father is in me.

And Paul said to the Christians of Rome (*i.*, 19. 20),

> That which may be known of God is manifest in them, for God hath showed it unto them; for what of Him are invisible, even His Eternal Power and Very Self, since the creation of the world are clearly manifested, cognition being had of them by means of the things that are created.

Athanasius said,

> We do not teach three principles [αρχαι, unoriginates], as our illustration shows; for we do not speak of three suns, but of the sun and its radiance.

Hippolytus says: speaking of the Word;

> Whom He had within Him, invisible to creation, till He manifested Him, uttering the Word, and begetting Light from Light, ... and so another stood by Him· not as if there were two Gods, but as though Light from Light, or a ray from the sun.

Basil says:

> If any one truly receive the Son, he will find that He brings with Him on one hand His Father, on the other, the Holy Spirit.   For neither can He be severed from the Father, who is ever of and in the Father; nor, again, disunited from His own Spirit, who operates all things by means of it.

Clement, also, speaking of the names by which the God of the Mosaic law was called, says:

> See to it whether the Son also be not signified by these names, being in His own right the Almighty God, in as much as He is the Word of the Almighty God.

In all which, the term "Word," Logos, very inadequately expresses the meaning, what is so styled being rather the Self-uttering of God, or the Divine Reason.

The whole Deity manifests itself limitedly, and in a particular phase, but no manifestation is all of Deity, and the Very Deity is said in the Kabbalah to have no name, and to be beyond the reach of any cognition. It is the whole soul of a man that thinks a thought; but no one thought nor any number of thoughts are the whole soul.   Every thought is a manifestation or revealing of the soul or intellect, an emanation from it, an utterance of it.   By these alone we have a knowledge of the soul; and though each is the soul manifested, yet each is also a thought, and as such has a distinct existence; and thus the emanations of the Kabbalah, God's Will, Wisdom, Understanding, Benignity and Severity, are personified, as distinct existences, as the thoughts are, when once uttered outwardly.

The root of this doctrine is in the old Aryan fire-worship. Fire is the essential unmanifested Principle, whose manifestations or emanations (i. e., outflowings) are the flame, light and heat. It is not correct to say that fire was to them the symbol of the First Cause.

In *Rig-Veda ii.*, 1. 3, it is said,

> Thou, Agni, art Indra, bountiful to the excellent; thou art Vishṇu, the wide-stepping, the adorable.
>
> *vii.*, 20. 2.—All divine potency, as that of the sky [in the special form it has in the sky, or as it is manifested or exists there], was completely communicated to thee, Indra, by the Devas [the stars], when Thou, O impetuous Deity, associated with Vishṇu [the heat], didst slay Vṛitra and Ahi [gloom caused by clouds and cold], who shut up the waters.

This *"divine* potency," is the potential energy of the celestial fire, as it exists in the sky, and manifests and displays itself in action as the lightning. Its use by Indra we shall learn hereafter.

> *v.*, 3. 1.—Thou, Agni, art Varuṇa, when thou art born; thou art Mitra when thou art kindled. Son of strength, in thee all the Devas reside. Thou art Indra to the man that sacrifices.

When we have discovered that Varuṇa and Mitra were the planets Jupiter and Venus; the Devas, the stars, and Indra, light, to read this verse aright is easy. I read it thus:

> Manifested outwardly and limited, O Agni, thou art Varuṇa: shining radiantly, thou art Mitra: as manifestations of thee, all the stars have place and local habitations; and to the sacrificer thou dost reveal and manifest thyself as Indra (light).
>
> Thou art Aryaman (Mars), when thou, self-controlled, possessest the "secret name of the maidens."

Nothing could seem more enigmatical; but nothing is simpler, when we have the key. I read the verse:

> Thou art Aryaman; and self-limited [i. e., manifested in small portions or stars of light, of definite shape]. Thou hast given to thee the special and particular name of the Pleiades.

In the *Atharva-Veda xiii.*, 3. 13, it is said,

> Agni becomes Varuṇa in the evening, and Mitra when rising in the morning. Becoming Savitṛi [the Moon], he moves through the expanse; and becoming Indra, he burns along the middle of the sky.

I am to tell you, now, how I attained the results that I have indicated. I am to remind you, however, that the philosophic notions contained in the Vedic conception of Agni had not suggested themselves to any commentator; and that, if I am right, no commentator knew what either Varuṇa, Mitra, Aryaman, Indra, Vishṇu or Savitṛi, really was.

I said, "if we collect from the *Veda*, and group together under different heads, what the hymns contain, in respect to the characteristics of Agni, and his relation to the sacrifices, to men and to the other Deities, we may learn what it was, that, as him, they worshipped, and be prepared to make, more intelligently, the same inquiry as to the other Gods." And I proceeded to do so, as follows:

As *simply* Fire, he is termed the *Radiant*, "the constant illuminator of truth, increasing thine own dwelling." "Illuminator of truth" means making visible the reality of things, which, as the daylight, and manifested through the sun, Agni does with constant regularity. And Agni *dwells* wherever the fire is and burns. His *dwelling* is the space it fills, and that space, when a fire is kindled, constantly enlarges, the fire spreading and extending.

He is generated by attrition, resplendent and young (for he never changes, grows feeble nor decays, and is continually re-created or re-born). He is wise, radiant, the remover of disease, the purifier, shining with pure radiance. He abides in the waters; for he illuminates them, so that the eye can look into the depths of the streams and lakes; and in them the stars seem to dwell at night, and the sun by day; and, as the lightning, he dwells among the rains, suspended in the clouds.

"Lord of sustenance," the poet says, "assume thy vestments, and offer this our sacrifice." His vestments are the visible shapes in which he invests himself, of the flame, to manifest himself withal; and he is lord of sustenance because his light and heat cause the earth to produce, and by his heat, what is produced is cooked for the support of life.

He is vast, illimitable, smoke-bannered, of variant splendor, brilliant-rayed, distributor of riches, manifold, for the benefit of all the world, the offspring of two mothers, and reposing in various ways for the use of man; pre-eminent over the world, become manifest to the worshipper. He is "wise and intelligent," because he explores everywhere, and sees and knows all that is and all that is done. The figure which represents him as seeing and knowing is as familiar now, as it was ten thousand years ago; for we say that the stars "look down" upon the earth, that the moon "smiles" upon it, and that the sun "sees" whatsoever is done in the light. He is manifold, multiplied into many particular fires, that all the people may be benefited by him; and while in the sky, high above the earth he also manifests himself in the sacrificial fire. So he is manifested in many ways and by many orbs, which also were supposed to shine for the benefit of man.

So Agni "announced heaven to man." This is called a *translation*. It is a perversion. The real meaning is that the light made the sky known to men, by enabling them to see it. How could the fire "announce heaven"? and what is "announcing heaven"?

"Irreproachable," it is said of him, "a vigilant God, in the proximity of thy parents." One would like to know what meaning Professor Wilson attached to "irreproachable." Fire commits mischief and ravages enough to deserve to be often *reproached*. But nothing is so pure, so free from the grossness of matter, so *immaculate*, stainless, taintless, of such tenuity and subtility, as fire and flame. That Agni is a vigilant Deva, in the proximity of his parents, requires more consideration. The fire is watchful, vigilant to gain an advantage, always on the alert, quick to evade men's watchfulness, and to extend and encroach, is open-eyed and wary. The "parents" of Agni, here, are the sky and expanse, in which he appears and shines and is conceived to have been produced: and he is "in proximity to them" (as the Word was προς τον θεον "near unto God"), by being manifested as the luminaries that dwell there.

He "instructs the disciple, and defines the limits of the horizon": which probably meant that he taught the routes over the plains and through the forests to the young herdsman. And he "defines the limits of the horizon," by making it visible, and extending himself to it.

"The good and durable actions which the Gods perform are all aggregated in thee." The word rendered "Gods" is *Devas*. *Deva* means whatever shines or emits radiance, but specially and almost always, the stars, "the good and durable actions" which these Devas "perform" are the beneficent results of their supposed influences, as for example, the causing of the spring-rains by the Pleiades; and all these are attributable to Agni, whom each star is, manifested limitedly, or like an aperture, through which he shines.

> Bright with thine own radiance, sit on the sacred grass [the particular sacrificial fire, shining with the light of the universal Agni]; shine forth! emit the curling and graceful smoke! Agni, with the burning rays, whose rays high-ascending shine.
>
> Manu detained thee, Agni, light to the various races of mankind. Denizen of the sky, Manu [the original of our word "man," the legendary ancestor of the Aryan race, the original of the Greek Prometheus, who stole the fire of the Gods from the sky, for men], Manu domiciled Agni on earth.

And *man* means, in Sanskrit and Zend, to "think, understand, know"; and *manas*, in each language, "mind, intellect, thought." *Manu*, *man*, was simply the human mind or intellect, and so was, at the beginning, the Greek Prometheus.

His flames are luminous, potent, inspiring fear, and not to be trusted. He is "the immortal sustainer (or cherisher and preserver) of the universe"; for to him generation and production are owing, by which continuance of all living races of beings is secured: and it was in this sense that Vishnu was the preserver, a meaning of that word which in later days was lost. He was the preserver, as perpetuator and constant renewer. Fire, light and heat are the very life of Nature. The word rendered "universe" means created beings.

Agni is "associated" with Ushas and the Açvins, and so he and Indra are said to be "associated"; but this word very inadequately expresses the original idea, which is that of duality in unity, the relation ascribed to God the Father and God the Son, and, as to the Trinity, expressed by our phrase, "three in one and one in three."

As a local fire, Agni is pictured thus:

> Armed with the flames and vivified by the wind, with his whole might, in a volume of flame, he rushes triumphant through the forest, swiftly devouring it, he climbs the dry wood: his blaze consuming, runs like a race-horse, and his roaring sounds as if high in the air.

He is "rich with righteous acts," which is simple nonsense. "Righteous acts" are either the observances of worship and sacrifice, to which the fire is indispensable, or beneficent results of the action of fire, light and heat.

Of him as the universal fire it is said: "all other fires are branchings of Agni. In him, being long-lived, they rejoice."

> The living Father hath sent me, and I live by the Father [Christ says in the Gospel of John vi., 57]: the only begotten Son is in the bosom of the Father [i., 18]: the Son can of himself do nothing, except he sees the Father doing somewhat, for whatsoever he does, the Son equally does [v., 19]. As the Father hath life in Himself, so hath He given to the Son to have life in Himself [self-existence, and a distinct personality, v., 26]. As the Father knoweth me, even so I know the Father. The Father is in me, and I am in Him [x., 15. 38].

> He is manifested as Vaiçvânara, the navel of men, supporting them like a column, deeply-planted. Treasures were deposited in him. He slew the stealer of the waters, and sent these down on the earth. [This is the special function of Indra, and here ascribed to Agni as Vaiçvânara.] All the Devas engendered him in the form of night, for the venerable sage: and as him, Agni, the head of the sky and navel of the expanse became ruler over both expanse and sky. Vaiçvânara, by his greatness is all men, and is to be worshipped as the diffuser of manifold light.

It is easy to know what was meant by *Vaiçvânara, Vaiçva* or *Viçva,* (in Zend *Viçpa*) meant "all, the whole, the aggregate." It means this in *Vaiçvadevas* or *Viçvadevas,* "all the Devas," Gods or stars. *Nara* means "a man," but also and often is applied to the Deities, in the sense of "an individual," "a single one of a class or number." Agni Vaiçvâ-nara, therefore, is Agni the universal, including in himself all individualities of fires or lights. Agni is manifested as the aggregate of the stars, personified as a unit, perhaps the starry heavens, or, to invent a word, "star-kind," the source of all individual stars, holding them up in their places as firmly as a column could. The "treasures" deposited in him is the light emanating from Agni. He slew Vṛitra and released the rains, by the lightning, with which Indra shatters the clouds and slays the gloom. All the Devas combined to engender the sacrificial fire for the venerable Ṛishi, when it shone enveloped by the night or darkness before the dawn; and, as Vaiçvânara, Agni reigns over both the sky and the expanse; Vaiçvânara being the head, or source of light, as the brain is of intellect, of the sky, and navel of the expanse, sustaining the stars in it by nourishing them with light.

And thus Vaiçvânara includes in himself all individual manifestations or stars, and is to be worshipped as diffuser of light by means of manifold and multitudinous luminaries.

Agni is the kind kinsman of the waters. He breathes amid the waters like a sitting swan. Awakened at the dawn, he restores consciousness to men. Born from the waters, like an animal with coiled-up limbs, he became enlarged, and his light flowed afar. He tosses about his rays, like streams of water. The rays commingle, visible in the sky. He is born in the woods, and hides in the hollows. He *upholds* the expanse and sky, and *props* up the sky with true prayers; and this he does "like the unborn." In his character as the unmanifested universal (for "like" is here put by error for "as") he fills the sky and expanse with light, and thus "upholds" them; for if utter darkness were perpetual, filling the expanse, there would be for man neither sky nor place between it and the earth. That "he props it up," and with "prayers," is mere nonsense. As the fire of the sacrifice, he adds to and maintains the light in the sky, with that which he conveys thither from the sacrifice, and into which the oblations are transformed, and with which the prayers ascend to the stars. That seems to me the meaning.

> Radiant among the Devas [by and through them], and in his single very self comprehending the potencies of all of them; born living in the dry wood, he who delights in the sacrificial chamber has studded the sky with constellations.

The potencies of all the stars are his, and emanate from him, through and *as* them. He exists, latent and concealed, in the dry wood, and is born from it by means of the generative attrition. Rejoicing in the chamber of sacrifice, it is he also that jewels the sky with constellations.

> He assumes all celestial natures [i. e., takes the shapes and forms in which he manifests himself in the sky]; is white-shining, the extinguisher of the dawn [which

as the light of the sun he overpowers]; the illuminator, is possessed of manifold
light [manifests himself variously]; and while filling the all with radiance, gives
homes to men, and enables them to descry the forms of the objects that surround
them.

In his essence, he is not perceptibly the senses; but is cognizable by the
intellect alone. This is unmistakably the Vedic idea, which elsewhere
speaks of things seen only by the mind. He is manifested as light, heat,
flame, and otherwise. He is in everything and everywhere, exerting
beneficent influences. He rules the night, and is all-knowing, knowing the
origin of Devas and men; for he is the source and origin of all the Devas,
which are rays or sparks from him, and all men owe to him their birth and
their life. He was before any of these were, and therefore may well be said
to know their origin.

Invested with actuality as a visible fire, everything augments him.
The *air* makes him bright (or, I think, the *flame* reveals him in *brightness*)
and to shine in every mansion; and he bestows light on his daughter, Ushas,
the Dawn.

He is "the golden-haired Agni," who shakes the clouds, when the rain
is poured down. As the lightning, he nourishes the earth with the milk of
the rain.

He is localized as the digestive agent in the human body, as the *vital*
principle; then among "the seven conspicuous mothers"; and, thirdly,
"the associated generate him, delighting in the ten quarters of space, to
produce rain or to send down light upon the earth." So he is called three-
headed and seven-rayed; and I think that the "seven conspicuous mothers"
are the seven colors, displayed by means of the prism, and in the rainbow.
The three "heads" are flame, light and heat, and from this innocent poetic
figure came afterwards the three-headed God of the Hindū Brahmanism,
Brahma, Vishṇu and Siva, of whom Vishṇu alone is known to the *Veda*, and
he retained his old character as preserver, originally meaning perpetuator, as
heat by which all animal life is perpetuated.

So he is "the living breath (the vitality) of three-fold Nature, co-extensive
with the sky, perennial heat." The word rendered "Nature" means living
creatures, as we speak of "the animal creation"; and the three divisions of
those of the water, earth and air, are the "three-fold Nature."

Professor Wilson applies to the actual fire produced by attrition, not to
the Universal Fire, the epithets, "far-seeing," "single-minded," "intelligent,"
"immortal," and "radiant-limbed." We plainly enough see that these
epithets are ludicrously inapplicable to a fire kindled in the woods, produced
by rubbing two sticks together; and may well conclude that they are equally
inapplicable elsewhere. It is simply impossible that the craziest poet that
ever lived could have applied to a fire burning on the ground, epithets with

some of these meanings. Translation is to express in one language, what that means that is written in another. These epithets are not translation. For *far-seeing* read "shining to a distance, or afar," for *single-minded*, "having, or being used for a single purpose." The other three epithets are not correct, but they can at least be understood.

Men have cognizance of Agni as white, in the chief place of his manifestation: i. e., he is manifested as light, and not as flame or colored radiance in the sky. That "men" have cognizance of him may simply and literally mean that human eyes behold him manifested as light, in the sky; or it may mean that the stars, each as a separate and distinct unit and entity, are in intimate union with Agni, and receive their light from him, or *know* him as light. The original meaning of *vid*, in Sanskrit and in the old Aryan, was to "see"; whence, derivatively, to "perceive, feel, know." The Latin *video*, "I see," and Greek ειδω, "I see" show the original meaning. In Zend, *vid*, means, also, to "possess," and to "get." The stars know and possess Agni, as light, and there chiefly manifested, he is Vaiçvânara.

Shining as such, with never-lessening splendor (which is his "immortality"), he pours light over both sky and earth. It is he who shines resplendent in the sun. He shines before the dawns come: he is latent in the waters, and enters into the nascent plants.

A vast number of epithets are applied to him, of which I shall repeat only a few. He is the high priest of the sacrifice, because it is the fire that consumes the offering. He is remover of diseases; for he dries up and disperses its causes. He is like a loving father to a son, a kinsman to a kinsman, a friend to a friend. He is first of the immortals, and friend of the Devas. He appropriates the prayers addressed to the eternal creator; i. e., to him the prayers belong, that are addressed to the perpetual renewer of life.

He has a visible existence, as the sun, who discerns all that is true, i. e., everything that is real, actual, material. In him is all existence. He is generator of men, as well as of heaven and the expanse. He becomes manifested, in place, and by self-limitation, where his glories are. It is he who, entering into the womb, procreates.

He is the first (the source or origin) of the Devas, and also, when kindled by man upon the altar, their nourisher. For he feeds them with the light into which the oblations are transformed by the fire. His chariot is the lightning; his hair, flame, and his glory manifested in the expanse. He is, like a great ocean, everywhere. Enabling men to find their way, he preserves them from error and wanderings astray, or, according to Professor Wilson, from "sin." And he bestows faculties, because in perpetual darkness men would have none, or the use of none. Varuṇa, Mitra and Aryaman kindle him, their messenger from of old. He is associated with Ushas and the Açvins. "By him Mitra, Varuṇa and Aryaman are animated; for at his origin they were all comprehended in him," in their wholeness, in all their functions; "he encompassing them as the circumference of a wheel does the spokes." "They have styled the sun, Indra, Mitra, Varuṇa, Agni. Agni is all the Devas." The first clause should read, it is clear, "They have called Agni by the several names, Sûrya, Indra, etc." "He is Indra and the adorable Vishṇu. He is the royal Varuṇa, the adorable Mitra, and Aryaman. He is Rudra, and the Deva Savitṛi, and, to the offerer of the oblation, Aditi."

Thus Agni was the Universal Fire, the Vital Principle of the Universe. Neither heaven nor the expanse, it is said, could *measure* him; i. e., were not equal to him in extension. He was *all* the fire, flame, light and heat, everywhere. And this *all* was regarded as *One*, having personality and self-identity of being, a *Unit*, of which all portions were the outflowings or emanations, and the orbs were manifestations, each of them Agni himself, manifested and limited in place and form.

He was Creator, for he caused reproduction. He was Preserver, for he both sustained and caused life; and as consumer, he was the Destroyer, and what he consumed became light and so lived again. Thus he was the origin of the Hindū triad. So Philo says that the Universal Light is the image of the Divine Reason, and from it all the planets and stars derive their light. He says:

> Even before the creation God saw, using Himself as light.

It will be easy for any one familiar with the ancient philosophies, to find passages in abundance, in which the ideas of the Aryan hymns are developed into doctrines, and become articles of faith or tenets of philosophy; and Paul only repeated the Vedic and Zarathustrian idea, when he said in his first letter to the Christians of Corinth,

> There are diversities of operations; but it is the same God which in His wholeness worketh in all; [and] as the body is one, and hath many members, and all the members of that one body, being manifold, *are* one body; so also Christ; [and] God has shined in our hearts, to the light of the knowledge of the glory of God, in His hypostasis, Yesus Christos.

The Greeks, to whom he wrote, understood what he meant by this, and by the expression that Christos was the *image* of God. And in a single sentence he stated to the Greeks of Ephesus the original Aryan doctrine,

> One God, and Father of all, who is above all, and through all, and in you all.

I shall have occasion to speak more of the outflowings of the Aryan ideas, in the philosophy of Greece, and in the writings of St. Paul, and of some of the Fathers of the Church.

All things are the progeny of one fire. The Father perfected all things, and delivered them over to the Second Mind, whom all nations of men call the First.

This is an ancient fragment, given by Cory. And Pythagoras held that there was one Universal Mind, diffused through all things, the source of all life, and in substance like unto light; and Heraclitus, that fire was the First Cause, the igneous principle of life.

The Deity next in importance after Agni, is Indra. The commentators say that he is the bright firmament; but they make no effort to support this hypothesis by the texts, or to reconcile them with it.

Agni and Indra are, as we shall see, continually associated together, said to be twin-brothers, and each exercising the functions of the other. Indra, Dr. Muir says,

> who is most frequently represented in the hymns as the patron and helper of the sacred race, and destroyer of their enemies;

for Indra is the Demiourgos, the manifestation of light by Agni, the very light itself, in and of Agni, the immediate agent by whom he acts. And in *viii.*, 38, 1, where the two are called *Yajnasya ṛitvija*, the two sacrificing priests, Indra shares in the character. There is no doubt as to the character of either; and nothing could be more expressly contradicted, than the idea that Indra was the *firmament* is by the Vedic texts.

The essence of the Indo-Aryan faith is thus expressed in *viii.*, 19, 16,

> *Protected by Indra, well-knowing the path that through Thy power, Agni, we should follow, we adore that of Thy Self, by which Varuṇa, Mitra, the Nâsatyas and Bhaga shine.*

Indra is once addressed as an Aditya (son of Aditi, Mother-Nature, or space without limit, as the mother of all things, because all things are produced in its womb). Except in this instance, the Adityas are the planets and in this, Indra is so called along with Varuṇa (Jupiter), is identified with Sûrya, the Sun, and receives once the epithet of Savitṛi, the Moon. There must be some sensible reason for this. There was no confusion or muddle of notions, with the composers of the *Veda*, and there is but one single, sensible reason possible to be imagined—that Indra was the light, and manifested himself by and through every luminary, and therefore was every one, as Yehuah was the Elohim and the messengers who talked with Abraham and Lot.

In *vi.*, 59, 2, Agni and Indra are said to be twin-brothers, having the same father, and whose mothers are, one here and the other there. It is strange that, in view of even one text like this, Indra should ever have been supposed to be the firmament. Dr. Muir remarks that the sense of this verse is not very evident, unless it simply means that the mothers are different. It is still not evident, until we know who "the mothers" are. The word rendered "father" is *janitâ*. The phrase as to their twinship is *bhrâtarâ yuvâm yamav ihehamatarâ*. I do not think that *ihehamatarâ* means "two mothers, one here and the other there," but that each has one father and two mothers, the earth and the sky or expanse.

The etymology of the name *Aindra* or *Indra* ought to indicate what he was. But as to that, also, there is uncertainty. Professor Benfey and M. Bréal are quoted by Dr. Muir as expressing the opinion that Indra was the *successor* of Dyaus, the Sky. The brilliance of the sky, in the original Aryan land, Benfey thinks, appeared to the people the most splendid of all things, and worthiest of worship; but in India, where its heat is destructive, and rain most beneficent, the Deity who caused *it* was deemed most worthy of worship. Indra causes rain, and in that name, he thinks, "we unhesitatingly recognize a word standing for *Sind-ra*," which again was derived from *syand*, to "drop." Professor Müller ascribes the same meaning to Indra. It admits, he says, of only one etymology, i. e., it must be derived from the same root that yielded *indu*, "drop, sap"; and meant originally the giver of rain, the Jupiter Pluvius. I do not find a Sanskrit word *indu*, meaning drop or sap, and but for the preconceptions in regard to the character of Indra, there would never have been a doubt as to the root of the word. It is the verb *indh*, to "kindle, shine." "Power" is a derivative meaning of *indriya*, as "virility" is; both owing to the attribution of generative potency to light. *Indu* was a name of the moon, as "shining," from the same root. *Indu* is also used, apparently as a synonym for Soma; or as a name of Soma; as in *R.-V. ii.*, 22, 1,

> He [Soma] has stimulated the great and vast [God, Indra], to achieve mighty acts. He, the God, the true Indu [Soma] has attended him, the God, the true Indra. [So in *ix.*, 90, 5.] Soma, Indu, purified, thou exhilaratest Varuṇa, thou exhilaratest Mitra, thou exhilaratest Indra, thou exhilaratest Vishṇu, thou exhilaratest the troop of the Maruts, thou exhilaratest the Devas and the great Indra, that they may be merry. [In *ix.*, 56, 4.] Indu, do thou flow, sweet, to Indra, to Vishṇu. Preserve from sin the men who praise thee.

The simple explanation is, that Indu was the Soma juice, "purified" by the fire, and ascending in the form of light, to feed the Devas and other Light-Deities. And *Sudh-ra* or *Aindh-ra* literally signifies "that which is kindled or shines, radiance, splendor, light." Varuṇa was Jupiter Pluvius.

Indra is said to be "apprehended by the understanding and appreciated by the wise." If this has any meaning at all, and is not mere nonsense, that meaning must of necessity be the philosophical one, that in his essence and Very Self, he is not cognizable by the senses, but is attainable unto by the intellect alone. It necessarily follows that he is not the firmament, nor any orb or luminary, nor any phenomenon of visible appearance, and that he must be something that is existent in the Universal Fire, an inseparable part of its substance, but emanating from it, and then with a distinct existence acting outwardly and visibly.

Dyaus was the Sky, and *Prithivi* the Expanse. The Hebrew word *Rakya*, absurdly translated "firmament," had the same meaning as *Prithivi*, which all the translations take to mean the earth. *Dyaus pitar* and *Prithivi matar* were personified, but neither of them was worshipped as a Deity. The chief Deities of the *Veda* are potencies, universals possessed of active energies or their manifestations that dispense light and reveal those energies.

Agni and Indra are "associated" together, and ride in the same car; and these expressions mean that they act with one action, to produce one effect—precisely what was meant by the phrase, "the Word was *with* God, and God *was* the Word." Together, they are pious ministers, present at the holy rite; for Indra, the Light, is in and of the fire, and emanates from it; but Indra alone is never the minister, the messenger or the invoker of the Devas.

He and Agni are "kinsmen" and "relations," conceived of as such by the intellect. What can that mean, unless that they are generated in the same womb (of the dry wood or elsewhere) together, and are of one essence, as human kinsmen are of one blood?

"Those stationed around," i. e., the various orbs, in their places, "associated with Indra, the mighty, the indestructible, the moving (πλανηται, the wanderers or journeyers, the Planets), and the Lights (fixed stars), that shine in the sky."

These harness to his car, side by side, his two bay horses. To him men owe their daily birth from sleep. For he, with the radiance of the morning, gives them anew the use of their senses, and literally arouses them from sleep.

He is the wielder of the thunderbolt, and his most noted function is, by shattering the clouds, to free from its bonds and confinement in them the rain, and send it upon the earth. He does this with the lightning or thunderbolt, slaying Vritra, who is said to be the demon of the clouds; and he also slays Ahi, and sets free the streams.

"The demon of the clouds" is a mere name without meaning; for who and what is this demon? The truth is that the whole of this is an error.

Indra is not primarily the Rain-God, but only incidentally or consequentially so; and Vṛitra and Ahi are not demons of the clouds. He is simply darkness or gloom, from *vṛi*, *vṛit*, to "hide, cover, conceal." When a heavy thundercloud ascends and veils the sky, gloom falls upon the earth. Darkness is the opposite and absence of light, and therefore the mortal enemy of Indra. To drive it away, and recover his empire, he must shatter the clouds, cause them to discharge their rain, and then to disappear; and he effects this by means of himself manifested as lightning, which shatters the clouds, and is called his weapon.

The only meaning of *Ahi* (Zend *azi*) that I can find, is "snake." In the first Fargard of the Vendidad, the opposition to Ahura Mazda's work in the original Aryan land is said to be a great serpent and winter. This makes it clear that Ahi or Azi had another meaning, at that time, than that of snake; and that this was either "cold" or "freezing." By making ice, Ahi obstructs the rivers. Ahi and Vṛitra are also spoken of as one. The reason is, no doubt, that cold and darkness are the absence of Agni and Indra. And Indra melts the ice and sets free the streams, because with his larger light in the spring comes warmth; and the spring-rains also, which serve to melt and break up the ice, in the season when the thunder-showers begin, and the flashings of the lightning.

Accordingly, in *viii.*, 89, 12, and *iv.*, 18, 11, together, we find Indra being about to slay Vṛitra, calling on Vishṇu for aid;

> Friend Vishṇu [he cries], stride vastly! Sky, give room for the thunderbolt to descend! Let us slay Vṛitra, and let loose the waters. Let them, when released, flow by the impulse of Indra.

He set the sun in the sky, because the sun is his revealing. He dwells in an eternal mansion, being never absent from the sky. How then is he the firmament?

From his ancient abode he visits many worshippers. Therefore he cannot be the firmament. He is sovereign of all the mobile and stationary (of all the planets and fixed stars). He enjoys both sky and expanse, investing the universe with his greatness; i. e., he occupies or possesses himself of both, and extends in every direction beyond the visible creation.

"He abides, the monarch of men"; i. e., becoming localized, in form, limitation and place, he is the essence of all light-beings, the substance of all individual lights or orbs. He makes the sky known, and is spread throughout the region of dew, and replenished in the sky by the libations sprinkled on the sacred grass, as its kindred rivers hastening to it fill the ocean. For the oblation and libations become part of the fire, ascend in flame, and go towards the stars as light. He abides in his might (in his very self), beyond the limits of the sky or atmosphere.

He is the counter-measure of the wide-extended expanse (i. e., is co-extensive with it, and filling it, measures it). He is the lord of the vast God-frequented; i. e., of the expanse in which the stars make their circuits (for the word rendered "God" is *Deva*, and the Devas are the stars). "Thy bulk," it is said to him, "fills the expanse; and no other being (luminary) is equal to thee." The word that I render by "expanse" is rendered by "firmament" by Professor Wilson; and yet he thinks that Indra is that very "firmament" which his bulk fills.

He "purifies" (i. e., makes bright and clear) the sky with his irresistible potency, sends showers, and by his bounty gratifies our desires. He is the expanse-inhabiting, the haughty one, taking precedence of all Devas. He is quick in action and puissant. His perfect and unfailing power to destroy shines in the conflict of the elements, as a mountain-peak, snow-crowned, glitters in the sunlight. He subjugates the malignant clouds, and with resolute vigor opposes the encroachments of night and darkness. In his essence and as his own, is all potency. He pervades the universe, is potent, swift, mighty, and resistless, and hurls the thunderbolt. The lightnings are called "his foe-prostrating *associate*, and brightly-gleaming spear"—the word rendered "associate" meaning that the lightning is himself manifested.

He is self-irradiating in his dwelling; i. e., wherever manifested and abiding in place and form, by whatever orb or phenomenon, the radiance thereof flows from his Very Self. It is he that with the dawn and the rays of the sun scatters the darkness. He makes straight, or smooth, the elevations of the earth, and strengthens the foundations of the ethereal regions. He divided in twain the eternal and united, the sky and expanse, as the sun in the brilliant and beautiful sky. If the word translated "earth" here is *Prithivi*, it means the expanse, and its elevations are the upper empyrean and I doubt very much there being in the original anything about "foundations" of the ethereal regions, supported by the light. The eternal and united is time, which the light divides into night and day.

We often hear these old poets say that Indra upholds and supports the sky and expanse. They knew that heat, which seems to be an *effect* of light, caused expansion and ascension, and might naturally think, knowing no other forces of Nature than those of fire, that the force which produces the bubble was competent to raise and uphold the hemispherical vault of the sky. Nor do I know why it might not, since that would be no more an extraordinary effect than those produced by other equally immaterial and imponderable forces, such as attraction and magnetism. He has begotten the sun and the dawn. Born in the highest sky, he pervades the sky and expanse, and became the first artificer. He manifested himself as the dawn and sun, and so produced or begat them. Mani-

fested, through its luminaries, in the sky, he diffuses himself through all
visible space, and he became the first maker or creator, since, so long as
all was darkness, there was no life and no creation of beings.

He overspreads the day with his radiance, he generates the day; he
illumines for man the banner of the days; he obtained light for the great
conflict. He animates the dawns and makes great their radiance. He
gave the sun, bestowed plants and days, gave trees and the expanse, and
shattered the cloud. His horses pasture in the two azure spheres of the
sky and expanse. He is parent of the sun, and "is clothed at night." The
commentator adds "with gloom." But he totally mistakes the meaning.
The soul "clothes" itself with the body. The sun, in the *Zend-Avesta*, is
the body of Ahura. The Divine Light, in the Kabbalah, clothes itself
with form; and form is the self-limitation of the Infinite. At night, Indra ·
"clothes" himself, not with *gloom*, but with the forms of the stars, planets
and moon, and so reveals himself limitedly as them. In the Kabbalah,
which only reproduces the *Zend-Avesta*, the limits of the manifested are
termed envelopes and garments, and were imagined to be like the shell
which contains the egg.

Indra and Agni sit together in their wonderful car which illuminates
all beings. Their names are "associated," and they are "allied" as slayers
of Vṛitra. They are the two "seated" together. "I consider you," one
poet says, "in my mind as kinsmen and relations."

The moral and intellectual attributes ascribed to Indra, are like those
of Agni. He is wise, bounteous, averter of violence or harm, always
gracious, showerer of blessings, handsome, a warrior, slaying the native
tribes and destroying their cities with the thunderbolt, performer of great
deeds, etc.

In one Sûkta he is addressed jointly with Varuṇa, in one with Vishṇu,
and in one with Soma. And Mr. Cox, in his *Mythology of the Ancient
Nations*, says, that to the Aryan poets,

> Indra, Dyu, Agni, Vishṇu, Varuṇa, were but names for one and the same Divine
> Being, who alone was to them the maker and preserver of all things.

That is precisely the same as if one were to say that the Father, the Son or
Word, and the Holy Spirit, of the Trinitarian Christians, are but names for
one and the same Divine Being, to them the maker and preserver of all
things. Varuṇa was a planet; but Indra, Vishṇu, Vayu and Rudra, though
all included in Agni, were yet, as emanations from him, as really distinct
from him to the Aryan mind, as the Logos was, to Plato and Philo, from
God the Father; and as much entities to them as the Amĕsha-Çpĕntas were
to Zarathustra, and the Sephiroth to the Kabbalists.

In the forty-seventh hymn of the sixth book, we find this prayer to Indra:

O Deva, have mercy! Give me my daily bread. Sharpen my intellect, like the edge of iron! Whatever I now may utter, longing for thee, do thou accept it! Make me possessed of thee! Let us meditate on the adorable brilliance of the creator in the sky! May he arouse our minds. Destroy not our future offspring, O Indra! For we have believed in thy great power.

Professor Max Müller says,

Another idea which we find in the *Veda* is that of faith; not only in the sense of trust in the Gods, in their power, their protection, their kindness, but in that of belief in their existence.

One with a reputation well-won, to maintain, as great as that of Max Müller is, ought not to utter mere verbiage like that. How could the Vedic poets trust in their Gods, and in their protection, unless they first believed them to exist? Every savage, even the lowest Australasian, believes that his God, fetish or idol exists. Gravely to advance that as a claim to consideration in behalf of our Aryan ancestors, can but provoke a smile. Of course they believed in Indra's existence and power, as they did in the existence and power of Mitra and Varuṇa. They ascribed divine attributes and especially intelligence and beneficence to the light and its manifestations, and even to the Soma juice, not because it intoxicated, for that quality it did not possess, but because the alchemy of the fire was believed to change it into light, which ascending to the sky fed and replenished the stars.

The notion of Mr. Cox substitutes another religion for that of the Indo-Aryan poets, and one much inferior to it. The attributes assigned to Agni, Indra, Varuṇa and Mitra made them veritable Gods, and it is no doubt true that these attributes imputed to Agni, his oneness of essence, the cognition of him by the intellect only, his identity with all his manifestations, his utterance of himself, or outflowing visibly and tangibly as light and heat, his sustaining and upholding the universe, led Zarathustra to the still higher conception of an intellectual undefined God, light, which each of his names means, but also intellect or wisdom, older than the earth and heavens, and maker and preserver of them, a moral being, author of the law of morals and righteousness for all mankind. But that conception, none higher and purer than which, of the Deity, has ever been attained unto by the human intellect, first appeared in the Zarathustrian teachings, and is not even remotely hinted at in the older *Veda*.

In the Hebrew Kabbalah, which contains only what the Jewish rabbis learned from the Median Magi, all the emanations or Sephiroth are contained in and produced from and depend from the Very Deity Ainsoph; and the nine emanations that succeed the first, Kether, are all contained in it. In each, the Deity is; but neither of them is, nor are all of them together, the whole Deity. The Indo-Aryan idea, if not as profound as that of the *Zend-Avesta* and Kabbalah, was the origin of it, the same in a simpler and less developed form. And in the Kabbalah, too, the very Deity, before Creation, was the universally diffused Light.

The fashion of fine writing, on subjects like this, is not favorable to accuracy of thought and expression; and it is peculiarly a subject, in the discussion whereof what is inaccurate is not only worthless, but mischievous. The speculations of Mr. Cox are, for this reason, so far as the Vedic mythology is concerned, utterly without value. So are those of the Brahmans, and of the modern commentators who find monotheism and the doctrine of the immortality of the soul in the *Veda*. Even in minor matters, the continual tendency is to exaggerate. For example, we hear of the Aryan poets being "startled" at this and at that, and among other things, at Indra having a mother. The word "startled" is a pet one, and it would be as well to relieve it from duty for a time. The Aryan poets were no more "startled" at that idea than they would have been "startled" to hear it said that the dew was *born* of the air, or that vapor was *born* of the water and had the sun for *father;* or that future events are *in the womb* of time, or that necessity is the *mother* of invention. Our daily language is so essentially and thoroughly figurative, that we are unconscious of it, and are "startled" at finding that the case was the same seven thousand years ago. We personify the objects of Nature every moment, in our daily and common speech. We make the old and new year, the days, the nights, the sky and the sea, joy and sorrow, hope and faith, poverty and power to be things and persons, whenever we speak of them. The sky *smiles* for us; the sea is hungry, ravenous and cruel, treacherous or angry, *sleeps* in the calm, and *wakes* when stirred by the winds. The stars *watch* over us; spring comes to us with her delicate fingers full of flowers; and time and death have all the attributes of personality. The phrase

Hail! heaven-born Light,

of Milton, precisely expresses the Aryan idea of the birth of Indra. It is the local manifestation of the all-pervading Agni, that is born of the wood, by attrition; and Varuṇa and Mitra were nursed in the lap of Aditi, space, mother of the Adityas, because these, the sun, moon and planets, had their origin in space.

Indra has golden locks and a quiver full of arrows; he holds a golden whip, his arrows have a hundred points, and are winged with a thousand feathers; for they are his rays; his beard flashes like lightning as he rides in his chariot, drawn by his tawny or glistening horses. And, Mr. Cox says, he is sometimes the father, sometimes the son, and sometimes the husband of the dawn.

That is but natural, because Indra was both the Universal Light, and every local manifestation of it. Besides, these hymns are not sermons propounding doctrines and notions already clearly defined and not to be departed from; but poems, full of the fancies as to the Gods, which occurred to each poet as he composed his hymn. It is evident enough that many of them had no sacred character attached to them, but were mere popular poems. We must not make the mistake of supposing them to have been all religious, when composed. For many of them were no more so than the poems of Hesiod, or Shakespeare's Venus and Adonis. I am quite sure that all the "hymns" addressed to Ushas, the Dawn, and the Maruts, the Winds, were simply imaginative poems, without any religious character at all. I do not believe that Çraddha, worship or devotion (not faith, as Müller supposes it); Brahmanaspati, prayer, silent or by sacrifice; Brihaspati, prayer recited or uttered; and still less Vanaspati, fuel; and Pitu, food, were believed to be, or really worshipped as Gods. Fire, light and heat were, as Agni, Indra and Vishṇu, the melting power of fire; as Tvashṭṛi, flame; as Vayu, and the rarefying and vaporizing power, as Rudra; each of these has gained individuality as distinct emanations.

Soma is also personified; but neither the Soma plant or juice can have been believed to be a Deity. Nor do I doubt that those hypostases or subsistences of Agni were originally poetic creations, invested with personality by the imagination. The symbols of the wise always become the idols of the vulgar, and so they came to be regarded as real entities; and out of that, again, grew the philosophy which regarded them as real emanations, and continued the original worship of the luminaries, but as organs of the manifestations and revealings of Agni and Indra.

Light or the fire, Indra or Agni, is the life of the heavens, earth and waters. It is vitality; and therefore these are said to owe to it their being, and it to be their creator. For Darkness, utter and entire, was deemed to be non-existence; and there was no contradiction between this idea and the distinct assertion elsewhere, that before any of the Devas, the sky and the earth were. The account of the cosmogony in the Hebrew book, Barasith, represents chaos, enveloped in utter darkness, as existing before "the beginning." Then the breath of Elohim moved or brooded on the surface of this oceanic chaos, and the genesis of things commenced. Heaven and earth *were;* but had no real existence for any save themselves, until light flashed forth and filled the great expanse.

Of course it is impossible, in the limits of a lecture, to discuss and interpret even the principal texts addressed or relating to Indra. I must content myself with a brief reference to a few others, examples of misconcep-
tion and mistranslation, or proving what Indra is not and is. *i.*, 4, 3, as
translated by Wilson, is,

> We recognize thee in the midst of the right-minded, who are nearest to thee. Come
> to us, pass us not by to reveal [literally, *mâ no atî khyâh*, "do not speak beyond
> us"]. Sacrificing or preparing to do so, by star-light, the worshipper says to the
> light, "We behold thee manifested by the stars, whose light comes immediately
> from thee. Do not utter thyself in radiance elsewhere, and not to us."

He is called "the Pervader." That epithet could not appropriately have
been applied either to the firmament, the Rain-God or a luminary. Elsewhere he is said to be "expanded like the ocean." This is equally inconsistent with the idea that he is the sun or any other orb. He is said to have
"engendered" the sun, the dawn, and the firmament; i. e., he manifests
himself as the sun and dawn, and makes visible the expanse. He irradiates
the firmament; in him the Devas have concentrated riches and worship
and power, manifesting his own sovereignty. These Devas are the luminaries, of which he is the substance and they his out-shinings, manifesting
his supremacy over them. A hundred skies and expanses, it is said, and a
thousand suns would not equal him, and these two regions could not attain
unto him (be extended beyond them), when he was born.

He kindled the sun, as the dawn, he filled both worlds, i. e., both regions, the sky and expanse. He is the mighty monarch of mighty creatures, i. e., sovereign and principle of the luminaries. He generated fire
in the clouds, made the earth visible to the sky, and being of vast bulk,
comprehends in himself the Vast. All powers whatever are aggregated in
him. Sustaining heaven and the expanse, he overspread them with effulgence and scattering the hostile glooms, ensouled the All. It is he who
gives birth to the light of the morning.

The "Victorious Associated" perceived a great light issuing from the
darkness. The dawns, recognizing him, arose, and Indra was the sole
sovereign of the rays. The radiant Indra, with the leaders, generated the
sun, the dawn, the earth and fire. The "Victorious Associated" were
probably the twin stars of Gemini, which, rising before day, saw the daylight begin to emerge over a great space of the eastern sky, from the darkness. The dawn seeing him, arose, and all the radiance was from Indra.
He, with the twins that had ascended, leading the way, caused the sun to rise
as he had caused the dawn, made the earth visible, and caused the lighting
of the sacrificial fire.

Among other boons, Indra is implored to give to the Aryans victory in war, which depends upon his will, it is said, and for which he is invoked by both the hostile armies.   In *x.*, 103, 8, etc., not he alone, but various Deities or personifications with him are invoked, enabling us to understand in what sense the light was an ally, and a warrior.   The passage is thus translated by Dr. Muir:

> May Indra be the leader of these (our armies); may Brihaspati (uttered prayer), Dakshina (largess), Yajna (sacrifice), and Soma march in front!   May the host of the Maruts precede the crushing, victorious armies of the Devas!   May the fierce host of the vigorous Indra, of King Varuna, of the Adityas, and the Maruts (go before us); the shout of the great-souled, conquering, world-shaking Devas has ascended . . . .   May Indra be ours when the standards clash; may our arrows be victorious; may our strong men gain the upper hand; preserve us, O Devas, in the fray!

He is represented as defeating the Dasyus, the men of black skin, and various other enemies of the Aryans, and with the lightning destroying their cities, for example, the hundred cities of Sambara.   Some of the texts that speak of this are:

> Indra, commanding a hundred modes of succor, protected in all the battles the sacrificing Ârya; chastising the lawless, he subjected the black skin to Manu (or the Aryans).
> Thou hast disclosed the light to the Ârya; the Dasyu was placed on the left side. Destroying the Dasyus, he has protected the Aryan color.
> With these succors thou hast subjected all the distracted hostile Dasyu peoples to the Ârya.
> Thou, Indra, art the destroyer of unnumbered cities, the slayer of the Dasyu, the prosperer of the Aryan, the lord of the sky.

The commentators imagine that Sambara, Sushna and other enemies of the Aryans, destroyed by Indra, were demons or spirits of the air, and that the cities of Sambara and other cities represented as destroyed, were cities in the clouds.

But it is very certain that the Dasyu were the native Indian tribes whom the Aryans conquered, and that Sambara and the others supposed by the commentators to have been demons, were native chiefs or kings. It is true that Indra is represented as destroying the cities by his lightnings; but this only proves that these songs were written long after the conquest, and when those engaged in the struggle had become legendary characters and the legends themselves had become half-historical, half-mythical.

In *Rig-Veda iii. xxxi.*, in the legend of the robbery and recovery of the cattle of the Angirasas, Indra, propitiated by mental devotion effected an entrance into the fastness where the cattle were hidden, and let loose the kine. He is said to have done this, simply because, as daylight, he evoked the owners to track, follow and find the stolen herds.

We learn, also, from several passages in the *Veda*, that the native tribes, like our North American Indians, were in the habit of making their attacks upon the Aryan settlements and homesteads, in the night, and retreating at daybreak; and this and the facilities which the light afforded for pursuing them, were enough to cause the Aryans to regard Indra as their ally and patron. The poetic imagination added all the rest. And afterwards, upon the foundation of the simple ideas of the hymns of the *Rig-Veda*, the diseased Brahmanic imagination and ingenuity created the most amazing superstructure of fable and extravagance of folly that the world has ever seen and human credulity believed in.

Permit me to direct your attention to two or three points of curious significance in the brief passages to which I have referred. In that relating to the robbery and recovery of the cattle, the credit of the recovery is given to Indra, and he is stated to have been propitiated and his aid secured by mental or silent prayer. In another passage, Brihaspati (prayer uttered aloud) is said to have recovered the cattle; and it seems also that the old Rishi, Angiras, while his seven sons were following the robbers and the cattle, made formal sacrifice for their success.

We thus learn the noteworthy fact that it was not believed that the Devas and great Deities, Agni, Indra and Vishnu were only to be propitiated by sacrifice and offering, or by formal offices of worship, performed by men set apart and sanctified to that service; but that the silent prayer of the heart, not even expressed in words, the mute orisons of the soul, were equally efficacious, in Aryan opinion, to secure the assistance and favor of the Gods. This ceased to be so after a time, when worship became a Brahmanic monopoly, for the tendency always is, in every religion, to exaggerate the value and efficacy of public worship, prayer and ceremonial as means of intercession with the Divine Grace, and in the same proportion to belittle the pious and devotional spirit that either prays in secret or does not utter aloud the petitions that the soul prefers to God, in obedience to the express command of Christ.

It is also noticeable that not only Indra led the Aryan forces to victory over the Dasyu, but with him also marched Brihaspati, and Soma, which, consumed by the fire and becoming radiance, invigorates and exhilarates the Devas and Indra himself. For men were, in those old days, possessed by a profound and earnest conviction that victory in war and success and prosperity in all the enterprises of life, were wholly dependent upon the Deities, and that piety and devoutness and worship were the only mothers of good fortune. Prayer fought for the Aryans, like a warrior armed in steel, and gave to the pious worshipper abundant crops, good pasturage

and increase of all his store, and success in all his undertakings. It necessarily follows that these undertakings, public and private, were such as it
was deemed fitting that the Gods should approve. It would be well for
us if we had no other national purposes, courses and policy, and no other
private pursuits and enterprises, than those in which success could properly
be regarded as the natural fruit and consequence of piety and prayer.

But also, and with Yajna, sacrifice or devotional ceremony, *Dakshiṇâ*
marched in front of the Aryan soldiery, against the fierce hosts of the infidel
Dasyus. In the Mahabharata and other Brahmanic books, *Dakshiṇâ* is a
present to the Brahmanas, as a sacrificial fee; a gift or largess, the efficacy
of which is especially praised in one of the hymns of the *Veda*. Originally
Dakshiṇâ meant the right, as contradistinguished from the left hand or side;
and thence, "clever, the south, upright, honest." Of course the time came
when gifts to the priests were deemed the most meritorious service to the
Gods. In the Vedic times, I believe, *Dakshiṇâ* meant an offering to the
Gods, or perhaps simply "reverence."

A profound confidence, also, in the beneficence of the Gods is constantly
expressed in the *Veda*. Indra is not only a friend, but a father, and the
most fatherly of fathers. He is the friend of the worshippers, as he was the
friend of their forefathers. "Now," it is said to him, "men resort to thee
continually, and the ancients born of old were beloved by thee." He is
the helper of the poor, loves mortals and is their protector. His friendship
and his guidance are sweet, and all men share his benefits. He is the deliverer
and the consoler of his servants, their strength, and a wall of defense.
One whose friend he is, is never slain or overcome. His powerful arms
are resorted to for protection; the loving praises of his worshippers, uttered
from the soul, go to him as messengers, and touch his heart; and the imploring poet with his hymn seizes the skirts of Indra's robe, as a son does his
father's.

I think there is not the least doubt that Indra was the universal *Light*.
There is not one text really inconsistent with this, and a multitude of texts
sustain it, and have on any other hypothesis no sensible meaning.

I can anticipate, nevertheless, that it will be thought that the conceptions
which I ascribe to the Aryan poets are too modern, too metaphysical, too
much in advance of their age.

It might be enough to say, that it is too plain to be denied that such
conceptions *were* entertained by them, unless the *Veda* is nonsense pure and
simple. Or to answer that these ideas and conceptions are found to have
been possessed by the Brahmans, the Bactrians, the authors of the Hebrew
Kabbalah, and the oldest among the Grecian philosophers; and that they
are the fruits, not of learning or scientific knowledge, but of reflection,

needing for their birth in the human mind only eyes with which to see the world, and intellect and imagination to speculate upon what the eyes see.

The relation between Indra and the luminaries, as conceived of by these old poets, is simple enough. If each luminary were an aperture, through which flowed a portion of one vast ocean of light, each would be that One Light seen in part, though individualized and called a ray. That the eye cannot descry the whole of that which is too great for the sight to take in at once, does not make what it does see not to be that, but something else; and a portion of the sea, confined in narrower limits, is still the sea, seen only in part. The moment we conceive of anything as a unit, we conceive of the whole as being where any part of it is. It is "the sea," that chafes against a particular shore, or lifts the pebbles gently on the shores of a particular bay. It is "the air" that breathes upon us, in at our window.

It is the whole soul that thinks each thought, and each is a manifestation of the soul, but not of the whole of the soul. So it is the whole light that utters a particular ray. A more familiar illustration is found in the expression attributed to Logan, the Indian chief, "my blood does not flow in the veins of any living being." Those of one family or race are said to be of one blood. And so it is the one light that manifests itself in all the orbs, and from each the radiance and splendor of Agni and Indra flow forth.

Each orb was conceived to be simply light, and not to be a luminous solid body. So Cicero considers the stars and sun, in his treatise of the nature of the Gods, and so, he says, did Cleanthes,

totaque sunt calida atque per lucida . . . . ea quidem tota esse igneas, duorum sensuum testimonis confirmari Cleanthes putat.

Each was accordingly conceived of as the Light-Unit or Light-Ocean, limitedly revealed.

The idea of emanation is equally as simple. Flame, light and heat are all conceived of naturally, even by the child, as separate and distinct things. Yet they are all included in the fire, and are of it, and flow forth from it. It is the fire, we say, that burns brightly, that blazes, that flames up, that shines, that burns us, that melts the metal, and changes water into steam. The flame, the light and the heat are distinct revealings of the fire, yet each the fire itself, in that particular mode and aspect, each a particular subsistence of the one substance; and when we, in our ordinary language, ascribe to the fire that burning of our flesh, that is the effect of the heat, we do precisely what the Aryan poets did, in ascribing the same potencies to Agni and Vishṇu alike.

I do not know how far I have succeeded in interesting you in this discussion. I have, I believe, shown you the true character of the great

Deities Agni and Indra, and expounded to you truly the leading doctrine of the *Veda*. We naturally think, however we may err in it, that what interests us will interest others; and for myself I profess that I have felt a profounder interest in learning what these remote forefathers of ours, unaided by direct inspiration, thought and believed, and in finding in the *Veda* the origines of ancient and modern religious philosophy, and of the great truths whose discussion has agitated the Aryan mind for seventy centuries, than I ever felt in the histories of the revolutions of empires, in the discussions of the schools or in the achievements of science; and it has been to me a source of increased pride and self-congratulation at being of a race that was even in its youth, if not in its infancy, possessed of such an intellect, vigorous, profound, acute, as these discoveries demonstrate; and even more because of its manly and heroic nature in those old days, and its freedom from degrading superstitions, idolatry and irrational faith. The race is rich in the glories of great deeds, done in all the ages, always deserving to be called by its ancient name, the Ârya. Its crowning glory is its ancient faith and the legitimate developments of that faith.

It yet remains to you to understand the other manifestations of Agni, and other of the Vedic Deities.

To these I shall devote the fourth lecture.

LECTURE FOUR

VISHŅU, VAYU, TVASHŢRI, RUDRA, VARUŅA, MITRA, ARYA-MAN, THE AÇVINS, USHAS, PUSHAN, AND OTHER DEITIES

I am, in this fourth lecture, to treat of Vishņu, known in the Hindū mythology as the preserver in the Trimurti, or Triad, of Brahma, Vishņu and Siva, of Vayu and other manifestations or subsistences of Agni, the Fire, of Ushas and the Açvins, of Varuņa, Mitra and Aryaman, Pushan, and other Vedic Deities. The space to be allowed for each must of course be brief.

In the twenty-second hymn of the first book of the *Rig-Veda*, this is said of Vishņu; as Dr. Muir translates it:

> May the Gods preserve us, from the place from which Vishņu strode through the seven regions of the earth. Vishņu strode over this; in three places he planted his step. Enveloped in his dust, Vishņu, the unconquerable preserver, strode three steps, bearing from thence fixed observances [upholding thereby righteous acts: *Wilson*]. Behold the acts of Vishņu through which this fitting [or intimate] friend of Indra perceived religious ceremonies [through which has accomplished vows: *Wilson*]. Sages constantly behold that highest position of Vishņu, like an eye fixed in the sky [as the eye ranges over the sky: *Wilson*]. Wise men, singing praises, and ever wakeful light up [amply glorify: *Wilson*] that which is the highest station of Vishņu.

Omitting what he adds in parentheses to the words of the original, Professor Wilson's translation of the first of these verses (the 16th) is: "May the Gods preserve us of the earth whence Vishņu by the seven meters stepped." The original of the phrase translated "by the seven meters," and "across the seven regions of the earth," is *prithivyāḥ sapta dhāmabhiḥ*, or *dhamabhis*.

> *Rig-V. i., 154, i.* I declare the valorous deeds of Vishņu, who measured the mundane regions [who made the three worlds—*Wilson*; *pārthivāni vimame rajāṅsi*; literally, Wilson says "he made the earthly regions"], who established the upper world [who sustained the lofty aggregate site—*Wilson*] striding thrice, the wide-stepping [thrice traversing; who is praised by the exalted—*Wilson*]. Therefore Vishņu is celebrated for his prowess, terrible like a wild beast, destructive, abiding in the mountains; he within whose three vast paces all the worlds abide. Let the hymn proceed strength to Vishņu, the dweller in the aerial mountains, the wide-stepping, the vigorous, who alone measured with three steps this wide, stable firmament [this spacious and durable aggregate—*Wilson*; and Professor Wilson also makes him abide in prayer, instead of dwelling in the aerial mountains]. Whose three

stations, replenished with honey [whose three imperishable paces, filled with ambrosia—*Wilson*], imperishable, gladden us spontaneously [delight with sacred food—*Wilson*]: who alone sustained the triple universe, the earth and the sky, all the worlds [who verily alone upholds the three elements (*tridhâtu*), and earth and heaven—*Wilson*].

The commentators are utterly confounded by these passages. Not one of them knows what they mean; nor has even a sensible conjecture as to their meaning been indulged in. The three steps or paces, were, Sakapûṇi says, on the earth, in the firmament and in the heaven. Vishṇu is the Sun, he says,

Becoming terrestrial fire, he paces or resides a little upon the earth, in the shape of lightning in the firmament, and in the form of the sun, in heaven.

Aurṇavâbha says,

at his rising, in the zenith and at his setting.

Mahidhara says,

going in the three regions, as Agni, Vayu and Aditya, or fire in the earth, air in the firmament, and the sun in heaven.

Wilson says,

there can be little doubt that the three steps here referred to are his rise, culmination and setting.

Prithivi did not mean the earth, but the expanse between earth and sky. And verses 5 and 6 of the hymn last cited are,

May I attain to that beloved heaven of his, where men devoted to the Gods rejoice [his favorite path, in which God-seeking men delight—*Wilson*]; for there is a spring of honey in the highest abode of the wide-stepping Vishṇu [in whose exalted station there is a flow of felicity—*Wilson*]. We desire to attain to these abodes of you two [Indra and Vishṇu] where the many-horned and swiftly-moving cows abide. Here that supreme abode of the wide-stepping Vigorous shines intensely forth. [Wilson has "many-pointed and wide-spreading rays," instead of the cows; and makes the "Supreme station shine of the many-hymned, the Showerer."]

Undoubtedly the whole of this seems to you utter nonsense. It had no sense to me, for a time. I am now to show you, if I can, what it all means. For it assuredly *had* a meaning, and that meaning, when we ascertain it, will tell us what Vishṇu *was*. And you will please to notice that no commentator makes the slightest attempt to inform us what Vishṇu really was, to the Vedic poets, except by quoting the notion of Hindū commentators, that he was the sun.

To interpret, if I can do that at all, the verses that I have quoted, I must deal somewhat with etymology, and see whether either of the translations (which as you have seen, very greatly disagree) is substantially correct. Without an example or two of this process, you cannot fully understand the subject; and for such an example no passages in the *Veda* are better adapted than these.

Returning to the beginning of the first of these two hymns, you find the poet saying, according to the translations,

> May the Gods preserve us from that whence Vishṇu strode.

I think it means in the original (*ato devâh avantu no yato Vishṇur*),

> May the Devas receive pleasure from this (sacrifice) whence Vishṇu strode.

For Benfey gives as meanings of *av*, to "please, satisfy, be pleased" (Vedic), as well as to "desire, take care and protect." Does *sapta dhâmabhih* mean "the seven *regions*" of the expanse? The verb *dhâ* has many meanings, and, among them, to "generate, carry, bear, nourish, preserve, get, show, put, grant"; and *dhâman* means "an abode, state, host, dignity, light, splendor." *Dhamâbhih* is the instrumental plural of this noun, and should mean the things (whatever they were) *with which* he strode. He strode from the sacrificial fire, and, I think, with the seven splendors of the expanse, i. e., with the seven colors of the light that ascended into it. *Vichakrame*, which is rendered "strode," means to "walk along, step, proceed." And Vishṇu is styled *Trivikrama*, or "he who took three steps or paces, or, who proceeded by three stages."

This, verse 17 continues, Vishṇu traversed (the same word *Vichakrame*). *Tredhâ nidadhe padam*, "in three places he planted his foot." *Samûlham asya pâṁsure*, which is translated by Muir, "and was enveloped in his dust"; and by Wilson, "and the whole was collected in the dust of his." There is no meaning whatever in either translation. *Samulham*, from *sam+uh*, to "bring near, bring together," may mean, "was collected, was gathered together, cohered." *Paṁcu* is "dust," or a particle of dust. *Asyâ* is the genitive of *idaṁ*, means "of this," and refers to the fire of the sacrifice; and the meaning of the phrase is, I think, "and all the particles that ascended from the fire adhered together with him."

In verse 18, we have *trîṇi padâ vichakrame Vishṇur*, "three steps Vishṇu stepped"; the epithets *gopah*, "protector, warder, concealer," originally "cowherd" and *adâbhyah*, "not to be checked or impeded," being applied to him. *Go*, in the plural, also means "rays"; and *gopah* may mean "keeper or guardian of the rays."

And then follows *ato dharmâni dharayau*, "upholding thereby righteous acts," according to Wilson; and "upholding thereby fixed ordinances," according to Dr. Muir. "Righteous acts," in Professor Wilson's translation, always misrepresents the original. *Dharma* means "virtue, merit, right, law, duty, justice," but these are all derivative meanings. Its original meaning is an act of worship, a ceremonial observance, a sacrifice: and such acts and observances are always the "righteous acts," of Professor Wilson, as the "sins," that Varuṇa, and other Deities are asked to forgive are the non-performance or neglect of them. *Dhri* means to "bear, carry, convey, maintain, support, retain, keep." And I think that the phrase means "carrying hence the sacrifice," or "giving effect to the acts of worship," causing the oblations to ascend to the sky, and become light.

Verse 19 is rendered,

> behold the *deeds* of Vishṇu, through which this intimate friend of Indra has perceived the established laws.

Such is Dr. Muir's reading. A slight objection to it is that it means nothing, but is simply a sound of words. Wilson's is,

> through which [the worshipper] has accomplished [pious] vows; he is the worthy friend of Indra.

Vishṇoh karmâni paçyata means "know the operation, or efficient action of Vishṇu"; *yato vratâni paçpase*, "whereby he has given effect to acts of worship." *Indrasyah yujyah sakhâ* means "the intimately united with," or "the closely united twin-brother of Indra."

Vishṇu, then, rising from the sacrificial fire, with the seven splendors of the flame, ascends by three successive steps or stages, the particles from the sacrifice being aggregated and ascending with him. Preserver of rays, whom nothing can hinder, he ascends by three stages, making effectual the acts of worship. Know, it is said, this efficient action of Vishṇu, whereby this intimately united twin-brother of Indra has given effect to our acts of worship.

Whither does he ascend? In verses 20 and 21 we are told. *Sadâ paçyanti sûrayah*, it is said, "the wise ones ever contemplate that supreme station of Vishṇu," *tad Vishṇuh paramam padam*, "that highest step." *Sûrayah* is "the sages"; but it is from *Suri*, *Sûrya*, the sun, the root being *svar*, "the sun, splendor, the sky." And these "sages" are *Sûrayah* because they have been translated to the sky, and shine there; and they do not "contemplate," but they *know*, and *have perception* or *intuition* of this last stage or step in the process by which Vishṇu makes the sacrifice effectual to nourish them with light, the great object of Aryan sacrifice, and for which the melted butter was poured into the flames to make a great blaze.

They do this, according to Wilson, "as the eye ranges over the sky"; according to Muir, the highest station "is placed like an eye in the sky." The original is *diviva chakshur atatam*. *Chakshas* is "an eye," and *chaksh* means to "see"; but also *chak* and *chakas* mean to "shine," and *ātatam* means "effused": so that I read this clause "effused as radiance in the sky," i. e., distributed there to the stars.

And verse 21 is,

> the Wise [or the Priest *vipraso*] ever vigilant and offering adoration, kindle [*sanainda-hate*] that which is the highest step of Vishṇu.

The meaning is, not that they kindle the station, but the sacrificial fire, which, fed by oblations, becomes the light in that supernal station.

In the other hymn (*i.*, 154), Vishṇu "measures" the regions of the expanse, as the sun is elsewhere said to measure the broad space, by journeying across the sky. Vishṇu measures the expanse, by ascending from the earth to the stars. But I doubt if *rajânsi* means either worlds or regions; and think that the phrase means "who poured out the colors of the expanse." He is said in this hymn, to have supported, or sustained the loftiest or upper abiding-place, stepping three times, because, ascending to it he supplied it with light. But the expression here is not *prathama pada*, but *uttaram sadhastham;* and *uttara* means "future," as well as "higher," and the meaning may be "the future abiding-place of pious men."

In this hymn Vishṇu is called *giri-sthah* and *giri-kshit*, which Muir considers to mean dweller in the aërial mountains; and Wilson says may mean dwelling on high, or abiding in prayer or speech. It means here that he abides above; and it is added that in his three paces all the regions or parts (of the expanse) abide. In verse 3, it is expressly said that he measured, either the firmament, according to Muir, or the spacious and durable aggregate, according to Wilson.

Dr. Muir has his three stations replenished with honey. Professor Wilson has them filled with ambrosia. *Madhu* means any thing sweet. In the next verse, the worshipper expresses the hope that he may attain that beloved heaven (or favorite path) of his, where men devoted to the Gods (or God-seeking men, *naro devayavo*) rejoice (or delight), "for there is a spring of honey in the highest abode of the wide-stepping Vishṇu" (in whose exalted station there is a flow of felicity). *Naro* means "individuals" as well as men; and *naro devayavo*, "the stars that once were sages, the deified men." They rejoice there (*madanti*): but *mad* also means to "become intoxicated," and the meaning is that these stars become exhilarated by the light that ascends from the sacrifice. Springs of honey could never have been imagined by the most frantic imagination to flow in the star-country, and ambrosia is a word that has no meaning.

Vishṇu sustains, according to Muir, "the triple universe"; according to Wilson, "the three elements." The word is *tridhatu*, and it means, according to Benfey, "three-fold." Here it means the expanse, composed of three parts, which are constantly called in the translations, the "three worlds." They are, the open space below the clouds, that between the clouds and luminaries, and that above the luminaries and below the sky, or, perhaps, that between the home of the planets and that of the fixed stars. It is not possible to speak positively as to the exact meaning of the different regions; but a safe rule is to assume that the division was the simplest and most obvious one. Any one could see at a glance that the clouds were below all the luminaries; and, with a little attention, that the morn came between the fixed stars and the earth, and I think that the three regions or "worlds," were the cloud-world, planet-world, and star-world. It is perfectly certain that the Vedic poets knew nothing of three worlds or a triple universe, in our sense of these phrases.

In verse 6, the abodes of Indra and Vishṇu are spoken of, according to Dr. Muir, in which the many-horned and swiftly-moving cows abide, the highest abode of the wide-stepping Vishṇu, which shines abroad with intense radiance. And in *iii.*, 55, 10, it is said,

Vishṇu the preserver, guards the highest abode, occupying the delightful imperishable regions.

Professor Wilson has many-pointed and wide-spreading rays, instead of horns, and he is right. Rather too much has been made out of the "cows" of the *Veda*, and the comparison of the clouds of the dawn or any other clouds to "cows" is often discovered where it does not exist.

In the hymn, *i.*, 155, Indra and Vishṇu are praised together,

who both stood, great and invincible, on the summit of the mountains, as if on an excellent steed.

Wilson has it, "upon the radiant summits of the clouds." In the upper region of the sky it is said, "the son has an inferior and superior appellation, and a third of father." Literally, I think, the line reads, "the Son bears a lower and higher name, the Father a third one." Perhaps, "the upper region of the sky" should follow this, the meaning being that the Father has his name there. There is no difficulty as to the literal meaning of the words or phrase. The question is, what the Son and Father are.

In the next two verses, the manhood of Vishṇu the preserver is praised, and he is said to have traversed the three regions with three wide steps, in different directions, for the many-praised existence. Man glorifying, it is said, tracks two steps of that sky-beholding (that which reaches the sky); but apprehends not the third, nor can the "soaring-winged birds." Dr. Muir has it that Vishṇu traversed far and wide the mundane regions (but the word is *parthivani*) for the sake of a wide-stepping existence: and that a mortal, *contemplating*, can *approach* two of the steps.

These passages make it perfectly certain that the steps are upward, through the expanse, to the sky; and that something *produced* (the son), having one name below and one above, and something that produces it (the father) having a third name, and still higher, occupy the three steps.

"Conceived of by his adorers," it is said in the next verse, "to be vast in body," i. e., conceived of by the intellect of his worshippers (of course his very self not being visible), as indefinitely extended, and not a luminary, "the youthful full-grown," i. e., recently manifested, yet of full stature, "advances to the combat."

Now who or what is this Vishṇu, that is the twin-brother of Indra, and so intimately united with him that the action of the two is but one action? They stand together, great and invincible. They attack together, and together avert from man (from the Aryans) the bolt of the archer *Kṛiçânu*. *Kṛiç*, to "become or make thin, emaciated." *Kṛiç-anu*, "the emaciator, he or that which makes thin or emaciates." There are, therefore, similitude and analogy between them, and one is not a principle or universal, and the other a luminary or manifestation.

Vishṇu is never said to *shine*. None of the attributes of light are ascribed to him. Yet he is evidently a subsistence of Agni, the Fire. For, in the next hymn, he is styled "self-born," is the mighty one, like a friend, accepter of oblations (receiving and consuming them), abounds with food, grants protection, and is every way accessible (within the reach of all). He is the *germ* of sacrifice, according to Wilson; by his nature the primeval *source* of sacred rites.

What is that but the *Heat*, which is the source and cause of the flame, and which consumes the oblation? When this thought occurred to me, I exclaimed, as Pythagoras did, "Eureka!" Everything was instantly clear to me. I saw why he was not said to shine, to be splendid or brilliant, but only to be mighty; why he and Indra were so closely united; why he was generator and preserver; and how he became the second person of the Hindū Triad, the preserver.

What, then, are the three "steps," and the son with two names in the two lower ones, and the father with one, in the highest? Clearly the son is the flame, and the father the light. The flame ascends and becomes invisible; reaching the sky, it is light, and nourishes the stars. Or perhaps the son of the fire was the vapor of the Soma juice poured upon the fire, which became cloud above, and light in the region of the sky. During all the steps of the process, the ascending heat carried with it the particles, these not separating and being lost, but adhering together, and reaching the sky as light. And it will be found that in this idea was the foundation of the practice of burning the dead. It was the fortunate destiny of the body to become light, by means of the fire, and so to reach the sky, which if denied cremation, and buried in the earth to rot, it could never do.

It is the heat, then, issuing from the sacrifice, that makes the three steps. Two of these the worshipper can follow with the mind; for he sees the vapor and flame, and can still conceive of it as existing when it becomes invisible, as the clouds melt away and disappear, but he cannot conceive of its reappearance as light, in the sky.

In *v.*, 3, 3, we find, in Wilson's translation, in an address to Agni;

For thy glory the Maruts sweep, when thy birth, Rudra, is beautiful and wonderful; the middle step of Vishnu has been placed, so those cherishest the mysterious name of the waters.

There is no attempt at explanation of this; but it must refer to the water or Soma juice, which had become vapor, finally becoming invisible.

It is quite likely that after it had been forgotten that Vishnu was heat, and when it was no longer known what was meant by his three steps, the texts in relation to them and to his "stations" were corrupted by emendations made for the purpose of suiting them to the supposed various meanings. The only real ground for wonder is, not that the texts are so obscure, but that they retain enough of the originals to enable us to say with certainty that Vishnu was heat.

In *i.*, 127, *i.*, it is said that Agni desires for the Devas the blaze of the clarified butter which is offered in oblation with his flames.

In many other passages "Indra-Vishnu" (so coupled together) are praised. They grow by the oblation; they have produced the sun, the dawn and the fire: together they slay Vritra, and smite the cities of Çambara, for both light and heat are in the lightning.

Thrice, it is said in hymn 100 of book *viii.*, Vishnu traversed Prithivi with its hundred lights. This single text suffices to prove that Prithivi was not the earth, but the expanse; and the next sentence, that he traversed it to give Manu a habitation, means that he ascended to the sky for Manu sacrificing, to procure for him a home among the stars. And, it is added,

the men who praise him are secure. He has procured for them an ample abode on high.

In one text it is said that Vishṇu strode his three steps by the force of Indra. He strode thrice, to where the Devas rejoice, i. e., to the sky, where they shine as stars. And that he is heat appears too clearly to admit of doubt, by the statement that, urged by Indra, he carried off a hundred buffaloes, broth cooked with milk, and a wild boar. "Urged by Indra," because, being sacrificed and burned, they would become light; "carried off," by conveying to the stars that into which the fire transmuted them.

> *ivi.*, 118. 11.—And his mother sought to draw back the Mighty (Indra), saying "My son, those Devas forsake thee." Then Indra, being about to slay Vṛitra, said, "Friend Vishṇu, do thou stride vastly!"
>
> *viii.*, 89. 12.—Friend Vishṇu, stride vastly. Sky, give room for the thunderbolt to descend! Let us slay Vṛitra and let loose the waters! Let them, when released, flow by the impulse of Indra!
>
> *vi.*, 20. 2.—All divine power, like that of the sky, was completely communicated to thee, Indra, by the Devas, when thou, O impetuous, associated with Vishṇu, didst slay Vṛitra and Ahi, stopping up the waters.

And in other passages the same united action is spoken of. The light alone does not always suffice to free the waters. For cold is the ally of gloom and darkness, and there is heat as well as light in the lightning that shatters the clouds, while heat alone can loosen the icy bonds of the rivers and cause the water to flow free in their channels in the spring.

In *v.*, 87, 4, and 8, it is said that,

> the wide-striding strode forth from the common abode [the sacrificial fire in which abide the light, heat and flame, and the other potencies of Agni] . . . . when by himself [separately manifested] he has yoked his emulous and vigorous steeds, he issues from his self, with his swift horses, augmenting our felicity.

Hymn 69 of the sixth book is addressed to Indra-Vishṇu, and styles them the generators of all prayers, and attributes to them jointly the taking vast strides, making the expanse wide, and extending the regions or splendors. They grow by the oblation, are swallowers of the essence of the Soma juice, are the receptacle and bowl in which it is held, are exhilarated by it, and are worshipped with reverence.

Vishṇu is the preserver of embryos: he envelopes the expanse on all sides with light; the Açvins abide in his strides: he is associated with the mountains and rivers, for the internal heat of the earth produces volcanic .eruptions, and the heat of the spring melts the ice in the rivers.

When once we have the key to what is said in regard to Vishṇu we find that everything is singularly appropriate and true to Nature. To extend and diffuse itself is a peculiar and striking faculty of heat. It penetrates everything. From the small fire kindled in a corner it extends into and warms every portion of the room. When the summer sun rises in the morning, the heat seems instantly to diffuse itself through the whole expanse. It is omnipresent. It is in the thermal springs, and in the depths of the earth under the mud-volcanoes of the Caspian. It is in the bodies and blood of all living creatures as the vital heat. It is produced by friction, and it is manifested before the flame, when fire is obtained by attrition. The herdsman driving his wooden-axled cart, had often seen the axles heated and at last taking fire, as he journeyed. Volcanoes then active and ages ago extinct, informed the Aryans that heat was in the bosom of the earth; and it filled the expanse and came from the sun in his station.

It was not inseparable from light. It exists where there is no light, in the deep bosom of the earth. There is light without heat, and heat without light everywhere. But they are together in the sun and in fire and lightning, and thus are often "associated." According to the later myth, when Bali had conquered the light, Indra, overcome, called upon Vishṇu, the heat, the potency and vigor of the universe, to re-conquer for him the three realms. As generator, Vishṇu was the preserver and perpetuator, and sustained, supported and preserved the universe. And it is certainly a fact of no little import and interest in the spirit-history of man, that upon a text or two of the *Veda*, ascribing this particular function to heat, personified by an imagination at once poetic and philosophic should have been built up in later days the whole vast mass of Hindū legend in regard to Vishṇu, and that he should have become for a hundred generations and many millions of human beings, the Very God, the second person of the divine Triad, as the preserver of all created things.

· Dr. Muir says that the *Rig-Veda* contains numerous texts in which the Rishis ascribe to Indra, Varuṇa and other Gods the same high and awful attributes and functions which are spoken of in others as belonging to Vishṇu. And he concludes that the latter occupied a somewhat subordinate place in the estimation and affections of the ancient Rishis.

Certainly, so far as the Vedic Deities have heretofore been defined by the Hindū, German or English commentators, all is lamentable confusion and uncertainty. Except as to Agni, Ushas, Sûrya and the Maruts, everything is chaos. Why the same powers and functions are ascribed to different Deities, and what seem to be contradictory functions sometimes to the same Deity, no one endeavors to explain; but all the modern commentators stare helplessly at the muddle which the Brahmanic blind guides have made of the whole matter.

Certainly such cannot be the real character of the *Veda;* and the notions of the Rishis as to their Deities *could* not have been thus confused, misty and unintelligible. There must be *some* key by which the meaning can be

laid open. But there is no such key, unless it be that Agni is fire, as a
universal substance and unity, invisible, extending everywhere, and including in and of his unity the flame, light and heat, in no wise distinct or
separate from himself or each other, until manifested by emanation from
him.   Then they become subsistences, persons or hypostases of the universal
substance, and each, as well as the substance itself in its unity that includes
them is deified. Each being Agni, manifested partially and limitedly as
the particular hypostasis, the functions of Agni, so far as they are those of
the particular subsistence, are sometimes assigned to it alone, or to both
together, when they are represented as equals associated together.

> The living Father hath sent me, and I live by the Father [Christ said, using language
> perfectly familiar to those who heard him]: I am not alone; but I and the Father
> that sent me; if ye had known me, ye would have known the Father also.   I pro-
> ceeded forth and came from God. . . . . O Father [he said], glorify thou me with
> Thine own self, with the glory which I had with Thee, before the world was.
>
>   God was in Christ [Paul says]: He was the Wisdom and the Power of God;
> who being in the form of God, thought it not robbery to be equal with God.

The Vedic doctrine is as little contradictory as this is; and if we add
that the substance, Agni, and its subsistences, Indra and Vishṇu, are also
conceived of and represented as by self-limitation manifesting themselves
in form and place, as the celestial luminaries, and out-shining by them, we
shall find, I think, no other unintelligibility or confusion in the *Veda*, than
so much as arises from corruption of the texts or ignorance of the true
meaning of words and phrases, in a great measure caused by Hindū mis-
interpretations.

VAYU

In seeking to ascertain what was meant by Vayu, I found but few passages
in the *Veda*, and nothing at all in the commentators, that could resolve my
doubts.   The latter told me that Vayu was "the gentler movements of the
air," or the air itself; and that there are only three Deities, according to the
etymologists: Agni, whose place is on earth, Vayu or Indra, whose place is
in the atmosphere, and Sûrya, whose place is in the sky. Sâkapûni thought
that these were the triple manifestations, the three steps of Vishṇu; fire on
the earth; lightning in the air; and the solar heat in the sky. It astounds
one to see how stupidly the human intellect can interpret its sacred books.

Vayu, in the *Veda*, yokes two red or purple horses to his car. He is
invoked to cause men to arouse from their sleep, to summon the sky and the

expanse, and to light up the dawn. How could "the gentle movements of the air" do that?

By means of thee [it is said], the brilliant dawns, from afar, display their welcome garmenting, in variegated and splendid radiance.

And Vayu and Indra are conveyed together, in a chariot drawn by the Niyut steeds. This was enough to prove that Vayu was not the air, but a hypostasis of Agni.

His horses are strong-limbed, youthful and full of vigor. They bear him through the space between heaven and earth, growing in bulk, and strong as oxen. They are not lost in the expanse, but continue on unretarded, with undiminished speed, difficult to be arrested, as the beams of the sun.

Vayu is pleasant to behold; and Indra and Vayu "abide in the sacrificial fire." Now, when we succeed in identifying ourselves, to some extent, for the time, with the Vedic poets, and become familiar with their processes of thought, we find their phrases to be deductions as to the effect and action of fire and light, that are singularly ingenious, and evince acute and profound thought, and we also find that plain and direct expressions as to the nature or office or relations of a particular Deity, are never loosely used, but always mean exactly what the words impart.

And when it is said that Indra and Vayu abide in the fire, this is not a mere meaningless expression, nor is it anywhere contradicted by any other expression inconsistent with it. There are no inconsistencies of that kind in the *Veda*. To *abide* in the fire, is to be *in* it, and not *of* it, as a component part of it. Light is so, and emanates from it; but *it* is Indra. Heat is so, and flows forth from it; but heat is Vishnu, and has no colors, and drives no red or purple horses. But these things *may* be said of the *flame* of the fire, of the flashings of the Aurora and the radiant orb of the sun. Vayu, therefore, must be the flame.

Indra and Vayu are invoked together, as abiding together in the sky, as swift as thought, having a thousand eyes, and being protectors of acts of worship and sacrifice. Vayu is said to beget the winds, the Maruts, though Rudra is regularly styled their father. For Rudra was the potency of fire to rarefy and expand and cause to ascend, and so to cause wind; and this same potency is ascribed to the flame. In the case of Tvashṭri, the potency of fire to soften and melt the metals, this special function was lost sight of in even the later Vedic period, and as melting is an effect of heat, Tvashṭri became invested with the general functions of heat, just as Vayu took the special function of Rudra.

Vayu defends from all beings, and protects from the fear of evil spirits. None precede him (for he is the first emanation of the fire, and from him the light and heat flow to a distance). So, the Devas hold back for him, as the Deity first to drink the Soma (for it must be poured upon the flames, to ascend thence to the stars in the sky). Proclus expressed the old Aryan idea, when he said,

> Fire dissolves the elements of that which it burns, and transmutes them into itself.

The horses of Vayu grow in bulk as they bear him through the expanse; are young, vigorous, strong, not to be arrested. For it is of the nature of flame to spread and expand. Every one who has seen great fires in the open air has noted how rapidly the flames flash from place to place, and seem, as it were, to revel in a delirious ecstasy. The steadiest flame, of even the household fire, is restless and unquiet; and to one who has seen herds of wild horses on the American plains, as the Aryans saw them on their native steppes, free as the wind, full of life and action, with luxuriant manes and tails floating in the morning-breeze, as they careered swiftly, "terrible as an army with banners" over the grassy ridges that stretched between the delighted observer and the glowing sunrise—to one who has seen the wild horse in his pride, it seems natural that to them, thus seen, the streaming glories of the rising sun and of the northern Aurora should have been likened.

Vayu and Indra are not only drawn in the same car, but Indra is the charioteer. Threefold Vayu and Agni concur in satisfaction with heaven; Vayu whom sky and expanse bore for the sake of riches; whom the divine language of praise sustains as a Deity, for the sake of riches. This unmistakably connects him with the sacrificial fire. The "riches" for which the sky and expanse produced the flame of the sacrifice, are the essence of the oblations, conveyed to the stars as light. And, for the sake of these riches, the divine language of adoration, that is, the sacrifice, sends the flame upward as a Deva, or as the Devas ascended, to become stars.

Indra and Vayu are munificent princes, and preservers of mankind. They confer prosperity, by gifts of cattle, horses, treasure and gold. The white-complexioned Vayu is intelligent and glorious, and bestows riches and male progeny.

The word Vayu is from the root *va*, *vah* or *vaj*, each of which originally meant to "move," and thence to "wave, fluctuate, etc.," and derivatively to "breathe or blow." But Vayu came to mean the air, as moving, inconstant, wavering, fluctuating, etc., and the name was equally applicable to flame, which alone, at first, bore the name. The epithets applied and attributes ascribed to Vayu are entirely inapplicable to the invisible colorless air.

After I had concluded that he was flame, I found that he was also adored in the *Zend-Avesta*, and styled in the translation, "the air that works on high"; and that there also it was plain that he was not and could not be the air. There, evidently, he was the flame. The proof of this is ample; and thus the interesting fact is established that the Indo-Aryans in the Punjab and the Irano-Aryans in Bactria or Bokhara worshipped Vayu, the personification of flame, the visible fire. And it follows, of course, that this Deity was adored by the Aryans before the separation of these two races, and is therefore an older object of worship than Agni or Indra.

Nor is that all. The same worship prevailed before the Greek emigration, and the Pelasgi or Hellenes carried it with them when they emigrated from the slopes of the Bolor Tagh. For Æschylus, in the Agamemnon says,

> And the altars of all our city-guarding Gods, of those above and those below, Gods of the sky and Gods of the forum, are blazing with offerings; and in different directions, different flames are streaming upward, high as heaven. Drugged with the mild unadulterated cordials of pure unguent, with the royal cake brought from the inmost cells.
>
> Zeus [it is said in the Orphic fragments], is the rushing of indefatigable fire . . . . He is the sun and moon. . . . . his eyes, the sun and the opposing moon, his undeceptive intellect the regal and incorruptible æther.

And the fifth Orphic hymn has this, which sounds like an old Vedic invocation:

> O Thou that hast the might on high, always untired, of Zeus, a portion of the stars and sun and moon, all-subduer, fire-breathing, that kindles all that live: æther, that givest light from on high, best rudiment of the world: O shining growth, light-bringing, star-radiant, calling on I beseech thee, tempered, to be serene.

And Orpheus is represented as saying:

> Light broke through the æther. The light was the Demiourgos, or being supreme above all others, and its name is Metis, Phanēs, Erikapæus. These three powers are the three names of the one power and strength of the only God, whom no one ever beheld. By this power all things were produced, both the incorporeal beginnings and the sun and moon and their influences.

Ârusha is the coruscating radiance, effulgence and beams of the flame, which send their light far forth, beyond themselves, and with it fill the sky and the expanse.

Tvashtri, the artificer of the Devas, the forger of the thunderbolts of Indra, is the softening and melting potency of fire.

> Thou, Agni, art Tvashtri [it is said in *ii. i.*, 5], of great wealth to the worshipper; these praises are thine. [In *vi.*, 97, 5] Yoking his horses to his car, Tvashtri shines in many places here in the three worlds; who, sojourning daily amongst his present worshippers, is their protector against adversaries [in *i.*, 84, 15, we find]: They

found on this occasion the light of Tvashṭri verily concealed in the abode of the moving moon.

Tvashṭri was an artisan, the most skilful of workmen, versed in all admirable and wonderful contrivances. He sharpened the iron axe of Brahmaṇaspati, and forged the thunderbolt of Indra. Brahmaṇaspati is prayer, and is armed with the axe, not as a weapon of war, but to cut down the trees that are to be the fuel for the sacrificial fire. As devotion moves the worshipper to fell the trees, it is imagined to be armed with the axe, and itself to fell them, by the arms and implement of its agent. This imaginary axe Tvashṭri sharpens.

He is the beautiful- or skilful-handed, the skilful worker, the multiform, or archetype of all forms. He has had more agency in creating Brahmaṇaspati than all other creatures, and with the sky, expanse, waters and Bhrigus, generated Agni. He is a companion of the Angirasas (the stars of Ursa Major), and frequents the paths of the Devas (the stars). He is supplicated to nourish the worshipper, and protect his sacrifice. He is *dravinodas* ("giver of wealth or strength," *dravina* meaning either of these, and *da*, to "give"). He possesses abundant wealth, and is supplicated to take pleasure in the hymns of his worshippers, and to grant them riches.

These passages leave no doubt that he is not a luminary; that he is a potency or function of Agni, the Fire, supposed to be in the sky as well as in the expanse and on the earth, shining or causing radiance, and by which the visible fire is kindled into activity; and that he is that particular potency by means of which weapons and implements are forged out of metals. And as in the *Zend-Avesta*, while Çpĕnta-Armaiti is the divine productiveness in Nature, Parendi, who accompanies her, is growth, germination, etc., so Tvashṭri was, evidently, at first, a peculiar function or potency of heat, the power of heat to melt and soften. Afterwards, if not at first, in addition to the power of melting ice, that of changing water into vapor was ascribed to him.

Having the potency of thawing in the spring, the snows and ice of winter and softening for the plough the frozen ground, and already invested, as forger of implements with the attributes of former and fashioner, we find that he imparts generative power and bestows offspring, as the vital heat. He forms husband and wife for each other, even from the womb, develops the seminal germ in the womb, and is the shaper of all forms, of animals and men. He produces and nourishes or maintains in life a great variety of creatures; all beings are his, and intimately connected with him, and he has given the sky and expanse and all created things their forms, and bestows long life.

Rudra is the father of the Maruts, the Winds. Priçni is their mother. Roth regards Priçni as a personification of the speckled clouds; and in his

Lexicon says that, like other designations of the cow, the word is employed in various figurative and mythical references, to denote the earth, the clouds, milk, the variegated or starry heaven. Sâyaṇa refers to a story of Rudra, as a bull begetting the Maruts on Pṛiçni, the earth, in the form of a cow. Benfey has "*Pṛiçni*, an adjective: of variegated color, delicate, feeble, thin, small, short, and a ray of light." He does not give its root, nor can I find any root for it, except *prish*, to "sprinkle."

> *Rig-V. ii.*, 34, 2.—Adorned with armlets (the Maruts), have shone like the skies with their stars, they have glittered like showers from the clouds, at the time when the prolific Rudra generated you, O Maruts, with jewels on your breast, from the shining udder of Pṛiçni.
>
> *v.*, 52, 16.—These wise and powerful (Maruts), who, when I inquired after their kindred, declared to me that the cow Pṛiçni was their mother, and that the rapid Rudra was their father.
>
> *v.*, 60, 5.—Rudra, their young and energetic father, and the prolific Pṛiçni.

Professor Wilson thinks that "the pure womb," or "pure udder" ("the shining udder" of Muir, *Pṛiçnyah çukra ûdhani*) means, "on the elevated places of the earth, in the mountains." According to Sâyaṇa, Pṛiçni is the many-colored earth. In the Nighantu, Pṛiçni is a synonym of sky, or heaven in general. Rosen thinks that in some texts it occurs as a name of the sun. In *i.*, 85, 3, the Maruts are called *Go-matarah*, "whose mother ·the cow (or earth) is."

> In *vi.*, 66, 1, and 3 [it is said that] Pṛiçni gives milk from her bright udder, once (in the year); [and the Maruts are called] the sons of the Showerer Rudra, whom the nursing to sustain, and of whom, the mighty ones, it is known that the great Pṛiçni has received the germ for the benefit.

Here, Wilson says, Pṛiçni is said to imply the firmament, which by the influence of the winds, sends down its milk, i.e., the rains, at the rainy season.

In *vii.*, 18, 10, the Maruts ride on parti-colored cattle dispatched by Pṛiçni. In *vii.*, 56, 1, it is said that the vast Pṛiçni bore the Maruts at her udder. In *viii.*, 20, 21, the Maruts are said to be the offspring of the maternal cow.

The Maruts are called by Müller "the storm Gods"; by Dr. Muir, "the Gods of the tempest"; generally, "the winds." They are supplicated to bring healing remedies; they are praised as beneficent; they are like blazing fires, unsoiled, white-complexioned, of golden or tawny hue, of sun-like brilliancy, playful as children or calves, have spears on their shoulders, anklets on their feet, ornaments or plates of gold on their breasts, luster in their cars, fiery lightnings in their hands, and golden helmets on their heads. Adorned with rings, they are conspicuous like the sky with its stars. They are decorated with garlands, every glory is manifested in their bodies, they are borne along with the fury of boisterous winds; gleam like flames of fire, split Vṛitra into fragments, are clothed with rain, create darkness, even during the day, with the rain-clouds distribute showers all over the world, water the earth and avert heat. They open up a path for the sun, cause the mountains and expanse to quake, rend trees, and like wild elephants devour the forests, have iron teeth and various weapons. Their horses are swift as thought. They ride with whips in their hands, in golden cars, with golden wheels, drawn by ruddy and tawny horses or by spotted deer. They have spotted horses, golden-footed.

They are called "the pious singers," "the beloved hosts of Indra, the blameless, skyward-tending." According to Müller, they are (*Viçve-devas*) "without guile," "wild ones who sing their song, unconquerable," are enthroned as Devas in the sky, in the light of the firmament, toss the clouds across the surging sea, and shoot with their darts across it. They are sportive, brilliant, unscathed, self-luminous.

And they grant favors, blessings and delights; they help the Aryans, against men and fiends, and are worshipful and wise, and bounteous givers. They are divine, blameless, pure and bright like suns. They confer power, are manly, majestic and wise. They devour foes, milk the udders of the sky, lead about the powerful horse, the cloud, to make it rain. They shake with their strength all beings, even the strongest, in the expanse and sky, make the rocks tremble and rend the kings of the forest, overthrow what is firm, and whirl about what is heavy. They chew up forests like elephants, when they have gained vigor among the red flames. They roar like lions, are far-sighted, handsome like gazelles, and all-knowing. They march in companies, and their anger through strength is like the anger of serpents. On the seats on their chariots, the lightning stands, visible like light.

They are brisk, bright, worshipful, active, the chasers of the sky, vigorous, impetuous, protect mortals and give food, treasure, strength and prosperity. They delight in the sacrifices and have their abode in the sky, make heaven and the expanse to grow, are strong and wild, sing their song, increase in vigor, and clothe themselves with beauty. They are beneficent, aiding Indra to slay Vṛitra, cleaving asunder and pushing along the clouds and giving rain, sheltering those who praise them, fulfilling the desires of the sages, and giving wealth and offspring. They are the guardians of him in whose dwelling they drink the Soma, and are propitiated by sacrifices and prayers. They carry off the offerings, strike the fiend with the thunderbolt, and create light.

The Maruts, it seems clear from these texts, are the winds, as embodied in and animating the clouds. They are not conceived of as merely the air in motion, but as invisible powers, armed with the lightning, of irresistible might when angered, beneficent when gently breathing, and bringing healing on their wings. Probably the ancient Aryans did not conceive of the cyclone, tornado and the cool breezes of the heated days, as merely the air in motion, but as masses of a nature unknown, rushing through it. The colors that clothe the clouds with beauty, were their golden ornaments; and the cloud, wind and storm seem to have been conceived of as one, i. e., that the storm-cloud bore the wind, and the summer-cloud the cooling and healing breeze in its bosom.

Of these clouds, Rudra, the potency of heat to rarefy the air and cause it to ascend and to move in currents, was the father: and Pṛiçni, who, I think, was the atmosphere, was the mother.

Rudra, begetter of the winds, is that potency of the fire which rarefies and causes it to ascend.

I have not space in which to detail the proofs, to be found in the texts, of the soundness of these conclusions. It must suffice to say that I have compared, and weighed and analyzed them, and hope to establish them to the satisfaction of competent judges, if I should ever publish what I have written upon these subjects. Of Rudra I shall speak in my next lecture.

I cannot resist, however, pausing to quote two verses of the 10th book, curiously illustrative of the Vedic fancy. They are the 1st and 2nd of the 17th hymn.

> 1. Tvashṭri makes a wedding for his daughter. At this the whole world assembles. The mother of Yama [or of the twins, *Yamasya mâtâ*], the wedded wife of the great Vivasvat, disappeared.
> 2. They concealed the immortal from mortals. Making one of like appearance, they gave her to Vivasvat. Saraṇyu bore the two Açvins, and when she had done so she deserted the two twins.

Benfey gives, as meanings of *Saraṇyû*, "air, wind, water or cloud"; and *Vivasvat* as meaning "the sun." *Vi* means "a bird, the eye and the sky," and *vas*, to "dwell, live, shine." *Vivasvat* probably meant, originally, "the eye that shines" or "the dweller in the sky."

Professor Kuhn thinks that Saraṇyû is the fleet, impetuous, dark storm-cloud, and Vivasvat, the brilliant, the light of the celestial heights. Professor Max Müller thinks Saraṇyû, "the running light," was a name of the dawn, and her twins were day and night. He thinks that the dawn and the sun were the chief burden of the myths of the Aryan race. Its whole theogony and philosophy he thinks, centered in the dawn. Professor Kuhn holds that clouds, storms, rain, lightning and thunder were the spectacles that most impressed the imaginations of the early Aryans. He makes Yama to mean the lightning, and his twin sister, the thunder.

It is clearly impossible to defend the theory of Professor Kuhn. Agni and Indra were never imagined to be the Açvins, or children of Saraṇyû. But Müller makes the dawn and the alternations of day and night play by far too large a part in the Vedic mythology.

The latter part of the text seems to me to repeat the former, and the whole seems to mean that Saraṇyû, daughter of Tvashṭri, married Vivasvat, and that she bore the Açvins, and then abandoning them disappeared, and, immortal, was concealed from mortals; whereupon one of like form was made and given to Vivasvat as a wife. But this is not entirely certain. The meaning may be that the first wife, the daughter of Tvashṭri, was the mother of Yama, and that the second was mother of the Açvins, and abandoned them. *Yama* means "a twin," and also "a pair." *Yamasya Mâtâ* may mean "mother of Yama," or "mother of the pair" possibly; but not of "the twins," because *Yamasya* is the genitive singular.

This is a late legend, like most of those in the 9th and 10th books. It is a mere poetical conceit in no respect of a religious nature. Tvashṭri had come to be regarded as heat, instead of a particular potency of heat; and the vapor arising from boiling water, or from the Soma juice poured upon the fire was poetically called his daughter. Living under the mountains, the Aryans knew, of course, that the clouds were composed of masses of similar vapor. Saraṇyû was probably the low, soft morning clouds, which, glowing with the light of the rising sun, were said to be wedded to him and which melt away and disappear as he rises; and the poem may have been composed when the twin-stars of Gemini, rising before the sun, seemed to be born of the soft cloud through whose rifts they shone when these began to be lighted by the radiance of the yet unrisen sun.

When the Soma juice was poured upon the fire, a cloud of white steam rose a little way and then disappeared; but it seemed to reappear in the white fleecy cloud, the soft glowing vapor often seen in the eastern sky at sunrise, or on the summits of the hills, and which as the sun rises, lose their beautiful colors and slowly melt away in their turn. The vapor and the cloud were Saraṇyû. It was the child, not of the flame, but of the heat, because it equally rose from water not touched by flame. So much we can yet understand, and that the verses were the work of some poet as diligently and laboriously seeking for new conceits, as our modern English poets seek for new and outré phrases and forms of expression, in which also they only imitate some of the Vedic bards.

I must pass from the consideration of this class of Deities, to that which includes the heavenly bodies. It is said by some commentators that Brahmaṇaspati and Bṛihaspati are names or epithets of Agni. This is an error. If, when we speak of the efficacy of "prayer," we should conceive of prayer not merely as the aggregate of all particular prayers, as "humanity" is the aggregate and mass of all individual human beings, dead, living and unborn, but as a unit (as we sometimes consider humanity), of which each individual prayer is a manifestation or an emanation, as a ray is of the one universal light, we should have precisely the idea expressed by the name Brahmaṇas-pati. *Pati* is "chief, head or principal." Bṛihas-pati is prayer spoken aloud. As to both these, the texts are perfectly clear, and those that seem to favor the idea that they are names of Agni, only seem to do so, because sacrifice and oblation also are prayer; and whether silent or spoken the prayer of the worshipper is conveyed with the oblation, by Agni, to the Devas in the sky.

We have lost the old Aryan faith in the perfect efficacy of prayer and worship, however much we pretend to profess it. Prayer is no longer a divine potency, nor are worship and devotion Gods, as Çraddha and Çraŏsha were to the Indo- and Irano-Aryans. The prayers of the latter were supposed to have been dictated by Ahura Mazda, and to have a singular and divine potency. We have one, also, dictated by the great Teacher of our faith, with prohibition against the use of any other, but for the most part we prefer those that are the fruit of the mere human intellect.

And we are so familiar with the phenomena of fire, as to see nothing marvelous in them. For us, the universe has no surprises. The performances of Deity in the physical world (I speak in no lack of reverence for Him but little reverencing an age that itself has little reverence for any deserving reverence), have lost the charm and gloss of novelty, the perpetual miracles of the natural world are like a play of which audiences are weary, and which, therefore, no longer *draws;* and we, miserable atoms of intelligence that we are, having invented *names* that have no sort of meaning to us, for the unknown powers and inexplicable phenomena of Nature, fancy that we know what they *are*, and what the natural causes that produce effects; and having substituted words and names for things, and made the universe still more incomprehensible, we look smilingly around upon its myriad marvels, imagine in our self-conceit that we know its processes, and can afford to dispense with God, whom we have also made a mere name, as a cause, altogether; and no more really *reverence* Him, than we do an ingenious mechanic who has succeeded in obtaining a patent for some new labor-saving invention.

When the Vedic hymns were composed, men had not begun to "explain" to themselves the great phenomena of Nature. We are supposed to have learned what light *is*, by solemn waggings of its head by that charlatan, science, and the oracular information that it is caused by the undulations of the ether, that fills all the space between this and the stars. How is it "caused" in a room where atmospheric air is, and ether cannot be, from the little taper that we light?   Who cares to know by what means God causes it?   *What is it?*   We no more know than the Aryan herdsman did.

There was no science, in those ancient days, to come between man and God with its poor little speculations, unable to explain a single phenomenon of the universe.   It can tell you learnedly now that objects form images on the retina of the eye; but it cannot tell how that causes us to *see*, nor *what* it *is* that sees.   It cannot even enable us to comprehend what it is that feels pain; and it is utterly powerless to comprehend what force it is that turns the magnetized needle to the north.   It no more knows what light or electricity *is* than our forefathers understood the phenomena of fire.

The old Aryan poets were nearer to God and to Nature than we are. We need not pity them because they had not the babble and jargon of science, the frivolities of metaphysical subtlety, doubts whether reality is real, or a theology that assassinates religion.   They were not amazed or startled at Nature, as some poetical and ambitiously fine-writing commentators indulge their fancy in imagining.   They simply accepted what they saw as a mystery, and the potencies of Nature as real and controllers of their fates and fortunes.   If one can imagine himself, a man in all the vigor of an acute and reflective intellect, with no idea even suggested vaguely to him of a creative divine intelligence, defying definition and eluding the grasp of the intellect, seeing after the long darkness of the night the light of the coming dawn faint in the eastern sky, growing and extending with gradually increasing glory, until it glows over the sky and makes the whole material world visible, seeing its many-colored radiance flashing far abroad, heralding the rising of the sun; and at length his brilliant orb rising with stately and calm majesty over the snow-covered mountains, or out of the bosom of the far-extending plain, bringing the great and beneficent gifts of light and warmth to a rejoicing world; and can also imagine himself utterly ignorant of the nature of light and heat, and without idea of any creative cause which the dawn and sun obey, he may feebly comprehend the ancient Aryan ideas of the light and heat and splendor of the sun.

If one can imagine himself conceiving of no other cause and origin of heat and fire, and flame and light, than strength, creator of motion, and motion of attrition, and utterly ignorant how the little fire so born feeds on the wood in which it lay concealed, and by what potency it grows, until it leaps, flashes and exults in its terrible and destructive energy and might, equally ignorant of its origin and cause in the blazing splendors of the sun, the Aurora unfolding and shaking its glowing, flashing, coruscating glories, and the crooked lightning, its origin and cause unknown, its momentary existence and capricious movements inexplicable—imagining this, he may in part conceive how the most ancient men came to worship fire as the highest God.

And, after all, we know as little about the nature of light and heat as the old Aryans did; and the jargon of science in regard to them is as unintelligible to us, as the jargon of alchemy or the Kabbalah. The final result of the old thought was,

There is a supreme mind above all these, the light-principle; and light is the Deity manifested.

Is it so certain as we think that we are wiser than they were? Does any theory explain to us the cause of the chemical action of light and of its colors blended in the white of its rays, or why it can only travel in right lines, or any other of its phenomena? and who shall dare say that it is not the very manifested presence of the living God?

The Goddess *Ushas* of the *Veda* and *Ushahina* of the *Zend-Avesta* is unquestionably the dawn. The texts themselves continually say so. The hymns addressed to her are, for the most part, merely poems, children of the imagination and not of conviction or religious fervor; and they are chiefly valuable for the aid they afford towards understanding what is said of other Deities, and in avoiding misconceptions.

She is *duhitâ divah*, the daughter of the sky. She brings horses and cattle, and is all-bestowing; for the light of morning, that enables men to see what, if darkness were perpetual, would be as if it were not, to them, may easily be conceived of as bringing and giving that which it enables men to possess and use. Like an active woman she advances, giving strength and arousing men and animals. She has yoked, i. e., she brings her rays, from the remote rising-place of the sun; and comes onward with a hundred chariots. Everything that moves bows down before her glance, i. e., every star and planet that traverses the sky, pales before her light. The beautiful female creates radiance; the potent daughter of the sky, appearing, drives away those hostile to the worshippers. For the natives, like our Indians chose the night-time for their predatory attacks, and disappeared at the dawn. She brings abundant prosperity; for she enables the husbandman to labor, and the herdsman to drive his herds afield, and wealth to be won by the other avocations of the day.

In thee [says one poem], when thou dawnest, are the life and the breath of all creatures:

for they wake from the death of sleep, when her light falls upon their eyelids. She is asked to hear the invocation and to come to the Soma-offerer's house, and to protect the prosperous man with her chariot, and she moves in a chariot drawn by light and ruddy steeds, and is asked to bring all the Devas to drink the Soma.

I regard this as simply a poem; and do not believe that it was one whit more devotional than the hymn of Coleridge to Mont Blanc. The dawn never could have been seriously conceived of as a being, having knowledge, power and sympathies: and that alone which *was* venerated in her, was the light, in which the dawn consists.

Ushas, says Professor Müller,

> is the image of undying youth; for day after day she appears, in unfading beauty, although they who daily look upon her, do daily grow older, and at last die.

Therefore she is said to conduct all transient creatures to decay. She is divine and ancient, born again and again, with unchanging hues, and she wastes away the life of a mortal, like the wife of a hunter, cutting up the birds.

We see in this, how, with these poets, sequences became causes and effects. As the dawns come and go, and the days pass, our life is taken, piece by piece, as it were, away; and the dawn is conceived of as *causing* these daily losses for which there is no reparation. Precisely thus, the light *creates* what it enables us to *see* and *know*, and *upholds* the sky, which in the darkness would, as it were, press down upon us.

Ushas is "endowed with truth," also, like Agni and Indra. She is visible and real to men; not an invisible principle, but an actual phenomenon, her return certain and unfailing. The word "truth" is but a false translation.

Unimpeding divine rites, though wearing away the ages of mankind, she shines, the likeness of the mornings that have passed, and of those that are to come. Night, her sister, prepares a birthplace for her elder sister, and having made it known to her, departs. Of all the sisters that have gone before, a successor daily follows the one that has preceded.

The hymn *i.,* 92, is perhaps the most poetical and interesting of the *Veda*, and I borrow here for your gratification the translation of it, interspersed with verses from other hymns, by Dr. Muir, with but here and there an alteration:

> These Dawns have become conspicuous: they display their luster in the region of the east. Like gallant warriors drawing forth their weapons, the ruddy self-multiplying flocks of rays advance. The rosy beams have flashed spontaneously up: they have yoked the self-yoked ruddy cows. The Dawns, as heretofore, have brought us consciousness: the crimson coruscations have assumed a brilliant luster. Like women active in their occupations, they shine from afar upon a common track, bringing sustenance to the pious and liberal worshipper, and all things to the man

who offers libations of Soma. Ushas, like a dancer, puts on her gay attire, and displays her bosom. Creating light for all the land, she has dissipated the darkness. Like a maiden glorying in her form, thou, Deva, advancest to meet the Deva who comes courting thee. Smiling, youthful and resplendent, thou dost unveil thy bosom. Like a fair girl adorned by her mother, thou displayest thy person to the beholder . . . . Awaking the sleepers like an inmate of the house, she has come, the most constant of all the females that have returned. As a woman who has no brother appears in presence of a man, as a man mounted on a chariot goes forth in pursuit of wealth, as a loving wife shows herself to her husband, so does Ushas, as it were, smiling reveal her form. Her bright radiance has become visible, it extends, and penetrates the profound of gloom. The bright, lucid Dawns with their radiant bodies put out of sight the black abyss. We have come through the darkness of the night. Ushas rises, restores consciousness; radiant she smiles like a flatterer seeking his own advantage. Fair in her aspect she has awakened all creatures to cheerfulness. The shining daughter of the skies, bringer of excellent songs, has been praised by the Gotamas. Ushas, thou distributest resources, in men, offspring, horses and kine. Directing her eyes towards all creatures, the Deva shines in their sight far and wide. Arousing to activity every living thing, she notices the voice of every adorer. Wearing out the lives of men, the lady shines with the light of her lover. The Sun pursues the shining Deva Ushas, as a man pursuing overtakes a woman. Daughter of the sky, mistress of the world, food providing, wife of the Sun, the bright and blessed one has widely diffused her rays, as if she were driving forth cattle in various directions, or as a river rolling down its floods, obeying the fixed laws of the creatures of the sky.

And in *i.*, 113 and 124, the poet says:

The fair and bright Ushas with her bright child has arrived; to her the dark one has relinquished her abodes; kindred to one another, immortal, alternating, day and night go on with alternation of color. The never-ending path of the two sisters, which, commanded by the Devas, they travel, is the same. They neither strive with each other nor rest, the prolific Night and Dawn concordant, though unlike. Ushas has awakened all the living; the prostrate sleeper to move, another to enjoyment, to the pursuit of wealth, those who see but a little way, to see far; one to seek the power of chieftainship, another to follow after fame, another for great exertions; another to pursue whatever may be his particular purpose. Ushas follows the track of the Dawns that are past, and is the first of innumerable Dawns that are to come, bursting forth, reviving life, awaking all that were dead in sleep. Alike today, alike tomorrow, they observe the same perpetual regularity as Varuṇa. Inasmuch as thou hast caused Agni [the fire of the sacrifice] to be kindled, hast shone forth by the light of the sun, and hast awakened the men who are to offer sacrifice, thou hast done good service to the Devas. How great is the interval that lies between the Dawns that have arisen and those that are yet to arise! Ushas yearns longingly after the former Dawns, and gladly goes on to shine with those that are to come. Those mortals are gone who saw the earliest Ushas dawning: we shall look upon her now: and the men are yet to come who are to behold her on future morns. Arise! our Life, our Breath has come! The Darkness has fled: the Light arrives! Ushas has come upward on the path by which the Sun is to travel: we have come to the point of time when men add another to their days. The priest, the poet, celebrating the brightening Dawns ascends with the measures of his song. Shine, therefore, O magnificent Ushas, on him who praises thee, and on us with life and offspring smile! Mother of the Devas, manifestation of Aditi, precursor of the sacrifice, mighty Ushas, shine forth! arise, and graciously accept our prayer!

Much is said of Ushas, as of the other Deities, which, as expressed in English, would seem to us senseless and absurd, in the translations. Thus it is said of her, that she "baffles animosities." You would hardly suppose that this means that she causes marauding bands of hostile natives to disappear.

Only four other passages in regard to Ushas I shall quote, because they seem inconsistent with her character as a splendid manifestation of Indra, are curiously fanciful, and a profound enigma to the commentators. Indra is said, in several places, to have created or lighted up Ushas. They are these: in *ii.*, 15, 6, he is said to have crushed her chariot with his thunderbolt: in *iv.*, 30, he is commended for a deed of might and manhood, in smiting her, a woman bent on evil, who was exalting herself. He crushed her, and she fled away in terror from her shattered car, when he had crushed it, and it lay broken and in pieces. In *x.*, 138, 5, it is said that the bright Ushas was afraid of the destructive thunderbolt of Indra, and departed, abandoning her chariot: and in *x.*, 73, 6, it is said that Indra destroyed certain foes, as he did the chariot of Ushas.

Müller has a very beautiful passage, in which he describes the dawn as a beautiful maiden, consumed in the too ardent embrace of the sun, her lover, his love proving more fatal to her than hate. But this is not the Vedic idea.

If we suppose that at the first faint glancings of the dawn in summer, a heavy thundercloud rises, and by degrees thrusts up its dark masses into the eastern sky, thus forbidding the sun to pour his light upon the earth, when he shall have risen: that in this war of darkness against light, Ushas, as she exalts herself, unites with the clouds, as the stars fade out of the sky or the cloud conceals them; and that flushing all the cloud-peaks with her golden glories, she makes these glories of the somber cloud her chariot, we can understand how the poetic imagination made her an ally of evil, the dark cloud, the enemy of Indra; and how he could be said to crush her chariot with his thunderbolt and compel her to flee in terror.

Mitra, Varuṇa and *Aryaman* are three Deities so closely united by some bond as to be very generally named together, Mitra and Varuṇa very often so, and each of these seldom and Aryaman hardly ever mentioned alone. They are called Adityas, as sons of Aditi, a female personification whom Müller thinks to be "the unbound or unbounded," "the free and unlimited," "the infinite"; and whom I understand to be precisely what we mean by "Mother Nature," the productive principle in Nature. They were sons of Daksha, "strength," the divine generative potency, who is also termed the father or generator of fire.

There are other Adityas besides these, and their names and number vary. Various epithets are applied to them. They are "shining, resplendent, white, golden, unswerving, blameless" (or never wandering); *ritávánah* rendered by Muir "possessing truth"; but the original meaning of *rita* is better preserved in the Latin *ratus*, "fixed, firm, stable, unalterable." They are rulers, lords, victorious, protectors, dwellers in the depth, sleepless, unwinking, many-eyed, far-seeing, and with uniform motion.

Mitra and Varuṇa support or maintain and preserve things, both moving and stationary. They see the good and evil in men's hearts, and know the sincere from the deceitful (for that they are worshipped implies that they know when they are *sincerely* worshipped). They are true and worshipful, and hate falsehood, and punish sin (or non-observance of ceremonial rites); and they give protection, length of life, offspring, guidance and light.

No attempt has been made by any commentator to ascertain, by a careful comparison of texts, the real meanings of these three Deities or of any one of them. Mr. Cox thinks that Varuṇa was "the veiling heaven," and Mitra, "the light-illumined sky." Sâyaṇa and other Hindū commentators make Mitra to be the God over the day, the sun, the producer of the days, the ruler of the terrestrial world; and Varuṇa, the representative of the night, the ruler over it, one who envelopes in darkness, the producer of the night, the setting sun, who by his departure creates the night.

The texts very clearly show that neither of these Gods is a principle or substance, or a potency of any sort, and that they are luminaries. The worshipper actually beholds them with his eyes. He sees the chariot of Varuṇa upon the ground. It is the long trail of the light of Jupiter upon the grass, when he is the Morning-Star.

> When I have obtained a sight of Varuṇa [it is said], I have regarded his luster as the face (or image) of Agni (*Agner anúkam*).

How often is it said by St. John, that the Son is the *image* of the Father?

Varuṇa is arrayed in golden mail, and surrounded by his spies or outlookers, the stars. Potent and punctual, he sits in his station, exercising sovereignty. Having form and place, he is indisputably a luminary. He and Mitra are called kings, and monarchs of all things. They are *Asuras*, which Dr. Muir renders by "divine"; but it means "blazing" or "shining ones," from *as, ash, ush,* to "burn, shine."

The grandest cosmical functions are, as Dr. Muir says, ascribed to Varuṇa. He measures and upholds the sky and expanse, and embraces all the three regions; for the light that flows from him is the manifestation of Indra, and it pervades and envelopes everything.   He is said to *cause* the sun to shine, because when he is the Morning-Star he *precedes* the sun, and sunrise follows *his* rising, as the effect follows the cause.   He opens boundless paths for the sun, because he goes before him, on the path that he is to travel.   He *sees* and *knows* various things, because he shines on everything, and to *shine* is to *see*, as *we* say that the sun and moon *look down* upon the earth, and that the stars are the *eyes* of the sky.

The expressions which seem to attribute divine potencies and moral qualities to him, and which at last came to be so understood, if traced back to their original and material meaning, and if we can catch and follow the thread of the poetic Aryan thought, will be found to have had, at the beginning, a sensible and natural application to him as a planet.   The potencies ascribed to the Soma plant are equally as great, and, to our way of thinking, much more extraordinary; and even these are all capable of explanation, and are perfectly simple developments of a luxuriant imagination, fettered by no rules, and by no consideration of well-ordered thought, or fear of exaggeration.

In the hymn *iii.*, 59, 1 to 8, the character of Mitra is defined with perfect distinctness.   Calling to men, he causes them to come forth to their labors. He fills the sky and expanse with his light.   With unwinking eye he looks upon all creatures; and what can more plainly say that he is a planet?   He is the son of Aditi, the great Aditya, who rouses men to their labors, confers benefits on his worshipper, and is to be approached with reverence.   With his radiance he transcends the sky; with his effluent glory the expanse.

In the *Atharva-Veda xiii.*, 3, 13, it is said:

> Agni becomes Varuṇa in the evening; rising in the morning, he is Mitra. [In *Rig-Veda vii.*, 36, 2, it is said], One of you (Varuṇa) is the lord and unassailable guide; and he who is called Mitra summons men to activity.

However it may seem to others, I, looking for the explanations of the texts of the *Veda* that are most consistent with the Aryan naïveté of thought, and the simplicity and material character of the primitive meanings of words, find in these passages conclusive evidence that Mitra was originally the Morning-Star and Varuṇa the Evening-Star.   And undoubtedly the reason for the close connection between them (the former being mentioned alone in only one hymn) was that originally whichever was the Morning-Star was called Mitra, and whichever was Evening-Star, Varuṇa, and that the former name was not exclusively applied to Venus and the latter to Jupiter, until a later day.   Thus interchanging functions, they were naturally always spoken of together.   Roth thinks that the distinction between the two was one that could not originally be defined with intellectual precision. That is a mere unfounded notion. The Aryan notions of all the old Gods were perfectly clear and distinct. He considers Mitra to be the celestial light in its manifestation by day, and Varuṇa, though lord of light, yet rules especially over the nightly heaven, though he is not relegated to the night alone, but continues to be lord and first. I neither repeat here his curiously hazy and indistinct notions, which Dr. Muir thinks "ingenious and interesting," nor what I have written in demonstration of their unsoundness. But I must say that the nebulosity of his notions is only equalled by that of the like prematurely-born conceits of Dr. Haug as to the *Zend-Avesta;* and that I have not encountered even one that was not palpably, and in general ludicrously erroneous.

Herodotus speaks of Mitra, not as a God, but as a Goddess, and says that she was identical with Urania. In the Vendidad, one meaning of Mithra is "a promise, contract." Afterwards it came to mean "an ally," with whom one contracts; and then, generally "a friend." The older meanings of Aryan words are found in the Zend, and I do not doubt that Mitra originally meant "the promiser," or "the forerunner"; because the Morning-Star, rising gives assurance of, heralds and foretokens the speedy rising of the sun, whose friend and ally he was considered to be.

Varuṇa meant "excellent, eldest, pre-eminent." It was a natural appellation of the largest and brightest of all the stars; and that this planet bore the name of the king of the Olympian Gods, proves the estimation in which it was held by the Aryan race.

It needs no argument to prove that the adoration of the visible luminaries preceded that of the universals, fire and light, which must at first have seemed to owe their being to the energy of these luminaries. The worship of the sun and moon still existed in the Punjab, for hymns of adoration are addressed to them. These had been adored by their ancestors, and had by degrees become subordinates. It is not possible to doubt, therefore, that the known planets and principal stars were also adored in Bokhara. There is abundant proof in these hymns that at least the principal ones were sung, and the most solemn sacrifices had, at particular times and seasons of the year; not only at early dawn, but when certain planets occupied particular places, and when particular stars rose in the east before the dawn, and led the way for the sun to ascend into the heavens.

The great sacrifices were held at the time of the vernal equinox. The Pleiades rose with the sun at that period of the year, about 3,900 years before Christ; the Açvins or Twins, about 5,500 years earlier, or perhaps 6,000. In those early days, the observations of the planets and stars were, we may safely conclude, only such as consisted in noticing, at evening and morning, the risings and settings of the principal stars and the known planets.

All the ancient nations made the planet Jupiter a God; and he would not have been the king of the Gods for the Greeks, if he had not been the royal Varuṇa of their Aryan ancestors. But his worship especially connects itself with the coming of the spring, when he was the Morning-Star, and rose before the sun, with or nearly at the same time as the stars of Orion, the Pleiades and the Açvins. For the Pleiades became, with the Hyades, the stars of rain, because they rose heliacally when the rains of the spring were to be expected, and so Varuṇa is in many passages invested with the function of causing rain, and thus became the Jupiter Pluvius of the Latin Aryans.

No luminary could have seemed more worthy to be adored in that old land of resplendent skies, than the Morning-Star, the Phōsphōr and Lucifer (light-bringer) of the Greeks and Latins, when large and brilliant in the clear, pure atmosphere, it announced to the worshipper waiting for the dawn, that the darkness was about to flee, discomfited away, when, casting long lines of light upon the tremulous waters and on the grass sparkling with dew, it seemed to their imagination to descend from the sky, and be present, by that light, at the sacrifice that waited for the first blushings of the golden dawn; when from the still bosom of the lake or the deep waters of the river, itself flowing as it seemed from the home of the stars, the beautiful orb itself, as real as its counterpart in the sky, smiled upon those who seemed to be its favorites.

The Evening-Star, Hesperos of the Greeks, Hesperus and Vesper of the Latins, lingered in the sky after the sun had set, to delay the coming of the darkness, and seemed to promise the worshipper protection. Unfailingly returning at the appointed time, according to "the fixed ordinances of Varuṇa," to him who watched and waited for them to appear, they seemed incapable of deceiving, and human truth was but the image of their faithfulness. Their calm, grave stateliness and regular march, and the ever benignant regard with which they looked on men and their affairs, gave the idea of power, of self-reliance, of judicial impartiality, of kindliness and of protection; and for the unfortunate, of grave sympathy and compassion. And it is curious, that the Phœnicians and all the people of Palestine and Chaldæa called the planet Jupiter Sydyk, Tsadūk, "just," and adored him by that name; and that Malaki-Tsadōk, whom we call Melchisedek, was his priest and king.

And we, the descendants whether of Aryan or Abarim still love these beautiful wayfarers of the unfathomable depths of heaven, in spite of all that science has done to make them for us mere dull globes like ours; and we look anxiously for and welcome their coming. To him who, waking before the dawn, waits upon the great plains for its coming, or on the ocean marks the hours that pass so wearily, by the slow progress of the three glittering kings of Orion, nothing gives such comfort and content as the rising of the Morning-

Star above the far horizon of land or water, with promise of the glorious coming of the dawn, and of the renewed life of the world.

If Mitra and Varuṇa are these two planets, then Aryaman must likewise be one. In the earliest Aryan times, it is not probable that Mercury and Saturn were known as planets, though they had become so in the Punjab. The Greek name of Mars, the planet and the God of War, was Arēs: Arya originally meant a warrior, and that red and fiery star no doubt had the same character in the older as in the later day. I do not doubt, therefore, that Aryaman was Mars. And as he has no known connection with the seasons, no particular functions are ascribed to him, and he appears merely as the associate of Mitra and Varuṇa.

Time, and the limits of this lecture, will not permit me to demonstrate the truth of my theory, by recitation and discussion of the various texts. I shall only add that they traverse the sky, and it is their abode. They wear vestments of light. They are Devas, eminent among the Devas, and their *forms* traverse the sky and expanse. They are twins, but not one and the same. They manifest vigor daily, and, finally, it is said:

> The royal Varuṇa, of pure energy, in the base sustains on high an orb of light, the rays whereof dart downward, while their base is above.

I was long at a loss to know what Pushan was. But I did not long doubt as to Mitra and Varuṇa. That they are originators of rain makes it certain that they are either stars, constellations or planets: and the sentences that I have quoted prove them to be planets, and the Morning and Evening Stars. How could the light of day and that of night originate rain? It is, in fact, somewhat to be wondered at, that their planetary character should ever have been doubted by anyone at all familiar with the modes of thought and expression of the Vedic poets. A single other verse completely identifies them. It is *iii.*, 55, 6:

> The child of the two mothers (night and day) sleeps in the west, the other infant journeys unobstructed: these are the functions of Mitra and Varuṇa.

The reference to the Evening and Morning Stars is unmistakable here, as it is in *iii.*, 61, 7,

> The mighty Ushas, the golden light, as it were, of Mitra and Varuṇa diffuses her radiance in different directions.

That Varuṇa had become invested, even in the Vedic times, with more eminent attributes than at first was only the natural result of poetic exaggeration and the fanciful conceits of the bards. And it was only the same process that in Greece made Zeus or Jove the king of the Olympian Gods, while the sun was but Apollo, son of him who was originally only the planet Jupiter. But it is still uncertain how much, in the later hymns to Varuṇa, was the utterance of sincere religious conviction, and how much mere poetry.

In two hymns in the seventh book of the *Rig-Veda* are supplications to Varuṇa, for pardon or indulgence for "sin" committed, the sin evidently being neglect to sacrifice to him, or negligent performance of the ceremonial observances of his worship. I quote from Dr. Muir, as translated by Professor Müller, part of one, the eighty-sixth, and the whole of the other, the eighty-ninth:

> 86, 3. Seeking to perceive that sin, O Varuṇa, I inquire, I resort to the wise, to ask. The sages all tell me the same; it is Varuṇa who is angry with thee. 4. What great sin is it, Varuṇa, for which thou seekest to slay thy worshipper and friend? Tell me, O unassailable and self-dependent God; and freed from sin I shall speedily come to thee with adoration. 5. Release us from the sins of our fathers, and from those which we have committed in our own persons. O King, release Vasishṭha like a robber who has fed upon cattle; release him like a calf from its tether. 6. It was not our will, Varuṇa, but some seduction that took us away—wine, anger, dice or thoughtlessness. The stronger perverts the weaker. Even sleep occasions sin.
>
> 89, 1. Let me not, O King Varuṇa, go to the house of earth. Be gracious, O mighty God, be gracious! 2. I go along, O thunderer, quivering like an inflated skin; be gracious, etc. 3. O bright and mighty God, I have transgressed through want of power; be gracious, etc. 4. Thirst has overwhelmed thy worshipper, when standing even in the midst of the waters; be gracious, etc. 5. Whatever offense this is, O Varuṇa, that we mortals commit against the people of the sky; in whatever way we have broken thy laws, by thoughtlessness; be gracious, O mighty Deva, be gracious.

But the finest hymn or poem is a later one, the sixteenth of the fourth book of the *Atharva-Veda*, with which I must conclude as to Varuṇa:

> 1. The great one who rules over these worlds beholds as if he were close at hand. When any man thinks he is doing anything in secret, the Devas know it all. 2. Every one who stands or walks or glides along secretly, or withdraws into his house, or into any lurking place. Whatever two persons, sitting together, devise, Varuṇa the king, a third party, knows it. 3. This earth, also, belongs to the King Varuṇa, and that vast sky, whose ends are so remote. The two seas are Varuṇa's stomachs; he resides in this little pool of water. 4. He who should flee far beyond the sky would not there escape from Varuṇa the king. His messengers, descending from the sky traverse this world; thousand-eyed, they look across the whole earth. 5. King Varuṇa perceives all that exists within the sky and expanse, and all that is beyond. The winkings of man's eyes are all numbered by him. He handles these as a gamester throws his dice. 6. May thy destructive nooses, O Varuṇa, which are cast seven-fold, and three-fold, ensnare the man who speaks lies, and pass by him who speaks truth.

After I had once studied the texts of the *Veda* that relate to *Pushan*, I found it impossible even to conjecture what he was. I discovered that, only when I returned to the texts again, after a considerable interval; and then only by the help of the Greek mythology.

Literally, he is the "nourisher, cherisher or augmenter," from the verb *push* or *pûsh*, to "nourish, cherish and augment." Dr. Muir frankly confesses his ignorance of what he was, saying,

> It will appear that the character of this God is not very distinctly defined, and that it is difficult to declare positively what province of Nature or of physical action he is designed to represent.

It seemed to me necessary first to ascertain what he could *not* be.

He conducts men over roads; protects them while they journey, driving away the wolf, the waylayer, the thief and the robber; he makes paths easy to traverse, and leads men over them to a country of rich pastures; he carries a spear of gold, and a *goad* with leathern thongs, for driving cattle; he follows the kine, and protects horses, and compels even the niggardly to be hospitable to the wayfarer. He brings the cattle home safe, and drives them back to the owner, when they have strayed; he has his hair braided, and is drawn by goats, is a skilful charioteer, and drives the golden wheel of the sun through the clouds; moves onward beholding all creatures, and with his golden ships that sail across the ocean of the air, acts as the messenger of the sun, desiring food and subdued by love. Him, vigorous and rapid, the Devas gave to Sûryâ, the daughter of the sun, and he and Soma force the hated darkness to hide itself, and drive the chariot with seven wheels. He was born to move on distant paths, on the far road of the sky and the far road of the expanse; and he goes to and returns from both the beloved abodes. He abides in the sky, and moves onward, beholding all things. Clearly, he is not "a province of Nature, or of physical action."

Is he a potency, a particular energy, of Indra, or a luminary? He is a radiant Deity. Indra and he are invoked together. Indra drinks the Soma, but Pushan prefers meal and butter. He is the friend of Indra, who seeks to slay his enemies in company with him. When Indra brought great rains, Pushan was with him, and they together bring prosperity.

No potency or energy of Agni or Indra abides in the sky, and moves onward, i. e., revolves, looking down on the earth; or is the messenger of the sun, or lord of roads, or carries a spear and goad. He is a luminary. That is clear. That he fulfils prayers, incites sages, promotes sacrifices, drives chariot-horses, is a Rishi friendly to men, a protecting friend of the sage, the ancient and unwavering friend of every suppliant, is consistent with either character. He is the lover of his sister, and the poet addresses the husband of his mother; and he is called the brother of Indra. It is doubtful whether these relationships can be explained.

The functions ascribed to him reminded me of the Deity whom the Greeks called *Hermes* and the Latins *Mercurius*. Cicero says that there were five of this name, the first of whom was the son of Cælus and Lux, of the sky and light. The planet Mercury is so close an attendant upon the sun as to be almost always within his radiance, and therefore seldom visible. The Mercury of the poets was the son of Zeus or Jupiter, by Maia, one and the most luminous of the Pleiades. This Mercury was the messenger of the Gods, and especially of Jupiter, as Pushan was of the sun. He was the patron of travelers, as Pushan was, and of shepherds. He conducted the souls of the dead, another function ascribed to Pushan. He was the patron of orators and merchants, and the protector of thieves, pickpockets and other dishonest persons, because when just born he stole and drove away the oxen of Admetus, which Apollo tended. Zeus, whose interpreter and cup-bearer he was, presented him a winged cap and wings for the feet; and he invented the lyre with seven strings, and gave it to Apollo, the Sun, receiving in exchange the celebrated caduceus, a rod round which two serpents entwined, each forming a semicircle. The Greeks had lost all memory of what it was the symbol. We have not recovered it.

Hermes was supposed to make all things fruitful, in the spring, by communicating the solar influences to the moon. Father of Pan, he was the God of flocks, herds and pasture-grounds, and called *Nomios*, "pasturer." The golden rod, whence he had the name of *Chrusorrapis*, was perhaps his spear of gold in the *Veda*. When he had restored the stolen oxen to Apollo, and given him the lyre, that God placed in his hand, to be his own, a shining *goad*, and put the oxen in his charge. He was the watchman of the night and guardian of doors, brought dreams, assisted at the birth of all beings, and showed the road to travelers, conducted, guided and escorted them.

Mercury, as we all know, is alternately visible and invisible, never being at a greater distance from the sun than 28°, 48′; and Cicero calls it and Venus *Comites Solis*, associates or companions of the sun. Copernicus lamented on his deathbed that he had never seen it; and Delambre, a great French astronomer, saw it but twice in all his life. But it was seen by the ancient Chaldæans, and well known to the ancient Greeks, and there was no reason why it should not have been discovered by the Aryan observers at Samarkand; for the atmosphere is peculiarly clear there, and few vapors dim the sky near the horizon, the consequence being that even small stars can be seen when only two or three degrees above it.

There is no doubt of the identity of Pushan and Mercury; and therefore that planet had been discovered before the Græco-Aryan emigration. How his peculiar functions, such as guiding travelers, protecting roads, and caring for strayed cattle came to be ascribed to Pushan and Mercury, will probably never be discovered. Nor can we account for his connection and that of Hermes, with goats and a ram.

Pushan is, as the original words are rendered by Dr. Muir, inspirer of the soul, abiding within the whole creation. I think that the meaning is "furtherer of meditation, praised by all living beings." The Greek Hermes was the God of eloquence and persuasion, and the suggester of shrewd devices, and cunning plans. He was also the instituter of divine worship and the first sacrificer.

Pushan is the nourisher, dispenser of food, blessings and prosperity, the beneficent; and one of the epithets of Hermes in the Iliad is "beneficent, greatly useful or profitable." So he is, in the Iliad and Odyssey, "astute, preserver, averter of danger, benefactor, protector, prosperer, giver of health." Pushan is especially called "wise," and Mercury is "of varied counsels, wise." Pushan is called *Kapondin*, said to mean "having braided hair," but the real meaning of which is not known. It probably meant wearing a head-dress, like the petasus, or winged cap, of Hermes.

The wisdom and beneficence ascribed to Pushan naturally seemed to belong to one who dwelt almost continually in the very bosom of that light which was the effluence of the highest Deity conceived of by the Aryans. And thus it naturally came that the Greek Hermes was regarded as the Divine *Word*, in which resided the creative potency of the Deity, and the Divine Intellect and Beneficence. And that he tended cattle, and stole those tended by Apollo, probably had its origin in the fact that in the Aryan language the same word *go* meant both "cattle" and "rays of light." The name "Mercurius" was given to quicksilver, because it represented the divine spirit or intellect in man.

Caesar informs us that similar potencies to those ascribed by the Romans to Mercury, were ascribed to him by the Gauls, who were Celtic Aryans, and the earliest emigrants from Asia.

We know the fact that these energies and functions were ascribed to that planet, and we know that there were sufficient reasons for it, although those reasons may never be discovered. The Vedic poets were as rational and keen of intellect as we are, and thought as coherently; and their imagination, though vivid, quick, and somewhat extravagant, was not the imagination of delirium. There were fitness, consistency, oppositeness, and logical congruity in their ideas; which will continually become more manifest to us, as we succeed in identifying ourselves with them, and in thinking as they thought, divesting ourselves for the time of all ideas which they had not, and, as it were, of all knowledge which they did not possess. To understand them, we must look at so much of the universe only as we can see, look at it with their eyes, think it to be what they thought it, know only what they knew of it, and conceive of no other divinity than that of fire and light.

Considering this planet as nearest of all to the source of light, and as the agent, herald and messenger of the sun, with whose rays his mingled and united, and light being the very life of men, the cause of all production, the cause of all reality, that whereby men are enabled to travel, to labor, to avoid dangers, and to search for and find what is lost, there is nothing in the hymns to Pushan which it was not natural for a poet to say.

Two verses are worth quoting, to show what nonsense can be imputed to these poets, and because they furnish additional evidence of the character of Pushan. They are *i.*, 23, 15 and 16,

> 15. Verily he has brought to me successively the six, connected with the drops, as repeatedly ploughs the barley. 16. Mothers (*ambayah*), to us, who are desirous of sacrificing, the kindred flow by the paths, qualifying the milk with sweetness.

The "six" are the Pleiades, only six of which are visible, and which were mentioned anciently as composed of six stars only; and they came to be considered seven only because they were supposed to be meant when the seven stars of the Great Bear were spoken of. *Ambayah* means "waters," and the verses mean:

> He (Pushan) has brought to us year by year the Pleiades, connected with the rains at the season of ploughing for the planting of grain. For us who desire to sacrifice, the kindred waters flow by the paths we travel, making rich and sweet the milk of our cattle.

Sûrya was the ordinary and usual name of the sun, from the roots *sur* to "dart, shine," whence, also, *Sûris*, "the sun"; the Greek, *Seir, Seirios;* Latin, *Sirius;* Gothic, *Sauil;* Lithuanian, *Saute;* and *su, sû* to "dart forth, produce," whence *Savas*, "birth," *Sunus*, "the sun."

Sûrya has seven horses, who bear him, the bright-haired, in his car; has yoked the seven mares that draw his chariot; dwells among the Devas (which shows what they are); traverses the sky and the broad expanse (*vidyam eshi rajas prithv*), by which phrase we have positive proof that *Prithivi* was not the earth, nor *rajas prithv* "the mundane regions." He is the most active of the active Devas, the swiftest (slowly as he seems to move), and *measures* the sky with his rays (which shows what *that* phrase' means); *measured* the worlds (*mame rajasi*), i. e., the regions of the expanse, for he "measures" where he journeys and his rays go. He *produced* the sky and expanse (*rodasi*) which are beneficent to all. He is great in renown, the divine leader of the Devas (*Devanam asury-ah*), the pervading, irresistible luminary.

What is said of Sûrya in the few hymns addressed to him, is of little interest, except so far as it enables us to understand what certain epithets mean, and certain adjectives, which are applied to other Deities also, and the meaning whereof, if they were not used in regard to some known luminary, forty etymological Œdipuses would never discover in the translations.

Savitar or *Savitṛi* became in the post-Vedic times, a name of the sun. All the commentators take it for granted that it is so in the *Veda*, where Savitṛi is often addressed in strains of adoration. Of course I took it to be so; but the texts themselves refusing to accommodate themselves to that theory, compelled me to a contrary conclusion, and to my surprise proved to me that Savitṛi was the moon. If it was not, the moon received no worship or adoration. It is quite impossible that this magnificent luminary could have been so despised, being connected with the measurement of the months, noteworthy for her changes of form, and adored by every people of antiquity.

Savitṛi is the golden-handed, son of the waters, dispenser of riches, re-. volving in the darkened expanse, arousing mortal and immortal, the Deva Savitṛi travels on his golden chariot, beholding the regions; travels by an upward and a downward path, with two white horses, removing all sins [i. e., enabling men to avoid being lost in the darkness]. He is many-rayed, and his chariot decorated with golden ornaments, and furnished with golden yokes.

> The regions are three, two are in the proximity of Savitṛi [for the third, the sky, is above the moon]. One brings men [sages translated to the sky] to the dwelling of Yama [i. e., to the region of the fixed stars].
> The well-winged, deep-quivering, etc., has illuminated the three regions. Where is Sûrya now? Who knows to what sphere his radiance has gone.

The meaning is perfectly clear, that the moon is in the sky, shining, after the sun has set.

Savitṛi is golden-eyed and golden-handed, travels between the two regions of sky and expanse, dispels diseases, approaches (follows) the sun, and overspreads the sky with radiance, alternating with gloom. Life-bestowing, well-guiding, exhilarating and affluent, Savitṛi, if worshipped in the evening, is at hand, driving away Rakshasas and Yâtudhânas. Having risen, he stretches forth his arms for the delight of all:

> he has stopped the traveler from traveling, restrains the desires of warriors for combat, for night follows the function of Savitṛi: i. e., he performs his functions at night . . . . the prudent man lays aside the work that he is skilled in, unfinished; but all spring up when the divine unwearied sun, who has divided the seasons [given up half of the hours], again appears.

The warrior, eager for victory, who has gone forth, turns back; all moving beings desire to return to their homes; the laborer, abandoning his half-wrought toil, returns, when the function of the Deva Savitṛi begins . . . . The ever-going Varuṇa grants a cool, accessible and agreeable place to all that move, on the closing of the eyes, and every bird and every beast repairs to its lair, when Savitṛi has dispersed beings in different directions.

Savitṛi, encompassing them by his magnitude, pervades the three-fold firmament, the three worlds, the three brilliant spheres, the three skies, the three-fold expanse; may he by his three functions of his own protect us.

I believe that all the former part of this verse is corrupted, and that the words rendered three and three-fold really apply to Savitṛi and not to the firmament, skies, etc. The texts have been forced, in more than one instance, to correspond with the theory that Savitṛi was the sun. In one verse quoted above, the phrase "Night follows the function of Savitṛi," is made by the scholiast by interpolation, to read, "Night follows the (cessation of the) function of Savitṛi"; and in another "when the function of the Deva Savitṛi" has added to it the words "is suspended." The interpretations by the scholiast of the stanza last quoted are not worth repeating. It is explainable by the fact that among the Greek and Latin Aryans, the moon, *Sĕlenē*, *Luna* or *Diana*, and *Hĕcatē*, was triformis, and some of her statues represented her with three heads—those of a horse, a dog and a boar. Diana, also, was drawn by two white stags, as Savitṛi was by two white horses. Hĕcatē was called *Diva triformis, tergemina, triceps.*

For the origin of the Vedic idea of the triple form and functions of the moon, we shall be wise to look to those changes and phenomena which the simplest herdsmen saw, and not to the silly conceits and nonsensical vagaries of the Brahmans. At one time the moon was seen as a simple thin crescent low in the west at the evening twilight. Half a month afterwards she rose in the east at the same hour, a huge red orb; and late in her third quarter she rose a little before day, a crescent in the eastern sky. At each of these periods she was accompanied by a different train of stars, and thus the sky, expanse, etc., may have been conceived of as three-fold.

One single text is enough to prove that Savitṛi was not the sun:

Either thou traversest, Savitṛi, the three regions, or combinest with the rays of Sûrya [Sâyaṇa says that Savitṛi is here the sun before he rises; Sûrya, the sun in general], or thou passest between the night on either hand [the sun does not journey in a lane, as it were, cut through the darkness]; or thou, Deva Savitṛi, art Mitra by thy functions [i. e., rising before the sun, performest the functions of the Morning-Star. So Savitṛi is said to precede both night and day; for in the short winter-days, the moon at times rises before the sun, and sets after him]. He puts forth his golden arms for donations, and stretches out his hands filled with water, in the various service of the world.

The golden arms are evidently the horns of the crescent moon; and the common people still judge whether the moon is to be a wet or dry one, by the manner in which the new moon lies.

And Savitṛi is peculiarly the cause of procreation and production, which has been considered the function of the moon in all ages. Finally, it is said,

> may the outspread, vast and golden arms of Savitṛi extend to the ends of the sky.
> . . . . May Sûras (the sun) impart energy unto him.

Sûrya is sometimes called the eye of Agni, as the sun is called in the *Zend-Avesta* the eye of Ahura. Each manifests the primal light, and so Sûrya is said to have been produced or caused to shine, or to have his path prepared, by Indra. Dr. Muir remarks on the fact that he is sometimes the chief of the luminaries and identified with Indra, and that in other places his dependent position is asserted. Plainly because he is sometimes regarded as Indra manifesting himself, and sometimes as merely the sun, caused and produced by Indra. There are precisely the same apparent contradictions in regard to the Logos or Word. And when Ushas, Dhatṛi, Mitra, Varuṇa and others are said to *cause* him to rise, the meaning simply is that they precede him. Dr. Muir speaks of "the divine personality of the sun" being sometimes thrown into the background, and his becoming little more than a part of Nature, created and controlled by those "spiritual powers" which exist above and beyond all spiritual phenomena. The poets of the *Veda* had no idea of any such spiritual powers, or of any divine personality of Sûrya. The highest idea that they had of the sun was, that he was a shining forth of Indra. They attributed intellect, power, benignity, to Agni and Indra *as* fire and light, and not to any Divine Being above them, their creator or cause. They had no word that expressed what we mean by "divine," and they attributed to Agni and Indra powers purely human, and human intellect and temper.

I know that it may be said that the original meaning of all our theosophic language was material, "celestial" meaning "sky" or "of or in the sky," and "spirit" being from *spiro*, "breathe": and that as these words have, nevertheless, other and higher meanings to us, so the Vedic words had. If I were reading the later Brahmanic books, I should translate such words by their higher meanings, because they had obtained them when those books were written: but it is equally manifest that they did *not* have them in the Vedic period, and that the ideas which they afterwards conveyed were then unknown. One cannot mistake Agni for God or a spirit; nor Ahura Mazda, in the Gâthâs of Zarathustra, for anything else than God.

Sûrya is made by Dr. Muir to be "God-born." But *devajataya*, like *dus-jata*, "miserable," and *yatha-jata*, "foolish, a fool," means merely "a deva," literally "born a deva." And he is called *deva-devatrâ. Trâ* here implies superiority, and as the Hebrew phrase *Kadosh-Kadoshim* means, not "Holy of Holies," but "the holiest," so this phrase means "the greatest Deva."

In the tenth book Savitṛi is styled *Sûrya raçmi*, literally "Sûrya-rayed," i. e., receiving his light from Sûrya; in the first he is said to declare men without fault before Sûrya, and to approach or bring Sûrya; in the fifth to be conjoined with the rays; and in the seventh he is prayed to arouse the innocent man, at the rising of Sûra, the sun. In the seventh book Savitṛi and Sûrya are separately mentioned; and in the tenth both are mentioned in juxtaposition with Dhatṛi and Vishṇu.

I have not found any text that is inconsistent with the theory that Savitṛi was the moon. On the other hand, many prove that it certainly is impossible to consider her as the sun. The word Savitṛi is masculine, and so the name is written in the *Veda*, but *Savitṛî* (with the accent over the final letter) is feminine, and means "mother." The Sanskrit *i* becomes *î* by the accent above it. *Savana* is "the moon"; *Sava*, the sun and the moon; and the root of all is *su* or *sû*, to "produce, pour out, impel, incite." The change from feminine to masculine was easily made, when Savitṛi came to be considered the sun, and the hymns were reduced to writing and compiled, three or four thousand years after they were composed. Mitra and Mithra became masculine in the same way; and while we are told by Herodotus that Mitra was originally a female Deity, we also learn that to some of the ancient peoples, the moon was a male Deity.

It cannot be ascertained from the *Veda* whether the planet Saturn had a name and was adored, or not. Mitra, Aryaman and Varuṇa are often called Adityas, sons of Aditi, and Sûrya is also called so in a few places, Indra in one passage, and the sun and moon in the *Atharva-Veda*. Why these should be specially designated as Adityas, children of Mother Nature, or of the infinite, or unbounded, unbound or unlimited or eternal, or whatever else Aditi may be imagined to have been does not in the least appear. It does not appear even, that the Adityas were the sun and moon and five planets; nor what their number certainly was. As specified in *Rig-Veda ii.*, 27, 1, they were Mitra, Aryaman, Bhaga, Varuṇa, Daksha and Ança. Daksha was not a planet, and we do not know what Bhaga and Ança were; and Pushan is omitted. In *ix.*, 114, 3, the Adityas are spoken of as seven in number. The number was at a later time increased to twelve. Professor Roth concludes that the

eternal and inviolable element in which the Adityas dwell, and which forms their essence, is the celestial light. The Adityas [he says], the Gods of this light, do not therefore by any means coincide with any forms in which light is manifested in the universe. They are neither sun, nor moon, nor stars, nor dawn, but the eternal sustainers of this luminous life, which exists, as it were, behind all these phenomena.

And so, behind this luminous life, which exists, *as it were*, behind the visible luminaries, exist several somewhats that are "sustainers" of it!!! *How* they *sustain* the luminous life, and what manner of beings they are, he does not hint. There is no such superlative nonsense as that in the *Veda*. Originally, I have no doubt, Mitra, Varuṇa and Aryaman were the only Adityas, being the only known planets; and subsequently other names were added, when the original reason for calling those three planets Adityas had been lost; and because of that, also, the number increased until it reached twelve. Perhaps Aditi was originally the vast expanse, supposed to be boundless in each direction, below the sky that was considered the domicil of the Devas; and the Adityas were the bodies that, being evidently below the stars, were denizens of the expanse. If so, the moon was an Aditya, but the sun could hardly have been. Ança may have been a name of the moon, and Bhaga of Saturn. But all that is entirely uncertain.

In the 72nd hymn of the tenth book, a comparatively modern hymn, is this legend:

of the eight sons of Aditi, who were born from her body, she approached the Devas with seven, and cast out *Mârttâṇḍa*. With seven sons Aditi approached the earlier generation [i. e., she placed them near the pre-existent stars]: she again produced *Mârttâṇḍa* for birth as well as for death.

The Hindū commentator, in the *Taittiriya Araṇyaka*, says that *Mârttâṇḍa* means one in consequence of whose birth the egg has become dead, or, he is called *Mârttâṇḍa* because he was born when the egg was dead. *Mri* means to "die"; *mṛita*, "dead, death." But also, from *mṛid*, "earth," are *mṛida* and *mṛittaka* "earth." The Çatapatha Brâhmaṇa says that *Mârttâṇḍa* was undeveloped into any distinctions of shape, as broad as he was long. Müller gives to the name the meaning of "addled egg." It was probably the earth, which not being radiant is lifeless because lightless; and having no limits to the ancients, could have had for them no definite shape.

Bhaga is often named with Mitra, Varuṇa and Aryaman. His rays are spoken of, and Agni is said to be Bhaga and Savitṛi. Mitra, Aryaman, Bhaga, the multi-present Varuṇa, the powerful Ança are invoked together. He is often named with Savitṛi, is all-knowing, abounds in health and distributes treasures. He is swift, the chief leader of rites; and it is said:

"Protected by Indra, well-knowing the path that through thy power (Agni), we should follow, we adore that of thine, by which Varuṇa, Mitra, Aryaman, the Nâsatyas and Bhaga shine."

The Nâsatyas are the Açvins. The dawns are asked to bring Bhaga, and Ushas is styled his sister. It is clear that he and Ança are luminaries;

but whether planets or stars is uncertain.   Etymology gives us no assistance.   Ança is a ray of light, and Bhaga, the sun, according to Benfey.

We at least know that, whatever they were, it was as manifestations of the light that they were adored.   There are others yet to be made known to you, before even this limited view of the *Veda* will be complete. These I shall speak of in another lecture.

LECTURE FIVE

THE VEDIC DEITIES

RUDRA: THE ANGIRASAS: THE AÇVINAU: SOMA: THE RIBHUS: PARJANYA:
VÂTA: SARAMÂ: SARASVATI: THE APSARAS: SINIVALÎ:
RÂKÂ: PURUSHA: PRAJÂPATI: HIRANYAGARBHA

We have thus far found the Indo-Aryans in the Punjab, and their
remote ancestors in the river valleys of Bokhara, on the steppes of Toorkhistan and the slopes of the Bolor Tagh, worshipping fire and the light,
in themselves personified and invested with intelligence, will, power and
beneficence, in other potencies of the fire, regarded as separate entities,
and in the sun, moon and planets, by which they manifest themselves.

Only one potency of Agni remains to be noticed. It is *Rudra*, father
of the Maruts, or winds.

Rudra is the encourager of hymns, the protector of sacrifices, possessed
of medicaments that confer happiness, wise, bountiful and mighty, accom-
plisher of sacrifices, who goes crookedly, radiant, with braided hair, has
strong limbs, assumes many forms, shines with brilliant golden ornaments,
is supreme ruler and lord of the world, bears a quiver and a bow, is destructive, fierce and formidable, cherisher of the world, all-knowing and
divine.

> Thou, Agni [it is said], art Rudra, the great Asura of the sky.

He grants increase of offspring, prosperity and long life, driving away
enmities, sins and diseases. He is the great physician, is mild, easily-
invoked, multiform, tawny and also white-complexioned, intelligent, dispenser of good and gracious.

I did not doubt that if we could but ascertain exactly what was personified as Rudra, all these enigmatical phrases, with many others, and
contradictory attributes, would become clear, consistent and harmonious.
It was positively certain, since Agni is declared to be Rudra, that the latter
is some manifestation of the former, some potency of Agni in action, Agni
possessing or performing certain functions, and producing certain effects.
He is a subsistence of that substance which is Agni. He can be wild, fierce,
destructive. He wields the thunderbolt, bends the bow, and hurls the
arrows, and yet he is gracious, easily propitiated, dispenses benefits, heals
the sick and gives long life. He is the most eminent of beings, vigorous,
energetic, source of his own renown. He slays, and he lengthens life.
He has divine power, and is lord of the universe, governing and possessing

the whole expanse. Nothing is more potent, and he is renowned and youthful, a brilliant form, brilliant as the sun, shining like gold, the best and brightest of the Devas, and he performs the last and final office of the sacrificial fire, in conveying the oblation to the sky.

Rudra is called "father of creatures," or of the world of the living (*bhuvanasya pitara*): he wears spirally braided hair (*kapardino*), and has a beautiful chin (or soft belly). He is arrayed in bright golden colors, is lord of this vast creation and cannot be deprived of the potency of light. In *ii.*, 1, 6, it is said,

> Thou, Agni, art Rudra the great Asura of the sky (*twam Rudro Asuro maho Divah*): thou art the strength of the Maruts: thou art supreme over food.

When we find what there is, among the phenomena of fire, that in appearance, action and effects fulfils all these conditions, we shall have found out what Rudra was. It is perfectly clear that he was not a luminary; and he was not light; nor does flame fulfil *all* these conditions. And there is another: this subsistence, hypostasis or potency of Agni must be that which could necessarily appear to the poets to be the cause of great movements of the air, and thus to be the generator of the winds.

I do not believe that *Rudra* is from the root *rud*, to "resound, groan, roar," or that it means either "terrible" or "roarer." I think it is from *ruh*, to "rise, ascend, swell up, grow, expand, increase," whence *rûdhis*, "growth." The old form of *ruh*, also, was *rudh*.

Two effects of fire no one could fail at once to notice. It expands water into vapor, and causes its own smoke and the vapor to ascend. A little observation would show that it caused an ascending movement of the air, because one would see small things of little weight, leaves and chaff, carried upward by the current so created. Above the flame he would see a visible rippling of a thin transparent substance, and this he could discern even in the warm sunshine. In the case of a great conflagration of the grassy plains or of the woods, he would find the fire, if long continued, causing wind and rain.

He would see the smoke and rarefied vapor eddy and whirl in the air, and whatever they took up with them carried in spiral circles higher and higher up, perhaps until all disappeared. He would soon attribute to a like agency the little whirls of wind that dance, of a summer day, across the plains and along the roads. And he would not long delay, after personifying the light, the heat and the flame, and deifying the softening and melting potency of the fire and heat, to consider the power of expanding and rarefying, of causing upward currents of air, and whirls, and even wind and rain, as a distinct function of Agni, if not a subsistence of his substance, an hypostasis, and so to deify it, as he deified Tvashṭṛi. He could call this personification "white-complexioned" because the rippling in the air caused by the heat is colorless and diaphanous, as one may imagine that silver, vaporized, would be. And when the smoke ascended with it, he could call it dark-hued and tawny. The spiral curls of vapor would suggest an epithet comparing them to ringlets, and that might, by and by, be taken to mean that the God who, in action and manifested, was this potency and energy, wore braided hair.

When once the conception of this immeasurable potency and force was attained, and Rudra became father of the winds, that sometimes brought the terrors of storm, and sometimes health on their wings from the snowy northern mountains—of the winds generated by him in the vast expanse, the imagination and fancy of the poet would have an unlimited field in which to display their powers. The mother of the Maruts is *Priçni*. I find no derivation for this but the verb *prish*, meaning, among other things, to "sprinkle." *Priçni* is said to mean "of variegated color, a ray of light," etc. I think it was the atmosphere. As the heat from the sun fills the whole expanse, so would Rudra be deemed to exercise his powers everywhere; and as there would be no known limit to his powers, so there would be none to their effects. The mode of action of the powers being unknown, the poets' conceptions of Rudra would be vague and indefinite. Father of the storm-winds, the simoom and the tornado, as well as of the zephyrs of spring and the mountain-breezes of the summer, and carrying the clouds hither and thither, the lightnings would be deemed his arrows, and the rains his gift. Issuing from the flame, he would still wear its colors as his golden ornaments, and be justly styled "beautiful" and "brilliant."

He could well be styled "lord of hymns" and "fulfiller of the sacrifices," for it was he who conveyed upward towards the stars the light into which the oblations were transmuted, to be the nourishment and exhilaration of the denizens of the sky, the Devas, to whom we give the unmeaning name of Gods, a word that should not be applied to any but *the ONE*.

In the later Indian literature the importance of Rudra is immensely increased, his attributes are more clearly defined, and the conceptions entertained of his person are rendered more distinct by the addition of various features, and are illustrated by many legends. Rudra has thrown most of the Vedic Gods completely in the shade, even Indra not competing in power and dignity with him, so that, together with Vishnu, Rudra now engrosses the almost exclusive worship of the Brahmanical world.

When the planets were adored as manifestations of Agni and Indra, and causers of rain, it was not possible that men should not also deem the stars worthy of worship. Many of these were deemed to have been from the beginning; but many were the ancient Rishis and sages, translated to the sky and immortal there as Devas.

The connection of certain stars and constellations with the regular recurrence of the Vernal Equinox, has caused them from the remotest times to be regarded with peculiar veneration. The Pleiades became to the Greeks the daughters of Atlas; the Hyades, one of which was the great bright star Aldebarán, were so named because, rising with the sun they brought the rains of the spring; and these with the many brilliant stars of Orion, the Twins, Sirius and Capella, all congregated in one portion of the sky, must always have attracted the attention and admiration of a people like the ancient Aryans.

Those who have slept month after month, of year after year, in the open air, in the forests and on the great western plains, who have risen habitually before day, and measured the hours of guard duty by the westward marches of Jupiter or the three Kings of Orion, can in some faint degree appreciate the sensations inspired in the minds of the old Aryan herdsmen and poets, leading the same life in nearly the same latitudes, by the bright armies of the skies. No one who has led that life and become familiar with the principal planets and constellations and single stars, will wonder that they were, almost from at first, regarded as protectors, consolers and guides of men, gracious, beneficent and bestowers of benefits.

Of the fixed stars those would become most noticeable which were largest and brightest, and, thence and from their groupings, of unmistakable identity, or those whose risings and settings marked particular seasons. In the Odyssey of Homer, who lived about 960 B.C., Ulysses, leaving Calypso, observes the Pleiades, Boötes, the Bear, called also the Wain, and Orion; and in the Works and Days of Hesiod, about 860 B.C., Orion, Sirius and Arktouros, the Pleiades, the Hyades, mark the times, by their times of rising, for ploughing and reaping, the vintage and avoiding the sea; and all these had of course been noted from the earliest times. In the time of Hesiod the Pleiades rose heliacally, or a little before the sun at the beginning of June; 3,000 years before Christ, they so rose at the Vernal Equinox, and portended rains, and were in the *Veda* and *Zend-Avesta* the rain-stars.

Perhaps the most constantly watched of all were the seven stars now known as Ursa Major or the Great Bear, which, in the north, traveling in a perpetual circle, never set. Never changing their relative positions, and always visible, no group could be, to the herdsman, so sure a guide, nor so easily conceived of as beneficent spirits of the dead watching over and sympathizing with the children of their race. And, accordingly, we find them called the Seven Rishis, and believed to be the seven sons of Angiras, holy and devout sacrificers, who had become Devas in the sky, immortal among the stars, in the only heaven conceived of or hoped for by the Vedic bards.

These "radiant rulers, bringing winter and summer to mortals," were, if not the very first, at least among the earliest objects of human worship. They were the "Heavenly Host," the Tsabaoth of the Hebrews, the sons of God, who sang the jubilee of creation; and the pre-eminent title of Yehuah was Yehuah-Tsabaoth, "the Lord of Hosts," as we translate it. But *Yahoh* or *Yahvah Tsabaoth* means the *Very Self* and *Being* of the stars, i. e., that *Substance* which is manifested by them: their *Life* and *Soul:* and *Yahoh Elohim* means that *Self* and *Substance*, of which the Elohim are potencies, attributes and emanations—their *Ens, Entity, Being.*

Oannes, Oe or *Aquarius* rose from the Red Sea to impart science to the Babylonians: and the bright Bull legislated for India and Crete. Zarathustra or the older teacher of the religion attributed to him, abolished the adoration of the stars; but the people clung tenaciously to it, loving the beautiful "eyes of heaven" still, and the old worship attached itself to the new, and the constellations Haptoiringa, Çatavaêça, Tistrya and Vanant were adored again as of old. Everywhere in the Orient the stars were believed to be animated intelligences, presiding over human weal and woe; the Potentates and Holy Ones of Heaven.

Among the many beautiful clusters of stars, none presented an appearance so brilliant as those of Orion and Taurus. There are seven great bright stars in Orion, three of which, in a straight line in his belt, the Three Kings, the same to the eyes of the first men that lived as they are to ours, and forming a part of the most splendid assemblage of stars in all the sky, must always have been familiarly known, and distinguished among the celestial watchers over men. To the Indo-Aryans they were three brothers, wise artificers and skilful, rewarded for their labors and services to the Devas by being made most conspicuous among these denizens of the sky.

We must remember, also, that we do not see the stars in all that beauty and brilliancy which they had to those of our race who worshipped them as Deities. The greatest among them differ in color, and the difference is perceptible to the eye. Seirios, Vega, Altair and Spica are white; Aldebarán, Arcturus and Betelguese are red; Capella and Procyon are yellow; and these differences are far more striking in countries where the atmosphere is clear and dry, not humid and hazy. In Syria, for instance, one star shines like an emerald, another like a ruby, and the whole heavens sparkle as with various gems.

There are two Deities, often invoked in the *Veda* and regarded with peculiar veneration, in intimate connection with the dawn, known only by the single name of *Açvinau,* "the twin horsemen." Dr. Muir says that these Açvins seem to have been a puzzle even to the oldest Indian commentators. But so were nearly all the Vedic Deities; and it is by far more noteworthy that the Açvins *continue* to be as great a puzzle to all the *modern* Vedic scholars. He quotes as follows, from Yáska in the *Nirukta:*

> Next in order are the Deities whose sphere is the sky. Of these, the *Açvinau* are the first to arrive. They are called *Açvinau* because they *pervade* (*Vyaçnuvâte*) everything, the one with moisture, the other with light. *Auraṇabhâva* says that they are called *Açvinau*, from the horse (*açvaiḥ*) on which they ride. Who, then, are these Açvinau? Heaven and earth, some say; day and night, others say; and others, the sun and moon. The legendary writers say, two kings, performers of holy acts. Their time is subsequent to midnight, whilst the manifestation of light is delayed; and ends with the rising of the sun. The dark portion denotes the intermediate (God), the light portion, Aditya (the sun).

Professor Goldstücker reads the latter portion of this differently, and does not think with Roth that Yâska identifies the Açvins with Indra and the sun. This is his version:

> Their time is after the latter half of the night, when the space's becoming light is resisted by darkness; for the middlemost Açvin (between darkness and light) shares in darkness, whilst the other who is of a solar nature, shares in light.

And he quotes Durga, the commentator, on Yâska, who so interprets the passage.

On which one cannot help remarking two things; first, that it is not probable that any one is at all the wiser for this reading, which only makes Yâska's nonsense more nonsensical: and, second, that if scholars so widely disagree as to the meaning of a simple passage of *classical* Sanskrit, of an author comparatively modern, there cannot be any great certainty as to their interpretations of much of the *Veda.*

Professor Roth also says:

> The two Açvins, though like the ancient interpreters of the *Veda,* we are by no means agreed as to the conception of their character, hold, nevertheless, a perfectly distinct position in the entire body of the Vedic Deities of light. They are the earliest bringers of light in the morning sky, who in their chariot hasten onward before the dawn, and prepare the way for her.

There is no doubt at all of the meaning of the *name.* *Açva* is "a horse," and *Açvinau* (dual) is "the two or twin horsemen." That they are called so "because they *pervade,*" is an idle Brahmanic conceit.

The Açvins are said to have been "born here and there," a phrase by which the translators make nonsense of the original. They have "striven forward" (whatever he who invented the phrase may have intended it to mean) with spotless bodies, according to their respective characters (which it is to be hoped are respectable).

> One of you, a conqueror and a sage, is borne onward, the son of the strong one; the other is borne onward, the son of the sky.

And then *both* are, in several places, called *divo napâtâ*, sons or grandsons of the sky. Their mother, in one place, is said to be *Sindhu*, the Indus. Their sister is mentioned also, by whom the commentator understands Ushas; and they are, in many parts of the *Rig-Veda*, connected with Sûryâ, the youthful daughter of the sun, called also, once, Urjânî, and represented as having, for the sake of acquiring friends, chosen them for her two husbands. What this wife of the Açvins was or represented, or what the wives of Indra, Agni, Varuṇa and other of the Deities were or represented, no one even endeavors to guess. In *i.*, 116, 17, the daughter of the sun, *duhitâ Sûryasya*, is said to have stood upon the chariot of the Açvins, attaining first the goal, as if with a race horse. All the Devas, it is added,

> regarded this with approbation, in their heart, saying, "Ye, O Nâsatyas, are in alliance with good fortune."

Pushan also is elsewhere said to be the lover of his sister Sûryâ, and brother of Indra. The Gods, it is said, gave him, subdued by love, to Sûryâ.

The Açvins, Pushan and the Devas, wedding one in the imagination of one poet, one in that of another, with this daughter of the sun, whose name, Sûryâ, is the feminine form of his. She can be nothing else than his radiance which, before he rises, glows over the eastern sky, and unites with that of the various stars. That fusion is their marriage.

Dr. Muir thinks that the Açvins represent the *transition* from darkness to light,

> when the intermingling of both produces that inseparable duality, expressed by the twin nature of these Deities.

It agrees, he says, with the epithets by which they are invoked, and with the relationship in which they are placed. They are the parents of Pushan, he says; they are the sons of the sky and also of Vivasvat and Saraṇyû; brothers of the dawn, Ushas, and husbands or friends of Sûryâ, whom he takes "for the representative of the weakest manifestation of the sun."

In *viii.*, 5, 1, it is said,

> when the rosy-hued dawn, though far away, gleams as if she were near at hand, she spreads the light in all directions. Ye, wonder-working Açvins, like men, follow after Ushas in your car, which is yoked by your will, and shines afar.

So, in *x.*, 39, 12,

> Come, Açvins, in that car swifter than thought, which the Ribhus fashioned for you, at the yoking of which the daughter of the sky is born, and day and night become propitious to the worshipper.

The twins are born, it is said, when the night leaves her sister, the dawn, when the dark one gives way to the bright. The Açvins are the two leaders of the sky, the presiders over this world. At the dawn they scatter the investing glooms to the ends of the earth. They come to the sacrifice together, lighting up the luster of their car, emitting vast and limitless radiance. Over the deserts, with water, they drive their horses. When the beloved Ushas, until then unseen, scatters the darkness from the sky, they are invoked and called Devas, and children of the sea whose appearance causes rejoicing. Even before the dawn, Savitri sends their car to the sacrifice. Ushas follows the luster of their approach. Their steeds awakened at dawn bring them. They send adorable light from the sky to men, and are invited to come when the fire of sacrifice is lighted ("when Agni is awakened on earth"), when the sun is about to rise and the dawn has dispersed the darkness.

Professor Müller, quoting one of the hymns, says that the dual character "of these Indian *Dioscuri*" clearly appears in it. I wonder that it did not occur to him that the Greek Dioscuri, Castor and Poludeukēs, the two fine stars of the constellation Gemini, the twin horsemen, worshipped both by the Greeks and Latins, sons of Leda by Jove and Tyndarus, in fact *were* the Açvins of the ancestors of those two great races. But his eyes were sealed by the theory that one of the Açvins was morning or dawn, and the other, evening or the gloaming. How could both *these* come to the sacrifice before the dawn and sunrise?

The connection between the Açvins is very different from that between morning and evening or the dawn and gloaming. They are like the two stones used for the single purpose of grinding the Soma; like two hawks rushing towards the same nest; like two priests reciting one prayer together; like twin-goats, and husband and wife; like two heroes on their chariot; like two horns in one head, two hoofs, two birds, two ships, two yokes, two naves of one wheel, two spokes, two felloes; like two eyes, two hands, two feet, lips, breasts, nostrils and ears, of one body.

They are said to be called *Dasras* and *Nâsatyas*. Indra-Vishnu are also called *Dasrâ*, and we also find the compound *Indra-Nâsatyau*, which Müller thinks must mean Indra and one *Nasatya*. I think that the two words mean "shining" and "not shining." Of the twin stars of Gemini, Castor rises before his brother, and when rising, not long before the sun, must have been visible at dawn, when Poludeukēs did not rise soon enough to be visible at all; and in the same way was sometimes visible, in the west, for several days in succession, after the latter had set. Even when both were seen, one would be visible before the other had risen, and continue so in the evening after the other had set.

The parent of the twins brings forth the twins; they two, dispersers of darkness combine, assuming bodies as a pair. Their resplendent forms bring prosperity; the hymn of the worshipper is associated with their forms, and they unite with the dawn; and the praiser wakes them and they precede the dawn. All this and especially that they have resplendent *forms* conclusively shows that they are celestial bodies. They are wakers at dawn. Their chariots appear at the opening of the dawn, scattering the surrounding darkness like the sun, spreading bright radiance over the firmament. How idle it is to talk of one of them *being* the dawn, and the other the gloaming! They *accompany* the dawn like leaders. They are *bringers* of the day, and are watchers and protectors.

> The ancient sages [it is said] praised them at dawn. Worship the Açvins at early dawn.

They are invoked to alight on the grass, like two swans, like two deer, like two wild cattle in a pasture. They are the two leaders of the sky, which Aldebarán became, twenty-five hundred years afterwards, when as many more years before our era, the Celestial Bull began to open the year, and the bull became an object of adoration. They are the magnificent lords of good fortune, showerers of rain and benefit, golden-winged, swift, never deviating, beautiful; lords of men and Devas, worthy to be adored. They cause the barley to be sown, by the plough. Their union is like that of the shining and the dewy, and one wheel of their chariot is on the top of the solid, while the other revolves in the sky. The translation is evidently defective, but the evident meaning is that one is on the horizon when the other is visible above it. They are called the circumambient Açvins, and asked where they desire to manifest their persons.

In another hymn they are said to have arrested one wheel of their car, for illumining the form, while with the other they traverse the spheres. And the same thing must be meant by i., 181, 4, very differently translated by Dr. Muir and Professor Wilson; the meaning of which seems to be that they are born here and there, i. e., rise at different points, and one is behind the mountains while the other is in the sky above them.

What is most peculiar as to these Deities is that their car has three wheels, and three columns for support, is triangular and has three fastenings and props; and some of the texts indicate that it is distinct from them, and goes in advance. It "traverses" the seven flowing ones, and is renowned among the five orders of beings; and in it they journey three times by night and three times by day, and are invoked to come three times, with the seven mother-streams.

The meaning of all this is very doubtful. The Açvins were clearly two great and noticeable stars, closely united to each other in the popular mind, and, at that day having a peculiar significance, as fulfilling peculiar functions or marking the recurrence of a particular season. And the triple character of the chariot may have meant that in the same constellation, or near them, was a third star, never associated with them in the popular mind as in close and intimate union, but still always accompanying them and noticeable with them.

Mr. Prescott says, in his *Conquest of Mexico*,

> As the eye of the simple child of Nature watches through the long nights the stately march of the heavenly bodies, and sees the bright host coming up, one after another, and changing with the changing seasons of the year, he naturally associates them with those seasons as the periods over which they hold a mysterious influence.

And Prometheus says, with Æschylus,

> and they had no sure sign, either of winter or of flowing spring, or of fruitful summer, but they were used to do everything without judgment, until I showed to them the risings of the stars, and their settings, hard to be discerned.

Plutarch tells us that the common time among the Greeks for the solemnization of the sacred rites was within that month in which the Pleiades appear. These were long esteemed the leading stars of the Sabæan year; long, even, after the colure of the Vernal Equinox had quitted Aldebarán and the other Hyades.

There is ample evidence in the *Veda* that the same custom, of celebrating the great festivals at the Vernal Equinox prevailed among the Indo-Aryans; and that very many of the hymns were composed for those especial occasions. That the *Açvinau* were the stars of rain, and announced the time to plough and sow, we have already seen.

There are but two stars in all the sky that answer all the other conditions. These are Castor and Poludeukēs or Pollux, and we shall find in the Græco-Aryan mythology the explanation of much of what is said of the Twin Horsemen in the *Veda*. The Greeks called Castor and the Dioscuri, children of Dios or Zeus, as the Açvins are called children of Dyaus, the Sky. They were the children of Leda, to seduce whom, Jupiter assumed the form of a swan; and it is curious that the Açvins are invited to come down and sit upon the grass like two swans, which is said to no other Deity. The Cephalonians called them "The Great Gods": and in Grüter is a Greek inscription which designates them as *The Great Gods, Dioskoroi Kabeiri.* Castor was mortal, his brother immortal. Castor being killed, Pollux entreated Zeus to restore him to life, or relieve himself of his immortality. He was permitted to share it with his brother; and thereafter each alternately lived and died, one remaining in the infernal regions as long as the other lived; the foundation of this legend no doubt being the enigmatical language of the old hymns as to one being below the horizon, while the other was in the sky. Finally Zeus rewarded them by transferring them to the sky, as the two great stars of the constellation Gemini. They were generally represented mounted on white horses, armed with spears, and riding side by side, their heads covered with bonnets, with a star glittering on the top of each. They were styled "the health-giving Divinities," as the Açvins are styled "physicians and givers of health." They were called "the divine helpers," and "the kings," as the Açvins were beneficent nourishers and guides, and "the two kings, performers of holy rites."

By the precession of the Equinoxes, the Equinoctial point is continually but very slowly moving along the Ecliptic, in a direction contrary to that of the sun's proper motion. This regression of the Equinoctial points on the plane of the Ecliptic, or constant shifting of the intersection of the Ecliptic and Equator, causes the annual arrival of the sun in either of the Equinoxes to be a little earlier than it would otherwise be. The amount of the precession is a little over 50 seconds of longitude annually; or for 30 degrees (a sign), requiring 2,156 years. The Equinoctial Colure now passes through the constellation Pisces; 390 years before Christ it passed through the principal star in the constellation Aries, and the worship of the Celestial Bull prepared to give place to that of the Celestial Lamb. About 2,500 years before Christ, it passed through the Hyades, in Taurus. Sirius then rose heliacally (with the sun) at the Summer Solstice, and became the Dog-Star; and the Hyades rose heliacally at the Vernal Equinox, and received their name, the stars of water, or the rainers.

About 4,500 years before Christ, the sun was in Gemini or the Twins, at the Vernal Equinox, and the Twin Horsemen then led the heavenly host, preceded by the constellations Taurus and Orion: and when they had ceased to open the year, supplanted by Aldebarán, they continued to be worshipped as before, not only in India, but in Greece and Italy.

The demonstration seems to me complete enough; but I will make it absolutely so. The present system of Hindū astronomy was compiled about 600 A.D., but it had existed long before. In that system, two small stars in Aries are called *Açvini*, and as all the stars of that constellation are of little magnitude and in no wise noticeable, that time-honored name could not have been given them on account of their brilliancy, or because simply as stars they were in any way notable. But from about the year 400 B.C., the stars of Aries had been rising, at the Vernal Equinox, with or at first a little before the sun, rising gradually earlier and earlier, at the opening of the year. And as these little stars thus performed the office of announcing the advent of spring, which had in succession been performed by the real Açvins and by Aldebarán, they received the name *Açvini* and are known by it still. It is impossible that they could have borne it during the Vedic period. It never suited them in any respect, and the cause of its application to them has ceased. The beginning of *Açvini* became the initial point of the fixed Hindū sphere, from which longitudes are reckoned, about the year 570 A.D., in consequence of its coincidence, then, with the Vernal Equinox. In the older lists we find, instead of *Açvini*, the dual *Açvinau, Açvayujâu,* "the two horsemen."

I think I need argue this no further. The triple chariot, I am satisfied, was composed of Castor and two stars in Auriga, the Charioteer, the splendid star Capella and a large star south of it, the two forming, with Castor, an isosceles triangle.

I think I will not apologize for the length of these demonstrations, however I may fear you have found them tedious. It would have been of little instruction and benefit to you, for me to have simply stated what I understood to be the meanings of these various Deities, and to have indulged in the inaccurate finery of language which has become somewhat fashionable in books and essays upon these subjects. If I had stated them, and told you that no commentator coincided with my views, you would have been justified in believing that whatever their views were, they were in the right, and I in error.

It would not have been just to myself, to make these conclusions public, without giving the grounds for them, as far as I can do so in the limited space at my command. Upon my mere dictum, they would be entitled to no very great respect. If they had been the views of others of infinitely higher authority, I could have stated them, and given my authority, and so made these lectures a mere compilation. As it is, I have been forced to endeavor to demonstrate their soundness.

Neither would it have been just to you, your object being to be instructed upon a subject almost entirely new, and to be put in communion with the thought of our Aryan ancestors. To do that, you had to know, to some extent at least, the meaning of their poems, their modes of thinking, their conceptions of their Deities; without which their figurative language would either be a succession of enigmas, not in the least understood, or which is far worse, utterly misinterpreted. You could only understand what they said in regard to Indra, by knowing first what Indra was. If he was the firmament, most of what is said of him cannot be interpreted, for it is simple nonsense.

The hymns to *Soma* are the most singular ones in the *Veda*, and that Deity is not much better understood than those which I have already mentioned. Dr. Muir speaks of

> The important share which the exhilarating juice of the Soma plant assumes in bracing Indra for his conflict with the hostile powers in the atmosphere, and the eagerness of all the Gods to partake of this beverage [and says]: Soma is the God who represents and animates this juice, an intoxicating draught which plays a conspicuous part in the sacrifices of the Vedic Age.

All the hymns in the ninth book of the *Rig-Veda*, besides a few in other places, are dedicated to his honor, and constant references to the juice of the Soma occur in a large proportion of the other hymns. Professor Whitney says:

> The simple-minded Aryan people, whose whole religion was a worship of the wonderful powers and phenomena of Nature, had no sooner perceived that this liquid had power to elevate the spirits, and produce a temporary frenzy, under the influence of which the individual was prompted to and capable of deeds beyond his natural powers, than they found in it something divine; it was to their apprehension a God, endowing those into whom it entered with God-like powers: the plant which afforded it became to them the king of plants; the process of preparing it was a holy sacrifice; the instruments used therefor were sacred.

The Soma plant was the *Asclepias acida* or *Sarcostema viminale* which grew upon the Indian mountains. In the *Zend-Avesta* it is called Haóma; and there seems no reason to doubt that they were the same, although, if the real plant was not to be found in the Irano-Aryan country, another may have been substituted for it. It is supposed by the commentators that the freshly-pressed juice had intoxicating qualities; but no one has taken the trouble to inquire as to the fact. I find in Baird's Cyclopedia of the Natural Sciences that the Asclepiadaceæ are a natural order of dicotyledonous flowering plants, of which 910 species have been described. They are chiefly shrubs, with a milky juice, having in general acrid, purgative, emetic and diaphoretic qualities. The milky juice is usually bitter and acrid, but occasionally bland and used as milk. Many of the species possess powerful medicinal properties. The bastard ipecacuanha of the West Indies is one of these, and the tuberous swallow-wort of Virginia another. The Syrian contains caoutchouc. The leaves of one kind are used to adulterate senna, and the roots of another in Madras, as a substitute for sarsaparilla. The Hindū medicine *mudar*, a diaphoretic, is procured from the bark of the root of several species; and another species is used to adulterate scammony, a purgative.

It appears, therefore, that the fact, which has been taken for granted, does not exist, and so the whole bottom of the theory drops out. Yet the hymns do describe enthusiastically the flowing forth and filtration of the divine juice, and the effects produced on the worshippers and Gods, by partaking of the beverage. Certainly the Devas and Indra were not believed actually to drink it: and you are ready to ask how, if it had no intoxicating qualities, it came to be sacred! Can any one answer that as to the mistletoe and vervain? It is a curious fact that the Creek or Muskoki Indians, before they eat the first green maize of the season, at what they call the green-corn dance, make from a weed that grows in the prairies a decoction called as-sī, and by the Americans "the black drink," said to be extremely nauseous and an emetic, which they drink, and after it has had its effect, feast on the corn. In Georgia and Alabama they used a different weed, which, not being found in the plains, was replaced by another. Nobody knows how the use of it commenced.

The Soma juice, nevertheless, is said to be sweet, honied, pungent, well-flavored and exhilarating. No one can withstand Indra in battle, when he has drunk it. When quaffed, it stimulates the voice (makes men talkative), and calls forth ardent conceptions. In one verse the worshippers say

> we have drunk the Soma, we have become immortal, we have entered into light, we have known the Devas. What can an enemy now do to us, or what can the malice of any mortal effect, O thou immortal God?

If the Asclepias had the effects of the Cannabis Indica, we could understand how the worshipper could, in a drunken frenzy, say this; but it seems to me much more reasonable to ascribe it to those ancient Rishis who had become Devas, become immortal in the region of light, and entered into the company of the Devas, fed there by the light into which the Soma juice was deemed to be transmuted by the fire.

Indra, of course, drinks it as light, and becomes generous; it impels him as the horses impel a chariot; the hymn comes to him, he turns it round in his heart, and quaffs the Soma; grows great thereupon, surpassing in size the sky and expanse; half of him is in the sky, the rest at the sacrifice, and he goes as a messenger to the Devas, bearing them the oblations.

Evidently he quaffs the Soma, here, when it is poured into the fire. The hymns, prayers and worship addressed to him are also described as stimulating his energies and invigorating him: and the worshippers are said to place the thunderbolt in his hands, and increase its efficacy. For the hymns and prayers ascend with the flame, and are also supposed to replenish him with light; for light was to the ancient Aryans, intellect and wisdom and strength. In *i.*, 187, savory and sweet Pitu is worshipped, and asked to protect the worshipper; and he was simply *food*. By *his* invigorating power, Trita slew the mutilated Vṛitra. The thoughts of the mighty

Devas are fixed on *him;* and by his kind and intelligent assistance, Indra slew Ahi; and he is exhilarating to the Devas. For the food, also, consumed by the fire, becomes of the fire, and ascends to the Devas as light.

Two things may be added. The Soma and Haŏma may not have been the Asclepias, but some plant whose juice really intoxicated. I imagine that it is identified with the Asclepias, only by uncertain tradition. And, if the juice furnished, by fermentation or distillation, an alcoholic liquor, it was no doubt used, not because it intoxicated, but because when poured upon the fire it caused a great flush and volume of flame and light, ascending high toward heaven: and so was changed into food of light for the Devas.

It is unnecessary to recite all the great deeds of Soma. He exhilarates and invigorates all the Devas, Varuṇa, Mitra, Vishṇu and the Maruts; and· all their powers are ascribed to him, for they are the powers of the light, which he becomes. The fuel that feeds the fire is adored, also, because when consumed it becomes fire. Wherefore Soma is king of Devas and men, all creatures are in his hand, his laws are like those of Varuṇa, and he is asked to forgive violations of them, to be gracious and deliver from death; and he is thousand-eyed and sees and knows all creatures; is hero, warrior and beneficent, a wise Ṛishi and the priest of the Devas.

He and Agni are said to have placed the luminaries in the sky; and he and Pushan to be generators of wealth and of the sky and expanse: and he and Indra dispel darkness, bring the sun and light, prop up the sky, and spread out the expanse, and hymn *vi.*, ·74, is dedicated to him and Rudra jointly.

I could not be made to believe that these poets actually believed Soma to be a God; or that they ascribed to him these powers because his juice intoxicated. It did not do so; and if it had been more potent than opium or Indian hemp, it would be simply preposterous to believe that these functions were imagined to belong to him because he made Indra and the Devas drunk. They were ascribed to the light which the Soma juice became by the action of the fire. I doubt if the worshippers ever drank it at all.

Three *Ṛibhus* are often spoken of in the *Veda*, men of the former days, who were artizans. In Professor Wilson's note to *i.*, 51, 2, the protecting and fostering Ṛibhus are said to mean the Maruts. They hastened to the presence of Indra, and uttered encouraging words, which means that they went from place to place, to the sacrifices, and recited hymns laudatory of Indra. Hymn 110 of Mandala *i.* is addressed to them, and they are invited by it to drink to their utmost content of the Soma juice, when it is offered in the fire. They are therefore Devas, i. e., stars. And they were men, translated to the sky as stars, for in verse 2, the Rishi Kutsa, author of the hymn, calls them sons of Sudhanvan, and says that when they were amongst his own ancestors, they went to the forest country to officiate, being desirous of enjoying, and while immature.   When they had become perfect, they went to the sphere of Savitri, who bestowed upon them immortality, and thence they came to him who is not to be concealed, i. e., to Indra manifested as the light of the sky, and there becoming stars ("and represented," i. e., invested with another form, that of stars), they partook of the libations, and made four-fold the ladle for the sacrificial viands, which the Asura had made single.   It was the work of Tvashtri.   They divided it into four. They made by the intellect the horses of Indra, and a car for the Nâsatyas, and a cow yielding milk.   They are leaders dwelling in the firmament, who, having equalled the velocity of the protector, ascended to the region of the sky.

Professor Wilson says that a text of the *Veda* identifies them with the solar rays; and that they are, indeed, said to be rays of the sun.   The text referred to does not identify them with the solar rays, and they are nowhere said to be rays of the sun.   The name itself is, I am satisfied, from *rebh*, to "praise," and not from *rabh*, *grabh* or *labh*, to "seize, take."

In *i.*, 161, the legend of the ladle is more fully given.   The Ribhus are advised that the Devas command them to make four-fold the single ladle; and that if they accomplish this, they shall be entitled to sacrifices with the Devas.   They replied, that having made a horse, a car and a cow, and two aged persons young, they were ready to execute the new order.   They did so, and Tvashtri proposed to slay them for profaning the·ladle for the drinking of the Devas.

> Then they made use of other names for one another, as the libation was poured out, and the maiden propitiated them by different appellations (*anyair enân kanya namabhih sparat*).   [*Sparat* means "protected" not "propitiated."]
>
> *Ribhu, Vibhwa* and *Vâja* [it is said], go to the Devas; doers of good deeds [skilful artizans] enjoy your sacrificial portion . . . . harness now your chariot and repair unto the Devas.   They have said, sons of Sudhanvan, drink of this water, or drink that which has been filtered through the Munja-grass, or, if you are not pleased with either of these, be exhilarated at the third sacrifice.   Waters are the most excellent, said one; Agni is the most excellent, said another: the third declared to many that which makes potent [*vardhayantim*, meaning the light into which the Soma is changed.   The scholiast says, either a line of clouds, or the earth]; and thus speaking true things, the Ribhus divided the ladle.

In another hymn Tvashtri is said to have been content, when he saw the four ladles.   In another, it is said to the Ribhus,

> There has been the drinking of the effused Soma, in consequence of your ladle.

They have gone the path of the undying, to the company of the Devas, and have obtained immortality among them. They cause the grass to grow on the high places, and the water to flow over the low places, for abundant production. Thus the spring rains are attributed to them. They repose in the dwelling of the unconcealable one, in the solar sphere, and inquire,

who awakens, *A gohyasya* [the unconcealable] to this office?

and the sun replies,

the arouser is the dog (*çvânam bodhayitâram*).

The commentator says that *çvanam* is the wind. It is Sirius, the Dog-Star.

The year being ended [it is added], you again today light up this region.

Prayer is a messenger to them. They bring nourishment to the devout. When, reposing for twelve days, they remained in the hospitality of the sun, they made the fields fertile, and led forth the rivers; plants sprung up on the waste places, and waters were on the low lands. Unmistakably this means that these three stars rose, for twelve mornings, so short a time before the sun, as to be enveloped in the light that preceded his rising.

They were named *Ribhu* or *Ribhukshin*, *Vibhvan* and *Vâja*. Vâja was the artificer of the Devas, Ribhukshin of Indra, and Vibhvan of Varuṇa. They have become Devas by soaring aloft in the sky like falcons; are "associated" with Indra, "with whom they are *intelligent*," i. e., their light is his manifestation, and they sympathize with Varuṇa, the Adityas, Savitṛi and others, i. e., they shine by the same light as they. They are intelligent, wise, showerers, munificent and givers of food.

We ascertain from these various texts and others, that the Ribhus were three stars, large and brilliant, and near enough to each other to be deemed a single constellation. They were in the same region of the sky as the Açvins, and Sirius rose before them, leading them up to perform their office of causing rain at the Vernal Equinox. All this points to the three stars in the Belt of Orion. Originally they were real or legendary persons, bards and artizans, to whom, if real, many legendary tales had attached. What was meant by their various works, I cannot conjecture. No doubt, those who heard the hymns recited, knew what it all meant, but for us the legends have lost their meaning.

The meanings of the three names of the Ribhus seem to be: *Ribhu*, "zeal, strength, sacrifice or praise"; *Vibhvan*, "power"; *Vaja*, "speed."

The word rendered by "ladle" is *chamasa*. Benfey gives it the meaning of "drinking vessel": Dr. Muir that of "sacrificial cup." The statement of the making the single new sacrificial cup into four (*i.*, 20, 6) is, *uta tyaṁ chamasaṁ navaṁ Tvashṭur devasya nishkritam akartta chaturaḥ punaḥ.*

Parjanya and *Vâta* are addressed together, and asked to send from the firmament waters to make the earth produce. All the commentators consider Parjanya to be a name of Indra, and Vâta only another name of the God of the wind. The glory of Vâta's chariot is celebrated, and its noise is said to come, rending and resounding. Touching the sky he moves onward, making all things ruddy, and he comes, sweeping the dust from the expanse; the gusts of the air rush after him, and congregate in him, as women in an assembly. Sitting along with them, on the same car, the Deva who is ruler of all the world (Indra) is borne along. Hasting forward, by paths in the atmosphere, he never rests on any day. Friend of the waters, first-born, true, in what place was he born? whence has he sprung? Life of the Devas (*âtmâ devânâm*), womb of created beings, this Devah moves as he pleases. His sounds have been heard, but his form is not seen.

He wafts healing to men, salutary and contenting the heart, prolongs lives, is the father of men, their brother and friend, who causes them to live.

Vâta is the perfect participle of *Vâ*, which means, according to Benfey, to "blow," and to "dry." It was perhaps, originally, the fire or heat, as producing dryness; and thence the summer wind, that dries all moisture. Its healing qualities indicate that it was the cool northern winds from the mountains: but how was the air or wind the vitality of the Devas, or, if Vâta was the air, how could the gusts of air rush after him and be gathered in him? How is air or wind the womb or source of production of living beings? How does it make the sky red? and how can the air travel by paths in the atmosphere? But the word "atmosphere" is, I think, not expressive of the meaning of the Vedic word *antarikshe*, which I take to signify the space which the atmosphere occupies. And I doubt also whether "the gusts of the air rush after him" expresses the meaning of the original. I think that Vâta was the atmosphere, supposed to extend to and touch the sky; that it was the vitality of the Devas by bearing to them, by the ascending motion communicated to it by the fire, the light-essence of the oblations; that the wind-gusts are not said to rush *after* him, for the very expression *Vatasya vishṭhaḥ* shows that they are *parts* of Vâta, and it is added that they are included in him, as portions of him, as women are included in and constitute an assembly of women. I think the meaning is that being congregated or aggregated in him, they as portions of him rush forward, or sweep onward. And probably the phrase "Let Vâta, the wind, waft to us healing (*Vâtaḥ â Vâtu*), etc.," means, "Let the atmosphere, as wind, waft to us." The atmosphere could well be called "shedder of rain."

Parjanya is. mentioned alone, and is conjoined with Vâta (*Parjanya-Vâtâ*) and with Agni (*Agniparjanyau*). Dr. Bühler thinks that from the etymology of his name and the analogy between him and *Perkunas*, the Lithuanian God of thunder, he was originally the Thunder-God. In another essay his conclusion is that he was "the God of thunder-storms and rains, the generator and nourisher of plants, and of living creatures." That is to tell us, not what he *is*, but what *effects* he produces.

He is *divas putrâya*, "the son of the sky." Benfey has *Parjanya*, probably *sphurj* + for old *sparj* + *ana* + *ya*, "a rain-threatening cloud, rain, the Deity of rain." But *sphurj* means, he says, to "thunder." Now *sphur*, from which it comes, means to "tremble, palpitate, struggle, break forth, flash, shine, sparkle"; and not to "thunder."

The texts tell us that Parjanya is the cause of fruitfulness in plants; that he splits the trees and destroys the Rakshasas; the whole creation (or rather, all creatures) are afraid of his mighty stroke, even the innocent man fleeing before him. He is the rain-impelling: thundering, he replenishes the earth with moisture: his praises as cause of rain are again and again repeated; but also, resounding and thundering, he slays' the evil-doers. What he *does* is plain enough. He *causes* thunder and rain. But what he *is*, is another thing altogether. He is a Deva, an Asura, and son of the sky. And to call him an *Asura* is to say that he is brilliant or radiant, and proves him to be an orb or some form of light.

Let us return to etymology. Benfey, who gives several Greek and Latin words as cognates of *sparj*, which are either not so or do not assist us, furnishes one that is identical with it σπαίρω, in the Greek, meaning "palpitate, vibrate, tremble." And under *sphur*, in his dictionary of the Sanskrit, we find *spharaya*, to "cause to flash"; *visphurita*, "tremulous, shaken"; *visphur*, to "tremble, glitter"; and *sphurita*, "trembling, glittering, shining, quivering, throbbing." And the Latin *fulgeo*, "lighten" and *fulgur*, "lightning," are identical with *sphur*, other forms of which, and older ones, are *sphal* and *sphul*, meaning to "tremble, throb," from which *sphalaya* means to "strike, crush."

Parjanya therefore means the lightning, as "flashing, glittering, vibrating, zigzagging"; and was Indra, the light, manifested and personified as the lightning.

The legend of *Saramâ*, whom Professor Müller considers to be the dawn, has become, in consequence of his interpretation of it, as worthy of examination as any one in the *Rig-Veda*. Professor Wilson says,

> Allusion is frequently made to a legend of the Asuras named Paṇis having stolen the cows of the Gods, or according to some persons, of the Angirasas, and hidden them in a cave, where they were discovered by Indra, with the help of the bitch Saramâ.

What we find in the *Veda* about her, is as follows:

> *i*. 6. 5.—Thou, O Indra, with the swift horses who break even into the fastness, didst find the cows, even in the place where they were concealed. [I translate *Vâhnibhih* "horses" on the authority of Professor Müller, Translation of *Rig-Veda i*. 27.]

We have in Benfey, *vah*, "carry, bear, have, proceed, move, flow, breathe"; *vaha*, "air, wind"; *vahni*, "a sacrificer, fire"; *vâh*, akin to *vah*, to "endeavor"; *vâha*, "a vehicle, horse, carrier, air, wind"; *vâhnî*, "an army, a body of forces, a river." In the text, the word means the outflowings, the rays or radiance of Indra.

> *i*. 62. 2, 3.—Through him (Indra), our forefathers, the Angirasas, worshipping him, and finding the foot-marks (the trail), recovered the cattle. When the search was set on foot, by Indra and the Angirasas, Saramâ secured food for her young. Then Bṛihaspati slew the devoured, and rescued the kine, and the Devas [i. e., the Angirasas, priests who afterwards became Devas, as the seven Ṛishis or Ursa Major], with the cattle, proclaimed their joy aloud.
>
> *i*. 72. 8.—The seven pure rivers that flow from the sky, skilled in sacrifices, found the entrance to the place where their cattle were concealed: through thee Saramâ discovered the abundant milk of the kine, with which man, the progeny of Manu, still is nourished.
>
> *iii*. 31. 5*ff*.—The seven intelligent sages, having ascertained that they were concealed in the fastness, propitiated by mental devotion, and recovered them all by means of sacrifice: for Indra, knowing, and being gracious to them, forced an entrance. When Saramâ led the way to the gap of the mountain, then Indra made great and ample for her young, as previously; then the sure-footed, first recognizing their lowing, followed on, and came to where the kine not fated to be killed were.

Indra made ample provision for the young of Saramâ, enabling the Angirasas to force their way into the stronghold where the cows were, some of which had already been killed, and part of the meat so recovered was thus given by Indra to her pups.

"The sure-footed," i. e., good at following a trail or scent, is the bitch Saramâ. The "most wise" and "valiant" and "destroyer" is Indra.

The Angirasas "followed the road that led to immortality," by that devout piety which at last caused their translation to the sky.

The Most Wise, desirous of their friendship, went to the fastness, and the mountain gave up to the valiant one the animals detained in it, aided by the young horses, equally eager: the destroyer recovered them, and immediately the Angiras sacrificed to him. The Angirasas, their thoughts engrossed by their cattle, sat down with hymns, following the road that led to immortality [among the stars]. This their perseverance was great, by which they sought for months to accomplish that. Contemplating their own giving milk to their young born before they were stolen, they were overjoyed: their shouts spread through sky and expanse: they replaced their recovered kine in their abodes, and stationed guards over the cows. Indra, the slayer of Vṛitra, liberated the milch-cows, the excellent, which contribute abundantly to sacred offerings, yielding butter for the libations, and milked for him sweet food. Indra . . . . discovered [enabled them to find] the cattle, and by his radiant effulgence drove away the glooms, and guiding the Angirasas with certainty to their own, he shut the gate upon all their own cattle [enabled them to place them in security in their place at home?].

v. 45. 6*ff.*—Come, friends, let us celebrate that solemn rite which was effectual in setting open the stalls of the cattle . . . . the ten months' worship, when Saramâ, going to the ceremony, discovered the cattle, and Angiras made all the rites effective [succeeded by means of the sacrifice]. When all the Angirasas, at the opening of that adorable dawn, obtained possession of the cattle, then milk and other oblations were offered in the august assembly, for Saramâ, following the true trail, had found the cows.

A later hymn represents Saramâ, when she had found the Paṇis, as holding a colloquy with them, to persuade them to give up the cattle. In it, Mr. Cox says,

we see unmistakably the dawn peering about through the sky, in search of the bright clouds, and restoring them in all their brilliance and beauty to the broad pastures of the heaven.

He should have added, "to suckle their young and furnish the Angirasas with milk and butter for oblations to Indra." By what right is that suppressed?

The Paṇis asked with what intention she came, for the way was far and led tortuously away. They ask what she wishes of them, and how the night was, and how she crossed the waters of the Râsa. They wished to know what manner of person in appearance Indra was; and said,

Let him come hither, and we will make friends with him, and then he may be the cow-herd of our cows.

She replied that deep streams would not stop him, and he would come to them and destroy them. They said,

> Those cows, O Saramâ, which thou desirest, fly about the ends of the sky, O Darling. Who would give them up to thee without fighting? for our weapons too are sharp.

She assured them that though their words were brave, and their bodies arrow-proof, neither would save them from the anger of Bṛihaspati. The Paṇis said that the booty which they had gained was securely bestowed in a fastness of the mountain, cattle, horses and treasure; that it was guarded by vigilant Paṇis, and she had come in vain. They proposed to Saramâ to remain with them and be their sister, offering to give her part of the cows. But she replied,

> I know nothing of brotherhood or sisterhood: Indra knows it and the formidable Angiras. They seemed to me resolved to have their cattle, when I came; therefore get away from here, Paṇis, far away. Go far away, Paṇis, far away: let the cows come forth free—the cows that Bṛihaspati, Soma, the stones (by which it was pressed), and the wise Ṛishis found, hidden away.

Professor Müller quotes the nonsense of Sâyaṇa and other Indian commentators, upon the subject of this old legend, and then gives his own opinions. He says, that there can be little doubt that Saramâ was meant for the dawn. I cannot see the least reason or ghost of a reason for any such notion. He says,

> in the ancient hymns of the *Rig-Veda* she is never spoken of as a dog, nor can we find there the slightest allusion to her canine nature.

This is evidently a later thought, and it is high time that this much-talked-of greyhound should be driven out of the Vedic pantheon.

Now, in *vii.*, 55, the watch-dog Sarameya, who guards the house, displays his teeth and tears the hog, is twice called the offspring of Saramâ, which one would suppose to be "an allusion to her canine nature." In *x.*, 14, 1, the watch-dogs of Yama are called the offspring of Saramâ; and it certainly seems almost inexplicable, on any ground other than that of hallucination, how any one could see *any* thing, in the Saramâ of the legend other than a dog.

> Sṛi is "to flow, to flow to, to blow, to go." From it are sṛika, "air, wind and arrow": Sara, i. e., sṛita, "who or what goes, going, a waterfall, water": Saraka, "going"; and various other words, all including the notion of going or moving; e.·g., Saraṭa, "a lizard," and Saraṭi, "wind, cloud": Saraṇi, "a path, a road." Saramâ is "runner, goer, swift, fleet."

Müller says that the root of Saramâ is no doubt *sar*, to "go"; but that the derivation is by no means certain, there being no other word formed in Sanskrit by *ama*, and with guṇa of the radical vowel. Bopp says that the feminine form of the suffix, viz., *mâ*, does not occur in Sanskrit, in substantives (§807); but the Greek μη corresponds to it, and the Latin like *flamma*, and the Lithuanian in *ma, mê*.

The etymology of *Pani*, he says, is doubtful. *Pan* means to "buy, play, stake, bet, risk"; whence *pana*, "play, a bet or stake, wages, hire, reward"; and *panitri*, "a trader." The *Panis*, Müller says, are mentioned together with Ushas, the Dawn. In *i.*, 124, 10, she is asked to wake those who worship the Gods, but not to wake the Panis: and in *iv.*, 51, 3, it is said that the Panis ought to sleep in the midst of darkness, while the dawn rises to bring treasures for man.

In the former passage, Wilson translates the word "traders"; in the latter "traffickers." In the latter place the word is *panaya*. In the former they are said to be reluctant to wake. No doubt the word meant "gamblers," who, wasting the hours of the night in gaming, and caring nothing for worship, were not desired to be wakened, nor would wake, at the dawn, but continued to sleep in darkened rooms.

In *vii.*, 6, 3, the irreligious Panis, with the Dasyus (*panin açrâddhân, avridhân, ayajnân*, "the undevout, not offering, not worshipping Panis") are said to be conquered by Agni. Therefore they were a people. In *vi.*, 13, 3, it is said that the man who has the aid of Agni destroys his enemy by his strength, and baffles the might of *Pani*: and in *vi.*, 51, 14, Soma is invoked to "destroy the voracious *Pani*, for verily he is a wolf." Here Wilson thinks that *Pani* may mean a trader or greedy trafficker.

In *i.*, 83, 4, it is said that the Angirasas acquired all the wealth of *Pani*, comprising horses, cows and other animals. In *i.*, 93, 4, it is said that Agni and Soma carried off the cows that were the food of *Pani*. Evidently the word meant a gambler, and was also a name given to a native tribe.

The proofs which Professor Müller adduces, of the identity of Ushas and Saramâ, are entirely inconclusive, and in fact of no weight at all. One is that Ushas is said, in two passages, to break open the stronghold and release the cows. So are Indra and Brihaspati said to do it. Professor Müller could easily adduce as much proof of the proposition that *all* the Gods of the *Veda* were *one* of them, and that *one all*. How he could write what I shall now quote, with much more about the bright cows of the dawn, I cannot but wonder. He says:

> The myth of which we have collected the fragments is clear enough. It is a reproduction of the old story of the break of day. The bright cows, the rays of the sun or the rain-clouds—for both go by the same name—have been stolen by the powers of darkness, by the night and her manifold progeny. Gods and men are anxious for their return. But where are they to be found? They are hidden in a dark or strong stable, or scattered along the ends of the sky, and the robbers will not restore them. At last, in the farthest distance the first signs of the dawn

appear; she peers about, and runs with lightning quickness, it may be, like a hound after a scent, across the darkness of the sky. She is looking for something, and, following the right path, she has found it. She has heard the lowing of the cows, and she returns to her starting-place with more intense splendor. After her return, there rises Indra, the God of Light, ready to do battle in good earnest against the gloomy powers, to break open the strong stable in which the bright cows were kept, and to bring light and strength and life back to his pious worshippers. This is the simple myth of Saramâ, composed originally of a few fragments of ancient speech.

Professor Müller admits that these imaginary fragments are peculiar to India, and not to be found reproduced in any other mythology. A sufficient reason for that is that they are merely inventions to support a theory that has no foundation.

The language of this legend is figurative; but the legend itself is a perfectly simple one. Its lesson is the efficacy of prayer to secure for the devout worshipper the assistance of Indra. The sons of Angiras, forefathers of the Rishis for whom the poet speaks, lost their cattle, "lifted" in the night by some predatory mountain band, whose name, Panis, has been preserved. They were driven to the mountains, across a river, by a long and rough and circuitous route, and there hidden in a gap or recess with a narrow entrance, in the mountains from whose fastnesses the Highland Caterans of the Caucasus had descended, and where they were guarded by vigilant warriors. The plundered owners cried aloud in prayer to Indra, for light, that they might see the way by which to recover their cattle; and Brihaspati, prayer, prevailed with Indra, as Ushas, to hasten the coming of the dawn. They mounted their horses, and the bitch, Saramâ, with them when they prayed, took and followed the trail, in advance of them. So the place in which the cattle were hidden was discovered. It seems from the text* that it was Angiras, the father, who sacrificed to Indra before dawn, praying his aid to recover the cattle. The hound is represented as having reached the stronghold of the Panis first, and as having heard the cattle lowing. The seven sages, afterwards the seven outflowings of light as stars, with their followers, attacked and defeated the robbers and recovered the cattle, and this success was ascribed to Indra, Ushas and Brihaspati, to the efficacy of prayer and the assistance afforded by daylight, which enabled the pursuers to see and follow the tracks.

---

*In *i*. 83. 4, it is said that the Angirasas first prepared the sacrificial food, and then, with kindled fire and a most pious act of worship acquired all the wealth of the Panis. *Atharvan*, first, by sacrifices discovered the path. Then the sun rose, the cherisher of pious acts of worship. *Atharvan* regained the cattle, *Kâvya* being associated with him. The comment identifies *Kâvya* with *Uçanas* and *Uçanas* with *Bhrigu*. *Kâvya* meant "of the sages," from *Kavi*, "wise, a sage"; and *Uçanas* was an ancient Rishi. *Atharvan* meant "a priest," and was the name of a Rishi. It was probably meant that the recovery of the cattle was due to the priest and bard, i. e., to the prayer and the hymns.

Returning, the Angirasas returned thanks by sacrifices, and their prayers, uttered aloud, ascended through the expanse to the sky. And when the stronghold was carried, Saramâ found food for her pups, Indra, by the aid he gave furnishing it in abundance, as he had done before. As the cattle were recovered "by the path of sacrifice," so Saramâ found the way to them "by the path of truth." It seems that some particular day of the year was celebrated as the anniversary of this recovery, at which the Soma juice was expressed, and the nine-month ministrants celebrated the ten months' worship.

I need not point out to you the various things in this legend which are utterly contradictory of the theory of Professor Müller. Not to see them, one must wilfully close his eyes, or else he must believe the *Veda* to be full of inconsistencies, and that it is no objection to a theory or notion that the texts are directly hostile to it. I believe, on the contrary, that there are no real incoherence and inconsistency in the hymns, though different poets, each giving his imagination loose rein, have often used figures and indulged in fancies so different as to seem inconsistent. Our own poets have compared the moon, for example, to many and different things, each comparison being, from the poet's own point of view, true and natural; and yet one very opposite to the other.

In *ii.*, 24, 6, where it is said that the sages, searching on every side, discovered their property hidden in the cave of the Paṇis, and forced their way in; that having seen through the false, and again coming (having detected the trick of a false trail, to throw them off the scent, and taken the true one again?) pursued the real track, and with their hand cast against the rock the destructive fire, which till then was not there, Professor Wilson says:

> The whole of this is, no doubt, allegorical. The cows hidden in the caves are the rains accumulated in the clouds, which are set free by the oblations with fire, of which the Angirasas were, no doubt, the authors, at least to some extent.

The only support that I know of, for this theory, is *i.*, 32, 11, where it is said:

> The waters, the wives of the destroyer [*dâsa patuyah*], guarded by Ahi, stood obstructed, like the cows by Paṇin; but by slaying Vṛitra, Indra set open the cave that had confined them. [And, in the next verse] When the single resplendent Vṛitra returned the blow, Indra, by thy thunderbolt, thou becamest like a horse's tail. Thou didst rescue the kine. Thou, Hero, didst win the Soma juice: thou didst let loose the seven rivers to flow.

But this is merely a comparison of the rivers, obstructed by ice, to the imprisonment of the cattle; and of Indra's exploits in the two cases, as of like importance.

Whatever these passages mean, they utterly demolish the theory of Professor Müller, leaving it not a leg to stand upon. The first passage entirely agrees with the others, in recounting an actual occurrence. It was the *property*, the cattle, of the sages that was shut up in the cave, stable or other place of confinement. And whatever is meant by the destructive fire cast against the rock, it equally destroys the conceit that the cattle were only the bright clouds of the dawn, to discover which the dawn ran peering about the sky. Professor Wilson does not understand what is said about the fire. Nor do I. He thinks it is a probable allusion to the dissemination of fire-worship by the Angirasas. But that is too far-fetched. So it would be. I am afraid to say that the meaning is that by means of sacrificing with fire, they gained entrance, flinging, metaphorically, the fire against the rock. Probably it means that they set fire to an abattis or other construction of wood that hindered their entrance.

It is only necessary to add that Saramâ is not invoked or spoken of as a Deity, and that her offspring Sarameya was plainly a watch dog, without sufficient discretion to know the worshippers of Indra from robbers, and therefore chidden for barking at them. What there is of real value in the legend is, the express and repeated references to the translation of the Angirasas to the sky as stars; and the profound conviction of the efficacy of prayer.

Of the Deities that were not manifestations, embodied forms, or potencies of light and fire, I shall notice but two or three.

Sarasvatî is both an actual river and a Goddess. A fabulous river Sarasvatî is to this day believed in by the Hindûs, said to run underground, and unite with the Ganges and Yumna at Allahabad. I cannot find that there is now any river called by that name. It could not have been the Indus, for that is the Sindhu of the *Veda*. It may have been the Sutlej, the hundred-channeled (*Sutudra*) once called the *Hesudrus*, which has a course of about 1,000 miles, and joins the Indus 470 miles from the sea, having a breadth of 700 yards or more, and being navigable for a long distance by small vessels.

Sarasvatî makes manifest (or manifests herself as) a mighty river; is the purifier and bestower of food, recompenser of worship with wealth, and is attracted by the viands offered as sacrifices. She is the inspirer of those who delight in truth, the instructress of the right-minded, and enlightens all understandings. Three undecaying Goddesses (rivers that never run dry), givers of delight, are invoked to sit down on the sacred grass, Ilâ, Sarasvatî and Mahi. In another hymn, Bharatî, Ilâ and Sarasvatî are invoked. In one Agni is said to be Hotra and Bharati, Ilâ of a hundred winters, and Sarasvatî, the destroyer of Vṛitra (or rather, I think, this must read "Thou, destroyer of Vṛitra, art Sarasvatí"). It is evident that he is said to be these rivers, because by melting the snows and sending down the rains, he fills them with water. Sarasvatí is prayed to come to the sacrifice, from the sky or vast expanse. She is called "Sarasvatí, dwelling with rivers," i. e., manifested locally *as* rivers. Rudra and she, with Vishṇu and Vayu, are invoked to send rain. She is, in one and the same hymn, a river, tearing away its banks, and the mountain crags, making land for men, and pouring water on them; and a divine Goddess, protecting her worshippers and riding in her chariot, filling the vast space of the expanse and sky, abiding in the three regions, comprising seven elements, and cherishing the five races. She is ever to be invoked in battle, and overcomes all enemies, has seven sisters, and is invoked to bring her water-laden sisters, as the sun brings the days. In one hymn she is called "mother of the Sindhu, and of those rivers that flow copious and fertilizing": and she is said to flow from the mountains to the sea.

She seems to have been a particular river, but also the Goddess, not only of that river, but of all the rivers of the Punjab; and she and the Ardviçura of the *Zend-Avesta* were the prototypes of all the Grecian and Roman River-Gods and -Goddesses.

I must add that it is very uncertain whether many of the texts in regard to Sarasvatí are correctly translated. One of these, with its various versions, will assist you to comprehend the difficulties of the *Veda*, and how an ancient Oriental book may be perverted and denaturalized by the Teutonic or Anglo-Saxon intellect of translators. It is *i.*, 3, 12, which I have already quoted. Professor Wilson makes it,

. Sarasvatí makes manifest by her acts a mighty river, and (in her own form) enlightens all understandings.

Sâyaṇa understood it of the river, and read it,

the Sarasvatí, by her act (of flowing), displays a copious flood.

Roth makes it,

a mighty stream is Sarasvatí; with her light she lightens, illuminates all pious minds.

He considers the commencing words as figurative, not as referring to the river. Benfey reads,

Sarasvatí, by her light, causes the great sea to be known; she shines through all thoughts.

He understands "the great sea" as the universe, or as life. And Dr. Muir thinks that

> the conceptions of Sarasvatí as a river, and as the directress of ceremonies, may be blended in this passage.

I think that the meaning is that Sarasvatí makes known or enables men to find the great sea or river, by being the means of reaching it; and that she removes all doubt as to the existence of it from all men's minds.

I am led to believe that the original Sarasvatí was the Oxus, chiefly because in the Vedic period the Indo-Aryans could not have known anything of the Indian Ocean, or of any other sea than the Aral and Caspian; because it does not appear ever to have been the name of the Indus; and if Sarasvatí was not the Indus, I do not know where else, except in Bactria, the land of the seven Kareshvares, there was a mighty river that could be called *Saptasvasâ, saptorthi-sindumatâ,* "having seven sisters," "one of seven rivers," or "mother of streams." Or it may originally have been the Sir Affshan, the river of Samarkand and Bokhara. We certainly do not find it in the Punjab.

In *Rig-Veda vii.,* 33, the Rishi Vasishtha is said to have sprung from *Urvaçi* the *Apsaras.* Böhtlingk and Roth describe the *Apsarasas* as female beings of a ghost-like description, whose abode is in the atmosphere. They are the wives of the *Gandharvas,* have the power of changing their forms, love playing at dice, and impart good luck. Professor Goldstücker says that originally they seem to have been personifications of the vapors which are attracted by the sun, and form into mist or clouds. In *x.,* 10, 4, Gandharva in the waters, and his aqueous wife are designated as the parents of Yama and Yamí. But this is a late hymn, and its notions are worthless.

Now, *ap* is "water." *Saras* is "a lake," *Sritas, Sri,* meaning to "flow, extend, spread, spread out." So *Sarasa* is "a pond," and *Sarasija* "a lotus," which grows in ponds. We call it the "pond-lily." *Sarasvant* is "the ocean"; *Sarasvatí* "the great river adored as a Goddess," *Sari,* "a waterfall," and *Sant,* "a river."

Thus *Apsaras* is simply "a lake or pond of water," as *Nabhas-saras* is "a lake or expanse of clouds"; and the *Apsarasas* were, no doubt, the lakes in which the various rivers or part of them had their rise. *Urvâ,* feminine of *uru,* is "large"; and *Urvaçi,* the *Apsaras,* was merely a larger lake, like *Seirikol,* out of which the main branch of the Oxus flows. Near it, no doubt, Vasishtha was born: and Yama near the Caspian, probably.

The thirty-second hymn of Mandala *ii.,* invokes, among other Deities, *Râkâ* and *Sinîvâlî. Râkâ,* according to Wilson, is the full moon, and *Sinîvâlî,* the moon on the first day when it is visible. It is said to these as follows:

I invoke Râkâ, worthy to be invoked. May she, who is auspicious of good fortune, hear us, and spontaneously understand. May she sew the work with an unfailing needle, and bestow a son with abundant wealth. Râkâ, with these thy kind and gracious intentions, wherewith thou grantest riches to the sacrificer, approach us today, etc.

To Sinîvâlî it is said,

Broad-loined Sinîvâlî, who art the sister of the Devas, accept the offered oblation and grant us progeny. Offer the oblation to that Sinîvâlî, the protectress of mankind, the handsome-armed and handsome-fingered, who is prolific and has many children. I invoke her who is Gangu, who is Sinîvâlî, who is Râkâ, who is Sarasvatî.

In another hymn it is said,

may the rivers carved out by Vibhu, may Sarasvatî and the brilliant Râkâ, the illustrious granter of desires, be willing to grant us riches.

The principal sources of the Indus and Ganges interlace with each other, as it were, north of the Himalayas. In Longitude 81° 30′ is the Lake Tso Mapham or Manasarowar, the confluence of the highest sources of the Yumna, the principal branch and real main river of the sacred Ganges. This lake is about 15,200 feet above the sea level, *circular*, with rocky coasts, and about fifteen miles in diameter. North, west and south of it are mountains from 22,000 to 25,000 feet in height above the sea.

From this lake a stream flows into another lake, Tso Lanak or Rakas-Tal, about five miles distant, of more irregular form, with several islands in its southern extremity, where it spreads considerably to the east and west. Its length is about twenty miles, its greatest width fifteen. From it flows the main stream of the Sutlej. The name Râkâ still survives in that of the lake *Rakas-Tal:* and as Sinîvâlî is said to be the Ganges, Râkâ and Sarasvatî, I think it was Lake Manasarowar out of which the Ganges flows, which supplies Lake Rakas-Tal, and from which, through that, the Sutlej may be said to flow. It is circular, and that agrees with Sinîvâlî, which is "wide-hipped" or "broad-loined." So she has many children, and handsome arms and fingers; which are the streams that run out of the two lakes, and those and the rivulets that run into them from the mountains.

There is one hymn in the tenth book of the *Rig-Veda*, known as the *Purusha Sûkta*, which is worthy of your notice. It consists of sixteen verses, of which all after the fifth are modern: They describe the origin of castes, and speak of the *Rig-Veda* and *Sama-Veda*, and were therefore composed after the compilation of those books, and ages after the Brahmanic period had begun. They detail the sacrifice of Purusha by the Devas, called Sâdhyas, the formation of castes, the sky, earth, worlds, etc., from his body, in all which it would be as idle to endeavor to find a meaning, as it would be to dream of finding any in the hundreds of pages of dreary Kabbalistic jabbering to be found in the Kabbalah Denudata, and which are perhaps the most pitiable specimens extant of the idiotic babble of the human mind, emasculated by superstitious follies and enervating speculations upon mysteries beyond the reach of the finite human intellect. No doubt there was originally a meaning, and probably a very simple one, to the allegory of the sacrifice (*yajna*) of Purusha; but that meaning is irretrievably lost.

Dr. Muir says of this hymn, that it is

> an important, but in many places obscure hymn of the *Rig-Veda*, in which the unity of the Godhead is recognized, though in a pantheistic sense.

All metaphysical speculation ends either in pantheism or atheism. There has never yet been discovered any solid middle ground. But I do not find any pantheism or unity of the Godhead either, in the Purusha Sûkta. The Hindū commentator, Mahîdhara, says that the *Deity* celebrated in the hymn is Purusha, the source of the universe; and Professor Wuttke thinks that

> the production of the world is here represented by the immolation of *Brahma*, who is dismembered by the Gods, the great powers who first came into being, and solemnly cut up as a victim, and the world fashioned out of his limbs.

Dr. Muir considers Purusha as the Supreme Being, and as immolated by the agency of the Gods,

> this immolation giving birth, by its transcendent power, to the visible universe and all its inhabitants.

The sacrifice was made by the Sâdhyas, who are called Devas. *Sadh* means to "finish, accomplish," and *Sâdhya*, "accomplishment, perfection." The Sâdhyas were Rishis, translated to the sky as stars; and if the text is to be literally read, they, while men, made the sacrifice of Purusha.

Dr. Muir says that the hymn is unmistakably an allegory. That is certainly true; but it does not mean, for example, that the Sudra or servile caste came from the feet of Brahma, either literally or allegorically. Nor are the mere ravings of a diseased fancy, the dreams of a distempered imagination, monstrous, incoherent, incongruous fictions, fitly to be called "allegories." Philo finds allegories in the dryest recitals of fact in the Hebrew writings, and St. Paul finds one in the account of the ejection of Hagar and Ishmael from the home of Abraham. But most of the Brahmanic fables and vagaries are not allegories, and never had any real meaning. To attempt to decipher the meaning of one such measure of nonsense as this, out of a thousand, would be as idle as to kill a single fly in the summer, to diminish the pest of their presence in myriads.

The first five verses of the hymn, I think, are of the Vedic period. I think so from the nature of the conception which they embody, and because their original meaning had been entirely lost, and that of Purusha was wholly misunderstood, when the modern portion was added. The hymn, with unimportant variations, is found in three of the Vedic Sanhitâs, to-wit, in the *Rig-Veda*, the *Yajûr-Veda* and the *Atharva-Veda*.

I will first repeat the ancient part of the hymn, as translated by Dr. Muir.

> 1. Purusha has a thousand heads [or, a thousand arms: *Ath.-V.*], a thousand eyes, and a thousand feet. On every side enveloping the earth he transcended [it] by a space of ten fingers. [So, in Vol. *v.* in Vol. *i.*, "everywhere pervading the earth, he overpassed a space of ten fingers."] 2. Purusha himself [alone], is this whole (universe), whatever has been and whatever shall be. He is also the Lord of Immortality, since through food he expands. 3. Such is his greatness, and Purusha is superior to [greater than] this. All existing things are a quarter of him [all creatures make a fourth of him], and that which is immortal in the sky is three-quarters of him [three-fourths of him are immortality in the sky]. 4. With three-fourths, Purusha mounted upwards: a quarter of him again was produced here below. He then became diffused everywhere, among things animate and inanimate. 5. From him Viraj was born, and from Viraj, Purusha. As soon as born, he extended beyond the earth, both behind and before.

Then follows the account of the Devas offering up Purusha as a sacrifice (*yajna*). Of course you wonder that I should admit these verses contain any sense or meaning, and are ready to ask what *can* be meant by *Brahma* transcending the earth by ten fingers' space? and how he expands through food, and is *therefore* Lord of Immortality? and what Viraj was; and how, if Viraj was born of Brahma, Brahma, the Supreme Being could be born of Viraj? How the Devas, or the Ṛishis called Sâdhyas, could sacrifice and cut up the Supreme Being, and have the sky and earth made from him, is perhaps so easy to be believed, that you accept it as a fact.

Let us see if these verses *are* mere nonsense. Dr. Muir makes them say that Purusha is the whole universe. The phrase is *Purushaḥ evedaṁ sarvaṁ yad bhûtaṁ yach cha bhavyam*. *Sarva* means "every, whole, entire, all"; and *bhû*, to "become, live"; and I have no doubt that *Purusha* meant, "man, mankind, universal humanity," and that the sentence in question meant that he was the whole *race*, all the individuals of the race that had lived or were to live, those that had been and those that were to be born.

Benfey gives, as the first meaning of *Purusha*, "a man generally or individually, a male, mankind." Other and later meanings are "the first man, the soul, the universal soul, the Supreme Being." But the word itself is from *puru* (Zend, *pouru*), meaning "much, many," whence *purudhâ* means "manifold." *Purusha* was at last used as a name of the Supreme Being or Universal Soul, only because he was the soul of universal humanity.

Sa bhûmiñ viçvato vṛitva plainly enough means that mankind are spread over the whole surface of the earth, not that they envelop or pervade it. But what is meant by *aty atishṭhad daçângulam*, if it is correctly rendered by Dr. Muir "he transcended it by a space of ten fingers," defies conjecture. Does it mean that "the Supreme Being," envelops the earth, as the rind does an orange, and being, *as* its rind, of the thickness of ten fingers' breadth?

Sthâ, to "stand," with *adhi* prefixed, means, to "stand on, inhabit, and surpass"; but also to "command, govern and lead." *Ati* and *adhi* alike mean "over, on," etc.; and the meaning of *adhishṭhita* being "fixed, established, occupied," I take the phrase in question clearly to mean, that man, who has before been said to spread over the whole earth, subdues it and subjects it to his will, cultivates it, and makes it yield for him, by the labor of his two hands, or ten fingers. The meaning is so perfectly clear, that I do not see how it could have been overlooked, unless Dr. Muir was misled by his notion that the hymn "recognizes the unity of the Godhead, in a pantheistic sense." It recognizes the unity of mankind, or, rather, of the Aryan race.

And man is also *utâmṛitatvasyeçâno*, i. e., *ut+âmṛitat+vaça+yeçâno*, "able to secure for himself long life"; for *annenâtirohati; annena* meaning "food," and *ati*, "abundantly," and *rohati* being the third person singular, present of *ruh*, to "grow"; causative, *rohaya*, to "plant, sow." *Rohati* is in the *Parasmaipada*, and means, no doubt, "raises," "sows and reaps." At any rate, the meaning is that, or that abundant food is grown or produced.

As soon as he was born, it is said, he extended beyond the earth, both before and behind. But the original is *sa jato aty arichyata paçchâd bhûmim atho purah;* and *rich* means to "separate, divide," and *aty*, "over" as well as "beyond"; and *paçchâd* and *purah* mean "backward" and "forward" and "westward" and "eastward." The meaning simply is, that from the beginning, mankind had spread in all directions by emigration.

Virâj means "splendor, radiance, light." It is *vi+râj. Raj* means to "shine, beam, shining," and *virâj*, to "shine forth, beam, illuminate." Man, dead and burned, becomes light, in the sky; and that light becomes man again.

All existing *creatures*, it is said, are a fourth of him. *Bhutani* means "living beings, creatures," but also "the elements"; and five *bhutas* are enumerated, earth, fire, water, air and ether. *Bhû* means to "become, spring up, be, etc.," and "earth, land, ground." All things that are or become are *bhutani*, whether living creatures or not.

I think, therefore, that the meaning is that the elements constitute one-fourth of Purusha, man. Three-fourths of him are immortal in the sky, and with these three he ascended, while the other fourth was produced again, entered into new bodies here below, and thus he was diffused among things inanimate and living beings.

One-fourth of man is his body. The other three are his vitality, his soul and his spirit, the two latter the *Psuchē* and *Pneuma* of the Greeks. The Hebrew Kabbalists called these three parts of man *Nephesch*, *Ruach* and *Neschamah*, or, in Latin, *Psyche*, *Spiritus*, *Mens*.

And, also, in the Kabbalah, the first Originate or Emanant, from the Very Deity, and in which all the ten sephiroth or divine emanations are contained, is Adam Kadmon, the anterior or primal man. But to this, it seems, only the form of the human head was given. The emanations were developed into the whole human form.

There is part of a hymn addressed to Yama (*x*. 14), the verses of which are addressed at funerals at the present day, to the souls of the departed, while their bodies are being consumed on the funeral pyre. The first six verses invoke the favor and presence of Yama, and of the fathers, the Angirasas, Navagvas, Atharvans and Bhṛigus, offerers of Soma.

> Mâlalî [it is said in *v*. 3], magnified by the Kavyas, Yama by the Angirasas, and Bṛihaspati by the Rikvans—both those whom the Devas magnified [*Vavridhur*, "made powerful, or exalted"], and those who magnified the Devas—of these some are gladdened by *Svâhâ* [invocation or formula of words, upon offering the oblation], and others by *Svadhâ* [the food offered]. [And in *v*. 4, accordingly, it is said to Yama] Let the texts recited by the sages bring thee hither! Delight thyself, O King, with this oblation! [And in *v*. 13, it is said] Pour out the Soma to Yama, offer him an oblation! To Yama the sacrifice proceeds, etc. [In *v*. 12, the worshipper prays] May they give us again today the auspicious breath of life, that we may behold the sun.

Between verses six and twelve are those now addressed, and supposed always to have been addressed to the dead.

Now, if you have noticed the verses, it appears that when the first six were repeated, the sacrifice was being prepared for. "To Yama," it is said in verse 13, "the sacrifice proceeds, when heralded by Agni and prepared." The fire had to be procured, by attrition, and these preparations, it is clear, were being made before sunrise. And what is supposed to have been said to the dead, was said when the oblation was ready to be offered. It is this, as rendered by Dr. Muir:

7. Depart thou, depart [rather, go, go!], by the ancient paths, thither where our ancient fathers went. Thou shalt see the two rajahs, Yama and the Deva Varuṇa, exhilarated by the oblation.

8. Meet with the fathers, meet with Yama, meet with the sacrifices thou hast offered [or, rejoin thy sacrifices which were stored up. The word so rendered is a single one, *ishṭâpûrttena. Ishṭa* is "sacrifice": *âpûrtta*, "accomplished, perfected." Benfey gives the meaning of *ishṭâpûrta*, "sacrifices and pious works,"] in the highest sky. Throwing off all imperfection, again go to thy home. Because united to a body, and clothed in a shining form. [Müller reads this: "Leave evil there, then return home and take a form, etc." Roth reads, "Enter thy home, laying down again all imperfection, etc."]

9. Go! Depart! Hasten hence! The fathers have made for him this place.

Other verses follow, that seem more modern. Yama gives him an abode, it is said; and he is urged to hasten past the dogs of Yama, off-spring of Saramâ, and so draw near to the benevolent fathers who dwell in festivity with Yama. And Yama is asked to intrust him to his dogs, and bestow on him prosperity and health.

But the word rendered "him" in "the fathers have made for *him* this place" [*loka*, "earth or land"]. "Bestow on *him* prosperity and health," is *asmai*, the dative singular of *idam*, "this." We find in the plural of *aham*, "I," *asmân*, "us"; *asmabhih*, "by us"; *asmâbhyam*, "to us"; *asmat*, "from us"; *asmâsu*, "in us." And I find in Zend the equivalent pronoun, meaning "this, this one," often used to signify the person speaking. I think that *asmai* is so used here; and as the priest or bard commonly uses "I" and "me," when he speaks for all the worshippers or people (each, perhaps, of the assembly repeating the words for himself), I think that it means "us."

Prosperity and health were certainly not asked for the dead. The "abode given" is the Aryan land.

The dogs of Yama, it is said, wander among men. The phrase is *charato janân anu*, which rather means that they follow after men or beings. I think that Yama was the constellation afterward called Boötes (Βοώτης, the herdsman) by the Greeks. It is for the worshipper the protection of his dogs is asked.

Nothing is said of any corpse being at this morning-sacrifice. I do not think that the invocation was addressed to a dead person, and I think it only came in later years to be so used, because it was misunderstood. It was part of a sacrificial hymn, not of a funeral one.

It was, I think, an address to the oblation, made when that was being thrown into the fire: that it is the *svâhâ*, spoken of in verse 3.

Go [it is said to it], ascend by the old paths, to the place whereunto our fathers were translated. Consumed by the fire, and so becoming light, ascend to the sky and feed the Devas. Go to the presence of the two regal ones, Yama and Varuṇa, who are always exhilarated by the oblation (*svadhâ*). Meet the fathers and Yama, in the heights of the sky, and the offerings completed heretofore. Having been freed of all imperfection of gross matter, by means of the fire, return to thy original home, in the sky, where the light abides. There unite with a star and a shining form. The fathers made this land for us. Yama gave us a dwelling-place, distinguished by days, waters and nights: go swiftly by a path unimpeded, past the dogs of Yama, to the presence of the fathers, who, become stars, are Devas, and feast with Yama. Commit us, Yama, to the care of thy dogs, who guard the roads and watch for the coming of enemies; and bestow on us prosperity and health. The two tawny dogs move now in the sky among the stars. May they bring up for us the light, which is the life of men, and enable us to behold the sun.

And then it is said,

Pour the Soma on the fire, as an oblation to Yama. Let the sacrifice to him proceed. Offer him an oblation with butter, and do it quickly. May he grant us to live a long life among the Devas!

In the *Atharva-Veda xi.*, 1, 36, it is said,

With these good deeds may we follow the sacrifice, which abides in the heaven with seven rays: *nâke tishthantam adhi sapta raçmau.*

In the *Atharva-Veda vi.*, 122, 4,

With my soul I ascend after the great sacrifice as it goes, ... May we, Agni invited, enjoy a festival in the third heaven (*trittye nâke*) beyond decay.

I have omitted the words *tapasâ sayoniḥ*, which Dr. Muir renders, "dwelling together with my austere fervor," because I doubt whether *tapasâ* has not its original meaning of "fire." I think the phrase means, "united with my fire."

At any rate, these passages conclusively show that the oblations consumed in the fire were deemed to ascend as light to the third region of the expanse, that of the stars, and there replenish with light and invigorate the Devas; and that to be translated to the same region, and become stars, and as stars Devas, was the only life after this, and the only heaven and immortality known to the Indo-Aryans.

And also it shows, as the Purusha Sûkta does, that the bodies of the dead were burned, that all except the earthy portion might ascend as light to the stars, and be united there with Indra and the Devas; an object that would be entirely frustrated by burial in the earth.

There are two hymns in the tenth book of the *Rig-Veda* which, though of a comparatively late period, are yet valuable because they contain the earliest conceptions of the creation of things and of a creative Deity. Whether they embody convictions already familiar to many, or only the speculations of the poets who composed them, cannot be known. It may be that in the first the fertile imagination of the poet created a new Deity, as his name would seem to indicate. If that were so, and each hymn were but the expression of the thought and speculation of a single mind, it would be curious and interesting, but not especially noteworthy, in a consideration of the Aryan faith. In every age and among many peoples of the intellectual races, there have risen single men who, more greatly gifted than those around them, recipients of a larger share of the Divine Light which is the life of the souls of men, inspired by rays of the Divine Intellect abiding in them, have uttered sayings far beyond the comprehension of those who heard them and have seen and known more of the Divine Truth than their fellows. These men have been the true seers and prophets of the race, uttering, as if it were intuitively, truths only to be generally acknowledged in later ages.

But each of these later hymns was understood by those who heard it, was not spoken to them in an unknown tongue, was but a response to what was already in the popular mind, and is the expression of ideas and conceptions that must already have become to some extent familiar, at least to the sages and the bards of the Indo-Aryans.

Each marks, therefore, one step of the steady advance of the Indo-Aryan mind towards the light; one step of that intellectual process which from the conception of fire and light as universals evolved at last the conception of an infinite God, and of the creation of the universe by the exertion of his sovereign will and power.

Dr. Muir remarks (*v.* 352) that when once the notion of particular Gods, Varuṇa, Indra, Sûrya and others, had become expanded so as to invest them with the divine prerogatives of omnipresence and omniscience,

> and had risen to an ascription of all divine attributes to the particular object of worship who was present for the time to the mind of the poet, the further step would speedily be taken of speaking of the Deity under such new names as *Viçvakarman* and *Prajâpati,* appellations which do not designate any limited function connected with any single department of Nature, but the more general and abstract notion of divine power operating in the production and government of the universe.

Prajâpati, "Lord of Creatures," is an epithet applied to Soma in *Rig-Veda ix.*, 5, 9, and to Savitṛi in *iv.*, 53, 2. Viçvakarman, "the Universal Architect," literally "all-doer," or "all-action or operation," is an epithet of Indra, in *viii.*, 87, 2, and of Sûrya, in *x.*, 170, 4. In *x.*, 81, 4, he is said to have produced the earth and spread out the sky, and to be all-seeing, having on every side, eyes, faces, arms and feet, and to blow with his arms and wings, when producing the sky and earth.

Hymn *x.*, 121, recites the creation of all things by Hiraṇyagarbha, who is also styled Prajâpati. The hymn, as translated by Dr. Muir, reads thus:

> 1. Hiraṇyagarbha arose in the beginning. Born, he was the one lord of things existing. He established the earth [*Pṛithivi*, expanse], and this sky; to what God shall we offer our oblation? 2. He who gives breath, who gives strength, whose command all the Devas reverence, whose shadow is immortality, whose shadow is death; to what Deva shall we offer our oblation? 3. Who by his might became the sole Râja of the breathing and winking world.

"Breathing and winking world"; *prâṇato nimishato jagato*. *Prâna* is "air, wind, breath, life"; and meaning to "breathe, blow, live," whence "ανεμος, "wind"; *animus*, "breath." *Prâṇin*, "life"; *prâṇavant*, "endowed with life." *Nimish, nimisha*, "twinkling of the eye." *Nimesha*, the same. Whence, derivatively, a Deva, i. e., a star.

Jagat, an old participle of the present of *gam*, to "move, go," and meaning "movable," and thence, "race of men, world." *Tri-jagati*, "the three regions." The whole phrase means "the living and twinkling that revolve."

> Who is the lord of this two-footed and four-footed (creation), [of human beings and the animals]: to what Deva shall we offer our oblation? 4. Whose greatness these snowy mountains and the sea with the *Rasa* [river, *samudram rasaya*, "ocean with its waters"] declares; of whom these regions [*pradiço*, intermediate points of the compass, half-quarters], of whom they are the arms, to what Deva shall we offer our oblation? 5. By whom the sky is fiery and the earth (*Pṛithivi*) fixed; by whom the firmament and the heaven were established, who in the atmosphere is the measurer of the aërial space; to what Deva shall we offer our oblation?

We have in this verse, *dyaur*, rendered by sky, *pṛithivi*, earth; *svaḥ*, firmament; *nâka*, heaven; *antarikshe*, atmosphere; *rajaso*, aërial space.

> 6. To whom two contending armies (*krandasî*) sustained by his succor, looked up trembling in mind; over whom the risen sun shines, to what Deva shall we offer our oblation? 7. When the great waters pervaded the universe, containing an embryo, and generating fire, thence arose the one spirit (*asu*, "radiance, splendor") of the Devas; to what Deva shall we offer our oblation? 8. He who through his greatness beheld the waters which contained power and generated sacrifice, who was the one Deva above the Devas: to what Deva shall we offer our oblation? 9. May he not harm us, he who is the generator of the earth (*Pṛithivi*), who ruling by fixed ordinances produced the sky; who produced the great and brilliant waters; to what God shall we offer our oblation? 10. Prajâpati, no other than thou is lord over all these created things: may we obtain that through desire of which we have invoked thee: may we become possessors of riches!

The hymn *x.*, 82, is:

> 1. The father of insight, wise in mind, impregnated with sap these two [worlds], as they bowed down [before him]. When their remotest ends were fixed, then the

sky and expanse were stretched out. 2. Viçvakarman is wise, energetic, the creator, the disposer, and the highest object of intuition. The objects of their desire inspire them with gladness, in the place where men say that the one dwells beyond the seven Rishis. 3. He who is our father, our creator and disposer, who knows all spheres and creatures, who alone assigns to the Devas their names, to him the other creatures resort for instruction. 4. The former Rishis, who fashioned these creatures in the remote, the near and the lower atmosphere [who *became* them, were *invested* with their *forms*], offered to him, like [as, while they were] worshippers, wealth in abundance. 5. That which is beyond the sky, beyond the expanse, beyond the stars and planets [or "the shining Devas," *paro Devebhir asurair*]—what earliest embryo did the waters contain, in which all the Devas were beheld? 6. The waters contained that earliest embryo in which all the Devas were included. One rested on the navel of the unborn, wherein all beings subsisted. 7. Ye cannot know him who produced these things: something else is within you. The chanters of hymns go about enveloped in mist, and unsatisfied with idle talk.

In this hymn as in that to Hiraṇyagarbha, I have ventured to suggest here and there an emendation of the translation. I am satisfied that the translations do not accurately reproduce the sense of either. But they enable us to see that the idea of a First Cause, great and intelligent, was beginning to assume definite shape in the Indo-Aryan mind. But as yet, all was matter of speculation and uncertainty, as the closing verse of the last hymn shows. So, in hymn 81, it is asked,

> what was the wood, what was the tree, out of which they fashioned the sky and expanse?

As translated, this is mere nonsense. The allusion must be to the production of fire by attrition, from the wood; and the meaning be, how the primitive light and fire of the sky and expanse were produced? It is added,

> Inquire mentally, ye sages, what that was on which he took his stand, when establishing *bhuvanani*, [the creatures, i. e., "the heavenly bodies"].

This "support" or "basis" is called in the *Atharva-Veda* "*Skambha*, on whom Prajâpati has supported and established all the worlds." And then it is said that Skambha established both these, the expanse and sky, etc., and pervaded (or was co-extensive with) the entire universe. The earth and sky stand, supported by Skambha. He is all this that has vitality, that lives and twinkles. Whatever moves, flies or stands, whatever exists breathing or not breathing, or twinkling, that sustains the expanse, containing all forms, that combined is one only. Thus Skambha seems to be the material universe, which a divine soul, fashioning it into forms, animates.

Hymn x., 129 of the *Rig-Veda* contains the most definite of these speculations, and reminds us of the Hebrew Genesis.

1. There was then neither non-being nor being; the sky (*rajo*) was not, nor the upper æther (*no uyoma paro yat*). What enveloped [all]? Where, in the delight of what? Was it water? the deep abyss?   2.   Death was not then, nor undyingness; there was no distinction of day or night: that, being One, breathed calmly, in self-dependence: there was nothing distinct from it or above it.   3.   Darkness was.   Originally wrapped in darkness, this all was undistinguishable water: that One which lay void, and wrapped in its envelope (of darkness), was developed by the power of warmth.   Desire first arose in it, which was the primal germ of mind: the wise, seeking by their intellect have discovered in their heart that to be the tie between non-being and being.   5.   The ray which stretched across these, was it above or was it below? there were impregnating energies and mighty powers, a self-supporting principle beneath, and energy above.   6.   Who knows, who here can declare, whence sprang, whence, this creation?   The Devas are subsequent to the development of this; who then knows from what it arose?   7.   From what source this creation arose, and whether it was created or is uncreated; He who in the highest sky is its ruler (*yo asyâdhyakshaḥ parame vyoman*), He knows, or He does not know.

Asya means "its, his."   *Adhyaksha* is said by Benfey to mean "perceptible, perception, or superintendent."   Its more literal meaning would be "overseer."   For it is compounded of *adhi*, "above, on high, over, on"; and *aksha*, "an eye."   *Aksh* means to "pervade."   "Its overlooker in the upper sky" was probably the sun.

The Semitic idea of the beginning of creation is the same.

The earth [it is said] was formless and confusion [*taho u baho*, shapeless and chaotic. The second word being composed of *bo*, "in it," and *hua*, "it is," it signifies, the rabbis say, that the germ of future development was contained in the shapeless matter]. Darkness covered the surface of this inane abyss, and the divine energy brooded (incubated) on the face of the waters.

It need only be added that *Prajâpati*, as an epithet, meant lord or master of creatures; but afterward, as a personification, that unity of which all creatures are the manifold: and *Hiraṇyagarbha* was the generative divine energy, in which that unity was contained.

There are in the tenth book of the *Rig-Veda* two hymns in praise of generosity, which for their quaintness, and as illustrative of ancient thought and manners deserve to be remembered.   One is 117, and it celebrates liberality to the destitute in general, in these words, as translated by Dr. Muir.

1. The Devas have not ordained hunger to be our destruction.   Even those who are abundantly fed are overtaken by various deaths.   The prosperity of the liberal man never decays; while the illiberal finds no comforter.   2.   He who, himself well provided with sustenance, hardens his heart against the poor man who

comes to him starving, and who has long courted him, desirous of food, such a man meets with none to cheer him.   3.   He is the bountiful man who gives to the lean beggar who comes to him craving food. Success attends that man in the sacrifice, and he secures for himself a friend for the future.   4.   He is no friend who bestows nothing on his friend who waits upon him, seeking for sustenance. Let every one depart from such a man; his house is no home; and look out for some one who is liberal, even though he be a stranger.   5.   Let the powerful man be generous to the suppliant; let him look down the long path. For, Oh! riches revolve like the wheels of a chariot: they come, now to one, now to another.   6.   In vain the fool obtains food: I tell the truth, it becomes his destruction. He nourishes neither his friend nor his companion. *He who keeps his food to himself, has his sin to himself.* 7.   The plowshare, furrowing the ground, brings man plenty. A man moving onward with his feet accomplishes his journey. A priest who speaks is more accept-able than one who is silent. A kinsman who is beneficent excels one who is stingy. 8.   A one-footed being advances faster than a two-footed. The two-footed comes after the three-footed. The four-footed follows in the rear of the two-footed, and moves on observing his steps.   9.   The two hands, though alike, do not perform an equal amount of work. Two cows with the same mother do not yield the same quantity of milk. Two men, though twins, have not the same strength. And two others, though kinsmen, are not equally liberal.

The other poem, 107, eulogizes liberality in giving presents to the priests.

1.   The great liberality of these men has been manifested. The whole living has been liberated from darkness. The great light given by the fathers has arrived. The broad path of benefaction has been beheld.   2.   The givers of donations dwell on high in the sky; the bestowers of horses live with the sun; the givers of gold attain immortality; the bestowers of raiment prolong their lives.   3.   A donation grati-fies the Devas, an offering to the Devas, and not from the illiberal; they bestow nothing; and many men who bestow donations are bountiful merely through fear of reproach. . . . .   5.   The giver of gifts, invited, advances first: he walks in the front as leader. I regard as the king of men, him who first presented a gift. 6.   They call him a Ṛishi, a priest, a reverend chanter of hymns and reciter of verses—he knows the three forms of the resplendent (Agni)—the man who was the first to propitiate with a gift.   7.   Bounty bestows a cow, a horse, and gleaming gold. Bounty bestows food, which is our life. The wise man makes largess-giving his breast-plate.   8.   Bountiful men neither die nor fall into calamity: they suffer neither wrong nor pain. Their liberality confers on them all this world as well as heaven.   9.   The bountiful conquer for themselves first, a pleasant abode, a well-dressed wife, and a draught of wine; they conquer those who walk before them, uninvited.   10.   A fleet horse is trained for the generous man; he obtains a brilliant damsel for his portion; this house of his resembles a lotus-pond, beautiful, embellished like the palaces of the Devas.   11.   The liberal man is borne along by rapid horses. The car of bounty [i. e., of the bountiful] rolls forward on easy wheels. Preserve, ye Devas, the bountiful man in battles.

Undoubtedly the fairer portion of my audience have already in their hearts commended the good sense and taste of this ancient poet, in giving as a reward for generosity, a well-dressed wife. Where men had a pride in seeing their wives well-dressed, there could not have existed that evidence

of barbarism, a menial condition of woman. Undoubtedly the expression
proves the poet's good sense and taste, because it is not true, nor ever was,
nor ever will be, either in man's or woman's estimation, that "Beauty,
when unadorned, is adorned the most." To dress well is one of the chief
triumphs of civilization: to dress in bad taste shows an intermixture of the
savage; and the barbarian taste for gaudy and showy finery, the instincts of
a South Sea Islander.

Where the husband prided himself upon his wife being well-dressed,
he must have desired that she should be seen so and admired. There must
have been at hand and procurable, the means of being so; rich stuffs in
shops well filled, and skilful fabricators of female gear; and there must have
been shopping, with all its excitements and charm. There must have been
fashions, too, perhaps as despotic, it is to be hoped not as capricious and
sometimes as barbaric, as now.

Here we may fitly end these outlines of the Vedic Deities. You will
not think the time wasted, I hope, that you have passed in the company
of the ancient ages, heretofore called pre-historic, in reading the ancient
records of our own race, surrounded by the shadowy forms of the grave
and majestic Deities whom they adored, and endeavoring to understand,
though but imperfectly, the old Aryan thought and its conceptions of the
great and mysterious potencies of Nature.

Without this chapter of the history of human thought, a chapter that
has been most grievously misread, and made so little and so paltry in comparison with its true and real greatness, and without that other and even
less understood and more wonderful chapter consisting of the compositions
of Zarathustra, that history is singularly incomplete. Every Sanskrit and
Zend scholar admits that the work of translating truly these ancient monuments of Aryan intellect and thought is hardly more than begun; that
even for etymology and comparative philology a great task yet remains to
be done, while philosophy has hardly as yet even undertaken its mission.

If I should be found to be wholly in error, my errors may at least serve
to indicate to more competent enquirers the way that leads to the truth.
I know that I have not seldom read imperfectly and erroneously these
ancient, obscure and enigmatical utterances; for I have not that thorough
scholarship that entitles me to speak *ex cathedrâ* as to the true meanings
of doubtful words, or can enable me to walk with entire confidence among
these mutilated fragments, so long beaten upon by the storms of Time and
subjected to the irresistible influences of decay and innovation.

I have, at least, all the time endeavored to keep in mind that the men
whose thoughts in the *Veda* and *Zend-Avesta* I have endeavored partially

to understand and interpret, were my own ancestors or of the same blood
as they, with intellects of like nature as my own; and who thought and sung
as Wordsworth and Shelley would have done, if they had been of that age.
To understand them even in part, it is necessary to identify ourselves as
perfectly as possible with them, to imagine ourselves, with as little knowledge
of the mysterious workings of Nature as they had, living when and where
they did, subject to the same influences, encompassed by the same surroundings, unacquainted with the causes, even proximate, of the phenomena of
the universe, having their intellectual wants and aspirations, their active
fancy and exuberant imagination, with no restraints such as modern good
taste or prim propriety of taste and artificial canons of refinement impose,
and with that ungovernable passion for personification which filled the
temples of Athens with statues of the male and female Gods, and peopled
the poetry of every subdivision of the race with a thousand graceful and
beautiful beings, creatures of the imagination and of a passionate adoration of the grand and of the beautiful, making the Seasons, the Years, the
Potencies of Nature, the Virtues and the Vices, Fortune with her blinded
eyes, Hope leaning on her anchor, and Faith and Charity and Love, and
even Death with his relentless scythe, persons and beings like ourselves.

When I have read the Vedic personifications, and seen the manifestations of the light invested with golden ornaments; and lakes and rivers
taking the forms of lovely maidens, clothed in radiant garments, and Indra
armed with the thunderbolt shattering the rock-built cities of the Dasyu,
I have remembered, for every bold personification and extravagant figure,
its counterpart in the writings of our own poets; for our poetry, like our
philosophy and our religious faith, is purely Aryan.   Did not Shelley sing,

> And others came—Desires and Adorations,
> Winged Persuasions and veiled Destinies,
> Splendors and Glooms and glimmering Incarnations
> Of hopes and fears, and twilight Phantasies;
> And Sorrow, with her family of Sighs,
> And Pleasure, blind with tears, led by the gleam
> Of her own dying smile, instead of eyes,
> Came in slow pomp—?
> . . . . Morning sought
> Her eastern watch-tower, and, her hair unbound,
> Wet with the tears that should adorn the ground,
> Dimmed the aërial eyes that kindle day;
> Afar the melancholy Thunder moaned,
> Pale Ocean in unquiet slumber lay,
> And the wild winds flew round, sobbing in their dismay?
> Lost Echo sits amid the voiceless mountains,
> And feeds her grief with his remembered lay?
> Grief made the young Spring wild, and she threw down

Her kindling buds, as if she Autumn were?
Death rose and smiled, and met her vain caress?
The golden day, which on eternal wings,
Even as a ghost abandoning a bier,
Has left the earth a corpse?

And did he not say of Night,

Wrap thy form in a mantle grey,
                          Star-inwrought!
Blind with thine hair the eyes of day,
Kiss her until she be wearied out,
Then wander o'er city, and sea and land,
Touching all with thine opiate wand.

And Wordsworth, most thoroughly Aryan of all our poets, overflows with
the Vedic personifications. Professor Müller is fond of his verse; and so
must every lover of the *Veda* be. Hear, for example, these fragments,
torn by me from their context, two or three among thousands like them.

With how sad steps, O Moon, thou climb'st the sky,
How silently, and with how wan a face!
. . . . this nipping air,
Sent from some distant clime, where Winter wields
His icy scimitar . . . . and bids the flowers beware,
And whispers to the silent birds, Prepare
Against your threatening foe your trustiest shields.

Nor must we only make ourselves to be, for the time, what our ancestors
were intellectually; but we must live their life, be with them herding their
cattle on the steppes, sacrificing at early dawn in the open air, cultivating
their fields, and subjugating the native tribes. We must be with them in
their own land also, the land of clear and brilliant skies, of mountains
unequalled in the world for the multitude and magnificence of their snowy
summits, and of crystal rivers, rushing from an immense height with terrible
power and rapidity, over precipices and through great gloomy gorges to
issue exulting and glorying in their power into the plains below, and forming
there the lovely alluvial valleys, which their waters annually made productive of all whereof the generous earth is fruitful for man in the most
favored climes.

What is of incalculable value to us, as a part of the Aryan race, in these
old poems, is this: that if the ontological conceptions which seem unquestionably to be contained in the *Veda* and *Zend-Avesta*, are really there, the
forefathers of our race were endowed by God with the intellect that was
sufficient unto itself to attain unto them without the aid of any special
revelation; and we are not indebted for them to any other race. And all
these ideas and conceptions were already mature, and understood by all

the people, familiar guests of every household, when the earliest Vedic poems were composed. "This is our prayer," the poet says, "the old, the prayer of our fathers." "Our fathers appealed to Indra, of old; they discovered the hidden light, and caused the dawn to rise; they who showed us the road, the earliest guides." "Now, as of old, make forward paths for the new hymn springing from our hearts."

For all our conceptions of God as a Universal Substance, a Supreme Unity, infinitely extended, and containing in itself all manifoldness, "as the sea its waves"; as the one essential light that is the life of the Universe; the one intellect, that is revealed and manifested in all intellects, angelic and human, as it is manifested as light, wherever light is; of a Deity who is a friend, a father, beneficent, indulgent, a protector and not merciless, forgiving and not cruel and vindictive—for our conceptions of the creative wisdom and of its utterance, the Word, that is the Deity's Very Self manifested; of Spirit, of the immaterial and undying soul of man, the Divine that comes from the great Source and Infinite Intellect, to inhabit for a limited time the body, and then to continue to exist, without loss of its identity or individuality; for all our philosophic ideas as to substance and its subsistences, persons or hypostases, and all of truth that there is at bottom in the emanation theory of the Hebrew Kabbalah and the speculations of the Gnostics—we must go back to the poets who chanted their devotional songs in the hearing of the herdsmen, when the morning-dew lay on the grass, and the sacrifice was solemnized with the stars for witnesses, to the blushing Dawn, to Mitra and the regal Varuṇa, to Indra or to Agni, their intelligent and beneficent Gods.

For all these are either their conceptions, or have grown out of theirs. This you will better know, and be more surely convinced of, when you are made acquainted with the real meaning of the compositions of Zarathustra and the Ahurian faith; without which even the most thorough examination and analysis of the *Veda* would be incomplete.

LECTURE SIX

THE ZEND-AVESTA—THE GÂTHÂS—THE DOCTRINE OF ZARATHUSTRA

I propose, in this and two other lectures, to make you in some degree acquainted with the doctrines of Zarathustra, and the history and legends of the Iranian branch (more familiarly known to you as the Medes and Persians) of the great Aryan race, as these are contained in the *Zend-Avesta* or Holy Scriptures of the Parsees. We shall find these writings even more interesting than the Vedic hymns, and that, while of greater antiquity, they contain the development of the Vedic faith, intermediate between it and our own philosophy and religion; and that all the ideas that have come to us from the Hebrews and the School of Alexandria, they learned from the teachings of the *Zend-Avesta*.

Few names of antiquity are oftener mentioned than that of Zoroaster, whose true name was *Zarathustra:* few ancient orders of priests than the *Magi*, who taught at Babylon the corrupted faith of *Zarathustra*. Every man of moderate acquaintance with the ancient religions has read of *Ormuzd* and *Ahriman*, or *Oromazdes* and *Arimanius* (names that he will hardly recognize in *Ahura Mazda* and *Aṅra-Mainyus*), principles of good and evil, light and darkness; of the creative Word *Honover* (which was not a *word* at all but a *prayer* of three lines, called *Ahuna-Vairya*); of the *Amshaspands*, *Devs*, *Izeds* and *Ferouers* (who were really called *Amĕsha-Çpĕntas*, *Daevas*, *Yazatas* and *Fravashis*); of *Zeruone Akhĕrēnē*, the primal time, of *Mithra* the Sun-God, and of *Sosiōsh*, the savior to come (who was really *Çaoshyanç*, a heroic chieftain that fought against the infidel Scyths and Tâtars).

The ancient Persians were conquered by, and received their religion from, the Medes, who were Aryan emigrants from Bactria. They called themselves, as the Indo-Aryans called themselves, simply "Arya": but as Iran, from *Airyana-Vaêja*, the name of the original country of both, came to be applied especially to Persia, I call the Bactro-Median branch of the race, *Irano-Aryans*.

We have an account of the faith and tenets of the Persians in the History of Herodotus, and other accounts, more or less brief, given by other Greeks, and by Armenian and Mohammedan writers. But even the first of these is comparatively modern, written when the religion had greatly changed; and we can ascertain the original tenets of the faith of the Irano-Aryans only from the *Zend-Avesta* itself, where it is called "the Mazdayaçnian

Law," and "the Ahurian Custom," and "Question"; and even from the oldest portions of that Parsee collection, alone.

Baron Bunsen decides that the Zend is the old Bactrian language. The only remnants of it are in the *Zend-Avesta*, where there are two dialects of it. This language was for many centuries the spoken and written language of Bactria, and was dying out in the third century before Christ. It is a pure Aryan dialect, the eldest sister of even the Vedic Sanskrit.

The ancient Persian language was developed from the Zend or Bactrian, and was spoken in Media and Persia and at Babylon. A few documents of it are still extant, in the cuneiform inscriptions of the Persian kings of the Achæmenian Dynasty (Darius and others), in the ruins of Persepolis, on the Rock of Behistun, near Hamadan, and at some other places of Persia. It is the mother of the modern Persian, but between the two there are great differences, and to read and understand the language of the inscriptions, Zend and Sanskrit have proved to be of greater assistance than the modern Persian.

The Pehlevi is the language of the Bundehesh and other Persian books, and, with variations, of many coins and inscriptions. It was that form of the Persian tongue that was current in Persia during the Sassanian rule (235 to 640 A.D.); and is a mixture of Iranian and Semitic elements, the latter identical with the Chaldee. The non-Iranian element is called by the Parsee priests *Huzvaresh*. The chief parts of the *Zend-Avesta* were translated into the Pehlevi, which ceased to be a living language, about 700 A.D., when the rule of a foreign dynasty had ended, under which the pure Iranian words were restored to the language, and the foreign words extirpated. The restored language was called Pazend, and was used from 700 to 1100 A.D., when the modern Persian took its place, composed of it and a vast number of Arabic words.

The Sanskrit is written as we write, from left to right. But Semitic influence caused the Zend to be written from right to left, like the Hebrew, Chaldee and Phœnician dialects.

The different portions of the *Zend-Avesta* are the five Gâthâs of Zara-thustra, ordinarily called *hymns*, and of different lengths; the *Yaçnas*, or devotional pieces, the *Vendidad*, the *Yashts* and smaller pieces and fragments, and the *Vispered*. I name these in what seems the order of their age; but they are not so arranged in the English translation of Bleeck, the only one we have. The Gâthâs are very much the oldest; but in that translation they are in the middle of the book, and counted as parts of the *Yaçna*, a collection of devotional effusions used at the sacrifices, which is not at all the character of the Gâthâs. The *Vendidad* (*vî-daêvo-datem*, "what is given against Daevas"), in twenty-two *Fargards*, or chapters, comes first in the translation by Bleeck: then the *Vispered*, a collection of modern prayers, in twenty-seven chapters: the *Yaçna*, seventy-five parts; and the *Khordah-Avesta*, containing, among other pieces, twenty *Yeshts* (*Yesti*, "worship"), addressed to and lauding various Deities, and containing various legends.

Parts of the *Vendidad* are much older than other parts of it; and the *Yaçna Haptanhaiti* is very much older than other parts of the *Yaçna;* the *Çrosh Yesht* does not belong in the *Yaçna*, and there are fragments of old lyrical compositions here and there in the younger Yaçna, some of them in the Gâthâ dialect, and of the age of Zarathustra.

The Gâthâs have been unintelligible to the Parsee priests for several thousand years. They were metrical pieces, odes, that were sung; patriotic effusions, intended to arouse and unite the Aryan population against the infidels, Drukhs or Toorkhs from the north, who had invaded and conquered part of the country, and marauded in that still held by the Aryans, and against the indigenous tribes, Turanians, Çaimirians and others, who had, at least in part, been conquered by the Aryans, and had revolted and joined the invaders. By means of these odes and otherwise, Zarathustra succeeded in inspiring with courage and the fervor of religious zeal the lukewarm and disheartened of the oppressed Aryans, was himself a brave soldier and skilful leader, and not a priest, and finally achieving complete victory, became the king both of the mother-country and its colonies.

I agree with Dr. Haug that he composed the Gâthâs. The reasons for this belief, which he gives, and the intrinsic evidence which the odes afford, are conclusive. In the very earliest of the other books, these Gâthâs are spoken of as sacred and adorable. The Yaçna Haptanhaiti, which Spiegel places among the Gâthâs, as the third, is in the Gâthâ dialect, and is treated as sacred in the later books, but is not, in them, counted among the Gâthâs. Dr. Haug thinks it the work of the immediate successors of Zarathustra.

The meters used in the Gâthâs are of the same nature as those used in the Vedic hymns. There are no rhymes, and the syllables are merely counted, without much attention being paid to their quantity; and a different meter is used in each of the five Gâthâs. In the first Gâthâ, each verse consists of three lines, each line comprising sixteen syllables; in the second, there are five lines in each stanza, each of eleven syllables; in the third, four, each of eleven; in the fourth, six, each of seven; and in the fifth there are various meters.

The language is improperly called *Zend.* The *Avesta* is the original text; *Zend*, a translation or commentary. In the Pehlevi translation, the whole scripture is called "*Avesta-Zend.*" Perhaps the most proper name of the language is Bactrian. For the Gâthâs were certainly first recited in Bactria, not very long after the Irano-Aryans crossed the Oxus and settled there, and when Bactria was the mother-country, and it and its colonies were under one government. I think there is ample and conclusive evidence of this in the writings themselves, in the old odes and later legends. Media had not then been reached by any stream of Aryan emigration; and consequently it was long before the Medo-Aryan race was in existence, and longer still before that race conquered Persia and afterwards Assyria.

It need not be deemed impossible that these old songs should have been preserved in the memories of men, and handed down unimpaired for the most part, from generation to generation. Thousands of Brahmins are now living, who are able to recite, with the greatest accuracy, even as to accents, the whole of one of the *Vedas*. To retain in memory the five Gâthâs was little in comparison with this. As long as the language was a living one and perfectly intelligible, there was no need of committing them to writing, and before writing was invented, such compositions were sure to be carefully preserved in the memory. We positively know that the Vedic hymns *were* thus preserved for at least a thousand years: and if they or the Gâthâs could be preserved during that time, it was equally possible so to preserve them during five thousand years.

The written text of the *Zend-Avesta* is to be referred to the reign of Ardeshir Babegan, who, originally a Persian officer of royal descent, and serving in the armies of Artaban the Parthian, revolted and liberated his country, re-establishing the ancient empire, about 226 A.D. To restore the ancient religion, he caused the Sacred Writings to be collected by the Mobeds. The language of the Avesta had ages before then ceased to be spoken. The Mobeds faithfully compiled all that remained of the ancient works, adding only here and there a word or two or a clause, where the original text was imperfect. Even these additions betray a want of real knowledge of the meaning.

We may therefore consider it certain that the text of the Avesta which we now possess, is such as had been preserved by tradition, from a very remote period, and although it has many imperfections, it is certainly genuine.

A colony of Fire-worshippers had fled from Persia to Bombay in India, in the tenth century. In Persia the Guebres have almost ceased to exist, for every Semitic faith is by its nature a persecutor, and exterminates when it cannot convert. We owe to *these* faiths that side of Christianity; to the Aryan religions, toleration. The consequence is that there are no settlements of Guebres now in Persia, except a few in Yezd and in parts of Kerman; and these are utterly ignorant of the old books, which were preserved at Bombay. It was chiefly through the Sanskrit, and with the help of comparative philology, that the ancient dialect of the Parsis or Fire-worshippers was deciphered.

King Ardeshir brought together, it is said, forty thousand Mobeds, from whose memory and recitation of the Scriptures, so much as was not forgotten, was collected and committed to writing. This is, in the main, no doubt, authentic. The condition of the collection indicates such a process. The books are incomplete and fragmentary, there are frequent want of connection, and interpolations, much of the text is hopelessly corrupt, the style awkward, and wholly ungrammatical in many portions—all showing the whole to be a collection of fragments.

The Zend alphabet is of Semitic origin, akin to the Syriac alphabets of the beginning of our era, and closely resembling that used in the inscriptions and upon the coins of the earliest Sassanides. The oldest existing manuscripts date from the early part of the fourteenth century, and most of them are even more modern. They all have substantially the same text, with only such disagreements as are due to the ignorance and carelessness of the copyists. They all represent a single original.

Little was known of the languages of Persia and Media, previous to the Shahnameh of Firdusi, composed about 1000 A.D. Here, comparative philology has had to create and re-animate all the materials of language, in which it was afterwards to work. It is due entirely to the inductive method of comparative philology that we now have contemporaneous documents of three periods of Persian language, deciphered, translated and explained, all now rendered intelligible; while, only fifty years ago, their very name and existence were questioned. After the Parsees emigrated to India, in the seventh and eighth centuries, Mr. Bleeck says, their ancient language remained in obscurity for upwards of a thousand years, and had become almost extinct.

Rather more than a century and a quarter ago, Anquetil du Perron, a young Frenchman, happened to see a few pages in the Zend character, copied from a manuscript of the Vendidad Sadê in the Bodleian Library, procured at Surat in 1718. He immediately conceived the idea of going to India, in search of the original Zend writings, enlisted as a soldier, to get there, was by the efforts of his friends released, and sent out with a pension from the king. He succeeded: procured copies of the Avesta and other works, made translations with the help of a Parsee, and returning, published them. His Parsee teacher had no grammatical knowledge of the Zend, and he and Anquetil conversed together through the medium of Persian. The case resembled that "of a man attempting to teach a language which he does not himself understand, by means of one which his pupil understands but indifferently."

He returned to Europe in 1762, his book was published in 1771, and a German translation of it in 1781. For many years afterward, the study of Zend made scarcely any progress. Erskine and other scholars regarded it as merely a corruption of Sanskrit, and this opinion was pretty generally received, until the Danish Professor Rask completely overturned it, and proved that Zend, though allied to Sanskrit, was a distinct language, and that modern Persian was derived from it, as Italian is from Latin.

But Eugene Burnouf was the real founder of Zend philology. He compared Anquetil's translation with the Sanskrit version of Neriosengh, and carefully analyzed every word of the original Zend. His labors continued from 1829 to 1852, other scholars meanwhile applying themselves to the study of the Zend. The discovery that it was one of the languages of the cuneiform inscriptions gave new importance to the language of the Avesta. Sir Henry Rawlinson translated a large portion of those inscriptions by means of it, and Zend philology made rapid progress. In 1852–1854, Professor Westergaard of Copenhagen published a complete edition of the Avesta and *Khordah-Avesta*, in Zend characters. Professor Haug published in 1862, *Essays on the Language, Writings and Religion of the Parsees*, at Bombay; and in 1852, Professor Spiegel published a German version of the Avesta, followed in 1859 by a version of the Vispered and Yaçna, and in 1863 by one of the *Khordah-Avesta*. An English translation of all these German ones of Spiegel by Dr. Bleeck, was printed in English, in England in 1864.

And it is a very striking fact, that, as Dr. Muir has written and published his five volumes of *Original Sanskrit Texts* to enable the Brahmans to understand the sacred writings of their own religion, so Dr. Bleeck's translation of the *Zend-Avesta* was made for a Parsee gentleman of Bombay, at whose expense it was printed, he permitting a few copies to be printed for sale in England.

Rask proved that the Avesta must have been reduced to writing at least previous to the Conquest of Persia by Alexander.

Professor Bopp's *Comparative Grammar*, a work of inestimable value, and the works of Burnouf, make it clear that Zend, in its grammar and dictionary, is nearer to the Sanskrit than any other Aryan language. Many Zend words can be re-translated into Sanskrit by merely changing the Zend letters into their corresponding forms in Sanskrit. Some particular letters in Sanskrit are uniformly other particular letters in Zend. *S* becomes *h*, and *v* becomes *p*, and sometimes *s* becomes *nh*. The Sanskrit *h* is never *h* in Zend.

The Sanskrit word for "thousand" is *sahasra*. It is not found in any Indo-European dialect; but it is *hazanra* in Zend. The German and Sclavonic have a word for "thousand," peculiar to themselves; and in Greek and Latin are many common words, not to be found elsewhere. These facts are full of historical meaning, and prove, in regard to Zend and Sanskrit, that these two languages continued together, long after the separation of the Indo-European tongues from the parent stock. We shall also find identities between them in mythology, but not all that have been imagined by the commentators, and yet others which they have not discovered. The Celtic, Sclavonic, Gothic, Germanic, Greek and Latin outflowings from the great source of Aryan life, took place before the worship of Agni and Indra had succeeded that of the heavenly bodies; and in each of the races that so flowed off and colonized and conquered, the original rude faith and Nature-worship were developed with different results; each, perhaps, even adopting in part the names given by the peoples whom they conquered and incorporated with themselves, to the sun, planets, stars, and other natural objects. The *Aser*, or Gods, of the Scandinavians, inhabiting *Asgard*, the starry sky, are identical with the *Asuras* (shining ones) of the *Veda:* but none of the individual Deities of the *Veda* appear by the same names in the *Eddas*. Each mythology, it is evident, grew up independently, after the separation; and although some of the Grecian Deities may be traced to the *Veda*, and many of the Grecian myths are founded upon expressions contained in it, the names of the Deities are almost entirely different.

There is no evidence in the *Zend-Avesta* of any schism, or hostility between the Irano- and Indo-Aryans, causing their separation. I think it will appear that while the Indo-Aryan mind, perhaps in the mother-country, before the emigration into Kabul and the Indus country, across the Hindu Kush, was slowly attaining to conceptions of a higher nature than those of the Star-worship, and the philosophical doctrines of the Agni- and Indra-worship were developing themselves, Zarathustra, or some one before him, after the separation, and in Bactria, advanced from the Fire-worship to that of an Infinite Uncreated Source of Light and Life and Intellect, of infinite beneficence as well as power; of a power of evil, not the rival of the Very Deity, nor co-equal or co-existent with him, but the opposite and absence of light and good and wisdom; with no other existence than that of the shadow, and therefore not created by Ahura Mazda; and to the philosophic conception of divine action by emanations, personifying his attributes and potencies, and whereby alone the Infinite God was revealed.

Nor, I am satisfied, did Indra become an evil spirit to the Irano-Aryans; nor the Devas of the *Veda* become the evil spirits known as Daevas. These are merely etymological resemblances, as I shall endeavor to explain to you. Neither is the Indus country mentioned in the *Zend-Avesta*, except in the first Fargard of the Vendidad, a comparatively modern recital of the countries occupied by the Aryans.

I do not agree with Professor Müller that the Vedic Sanskrit is the mother of the Zend and that the Irano-Aryan emigration took place from the Indus country, after the united race had settled in that region. I think that the contrary of both propositions is clearly and certainly demonstrable, that Zend and the Vedic Sanskrit are sisters, from one mother-tongue, many of the roots of which, and more of the meanings of roots are preserved in the Zend, as many are in the Greek and Latin, than in the Sanskrit; and that when the Irano-Aryans emigrated into Bactria, on their way to Media, those who became Indo-Aryans remained in Sogdiana, in the vicinity of Samarkand and Bokhara, and only emigrated when, perhaps long subsequently, they were crowded out by a great Tâtaric or Toorkhish invasion from the north, which even flowed over into Bactria.

There is no doubt that Westergaard and Spiegel are right in considering the *Veda* as the safest key to an understanding of the *Zend-Avesta*. It is a constant cause of surprise to find so generally and so readily the meanings of Zend words by means of the Sanskrit roots. The two languages are very much to each other as the Spanish and Portuguese are. But Professor Roth had not sufficient data on which to say, with his limited knowledge of Zend, "that the Vedic Sanskrit was purer, and had remained truer to its original character, while the stream of the Zend had been in various ways polluted, had altered its course, and cannot with certainty be traced back to that source." In fact, the speculations of this professor, so far as I have seen them, are singularly unfounded and worthless.

Du Perron's translation was a French one, of a Persian rendering of a Pehlevi version of the *Zend-Avesta*. It has ceased to be of use. Nevertheless, it did a great work, by preparing the way for other scholars; and without it the Zend might still and always have remained an unknown tongue to us, in an unknown alphabet, and the Achæmenian Inscriptions might still have been to us only "a quaint conglomerate of nails, wedges or arrows." For these groups or bundles of arrow-headed or wedge-like marks were only deciphered by means of the Zend and Sanskrit, by a process much like deciphering an Italian or Portuguese inscription without a knowledge of Italian or Portuguese, simply by means of classical and mediæval Latin.

There is no Zend-English Dictionary, nor any Zend Grammar in English, except one of a few pages in the *Essays* of Dr. Haug, and so much of Professor Bopp's *Comparative Grammar* as relates to the Zend in connection with Sanskrit, Greek, Latin, Gothic, German, Sclavonic and Lithuanian: and these, probably give us all that is to be known.

Professor Müller, while awarding to Dr. Haug great credit for his having "extracted" the most ancient Zend relics, and attempted a complete translation of them, adds these remarks, certainly quite favorable enough to that translator:

We by no means think that the translations here offered by Dr. Haug are final. Many of the passages as translated by him, are as clear as daylight, and carry conviction by their very clearness. [I find these at very rare intervals, so wide apart as to be phenomena to excite admiration.] Others, however, are obscure, hazy, meaningless. We feel that they must have been intended for something else, something more definite and forcible, though we cannot tell what to do with the words as they stand. Sense, after all, is the great test of translation. We must feel convinced that there was good sense in these ancient poems, otherwise mankind would not have taken the trouble to preserve them; and if we cannot discover good sense in them, it must be either our fault, or the words as we now read them were not the words uttered by the ancient Prophets of the World.

The truth is that Dr. Haug engaged in his labor with a preconceived theory as to the character, nature, meaning and purpose of the Gâthâs, and as to the doctrines of Zarathustra, and the relations between the Iranic and Indian branches of the race, that was utterly, *intus et in cute*, wrong; and this made it simply *impossible* for him to translate correctly one line in twenty of the Gâthâs. I am quite sure that he has not correctly translated one in fifty. For even where his theory does not compel it, he does not seem to have the faculty of discriminating between sense and nonsense, of which latter a large part of the translations in his essays consists; and the portions that are not nonsense in parcels are nonsense in the aggregate, while the parcels themselves, judging each by itself, and all of them together are such miserable, poor, pitiful tatters of thought and bald disjointed chatter as to give one the same uncomfortable feeling that we have when listening to a speaker whose helpless imbecility makes his utterances pitiably ridiculous, and painful to hear.

Dr. Haug declares the translations of Professor Spiegel worthless, because he has been governed by the Parsee tradition; lays it down that a thorough knowledge of the Sanskrit is indispensable to qualify one to interpret the Zend, and that the only certain means of discovering the meaning of Zend words is by finding their equivalents or roots in Sanskrit; and explains by what continuous and persistent study he perfectly qualified himself for the task. Nevertheless, I believe the version of Professor Spiegel to be much more true to the meaning of the original. You will find, in the specimens of the two that I shall give, that they continually disagree as to significations of single words, as to the syntax of sentences, as to the cases and numbers of nouns and pronouns, and the modes, tenses and persons of verbs, proving that there is immense uncertainty as to the grammatical forms of the Gâthic Zend; and it is often the case that the two translations of the same verse are so utterly and entirely at variance as that no one would believe if they were presented to him by themselves, that they were attempts to translate the same text. Neither, I must say, have I been able to discover in Dr. Haug's translations a devotion to the Sanskrit as a means of interpretation greater than that of Professor Spiegel.

Baron Bunsen has inquired as to the time at which Zarathustra lived, whose very name, by the way, Dr. Haug proposes to take from him, insisting that it was the name of his family, and that his own real and particular name was *Çpitama*. Professor Spiegel, also, rather leans to this. I find no warrant for the conclusion. There is a multitude of names of individuals in the *Zend-Avesta*, and one only for each individual. *Çpitama* is an adjective, in the superlative degree (which is formed regularly by the suffix *tema* or *tama*, and means "most noble," "most excellent," or "most illustrious."

In the year 1903 before Alexander, or 2234 B.C., a Zarathustrian King of Media conquered Babylon. The religion had even then degenerated into Magism, and was of unknown age. The unfortunate theory that *Vistaçpa*, one of the most efficient allies of Zarathustra, was the father of Darius *Hystaspes*, has long ago been set at rest. In the Chaldæan lists of Berosus, as found in the Armenian edition of Eusebius, the name Zoroaster appears, as that of the Median Conqueror of Babylon, but he can only have received this title from being a follower of Zarathustra and professing his religion. He was preceded by a series of eighty-four Median kings, and the real Zarathustra lived in Bactria, long before the tide of emigration had flowed thence into Media. Aristoteles and Eudoxus, according to Plinius, place Zarathustra 6,000 years before the death of Plato: Hermippus, 5,000 years before the Trojan War. Plato died 843 B.C.; so that the two dates substantially agree, making the date of Zarathustra's reign 6300 or 6350 B.C.: and I have no doubt that this is not far from the truth. The Vedic hymns certainly preceded the time, 2500 B.C., when the Stars of the Bull rose with the sun at the Vernal Equinox. They, or at least the oldest of them, were composed at a time when the Açvins, Castor and Pollux, of the constellation Gemini, so and then rose with the sun, i. e., 5000 years B.C., or at least before those stars had ceased to be objects of adoration on that account. In later times than that of Zarathustra, Tistrya, the three stars in the Belt of Orion, became the constellation of rain, because it rose with the sun at that time of the year.

And I consider it certain that the Irano-Aryan, an emigration under Yima, took place before the institution of the worship of Agni, Indra and Vishṇu, and when Mitra was the Morning-Star and Jupiter had no separate name, or at least was not called Varuṇa. It is quite certain that the land of the seven Kareshvares, bordered by the great river Ardviçura, running to the Sea Vouru-Kasha (near which and connected with it was the Sea Piritika) the land to which Yima or Yama emigrated with the Fathers, was Bactria;

and Bunsen has proven the absurdity of supposing a *return* of the Irano-Aryans, across the Hindu Kush, from the Indus country into Bactria.

If we add to this that the Zend has older forms than the Sanskrit, and that the Gâthâs give positive and ample evidence of a general state of society much more primitive and simple than that of the Punjab, as reflected and painted in the *Veda;* that there is not even one little allusion in the whole *Zend-Avesta* to the mode of life, the wars, the surroundings, the legends, of the Indo-Aryans in the Punjab, but the names of the heroes and those of the native tribes are all different; and finally, that the description of the Iranian land, divided into seven Kareshvares, and of the mountains south and east of it, and the rivers that traverse it, all agree with Bactria and suit no other country, we shall have ample reason to conclude that Zarathustra lived, fought and reigned in Bactria. I have examined carefully and discussed, point by point, all that has been written on this subject by Bunsen, Müller, Haug, Rawlinson, Donaldson and others, and have not hastily come to these conclusions. But in a lecture of an hour and a half it is impossible even summarily to present these various and discrepant views.

Let me give you some idea of the post-Gâthic Avesta, by quoting a few verses of the Mihr Yesht, which is a laudation of Mithra, the Morning-Star.

> Mithra, who as the first heavenly Yazata [adorable or worshipful one] rises over Hara before the sun; the immortal, with swift steeds, who first, with golden form, seizes the fair summits, then surrounds the whole Aryan place, the most profitable, where rulers, excellent, order round about the lands, where mountains, great, with much fodder, abounding in water, afford wells for the cattle, where are canals, deep, full of water, where *flowing* waters, broad with water, hurry to Iskata and Pouruta, to Mouru and Hareva, to Gau, Çughda and Qâirizâo, to Arêzahê to Çavahê, to Fradad-hafshu, to Vidad-hafshu, to Vouru-barsti, and Vouru-jarsti, to this Kareshvare Qaniratha, the lofty. The dwelling-place of the cattle, the dwelling of the cattle, Mithra the health-bringing goes round; who marches into all Kareshvares, as a heavenly Yazata bestowing brightness.

The meaning of this seems to me not to admit of doubt. Mithra (the Morning-Star, the promiser, herald or harbinger of the sun), as the chief or prince of the celestial luminaries, is represented as rising before the sun and lighting with his rays, as he appears over Hara-bĕrĕzaiti, the great Bolor Tagh Range, the tall and snowy peaks of that range and the Hindu Kush, and then as flooding with his radiance the whole most fertile and productive Aryan land—a land in which the wise rulers have partitioned the arable and pasture lands among the people, by boundaries; in which great mountains, heavily wooded and abounding with water, afford springs for the cattle; and where there are deep channels or canals, full of water, in which the waters flow in broad currents to Iskata and six other towns, or places, and watering by irrigation Arêzahê and six other Kareshvares or divisions, formed by these rivers; a country of healthful climate, and of abundant pasturage on the lower slopes and in the valleys of the mountains.

In the same Yesht (*v.* 67), Mithra is described as riding in his chariot from the Kareshvare Arêzahê to the Kareshvare Qaniratha (the lofty), which shows that in the former passage, these subdivisions of the country are named from east to west.

It is to be added, also, that the Drukhs, who had possessed themselves of part of the Aryan land, and made forays into that which the Arya still held, were horsemen, who had come from the north, the region of darkness and home of the Daevas, infidels not worshipping Ahura. A fierce, wild, cruel race, but not of dark complexion, and evidently those who afterwards bore the name of Tâtars, Scyths or *Toorkhs*, the latter perhaps identical with *Drukhs*.

I must content myself with so much of preface, a small part only of a very large discussion, and address myself to the main purpose of these concluding lectures.

What is *meant*, when it is said that this or the other God of one people *is* this or the other God of another?—that the Egyptian Hermes was the Mercury of the Romans, Mitra the Venus of the Greeks and Astarte of the Phœnicians, and the Greek Hercules the Tyrian Malkarth? It never meant that this and that nation originally worshipped the same God by the same name, and continue to worship him, with mere change of name, by one or the other, as they might remember one and the same man, Noah, Menes or Sesostris, who had actually lived, only calling him by different names. The Gods have not that actual human personality. The God *was* the same, if the embodiment of the same conception, if he represented or was the same potency or principle; if the name by which he was called by each people, conveyed to each people the same idea. The *God* of the English, the *Dieu* of the French, and the *Dios* of the Spaniard, *are* the same Deity, though *Dieu* and *Dios* are identical with the Sanskrit *Dyu*, the Sky. And if the ancient Aryans had worshipped the sky, by the name *Dyaus* or *Dyu*, and the ancient Greeks worshipped it by the name *Ouranos*, and the ancient Latins by the name *Cœlum*, these would have been one and the same God, as the Vedic *Pushan*, the Greek *Hermes* and the Latin *Mercury* were. The *Sûrya* of the Indo-Aryans, the *Mithras* of the Persians, the *Baal* of the Phœnicians, the *Apollo* of the Greeks and Latins, the *Osiris* of the Mitzraim, were originally one and the same God, as each originally represented simply the visible sun. But when new and different and higher attributes were ascribed to each, the same God became to each people really a different God.

Dr. Haug calls the Amĕsha-Çpĕntas "Archangels." He might, with the same propriety call them "Adjutants General." The Hebrew *Harashim* or *Malakhim* had a definite and precise character and definite and precise functions, entirely different from those of the Amĕsha-Çpĕntas, though they were attributes of the Hebrew Deity *El* or *Al*, *his healing, might, glory*, etc., were in number the same as the Amĕsha-Çpĕntas, and were conceived of during the Captivity at Babylon in imitation of these. We have, in fact, no right to use any English word, to represent a Vedic one, unless it conveys and represents, to us, the same idea which that Vedic word conveyed and represented to the Vedic poet who used it. If we offend against this rule, we deceive and mislead the reader; and with this kind of fraud the current translations of the *Veda* and *Zend-Avesta* swarm.

It will be no fraud on you if I should call Ahura Mazda, "God." For this is what I propose to show you: that he and the God we worship are one and the same, because the two names embody and represent the same conception; and the nature, character, attributes, pre-eminences, splendors and powers, intellect, wisdom, and action and manifestations, of Ahura Mazda were, in every respect, fully and perfectly, those which we conceive of, as of and possessed and exercised by, the God whom we adore as our Father, in whom is life, and that life the Light of men. Ahura Mazda is the very Deity, the Ainsoph, not cognizable even by the intellect, of the Hebrew Kabbalah, but neither nor our God is the *Yehuah* of the ancient Hebrews, any more than he is the *Zeus* of the ancient Greeks.

The Zarathustrians were not Fire-worshippers, any more than Saint John was a Light-worshipper. Fire was to them the son of, or an outflowing from, Ahura Mazda. In the visible fire they revered the invisible God. In all the wide universe, His was the only intellect, His the only intelligence and wisdom, His the only power and energy. "The forces of Nature were," truly, to them, "only the varied action of God." The worship of the Fire-principle, whether in public as in the Vedic period, or in secret by the priests, was that, perhaps, which led Zarathustra to the conception of an intelligent creative First Cause, self-existent, uncreated, unlimited, supreme. What he understood by this cause, and by the Amĕsha-Çpĕntas that were its agents, and what Zarathustra really said to those who heard him, in his five Gâthâs, it is my principal purpose to inquire.

––––––––––

I have endeavored, in my inquiry into the doctrines of the Zarathustrian religion, to ascertain the meaning of the five Gâthâs and the Yaçna Haptanhaiti. Mr. Bleeck warns his readers that the Gâthâs are extremely difficult and obscure, and that many passages are quite unintelligible, and more very nearly so. When it is frankly admitted that, literally rendered, according to the later meanings of the words, a sentence is unintelligible, it may be permissible to endeavor to find a sensible interpretation of the letter of the sentence, even if only by way of conjecture.

The Gâthâs are prefaced by this sentence, as translated by Bleeck from Spiegel, and by Dr. Haug:

> *Spiegel–Bleeck:* Good is the thought, good the speech, good the work, of the pious Zarathustra. May the Amĕsha-Çpĕntas accept the Gâthâs. Praise be to you, pure songs.
>
> *Haug:* The revealed thought, the revealed word, the revealed deed, of the holy Zarathustra: the Archangels first sung the Gâthâs.

Thought, Word, Deed or Act, we hear it often said, *is the Trinity of Zarathustra.* The three are often spoken of in their natural sense, as the thought of a man, the word spoken by him that expresses it, the act that carries into effect the thought so uttered. But also, the Thought is often the Divine Wisdom, resident, abiding, immanent, in the Deity's Very Self, unmanifested, unuttered: the Word is an utterance outwardly, and speaking, of that Wisdom (not what is spoken, but the Wisdom that speaks); and Acts or Deeds are what is spoken or dictated, as prayer or sacred songs. These are the "deeds" of Vohu-Manô, the Divine Wisdom (*Çpĕnta-Mainyu*) manifested in man, as the human intellect. For all intellect is, by this creed, divine: all truth is uttered by the Divine Wisdom, though by the lips of man. It will be well for you to remember this meaning of the word rendered by "deeds," and, also, that the words invariably rendered "pure," "purity," as invariably are mistranslated—"pure" meaning "religious, pious, a true believer"; and "purity," "the Ahurian religion, pious devotion to that religion, the true Faith."

This prefatory sentence is not in the Gâthâ dialect, but in the common Zend. It was written by the collector or compiler of the verses, long after their composition. It shows that the authorship of the Gâthâs was attributed to Zarathustra, when it was written.

The *Amĕsha-Çpĕntas,* formerly known to us as the *Amshaspands,* are, it will be well for you to remember:

1. *Çpĕnta-Mainyu,* the Divine Wisdom, immanent in Ahura Mazda, commonly deemed to be only a synonym of that name, or a mere appellation of Ahura.

2. *Vohu-Manô* (formerly known as Bahman), said by the commentators to be "the Protector of all Living Creatures."

3. *Asha-Vahista* (*Ardibehest*), said to be the Genius of Fire.

4. *Khshathra-Vairya* (*Sharever*), said to be Lord and Protector of the Metals. The care of the poor is also said to be entrusted to him.

5. *Çpĕnta-Armaiti*, female (*Sapandomad*), said to be the Goddess of the Earth. In the older writings, she is, it is said, especially the Goddess of Wisdom; in the later, she bestows a good way of life, fluency of speech, etc. She is really the Productive Power of the Deity, manifested by and acting through Nature.

6, 7. *Haurvaṭ* or *Haurvatâṭ*, and *Amĕrĕtâṭ*, who are almost always named together. The former is said to be Lord of the Waters; the latter, of the Trees. Formerly called *Khordad* and *Amerdad*.

Not understanding the Zarathustrian theory, nor knowing what Çpĕnta-Mainyu was, those who have undertaken to explain the doctrine have sometimes counted Ahura himself, and sometimes Çraŏsha ("Worship or Devotion," the *Çraddha* of the *Vedas*) as an Amĕsha-Çpĕnta. Neither was so or is said to be so in the texts.

I have here my own interpretation of the whole of the Gâthâs, of which I can, of course, read but a part. I shall give you only a few specimens of the translations of Spiegel, and of some texts, both his and Dr. Haug's. Without this, I should give you little idea of what I have endeavored to effect. As we come to mention of Ahura Mazda and the Amĕsha-Çpĕntas, we can pause, at intervals, to consider what each was, with less of tediousness to you than a formal and consecutive dissertation would cause, and more satisfactorily. Of course I should much rather not have to ask you to take it for granted (but necessity is omnipotent) that my interpretations are correct.

The five Gâthâs have their names from their respective beginning words, except the first, which is named from the Prayer *Ahuna-Vairya*, or *Yatha Ahu Vairyo*, which precedes it—the first of the three most sacred short prayers, dictated and taught, it is declared, by Ahura himself, and which has erroneously been called the creative "Word" *Honover*, being neither *creative* nor a *word*, nor *Honover*.

This Gâthâ consists of seven sections, called *Hâs* (*hâ* meaning a section or what is cut off), numbered Yaçna 28 to Yaçna 34, and comprising 101 verses, all in one meter.

The Prayer *Ahuna-Vairya*, so celebrated as the Word *Honover*, was believed to have been spoken or dictated by Ahura himself, was deemed to be of the utmost sanctity, and to possess immense potencies, sufficing for the cure of diseases, the subjugation of Daevas and victory over the hosts of the infidels in battle. The same efficacy and sanctity are still ascribed to it. Dr. Haug says of it and the other two great prayers, that they are very short, and it is therefore somewhat *hazardous* to venture a translation of them. On the score of age, it is the most venerable formula of words in the world, and worth knowing, if only for the immense length of time during which it has been deemed most holy and all-powerful.

There seems to be little in its words to have made it so; but the interpretations of it are so different as to persuade one to suspect that there must have been some secret and mysterious significance attached to the words, which was lost ages ago. But sacred formulas of words have not been unknown to any people, any more than *signs* of marvelous efficacy, and *rites* originally symbolic, grown into the indispensable means of spiritual salvation. After all, whatever men *believe* to possess mysterious potencies and efficacy to secure success, does possess them; for faith in their virtues gives hope, confidence and courage: and it is symbols and signs, and ceremonies and formulas, that always have governed and always will govern mankind. Let us look with somewhat of reverence, then, upon this old formula of words. In the original it is:

> 1.—*Yathâ âhu vairyô athâ ratus ashatchit hachâ.*
> 2.—*Vanhêus dazdâ manaṇhô skyaothnanaṁm anhêus Mazdâi.*
> 3.—*Khshathremchâ Ahurâi â yim dregubyô dadât vâçta rem.*

Dr. Haug, in his *Essays*, translates only the first line, which he makes to mean,

> Both the two lives, and the master of every pure thing, are to be believed in (*vairyo*, literally, he says, to "be chosen").

In the Spiegel-Bleeck translation of the *Khordah-Avesta*, the same line is rendered,

> "As is the will of the Lord, so the Ruler out of purity."

And the other lines:

> 2.—From Vohu-Manô gifts for the works, in the world for Mazda.
> 3.—And the kingdom to Ahura, when we afford succor to the poor.

You see that the first line is thus made to mean two utterly different things, and such is also the case as to a great number of verses of the Gâthâs. Dr. Haug's notion of *âhu* meaning the two lives, is mere nonsense. *Var* means to "choose," and *vairyô* might mean to "be chosen," being participle of the future passive, as in Sanskrit, *varya* is of *vṛi, var*, to "choose." This disagreement of the translators as to the entire sense of a verse and of every word in a line, gives you a faint idea of the difficulty which any person must labor under, who, having only these guides, endeavors by their confused utterances, to understand the Gâthâs.

But that you may fully appreciate *all* the difficulty, by one example not more striking than hundreds of others, I ask your indulgence for delaying

you a little longer, upon these three lines, the oldest recorded prayer of
man to God, the oldest extant monument, by far, of the human intellect,
the true meaning of which, if I *have* discovered it, I did not discover until
I had commenced the page that immediately precedes this.*

I shall first read to you, in the order of the original words, what I consider to be the literal meaning of each, and then what I think to be the
real meaning of each line.

> 1. As. Light. The virile. so. Ruler. The All-Pure. from, out of.
> 2. of the good. the gifts. of the intellect. of works. of life. for Mazda.
> 3. and the dominion. for Ahura. to. whom. from the enemies. may he
> give. pasture.

And I read these hieroglyphics thus:

> 1. As the procreative Light is, so the good ruler is, an emanation from the
> All-Pure.
> 2. May he give us, as the instrument of Mazda, the gifts of the good intellect
> (the Divine Wisdom), and of the blessings of life (or the divine gifts that sustain
> life).
> 3. And, as the instrument of Ahura, dominion to him unto whom he gives the
> pasture-grounds of the infidels.

The Ruler or King divinely commissioned, his intellect the Divine
Wisdom manifested; his teachings the teachings of God; he the source
from which flow to the people all that makes men happy; the security and
peace and holy quiet and content of home, the fruitfulness of the fields,
the increase of the herds, the grain whose undulations reflect the sunshine,
the victory that gives immunity from harm; the duty of the true believers
to propagate the true faith; the extension of the dominion of Ahura by
their conquests, the right to annex to *his* dominions the pasture-grounds
of the infidel—all this is in the prayer, with the profound conviction that
man has within him that which is from God and is immortal, a ray of the
great Primal Light, of the Divine Intellect that dwells in the Infinite Light;
that all that is good, whether as the food for the mind or for the body comes
from God, and is not the reward and compensation, but the effect and fruit
of faith and devotion, of loyal obedience and adoration.   Do you wonder
that two hundred generations of men, each generation for sixty or seventy
centuries numbering many millions of men and women, have devoutly
repeated this prayer many times a day, with an abiding faith in its Omnipotent Holiness?

The first verse of the Gâthâ *Ahunavaiti* is a paraphrase of it.

> I pray for this [it begins; and it is Zarathustra who asks for] the entirely pure
> works of the Holy Spirit,

---

*These lectures were in manuscript in the author's handwriting.—*Transcriber*.

which are the same "gifts of Divine Wisdom," asked for in the second line
of the prayer; and for the understanding of Vohu-Manô, the knowledge
of the true faith whose conquests and extension, annexing new and fertile
regions, rejoice the Aryàn cattle; *Gêus Urvâ*, the life of the cattle, cattle-
kind, and not "the soul of the Bull."

Verse 2 is thus translated by Bleeck:

> I draw near to you, Ahura Mazda, with good-mindedness. Give me for both these
> (worlds), the corporeal as well as the spiritual, gifts arising out of purity [i. e., Spiegel
> says, "gifts that will rejoice us in the other world"].

There is nothing about "worlds" or "the other world" in the text.
The corporeal and spiritual are the body and intellect. The benefits and
successes, fruits of the true faith, that are asked for, that make men glad
by prosperity, are those mentioned in the prayer and first verse, intellectual
wealth and material abundance. We shall often meet with "brightness,"
always meaning the prosperity and glory born of success; and with "world"
and "worlds" continually intruding where they do not belong.

> 3. I praise ye first, O Asha and Vohu-Manô, and Ahura Mazda, to whom belongs
> an imperishable kingdom [eternal rule and dominion, the Divine Royalty and
> dominion, *Khshathra Vairya*, which is also the Aryan rule and dominion, as we
> shall see]. May Armaiti, to grant gifts, come hither at my call.
>
> 4. I who have entrusted the soul to heaven, with good disposition, acquainted
> with the reward for the actions of Ahura Mazda, so long as I can and am able, will
> I teach according to the wish of the Pure.

That is: I, Zarathustra, who have in my heart addressed myself devo-
tionally to heaven, knowing what the fruit is of the religion of Ahura, will
continue while I have strength to do so, to teach that which is desired by
the Faithful.

> 5. Asha, when shall I behold thee and Vohu-Manô with knowledge, the place
> which belongs to Ahura Mazda, the most profitable, which is shown by Çraôsha.
> These Mañthras are the greatest thing, we teach them to those of evil tongue.

The Amĕsha-Çpĕntas, divine attributes personified, or emanations,
the Sephiroth of the Kabbalah, are cognizable by the intellect only and not
by the bodily senses.

That is, they are wholly intellectual conceptions, have only an intellectual, immaterial existence like thoughts, ideas, images and attributes.
They are comparable to and explainable by, nothing material. The seven
colors of the rainbow in the sky, subdivisions of the one white light immanent
in the sun, come as near the nature and mode of being of the Amĕsha-
Çpĕntas, as any thing visible can; and this because they are *effects*, and not

things or *beings.* The worshipper can *believe* that they have a genuine and actual being and personality; but he cannot *know* it. "To behold them with knowledge" probably meant not to see them with the eyes, but to behold what it was hoped they would effect for the Aryan people.

The place that belongs to Ahura Mazda is termed the "Most Profitable," which will be found to be always applied, in the sense of "fertile, productive," to a particular part of the Aryan country, then in the possession of the hostile infidels. I think it was the country around Balkh, and it belonged to Ahura, because the Ahurian faith had been carried there by Aryan colonists, who had been overcome and subjugated. In this same section we find the phrase, "Yours is the unbounded rule over the profitable."

Here, and very often in other passages, the phrase is applied to persons, and has, I think, a general meaning of "beneficial or serviceable to the country"; it being probably applied sometimes to the soldiery and sometimes to the husbandmen and other laborers. It is also applied to Deities, in the sense of "beneficent givers of benefits and blessings." I think that the longing desire expressed, is to be restored to the possession of that fertile region, south of and along the Oxus, which other passages of the Gâthâs distinctly show to have been then in the possession of Scyths or Tâtars, from the northern land beyond that river.

Asha-Vahista, we shall see, is the Divine *Strength* or *Power.* Also, Asha is the Fire, called the son of Ahura; and as arms are forged from metal, by means of the fire, the notion grew up in later days, that he was the protector of metals. As the divine power or strength, and fire, he was the force or strength of arms and armies, the divine strength thus manifested and acting as a force; the same idea being expressed in the Hebrew book of Judges, by the phrase, "the sword of the Lord and of Gideon."

Vohu-Manô is the *Divine Wisdom, manifested.* The military skill of the leader, fruit of the intellect or intelligence, was the "work" of Vohu-Manô, all human intellect being Vohu-Manô manifested and acting in man. So also all Manthras or devotional hymns, and prayers, were works of Vohu-Manô, i. e., productions of the intellect—of the *Divine* Intellect, resident in man. All this will be found plainly expressed in the Gâthâs and elsewhere in the *Zend-Avesta.*

The fertile region which it was the cherished purpose of Zarathustra to recover from the infidels, was "shown by Çraôsha," because it was through religious devotion and worship that it was to be recovered. Success and victory were, to the Irano-Aryans, not the reward, but the consequence and effect, the product and issue, of devotion. The Manthras, the prayers chanted or sung, were the most efficacious means to attain victory, and the Aryans taught them to those whom they converted, of the tribes that spoke, not the Aryan language, but barbarous tongues.

I am giving you now, not the conclusions that I came to on first reading these verses (for they at first had no meaning to me, and I had no theory nor a single preconceived idea to support), but those which gradually became plain to me, after long consideration and study of the whole book. It was not until then that I became convinced that these "hymns" had for their object to arouse and incite the Irano-Aryans to unite against, and endeavor to expel, the invaders who had possessed themselves of part of their country. To effect this, he endeavored to intensify their faith. It did not need to create the *desire* to put an end to the marauding, plundering and murdering of those not actually under infidel rule, the exaction of tribute from some, and the absolute subjugation of others, more galling, of course, because the native tribes, whom they had conquered, and whom they regarded as inferiors, had now become the allies of their infidel masters. It was, first of all, courage, confidence, enthusiasm, that were needed; and these Zarathustra "teaching" what the unconquered Aryans desired, exerted himself to inspire, by assurances that faith in Ahura, devotion, and obedience to the Mazdayaçnian Law would make it impossible for them not to succeed.

The *Çrosh Yesht, Yaçna lvi.*, calls Çraŏsha "the Strong, whose body is the Manthra." He is the unity of all worship and devotion, and inspires the Manthra, as the soul inspires the human body; is expressed by it, as thought is expressed, clothed and embodied in words. He is said to have been the first who offered sacrifice to Ahura and the Amĕsha-Çpĕntas; and he first sang the five Gâthâs of the faithful believer, the most noble Zarathustra; for prayer, and hymns and sacrifices are all alike utterances of worship and devotion. They all, and incense, are prayer. The heart can offer its adoration and prefer its petitions to the Beneficent Infinite, without one's employing and paying a professional expert to bawl them out for him, or vociferating them himself, in the hearing of the multitude. With the Indo-Aryans, the silent prayer, by thought or sacrifice, Brahmaṇaspati, was of equal eminence with that which by resounding voices was made echo among the stars. And Çraŏsha and Çraddha, devotion, worship, are by far greater Gods than these personifications of prayer or than the Manthra-Çpĕnta, the unity of the Manthras, of the Zarathustrian Gâthâs.

6. [*Spiegel-Bleeck*]: Come with Vohu-Manô! Give, O Asha, as a gift, long life. Through thy true words, O Mazda, great joy is prepared for Zarathustra, and to us also, we who destroy the plagues of the foes.

[*Haug*]: Come with the good mind, grant prosperity, for life long, by means of thy mighty words, O thou Wise, give both, Zarathustra and us, thy powerful assistance, to put down the assaults of our enemy.

And I thus read the verse:

O Asha, come unto us, with Vohu-Manô, and graciously give unto us security of life. By means of the words of truth revealed by thee, O Mazda, a great triumph is being prepared for Zarathustra and for us, who shall cause to cease the oppressions and cruelties of the infidel enemies.

7. Give, O Asha, that reward which men desire. Give thou, O Armaiti, his wish to Vîstâçpa and also to me. Make, O Mazda, those mighty, who sing your Manthras.

Which I read:

Give, Asha, that blessing (of victory and freedom), which the Aryan people hunger for. Give thou, O Armaiti, unto Vîstâçpa and myself, that for which we strive: and make, O Mazda, those mighty who sing your Manthras.

Armaiti, the productive potency of Ahura, acting through Nature, was invoked to give success, because food was as indispensable in war as arms and prayer, as wise counsels and the power of muscles and numbers; the husbandman as the man at arms. The Manthras, like the Mantras of the *Veda*, were devotional hymns, chants or invocations. They were the mighty or true words of Ahura Mazda, the deeds of Vohu-Manô; and *khratu*, power.

8. I pray thee, the best, for the best, thee. Thou who hast the same will with Asha-Vahista. I pray to the Ruler that he will be gracious to Frashaostra and to me, and to those unto whom I am well disposed, during the whole continuance of Vohu-Manô [i. e., Spiegel says, "as long as the corporeal world itself endures"].

Which I read:

I pray to thee, O Supreme Good, for that which is best; to thee, O thou whose will is that of Asha-Vahista. I pray to Khshathra Vairya, that he will be gracious to Frashaoçtra, and to me, and to those whose welfare I have at heart, while we continue to obey the law of Vohu-Manô.

I read verse 9:

On account of (or, that we may obtain) these blessings, we, who serve you by worship, will not offend Ahura Mazda nor Asha-Vahista nor Çpĕnta-Mainyu; for the fate of the fertile country which we seek to recover is entirely subject to your will, and you are sovereign over it.

Spiegel's rendering of this is:

On account of these blessings we will also not grieve Ahura Mazda and Asha, nor the Best Spirit, which are helpful to you in praise. Yours is the will, and the unbounded rule over the profitable.

He translates verse 10 thus:

> Whom thou knowest, O Asha, as the creatures of Vohu-Manô, the truthful, Mazda Ahura, to them fulfil completely their wishes. I know that ye are without want of food and friendly words.

The "creatures" and "the creation" of Ahura Mazda, "the good creation," are the Aryan race. They only were regarded as his creatures. The infidels were creatures of Aṅra-Mainyus. The creatures of Vohu-Manô were those in whom the Divine Intellect abided, and not Ako-Manô, unreason, the first or oldest of the progeny of Aṅra-Mainyus. "The Truthful" means those of the true religion. And I read the verse thus:

> O Asha, Mazda Ahura, do thou be pleased to give effect to the desires of those whom thou knowest to be inspired by Vohu-Manô, to those who are of the true faith. I know that ye do not need for sacrifices of food or words of adoration.
>
> 11. [*Spiegel*]: I keep forever purity and good-mindedness. Teach thou me, Mazda Ahura, from out thyself, form heaven through thy mouth, whereby the World first arose.

Thought, Word, Deed—these, it is said, are the Zarathustrian trinity; and we here find clearly expressed the doctrine that the universe is the uttered thought of God.

> I do not ask for success as the reward of sacrifices and prayers. These [he had said to Ahura and the Amĕsha-Çpĕntas] I know you do not need. [And he now adds] I am a sincere devotee of the true faith, and of loyal devotion to my God and people. Teach me from out thyself. Be thou, thyself, my teacher and inspirer, by and through thy Creative Word, whereby the universe first came into being.

This ends the first section. The second is very curious; and not so long but that I can give it to you entire, as I understand its meaning to be, from the supposed literal rendering of Dr. Bleeck. Dr. Haug says that it represents *Gêus Urvâ*, the soul of the animated creation, as crying aloud in consequence of attacks upon his life, and imploring the assistance of the Archangels. To this notion he forces the text of the whole section to accommodate itself. He makes the greatest possible nonsense of it, as, in fact, he makes of every part of the Gâthâs, with very rarely the exception of a verse, so far as I have seen his translation. Who could have been murdering "the soul of the animated creation"?

The simple truth is that the section is an allegory or parable, ingeniously putting forward Zarathustra's divine commission of military leader and sovereign. I must read you the first verse of Bleeck's translation, and for the rest shall have to ask you to accept my interpretation without the opportunity of comparing it with his translation, which I wish you could do throughout; but time will not permit it.

1. Towards you complained the soul of the Bull: for whom have ye created me, who has created me, *Aëshma* (wrath), defiles me, *Haza* (robber), *Remô* (suspicion), *Dĕrĕ* (suffering), and *Tavi* (thief). I have not fodder save from ye, teach me then the good things which know herbage.

Urvâ is said by Bopp to mean "mind," and by Haug to mean "soul." But it does not mean the soul, in our sense of that word, but the life-principle or vital principle. *Urvara* means "a tree," in Zend, and *Zaurva*, "old age." *Gêus Urvâ* is the one life of all the cattle, and means simply the cattle-kind, or the Aryan cattle, considered as a unit, as when we speak of the American people, we regard it as a unit, having one life, one intellect, one will and a single voice. I read this verse thus:

1. To you the Aryan cattle complained: for whom have ye created us? Who has created us? Rapine impoverishes us; the robber, fear of danger, suffering, and the thief. We have no food unless we can obtain it from you. Cause us, then, to have enjoyment of the fertile regions where herbage is abundant.

And I read the residue of the section, as follows:

2. Then the maker of the cattle inquired of Asha: Where hast thou a protector for the cattle, who will win victory, and enable the breeders of cattle to have food for them—whom [be thou blessed!] for a leader, to drive the marauding freebooters to the land of the infidel?

This verse is thus translated by Spiegel:

3. Asha answered him: there is not a ruler for the cow, who might be without tormenting: it is not known to them what manifestly rejoices the righteous. He is the mightiest among beings, at whose call come the workers.

This may mean: there are no rulers in the land, who do not harass the people. That which rejoices the true believer is not cared for by them.

Or it may mean: Asha answered him; there is not an owner of cattle in the land who can be free from the plaguings of marauders. The prosperity, evident and unmistakable, of the true believer is not known to them. He is the most powerful among the people, at whose call the laborers assemble. And I think this means that he is strongest and best able to resist marauding parties, who, employing many persons, follows the occupation of husbandry.

4. [*The cattle speak*]: It is Mazda who remembers the words of prayer which he dictated, long ago, before Daevas and the men who adore them were, and which he will speak again hereafter. The end of the matter will be as he pleases. Let that fortune happen unto us which he may permit.

5. I appeal now urgently, with uplifted hands, for my life and the life of the cattle, and for wisdom to decide what course to pursue in cases of doubt. Let not

those be slain who practice faithfully the duties of the true religion; nor the Aryan laborer and soldier, while the infidels are let to live.

·The phrase in Spiegel is, "nor the active without the wicked." The designation "active" often occurs, and seems generally to mean the soldiery in the field; but sometimes the husbandman and herdsman. "The wicked" are *always* the northern invaders, or unbelievers generally.

> 6. Then Ahura, who by his wisdom knows who are unbelievers, said: There is not a ruler or chief in all the land, whose conduct is governed by the precepts of the true faith. I, the creator, created you for the laboring man and the soldier.
> 7. This Manthra, of which prosperity shall come, Ahura Mazda made, his wisdom and power acting in unison [or, manifesting himself conjointly with Asha]; for the benefit of the cattle, and for milk for those who delight in obeying thy commands. What man is there, who can, by the Divine Wisdom, speak aloud this Manthra to the people?
> 8. [*Ahura Mazda speaks*]: This man communes with me here, to whom alone our religious teachings have been communicated, the most noble Zarathustra. He asks from us, Mazda and Asha, assistance in teaching and propagating the faith. I will make him cunning of speech.

Ahura Mazda had communicated or revealed to Zarathustra the Mazdayaçnian Law, or body of doctrine and truth, of the tenets of the true faith. This was the "Manthra of increase," which was to bring to the Aryans prosperity and greatness. To promulgate and enforce it, he was to be gifted with eloquence and the persuasive power of speech.

This song is one of a series, composed during the struggles against the invaders, to dispossess them of the country, at various periods, from the beginning, even to the end of the long conflict. When it began, Zarathustra had few to assist him. We shall find him saying so. The people were enslaved or discouraged by constant plunderings, the land impoverished, the leaders and chiefs had for the most part submitted, and some abandoned the Ahurian faith; and the revolted native tribes had joined the Drukhs, and marauded at pleasure. This is not fanciful or conjectural. These songs prove it to be historically true.

To arouse the people, to induce the lukewarm and dispirited to take heart, and the chiefs, of settlements remote from each other, to unite in one grand effort to liberate the country, these songs were composed, chiefly by Zarathustra himself, but in part by Jâmâçpa, a missionary, it seems, sent out by Zarathustra, at any rate acting as his subordinate and preaching the true faith. Victory and liberation were to be won, only by the assistance of Ahura Mazda, Vohu-Manô and Asha, or rather, by them using the Aryans as instruments, inspired by the Divine Wisdom and invested with the Divine Strength. To secure this, it was necessary to propagate the faith; by which and by prayer success was to be achieved. Without faith and prayer, armies could not be raised nor fed, nor strength be possessed by the soldiery, nor strategical skill by the captains and commanders, of whom Kava Vistaçpa, "the warlike," was Zarathustra's lieutenant.

Zarathustra had therefore to prove himself to be commissioned by Ahura Mazda, and to annunciate the claims of his Supreme Deity and the emanations from him to worship and adoration. So far he has ingeniously followed this path: and it remains for him to prove his right to lead, command and reign. Ahura proposes to send him to promulgate the true faith, the Mazdayaçnian Law, dictated or revealed by the Divine Wisdom, and invested with the divine potency and might, the embodied and uttered wisdom and power of God; and Zarathustra its Apostle. And to enable him to perform well his task, he is gifted with persuasive eloquence, is made "cunning of speech."

Thus accredited to and accepted by the people as an Apostle of the Truth, by whose mouth Ahura dictated prayers and sacred hymns, and taught the great truths of a spiritual and pure, a grand and sublime creed, the perfection of monotheism, the deification of Light and Truth and Infinite Wisdom, Zarathustra was the incarnation of Vohu-Manô, the Divine Reason, Mind and Intellect uttering itself through him in words of wisdom. But he knew that to expel the invaders, and liberate the country, and afterwards to maintain peace, order, domestic tranquillity and prosperity, and at the same time to extend the Aryan dominion by colonization, it was indispensable that one will should govern, and that will his own. He was the priest (prophet, though so called now, he never pretended to be); but he needed to be also general and king: and he proceeds ingeniously to announce his divine commission as each. *For*

9. Then thus remonstrated the cattle-kind: we are not content with a lord possessing no actual power, with the mere words of the man who can accomplish nothing; since our need is for an absolute ruler. In what condition is one who now brings to Zarathustra men of war [i. e., to what use bring them, when he is only a priest, and not commander and king]?

In Bleeck's translation, this last line is, "How shall now be he who brings to him active help?" The reply is in the next verse.

10. Give, O Ahura Mazda, to this Zarathustra, for co-adjutors, *A sha* and *Khshathra* [*power* and *dominion* or *rule*], *together* with *Vohu-Manô*, that he may create peaceful and comfortable homes, and prosperity and content. For I am assured that thou, O Mazda, art the primary possessor of these things.

Enslaved, or, where not so, continually harassed, plundered, beaten, their fields ravaged, their cattle driven off, their houses destroyed, and leading uncertain and precarious lives, the Aryan common people were in large measure homeless, and everywhere without the comfort, quiet and permanence of home. Wherefore, in addition to the assistance of the Divine *Logos* or uttered *reason* and *wisdom*, *Vohu-Manô*, which abode with him and inspired him as teacher, and made him eloquent and wise to disseminate the truth, that of *Asha-Vahista*, the divine *strength* or *omnipotence*, and of *Khshathra Vairya*, sovereign and supreme *dominion* is asked for him, that by freeing the land of its oppressors, exterminating the marauders, driving back the Drukhs across the Oxus, and restoring the reign of law, order and security, he might give the people comfortable and safe homes, and peace and pleasant quietude and content.

For, says the worshipper, in the plenitude of his faith,

> I am assured that it is thou, Ahura Mazda, as the Very Deity of whom these others are but emanations, it is thou that hast in reality these blessings in gift, though they must come to us from thee through them; and therefore it is thou unto whom I pray for them.

This apologue shows that Zarathustra claimed, as other reformers have done, to be inspired, Ahura Mazda and Vohu-Manô speaking by his mouth. But he did not claim, as Mohammed did (who pretended that the Archangel Gabriel wrote the Koran for him), to be inspired as no other men were; or to be himself the Divine Logos, in its very self and entirety. For his doctrine was that Vohu-Manô, the divine reason manifested, was *all* human reason, the reason of every man being the divine reason resident in him, by a spark or ray, as it were, of itself, he necessarily held that every true word, by whomsoever spoken, was inspired.

> 11. When will the land have the blessings of the true religion, good neighborhood, and law and order? Give greatness, O Mazda to Zarathustra, that the land may become great, and may Ahura be gracious to us on account of our loyal adherence to you, Zarathustra.

Of course the composer of this apologue did not expect it to be understood as a true account of actual conversations. It is obvious that it was meant to be understood as a parable. Only a people of a very low order of intelligence could have accepted it as true; and only a charlatan, which Zarathustra was not, could have gravely repeated it as true. That the cattle complain to Ahura of the evils that afflict the country, not only shows it to be a fable, but also, that a grave lesson was intended to be taught by it—the necessity of union, and of zeal and devotion in the cause for which Zarathustra was contending; the necessity for the government of a single will, and that the will of the wisest, as the only means of rescuing the land from its perils; and the value and efficacy of prayer and the true faith as the only efficient instrument of the regeneration of the people; but, above all, an implicit trust and confidence in the divine providence, in the infinite power, wisdom and beneficence of Ahura Mazda.

Dr. Haug says that the third section of the first Gâthâ is one of the most important pieces of the Gâthâ literature, being a metrical speech delivered by Zarathustra himself. As it speaks of what are ordinarily called the Two Principles, of Good and Evil, of the Persian theology, I quote some of the verses.

1. I promulgate this, for those who desire to know what Mazda revealed to the wise; the hymns of adoration of Ahura, that are to be uttered aloud by men, that are to be kept in the memory with sincere faith and devotion, that are beautiful in their excellence, and are beneficial to the worshipper.

2. Let every man listen to what I teach, because it is the best, and with his mind see the light of the truth; that each may determine for himself what course it is best for him to adopt [in regard to the struggle in which the speaker was engaged]. For in order that a great work may be done, those who know it to be such must convince others.

3. At the beginning these intellect-beings, the pair were, each alike, the causes and creators of both good and evil in thoughts, words and deeds; between which the wise rightly distinguish, knowing the one from the other; and the unwise do not.

4. When these two beings came together to create life and mortality (dyingness, caducity), thereafter to belong to the world that was to be, the Evil Spirit for the unbelievers and the Best Spirit for those that were of the true faith.

5. The unbelievers chose the Evil One of these two beings, as manifested in action; and the believers, who propitiate Ahura by devotional ceremonies, believing in Mazda, chose the Holiest Spirit [Çpĕnta-Mainyu], which embellished the stable sky.

6. The Daevas and those deceived by them chose the False One of these two. When one had made his election Akem-Manô inspired him with his teachings, and those tribes of men that were to work harm and mischief to the Aryan land, united themselves with the spirit of violence and rapine.

7. To the others came Khshathra, with Vohu-Manô and Asha, and Armaiti gave them permanent physical vigor. May it, O Ahura, continue so to fare with those who are thy creatures and thy people, as it did when thou didst first begin to create.

8. When the time for the punishment of these miscreants arrives, Khshathra and Vohu-Manô, who execute thy behests, do put themselves at thy service and disposal, O Mazda, and do give the invading unbelievers into the power of Asha.

The word of the original, which I render by "unbelievers," is *Drukhs* or *Drujas*. *Drukh* is taken to have meant, and even when the Vendidad was composed, had come to mean Demon, a spiritual evil being. But it never means that in the Gâthâs. *Dru*, in Sanskrit, means to "run, hurt, attack"; and *druh*, to "hurt, seek to injure or grieve, an injurer." The Zend *druj* is the same word. The double meaning of *dru*, to "run" and to "harm," caused the noun *drukh* to be fitly applied to the marauding northern

riders, Tâtars, Scyths or Toorkhs, between the Oxus and Jaxartes, whose
original habitat was on the immense steppes of Tâtary. I have no doubt
that the name *Toorkh* is *Drukh*, modified, or that it being their name in
their own language, they were called *Drukhs* by the Aryans, from similarity
of sound of the two words. As *we* call the *Shekapo* Indians *Kickapoos*, and
the *Oponaghke, Wabanocky*, we need not wonder at like changes of letters
in foreign words and names adopted by the Aryans.

9. May we be thine own [or, be under thy protection], who are striving to liberate
and make prosperous and strong, this Aryan land. May the powerful chiefs come
to our assistance with troops [May the strong chiefs bring help through Asha:
Spiegel]. Whoever is a true worshipper of Ahura, in this part of the land, will join
the forces that shall be raised there (in that part of the country where the infidels
ruled). [The translation of *Spiegel* is, "whoso is obedient here, he will there unite
himself with power."]

10. When the Aryan chiefs and people shall thus rally to the standard of
Zarathustra, the destruction of annihilation will fall on the Drukhs; and those who
thus cause the Aryan arms to triumph, will possess the land in which Vohu-Manô,
Mazda and Asha dwell.

11. Teach the two perfect prayers which Mazda gave to men; as many as there
are which by their own efficacy have long smitten and slain the infidels; for these
prayers do make the faithful to prosper, and through them peace and prosperity
will hereafter come to the land.

The fourth section is:

1. Reciting to you these prayers that have not before been heard, we teach
the words against those who bring calamities upon the Aryan land, with the religious
doctrines of the idolatrous Toorkhs; that these prayers may be the most potent
auxiliaries of those who devote themselves to the cause of Mazda.

2. If the good man, with faith undoubting, places his trust in that which the
eyes cannot perceive ["Faith," Paul said, "is the substance of things hoped for, and
the evidence of things not seen"], he will attain unto intercourse with all you Amĕsha-
Çpĕntas, because he addresses his petitions to Ahura Mazda, in whose disposition
are all these blessings, the fruits of faith in the true religion, by means of which our
life is prolonged.

3. Communicate to us, O Mazda, in words spoken by Vohu-Manô ["the tongue
of thy mouth"], that instruction which thou, manifesting thyself by the fire and Asha,
givest us to be strength for the warriors and worship for the intelligent, that we
may know it, and that I may teach it unto all the people.

The *Spiegel-Bleeck* translation of this is,

What thou in heavenly way, through the fire and Asha, givest as might for the
warriors, as perfection for the intelligent, that announce to us, O Mazda, that we
may know it, with the tongue of thy mouth, that I may teach it to all living.

4. When the people, with renewed faith and piety, shall invoke the aid of Asha,
Vohu-Manô and Khshathra, then I will ask, with sincere faith, with wisdom and

good intentions, that the powers of government may be vested in me; that by the concentration of force and energy which this will give, we may conquer the Drukhs.

5. Give me assurance as to what success I shall achieve through the true faith. Give me to know, through Vohu-Manô, what measures will give me victory, and, O Mazda, what will be and what will not be.

The cattle had demanded that he should be invested with capacity to command in war; and he now asks of Ahura assurances as to the results, and that through the divine wisdom in him, he may be enabled to determine on the measures and movements that will secure victory and to foresee results. It is a prayer for military sagacity and generalship.

6. May that sage [probably Jamaçpa] receive the highest reward, who, in aid of my undertaking, recites aloud the Mañthra that petitions for plenty, for the spread of religious faith, and for safety to life, in the land.

7. Dominion belongs to Ahura, so far as it inures to him, by means of the divine wisdom (Vohu-Manô). [To Mazda belongs the kingdom, so far as it prospers to him through Vohu-Manô: *Spiegel.*]

I do not believe that the meaning simply is, that when dominion is gained for him, prospers to him: it belongs to him. *Cela va sans dire.* I think Zarathustra meant that Ahura only obtained dominion, through his wisdom. In that sense, the thought has been repeated since. St. Thomas Aquinas said,

A thing is not right, because God wills it, he wills it because it is right.

Bossuet said,

Under a just God there is no purely arbitrary power.

And Fénélon said,

The absolute dominion of God is not founded on a blind will. His sovereign will is always regulated by the immutable law of his wisdom.

It is a grand old truth. There is a better foundation for power, than even a popular vote.

The residue of the verse is, according to Spiegel,

He came as the first fashioner; brightness mingled itself with the lights; he the pure, he upholds the best souls, with his understanding. Thou causest both to increase in heavenly way, O Mazda Ahura, thou who art also now the lord.

You think this unintelligible. No more so than nineteen verses of every twenty. It means this, I think: Vohu-Manô emanated as the first fashioner [the *Demiourgos*, the Creative *Logos* or *Word*]; and splendor, flowing into the celestial luminaries, was manifested through them. He sustains in existence the Aryan race (which is everywhere what is meant by "the pure creation," and "the good creation"): he maintains sound reason in them, by his wisdom that is incarnate in them; and Ahura, who is above all his emanations, causes both by his divine influence dispensed by these emanations, to increase.

8.　So I acknowledged thee, O Ahura, to be first in greatness, to be worshipped by the intellect, as the source from which Vohu-Manô emanates; wherefore I saw thee, revealed to my eyes as the truth of religion, and the creator of existence, thy Self manifested in the material world.

9.　Of thy substance was Armaiti, with thee was the wisdom that made the cattle, when thou, Mazda Ahura, the Heavenly One, hadst made for them pastures, over which to roam.

10.　To the active [the industrious, or those who by arms actively labor for the faith] sons are born who are not active. Among all the people, thou hast selected the active workers to possess, as truly religious, the many blessings in the gift of Vohu-Manô. The inactive did not, O Mazda, endeavor to extend the true faith among the impious.

11.　When thou, Mazda, didst create for us our Aryan land, and the true religion, and through Vohu-Manô the Aryan intellect, then thou didst invest the living souls with bodies, and createdst prayers and Mañthras, that should give effect to the desire for the acquisition of lands not yet possessed.

12, 13, 14.　Into this Aryan country, so created by Ahura, came teaching the false teachers as well as the true ones; he who is inspired by the Divine Wisdom, as well as he who utters the words of Akô-Manô (unreason). Those who, hearing, are convinced by and obey the Divine Wisdom, so speaking, will unite in the endeavor to regain possession of the land of Ahura. Thou, O Ruler, the True, seest and knowest what questions asked are sincere, and what are insincere. And thou seest also and knowest who they are that commit great sins, in order to cover small ones. Reveal to me, Ahura, the present condition of the cause, and what will be the result [or, more probably, the present disposition of men, and what will in the end be their course]. What will be the justly-due reward, by thy determination paid to the loyal believers; what to the unbelievers in thee, when the struggle shall be ended?

15.　As to this, reveal to me what will be the punishment of those who abet and countenance the establishment of the rule of the infidels? who, influenced by false teachings, do nothing, even the least thing, to sustain the life of the people; and what the punishment of the marauders who harass and impoverish the industrious, and those who, remaining quiet and neutral, do not vex and slaughter the Aryans and their cattle.

16.　Reveal this to me, O Mazda Ahura: Is the wise man, who, zealous in the faith, has striven to free from subjection and oppression the homes, the confederacies and the regions of the Aryan land, if he has proven his zeal by actual deeds, is he like unto thee?

17.　Which is the more potent, the faith of the Aryans, or that of the idolatrous invaders? Let one priest declare it to another, and let there be hereafter no one ignorant of it, among the people. Enable us to know, Mazda Ahura, the evidence of loyalty!

18. Let none of the people listen to the hymns and teachings of the impious; for into the home, clan, confederacy and region they bring the idolatrous religion which causes death. Expel them from the land by force of arms.

19. Let the wise Ahura be listened unto, who has assigned the faithful to both the mother-country and the providence ["to both worlds"], to inhabit and possess them, who, by the words of truth that he has spoken to men, is dominion; and in whose words is power. Through thee, the red fire, Mazda decides the fate of battles.

20. Those by whose abetting the devout Aryans are despoiled, shall, when the invaders are expelled, have for their home, for a long time, the northern land of darkness, with bad food and contemptuous words. To that region, ye unbelievers, the law of Ahura exiles you, as the reward of your own acts.

21. Ahura Mazda created abundant production and security of life, that the devout Aryans might be prosperous and happy—he, from whom as a source, his dominion emanates; and wealth of wisdom for him who by acts of worship conciliates his favor.

22. Both of these are actually possessed by the wise, that is, by those who have intellectual cognition of Ahura Mazda and the Amĕsha-Çpĕntas ["who knows through his soul"]; he is the good ruler who by his edicts and acts advances and extends the true faith; and such an one, O Ahura Mazda, renders to thee most efficient service.

From the fifth section I take the following:

1. Let the allies of Zarathustra, with devout worship, invoke the aid of Ahura and his emanations. We, ye Daevas, are obedient to his will, and he is content with us. May we be thy instruments, Ahura, to execute thy will, the subduers to inflict punishment on you, Daevas.

2. To them replied Ahura Mazda, directing affairs through Vohu-Manô, and by Khshathra Vairya, who is intimately connected with the Divine Power, the glorious Asha: We will reveal to you by her fruits Armaiti the perfect [the admirable divine productive power of God in Nature]. [And they reply] Permit her to be ours, and to abide with us.

3. Ye Daevas are all the issue of the unreason [Akô-Manô] of Añra-Mainyus. Whosoever pays tribute to you, he is an ally of the Drukhs and has become an enemy of the Aryans. You, who propagate unbelief over all the land of the seven Kareshvares, do even come to me with false professions of friendship.

4. The false teachers pervert everything that is good. Their true designation is, devotees of the Daevas, in revolt against the Divine Wisdom, who have cast away all knowledge of Ahura and of the true religion.

5. The evil spirit, Akô-Mainyu, despoils the people of both plenty and security of life, when by Akô-Manô he teaches you, Daevas, to do and to teach evil and error, which are the supremacy of the heathen.

6. The people will obtain abundant vengeance for their wrongs, if Ahura, who knows the hearts and motives of all through Çpĕnta-Mainyu, shall, as he has declared he will do, hold his enemies to account, by open execution of judgment. Of thy sovereignty, O Mazda, the determinations of Asha-Vahista (the Divine Power) are a part.

7. No one of these wretches knows the use of the arms with which we shall smite them, of the death-dealing weapons which Ahura has taught us to forge; of those made of the best metal, with which we are familiar. Thou, Ahura, best knowest the failure of their attempts to make them.

Am I right in this interpretation? You must judge. This is the *literal* rendering by Bleeck from Spiegel:

> Among these wretches no one knows anything, namely, that which is manifest at the stroke, what deadly he teaches, what is known as the best steel, their going astray knowest thou, Ahura, best.
>
> 8. To these infidels Yima spoke, the son of Vivanhao, who taught the Aryan people to eat flesh in morsels: From these I shall be distinguished by thee, O Mazda. [That he taught them to eat meat by morsels, means that he instituted sacrifices.]
>
> 9. The prayers of infidels cause by their teachings the destruction of life among the people. They prevent my success, which the Divine Wisdom ardently desires. Wherefore, with these prayers, children of my intellect, I invoke your favor, Mazda and Asha.
>
> 10. He makes my words to be of no effect, who there utters that which the cattle and the sun may plainly see to bear evil fruit: who pays tribute to the oppressors that devastate the fields and make them deserts, and by acts of violence do mischief to the true believers.
>
> 11. The deaths of those of us who are slain lie at his door, who thinks the life of the heathen to be the best to lead, the depriving men and their wives of the cheerful comforts of home; he, O Ahura, who endeavors to make wretched the life of the true believer.
>
> 12. The men who dissuade others from serving their country in arms, to these Mazda has threatened punishment; to those who slay the cattle of the Aryans, while professing to be our allies; who prefer meat to the true faith; the Karapas, who are become part of those who seek by violence to become masters of the country.
>
> 13. Whoever is willing to see the kingdom divided, he is of the household of Añra-Mainyus, as aiding to ruin the Aryan realms; and whoever proposes to rely on tears and supplications, instead of resorting to arms, and wishes to prevent the missionaries charged to teach the Mañthras, from seeing the extension of the true faith, he is guilty, as an accomplice, of the utter dismemberment of the realm and he co-operates with the Kavayas.
>
> 14. He is guilty, as an accomplice, of the utter dismemberment of the realm, and co-operates with the Kavayas: he who misleads the laboring man, if he induces him to submit to the infidels, and accept them as protectors; if he promulgates the doctrines that were uttered to induce the native tribes to become pillagers and slayers of the Aryan cattle, to be a protection for those who (as children of Ahura) are far from death.
>
> 15. I will drive you also, Karapas and Kevitayas, as well as the Toorkhish invaders, out of the Aryan land, to the country of those who are not invested with the power to preserve life [because they are creatures of Añra-Mainyus, who does not create life, but perishability], they who led astray both these tribes in the Aryan land.
>
> 16. All that is now seen to occur, and all that is to take place hereafter, is controlled and directed by Ahura Mazda; and the punishment which it is decreed shall overtake the oppressors . . . .

I take the following from the sixth section:

1. He, the Master, who created the original Aryan land, administers perfect justice to the infidel and to the faithful alike; on the faithless, that are to be found intermingled with the good and true that are his own.

2. Whoever acts in obedience to the desire and will of Ahura, who inflicts injury on the infidels, whether by the recitation of prayers and Mañthras, or by blows struck in the ranks of the soldiery, and whoever supplies food for the body. [For without food, war could not be carried on; and the service of the husbandman and herdsman was as efficient, and as much the cause of victory, as that of the priest or soldier.]

3. Whosoever renders good service to the Aryan patriots, whether by continuing to be their allies, or by military service, or as a hired man, pasturing the cattle, the work he does is that of Asha and Vohu-Manô.

4. I curse, O Mazda, disobedience of thy law, and disaffection, disregard of the obligations of the Aryan blood, the Drukhs whose inroads harass the husbandman, the hired men who are faithless, and stint the cattle of their food.

This, and other things said about "fodder" for the cattle will be better understood, if you remember that in all the region of the Zer Affshan and Oxus there is no pasturage for the cattle, and that what grass they obtain has to be cultivated in fields, by means of irrigation. All except the irrigable lands is a desert. Of course, faithless servants could rob the cattle of their food.

5. I call for help to the Spirit of Devotion, thy emanation (Çraŏsha) as the most efficient of all helpers. Give us security of life in the Aryan land where Vohu-Manô reigns, unto the due observances of religious worship, in which thou art revealed, Ahura.

6. What the priest (Zaŏta) in the religious observances, desires to have revealed to him from the Paradise of the Sky, that Ahura Mazda imparts to him through Vohu-Manô, who forms in thought the hymns, that are to be uttered; the visible ceremonies and the spoken adoration, which thou desirest, O Ahura Mazda.

7. Come to me, ye who are supreme! May Mazda, self-limited, manifest himself to us [of himself may Mazda show to us: Spiegel], with and through Asha and Vohu-Manô, who are to be adored as above Khshathra Vairya. May the outflowings of the Deity [his manifestations] be manifested to us, who adore him with sacrifices.

Verse 8 is thus rendered by Bleeck:

Teach me to know both laws, that I may walk with Vohu-Manô; the offering of thy equal, Mazda, then your laudable sayings, O Asha, which were made by you as help for Amĕrĕtât, as reward for Haurvat.

Here is a verse full of difficulties. What are "both laws"? Who is "the equal" of Mazda, and how can he, the Supreme, have an equal? What are the "sayings" of Asha? What is "help" for Amĕrĕtât, and what is "reward" for Haurvat?

"Laws" are always teachings or doctrine. The equal of Mazda is Çpĕnta-Mainyus, whose "offering," whose revealing, Vohu-Manô is. Zarathustra beseeches Ahura to teach him to know, first the Mazdayaçnian Law, the whole body of religious instruction and devotion, that he may thereby commune with Vohu-Manô, the out-shining, out-acting of Çpĕnta-Mainyus, the immanent Divine Wisdom, which separately acting is Vohu-Manô; and next the efficient and profitable odes or patriotic exhortations, which are ascribed to Asha-Vahista, as utterances by him, because he is the Divine Power, and the God of battles, and he inspired them. And these he made to assist Amĕrĕtâṭ, the divine spirit of Life, in making the life of the Aryans safe, that they might live long, which could only be effected by means of victory and the consequent restoration of peace, order, quiet and immunity in the land: and to be the efficient causes of the benefits flowing from Haurvaṭ, the divine spirit of Health, to which the plenty that is the fruit of peace, and comfortable homes, are as essential as they are to length of days.

9. May dominion over the Aryan land increase and extend, to thee, Mazda; and to this land, created by thee, let enduring prosperity come, and power, through Vohu-Manô—the accomplishment of that whereby the lives of the people will be secure and prolonged.

10. All the enjoyments of life, which were, and still are, and will be, these distribute, according to thy good pleasure. May we increase, through Vohu-Manô, Khshathra and Asha, and have abundance of the comforts of life.

11. Ahura Mazda, thou who art the most beneficent, and Asha, who makest the land greater and more prosperous, and Khshathra and Vohu-Manô, hear us, and pardon us all, whatever it may be.

12. Increase our faith, O Lord! Through Armaiti give the people and the cause strength! Holiest, heavenly Mazda, give us, in response to our supplication, strong military power through Asha, and through Vohu-Manô abundant prosperity.

13. To the end that I may carry to distant places the divine teachings that create good fortune, give to our land peaceful order, which is the fruit of the divine sovereignty, O Ahura, and the issue of the sacred utterances of Vohu-Manô, that bless us! Teach the people, O Çpĕnta-Armaiti, to obey with piety the divine law.

The remainder of the section contains prayers for the prosperity and peace of the country; and it concludes thus:

14. Zarathustra will gladly lay down his life, as a gift to his country, to secure to it the supremacy of Vohu-Manô, O Mazda, the true religion in conduct and in teaching, devotion to thee, and self-government.

The prayers and Maṅthras, we see, though the productions of the human intellect, were the thoughts of Ahura Mazda himself, uttered by Vohu-Manô, his revealed intellect, speaking by the mouth of the priest, whose own intellect was deemed to be the Divine Intellect itself, manifested and abiding in the soul of man, as the light is manifested and abides in the stars.

Now, this will have a profounder interest for you, as it has had for me, if you compare it with some utterances, five thousand years later, which are familiar to you, perhaps so familiar, that, as is very commonly the case, you hear them repeated without being impressed by the real meaning of the words: for the *Veda* and *Zend-Avesta* are little more misunderstood than our own Scriptures.

The author of the Epistle to the Hebrews, says:

> God, who at sundry times and in divers manners, spake in times past, unto the fathers, by the prophets, hath in these days spoken unto us by the Son, whom he hath appointed heir of all things, by whom also he made the worlds.

And Paul said, in his first letter to the Christians at Corinth:

> There are diversities of gifts, but the same Spirit . . . . and there are diversities of operations; but it is the same God which worketh all in all: but the manifestation of the Spirit is given to every man, to profit withal. For to one is given by the Spirit the word of wisdom, to another, the word of knowledge, by the same Spirit . . . . but the same Spirit worketh all these, dividing to every man severally, as he pleases . . . . know ye not that ye are the temple of God; and the Spirit of God dwelleth in you . . . . We speak the wisdom of God, in a mystery, the hidden, which God ordained before the world, unto our glory . . . . God hath revealed unto us by his Spirit . . . . We have received, not the Spirit of the material universe, but the Spirit which is of God, that we might know the things that are freely given to us from God, which things also we speak, not in the words which human wisdom teaches, but in those which the Holy Spirit teaches.

In the second letter to the Christians at Corinth is this verse, which sounds as if taken word for word from the *Zend-Avesta*, and can only be understood by a paraphrase:

> God, who commanded the light to shine out of darkness, hath shined in our hearts, to the light of the knowledge of the glory of God, in the person of Yesous Christos.

So Paul said, writing to the Christians of Galatia:

> When it pleased God to reveal his Son in me, that I might preach him among the heathen.

Saying to Timotheus, "one God, and one mediator between God and men, *the man* Yesous Christos," he said to the Christians of Colossē, that in Christ abided as in a body, all the plenitude of the Very Deity. In the letter to the Hebrews, the Son is said to be the radiance of the glory of the Father, and the express image of his person. And when Çpĕnta-Mainyus, the Divine Wisdom or Intellect, is styled the equal of Ahura, we are reminded that it is said that Christ thought it not robbery to make himself the equal of God. Of the signification of these phrases in these letters, according to the authorized interpretation of them, I say nothing; but they were perfectly familiar to the Greeks of Asia Minor and the Alexandrian Jews, und had to them the same meaning that they had to Philo; and to him the ame that they have in the *Zend-Avesta*.

The seventh section of the first Gâthâ begins with laudations of Ahura and Asha. In verse 5 Zarathustra asks what service Ahura requires, and declares that the people will, with true piety and zealous endeavor, protect the distressed people of the land, and renounce all Daevas and apostates, and then,

6. If you really exist, O Mazda, together with Asha and Vohu-Manô, give us the conclusive proof of your real being, by repossessing us of all the inhabited Aryan land, that by means of worship and sacrifice we may gain your favor, and draw nigh to you.

vii. 1, 2. The security of life, as the fruit of ceremonial observances, of sacred recitations and of sacrifices, and the prevalence of the true religion, and the reign of prosperity and abundance, these we ascribe to thee, O Mazda! these we acknowledge to owe, Ahura, primarily to thee; and so unto thee we also ascribe all the blessings which, through the mind we receive from Vohu-Manô. So also, with the observances of the pious, whose minds are devoted to the true religion, we come to worship and adore thee, O Mazda, with ample prayers.

3. Offering this with prayers to Ahura and Asha, Zarathustra prays that all things useful and beneficial, which owe their increase to the Divine Wisdom, may be bestowed upon the Aryan land, the realm of Ahura, for that whosoever sacrifices with offerings to Ahura and Asha, and the other Amĕsha-Çpĕntas, does it wholly by inspiration of Çpĕnta-Mainyu.

4. We beseech thee, Ahura, and Asha as one with thee, to send us thy potent fire, the swiftly-spreading, puissant, which gives manifest protection to him who, feeding it, makes it glad.

5. In what does your sovereignty consist? What good actions dost thou demand of us? For we, O Mazda, are thy servants, we will, with true piety and zealous endeavor, defend and protect the poor people of the land. But all of ye Daevas and apostates we renounce.

The remaining verses of this Gâthâ contain prayers for the prosperity of the country and people, and for the extension of the true faith. Part of the emanations are spoken of in them, but not in such terms as to aid us in determining what they were; so that we may pass to the other Gâthâs. In the next lecture I propose to explain them briefly, with a few quotations, and to state to you what I understand to have been the Zarathustrian conceptions of Ahura Mazda and the Amĕsha-Çpĕntas, and what their names mean, as far as etymology enables us to ascertain their meanings.

7. Where are thy worshippers, Mazda, whom the Divine Wisdom dwells in? In prosperity or adversity, the man so enlightened governs his conduct by the

excellent teachings of that Divine Wisdom. You only we know, O Asha! Wherefore be thou our liberator!

8. By means of those hostile preparations they put us in fear, which threaten the extermination of great numbers of our people, made when the oppressor of thy faith, O Mazda, was mighty there as leader of the infidels [or, by means of those irreligious teachings and observances, in which the destruction of many Aryans is involved, they cause us alarm, the oppressor of thy religion being mighty there to mislead]. From those who are not in their hearts devoted to the true faith, Vohu-Manô goes far away.

9. So long as these evil-doers destroy the Holy Wisdom, and are thereby infidels and apostates, they are wholly without religion, so long as they are thereby wicked and corrupt.

10. Let the priest, him who is inspired by wisdom from Ahura, the skilful of speech, in whom abides the true faith, urge it upon the people to be governed in their actions by the Divine Wisdom. But let them expel from the Aryan land all the teachers of evil.

11. For both health and security of life are means by which food for the offering is abundant. Increase the realms of Vohu-Manô, Asha and Armaiti; and let them be energetic and potent! Then, O Mazda, thou wilt no longer be affronted.

12, 13. · What hast thou ordered? What is it thou desirest of us, whether uttered praises or offerings? Let it be proclaimed, O Mazda! and do thou declare who most religiously fulfils your commands! Teach us, O Asha, the ways which are reveal ings of the divine reason; that path of Vohu-Manô, of which thou hast spoken to me; that law of the profitable, in which he who acts right wisely, from religious faith and principle, finds it to be well with him; and where the reward which thou hast promised to the wise, is given to those who are thy creatures.

14. Vouchsafe, O Ahura, to grant this that I shall now ask, to the minds, endowed with bodies, of the Aryans; intelligence and good sense, for those employed with the moving cattle, your wisdom, Ahura, that vigorous energy of the mind, which extends the true religion.

15. O Mazda, make known to me the best lessons and observances; for they are the worship that is due to thee, and to Vohu-Manô and Asha, with thee. Throughout the whole Aryan land, thou, Ahura, enlarging it according to thy pleasure, thou makest greater the extent of cultivated land.

I have thought that in this lecture I best respond to your desires, by repeating to you as large a portion as possible of the first, longest and oldest of these most ancient monuments of human thought, according to my understanding of their meaning, and with, for the present, only so much of comment as was necessary to make my reading of them intelligible. If they are of any value to us, and have in them anything that ought to interest us, the first great end to be attained is, accurately to reproduce in our own language and so acquaint ourselves with, that which these songs said to those who heard them when they were first repeated. As translated by Dr. Haug, they are worthless, for there is nothing in them to pay a man for even half a day's labor. Indeed, as translated by him, I should say that the Zend-Avesta had better be forgotten as soon as possible. Neither has it, as translated by Spiegel and Bleeck, any especial value as a record of ancient thought.

There is no *soul* in it in their translation: for it has no coherent sense, no intellectual purpose, and teaches nothing; but is for the most part merely feeble and insipid twaddle.

But if the meaning of the Gâthâs and the doctrines, ideas and conceptions of Zarathustra are what I think they are, then these old records are of priceless value and unequalled interest. To prove my interpretation right is the only possible means of justifying myself for engaging your attention and occupying your time in hearing that which is utterly valueless and for the most part nonsense, if I am in error. Every audience is a jury for me, to whose decision I have to submit the question whether I read these old books correctly; and therefore I must *prove* to each, if I can, that I do not misinterpret them.

For, *prima facie*, as my interpretation is wholly new, the presumption is that it is wholly wrong; "for," it may be fairly put, "if it be correct, it would not have escaped far more competent interpreters." I have therefore been in a measure constrained to place before you most of the first Gâthâ, as I read it, with occasionally the readings of Spiegel and Haug, that you might be in possession, as far as I could, in the time and space at my command, put you in possession of the materials for judgment upon the question whether the Gâthâs mean what I think they do. I have done this, in part. When I shall have concluded, you must decide.

I will quote no opinions to you, of other judges. Whether for or against my views, they are not what the lawyers call "authorities" for you. You must decide upon the case itself, upon the whole case. If these hymns become, as I read them, a connected and coherent whole, composed for a purpose evidently desirable to be attained, and of interest enough to enlist the attention of those who heard them: if they are no longer nonsensical, unmeaning, idle verbiage, but contain a doctrine, a philosophy and a religion worthy to be taught and worth knowing and remembering; and if the dictionary and the grammar, etymology and comparative philology do not contradict my reading, it may be deemed to prove itself correct. For, even of isolated passages of ancient works, constantly we know, instinctively, as it were, that a particular reading or interpretation *cannot* be right; and as constantly that another *must* be so. And if of a whole composition we conclude that reading to be correct which makes it to have a meaning, coherency and good sense, of interest when first heard, to those who heard it, and worth preserving in the memory, it is not likely that we shall be found very greatly to err.

The singular interest and value of the hymns consist not alone nor even chiefly in the intrinsic value of their doctrine and religious philosophy. That value and interest are very great, even when so considered, and still more so when we consider the age in which those doctrines were promulgated. But they are immensely enhanced by the fact that we find in them the source of much whose origin has been heretofore unknown, and doctrines, ideas and conceptions fully developed that have been reproduced in identical terms, in all the later religious and philosophical systems of the world. *"Ex Oriente Lux"* proves truer than the world has believed. It is the light of the *Zend-Avesta* that illuminates the pages of Pythagoras and Plato, of Philo and Plotinus and Proclus. Its ideas are theirs, as they are the ideas of the Kabbalah and the Gnostics, of Saint John and Saint Paul: and we, in our conception of the Deity, worship, only by another name, the Ahura Mazda adored by Zarathustra. It is a new chapter in the history of human thought, as it is an entirely new chapter in the material history of the world and of our race. I hope I read it aright.

LECTURE SEVEN

AHURA MAZDA AND THE AMĔSHA-ÇPĔNTAS

Before I proceed to make you acquainted with the contents of the other four Gâthâs of Zarathustra, I shall endeavor to explain to you the Zarathustrian conceptions of the Deity and his emanations, as I understand them.

And I shall say nothing by way of preface except this: that when I commenced the attempt to understand the *Zend-Avesta*, I had not the least idea of finding in it anything more than I had already read in Guigniaut's *Creuzer* and other works, in regard to the Persian religion; I had no theory to support, and did not dream of finding in the Zend writings the ideas reproduced in the Kabbalah, any more than I expected to find the Gâthâs to be what they are; nor did I find in the commentaries anything to lead me towards the conclusions that were forced upon me; and most certainly I had no thought of gaining notoriety by making new discoveries, either here or in the *Veda*.

I inquire first as to the Deity himself.

We find in the *Zend-Avesta* no attempts to *define* Ahura Mazda. Whatever he and the Amĕsha-Çpĕntas were, they were spoken of familiarly, their names evidently needing no explanation, any more than the need of explanation is now felt when God and his angels are spoken of. And this is a clear proof that the names were not new to the people, and that the religion was not recently established; so that we may well give credence to what is said in the Vendidad as to its having been taught by the father of Yima who lived at a time long before Zarathustra.

There are in the *Zend-Avesta* no discussions as to the nature of Ahura Mazda, and no legends in which he has a part. He is not invested with the form, the passions or the affections of humanity. He speaks to Zarathustra, but he is not visible to him. He acts and speaks through the Amĕsha-Çpĕntas. He is the Creator, wise and beneficent; but he creates by them, and his wisdom and beneficence are personified by them. He is the essential, pure and primal Light-Substance, in which is included a supreme and perfect mind or intellect. He is omnipotent and has supreme dominion. He is the productive power, which is manifested in Nature, and in him are health and life; and all the attributes and potencies are his emanations. All this we know from the names of the Amĕsha-Çpĕntas, whose functions are not at all enlarged upon or explained, but are spoken of briefly, as being perfectly well known.

"Through my wisdom," Ahura says to Zarathustra, in the Ormuzd Yasht, "through which was the beginning of the world, so also its end shall be." From his understanding the Manthra-Çpĕnta proceeds (the whole body of devotional composition), and the potent superiority of the Aryan race; the God of the creed of Zarathustra was veritably displayed and acted, in Nature and man.

In this Yasht a vast number of names is repeated, by which he is said to be called. Among these are "the understanding," "the endowed with understanding"; "wisdom," "the endowed with wisdom." If any critic should say that there is no foundation for my opinions, I shall ask him to tell me what else can by any possibility be meant by this, than that he is, himself, in his Very Self, wisdom and understanding, and has each of them also as his emanations, and *is* each of such emanations? He comes to his servants for protection and joy, and promises Zarathustra that he shall conquer the Drukhs; and the passages of this Yasht, in regard to that, show that there are incorporated in it portions of a composition of the time of Zarathustra himself.

In the Sirozah, the stars Vanant and Haptô-Iriñga are said to proceed from Mazda, though elsewhere they are said to be self-created and without beginning; and are, in the Sirozah itself, "the lights without a beginning, which follow their own laws." Thus, though *created* by him, they *proceed* from him, as his emanations do, and like them are immortal, as he is. For, as he never *began* to exist, so he never *began* to create. To think, with him, is to create; and being Mind, Intellect, Wisdom, he never was nor could be without thought. To exist, to think and to create are, with him, one and the same thing.

Benfey gives the Sanskrit verb *as*, as three different words: 1, to "be, exist," whence *asmi*, "I am"; Zend, *ahmi;* Greek, ειμι; Lithuanian, *esmi;* Old Sclavonic, *yesmy;* German, *im;* English, *am;* 2, to "throw, leave"; and 3, as the same with *ash*, to "go, take, shine." Eichhoff gives *ash*, with the meanings "*briller, bruler*"; and thence the Greek "αʒω, "αʒομαι, "dry up"; Latin *asso*, "roast, broil"; Greek αστηρ, αστρον; Latin *aster, astrum*, "a star."

The suffix *ura*, in Sanskrit, forms base words, adjectives, and nouns;. and as *vidura* means "knowing, wise," and *bhidura*, "a thunderbolt," as "cleaving"; so *asura* meant "burning, blazing, shining, radiant," or "star, luminary," as "shining"; or "being, existing," according as it was formed from the third or first verb. In Zend, *Asura* became *Ahura*, the *s* in Sanskrit commonly becoming *h* in Zend; and the *Asuras* of the *Veda* and *Aser* of the Scandinavians, were originally the luminaries of the sky.

As Ahura was, to Zarathustra, the father of the fire, he was the primal and essential light, from which the visible light flows and is manifested. And, as he was also the source of life and intellect, he was also life or the

Living One. I think that Ahura meant both "the Living One," and "the Light Being."

And these names were synonymous, so that one word might well express both, since light was deemed to be the life of all things: the Zarathustrian idea being exactly expressed by St. John, in the phrase, "In him was life, and the life was the light of man." Ahura was this light and life, the Light-Substance, the Life-Subsistence, of the universe.

The Hebrew Kabbalah had its source in the doctrines of the Median Magi of Babylon; and these had theirs in the *Zend-Avesta*. And the Rabbi Yitzchak Loria says (*Tractatus i., of the Book Druschim, or Metaphysical Introduction to the Kabbalah, Chapter i.*):

> The Light, supremest of all things, and most lofty and limitless, and styled infinite, can be attained unto by no cogitation or speculation, and its Very Self is evidently withdrawn and removed beyond all intellection. It was, before all things whatever, produced, created, formed and made by emanation; and in it was neither time, head nor beginning; since it always existed, and remains forever, without commencement or end.

And in Chapter *ii.*,

> Know, that before the emanations flowed forth, and created things were created, the Supreme Light was infinitely extended, and filled the whole Where; so that with reference to light, no vacancy could be affirmed, nor any unoccupied space; but the All was filled with that Light of the Infinite, thus extended, whereto in every regard was no end, inasmuch as nothing was, except that extended Light, which, with a certain single and simple equality was everywhere like unto itself, and was called *Aur h'Ainsoph*, the Light of the Infinite.

Mr. Dunlap says, in his *Vestiges of the Spirit-history of Man*,

> The Light was to the reflecting minds of antiquity, something higher, subtler, purer, nobler, than the orbs or beings whose essence it was. It was regarded as the First Light, the First Cause of all Light, the Supreme Light of all Light.

The Emperor Julian says,

> He uttered out from Himself the Sun, the greatest God, in all things like Himself.
> The doctrine of the emanation of all creation out of the Godhead [Mr. Dunlap says] is one of the oldest theories of religion. It is found in all ancient religions in which Sabaism was prominent. Hence all these religions were light-religions; for the human mind could only picture the Deity to itself as the purest light.

Accordingly, the rigidly orthodox Tholuck says that

> the theme of the Gospel according to St. John is the eternal conflict between the Divine Light and the corruption of men . . . . protracted until the light is victorious;

and that its doctrine is that everything existed through the mediation of the Logos, or, as Paul says, all things were created *in the Word.*

And in the Creed, Christ is called, "Light of Light, Very God of Very God," to denote his identity of substance with the Father. The Word, the Father and the Holy Spirit have one essence—Light.

As to the name *Mazda,* we have, in Sanskrit, from *mah* (the original form of which was *magh,* to "be great, powerful"), meaning to "adore, honor," *maha,* "great," and "light," and *mahas,* "light, radiance"; *mahasa,* "knowledge," *mahiman,* "majesty." And the fact that *mahas* and *maha,* changing to *Mazda* in Zend, mean "light," as well as "great" and "excellent," explains why neither Ahura nor Mazda is an adjective; but both are nouns, and the Deity is styled, indifferently, *Ahura Mazda* and *Mazda Ahura, Ahura,* and *Mazda.*

The primitive word which is the real root of Mazda, was not the verb *mâh, mad,* to "measure." The derivatives and compounds in which the root appears, *ought* to tell us its true original meaning. Among them are these: *mâhâtmika,* "majestic, of great honor, glorious"; *mâhâtmya,* "majesty, might"; *maharaja,* "a great king"; all which seems to indicate, as many other words do, that the original root or word expressed the idea of *magnitude.* Benfey says that the original signification of *magh* and *mah* was to "be great, powerful," and he gives as derivatives in other languages; Gothic and Anglo-Saxon, *magan;* Latin, *magnus, magis, major,* etc.; Gothic, *mikils* (whence the Scottish *mickle*).

So in Zend we find *mazas,* "great"; *mazda,* "great, greatness, creator, wise"; *mazisto,* "greatest"; *maz, magh,* to "be great"; *maghavô,* "Median Priest."

On the other hand, *mahas* is found with the meaning of "light, luster, radiance"; in *Rig-Veda vi.,* 64, 2: *Mitra-mahas,* "having a friendly light or luster," *i.,* 50, 11; *Vi-mahas,* "very resplendent," *i.,* 86, 1. Eichhoff gives as a root, *mâ,* "light," whence the Latin, *mane,* "morning, dawn," and the first syllable of *matutinus,* "early in the morning," *maturo,* "ripen"; Greek, μαιρω, "shine, glitter"; μαιρα, "the Dog-Star, intense heat"; μαρμαιρω, "glitter, coruscate, vibrate with splendor."

I am convinced, therefore, that there were two roots, from one of which *maha* in Sanskrit and *Mazda* in Zend had the meaning of "light." And in the name *Ahura Mazda,* I am quite sure that *Mazda* meant "light."

That *mâs* in Sanskrit and *mâo* in Zend mean the moon, are additional proofs that this is the true meaning. And the fact that in both the ancient and later writings, a Fravashi is assigned to Ahura Mazda (the Fravashi of a man being his pre-existent spirit), shows how little has heretofore been known of the true Zarathustrian conceptions in regard to Ahura. I do not find in the *Zend-Avesta* any hint of the beginning or origin of Ahura himself, or of the pre-existence of his Fravashi, as to which I will speak hereafter.

The creed of Zarathustra was eminently a religious one. Devotion and worship are constantly inculcated, and were regarded as a divine force and power. The Maṅthra-Çpĕnta, Prayer, as the unity that is the very self of all prayers, is "the body of the Fravashi of Ahura Mazda," and of Çpĕnta-Mainyu. It is prayer that wins victories, restores peace, makes abundance. Çraŏsha (Devotion), sleepless, watchfully protects the creatures of Ahura, the Aryans. He

> no more sleeps softly, since the two heavenly beings Çpĕnta-Mainyus and Aṅra-Mainyus, created the world; because he is resolute to protect the land of Iran, and wars day and night with the Mazanian Daevas, conquering and converting them.

Aṅra-Mainyus is not represented as a fallen angel or spirit, nor as created by or the antagonist and rival of Ahura Mazda. All that has been written about Ormuzd and Ahriman, as the good and evil principles, hostile to each other, and represented by light and darkness, is a mere mass of error. Aṅra-Mainyus and Çpĕnta-Mainyu are co-eternal; but the former and his emanations are always represented as overcome by the latter and his. Dr. Haug thinks that Ahura Mazda is the absolute Unity, from which both Çpĕnta- and Aṅra-Mainyus proceeded. But the ideas of Zarathustra were clear and precise enough. Ahura Mazda was the absolute and perfect light and life, the good and true. Zarathustra did not conceive of darkness *emanating* from light; for that which *is* the emanent emanates from *itself;* nor did he conceive of death as emanating from or produced by life; nor of evil, as emanating from, flowing out of, the good; nor of falsehood flowing out of the perfect truth. And Ahura did not make or create darkness, death, evil or falsehood; for he *makes* or *creates* only that which he *produces* forth from himself.

But the absence or non-existence of the light *occasions* darkness and *is* the darkness; and Zarathustra did not conceive of Ahura Mazda, the Supreme Light, as creating this darkness which was the absence of himself, or of his effluence. By withdrawing himself and his outflowing, he gave *occasion* for the darkness; which thus existed co-eternally with himself, and uncreated like himself, the twin of Çpĕnta-Mainyu, but not of the same father. So he deemed evil, death and falsehood, to be but the absence and non-existence of good, life and truth. If Ahura had created the light, or if his own existence had had a beginning, there would have been, before that creation or beginning, an eternal pre-existence of darkness, not his creature, but independent of him, and self-existent. So cold is only the absence of heat, sickness the absence of health, ignorance the non-existence of knowledge; and if Zarathustra, considering these, and evil and death and vice and

cowardice as but negations, still personified evil and unreason and submission, we still do the same in our daily language.

Ahura Mazda is a merciful and beneficent Deity, who commands none
of the atrocities that dishonor even war. The unbelievers are not his
creatures, but creatures of Aṅra-Mainyus and the Daevas, and he smites
them in battle; but he does not order religious persecution, nor the slaughter-
ing of women and children; the conversion of the infidels is more desired
than their destruction, and he even empowers and advises Zarathustra to
settle unbelievers in the conquered country, that it may be improved.

Of Ahura it could truly be said that he was a spirit, and to be worshipped
in the spirit and truth. Spirit was no more definable then, than it is now;
but he was power, wisdom, beneficence, dominion, life, health and the power
of production; and then, as now, he was, while profoundly hidden in the
inscrutable mystery of his nature, represented to the Aryan mind by these
attributes, which it personified.

There was no idol-worship; and we find no trace of the deification of
men. Nor does there seem to have been, in the original Zarathustrian
faith, any worship of the sun, moon or stars. Mithra was not then the
sun, originally the Morning-Star, he seems to have become the light.

The *Amĕsha-Çpĕntas* are (in *Visp. ix.*, 1) "the good *Yazatas*" (adorable
ones, worthy to be worshipped), "who have good empire, good wisdom."
Victory, power, rule, as well as truth and wisdom, are in and with them, and
flow from them. They are (*Visp. x.*, 20 to 22)

> The strong Yazatas, endowed with good rule, wise, immortal, ever beneficent, who
> dwell together with Vohu-Manô [for they are all contained in the first originate
> Çpĕnta-Mainyu], including the females [Çpĕnta-Armaiti, Haurvât, and Amĕrĕtât].

They are (*Visp. xii.*, 23)

> The good rulers, the wise, the givers of good, which dwell together with Vohu-Manô,
> which are hereafter to be created, hereafter to be formed, by Vohu-Manô.

By which it is perhaps to be understood, that notwithstanding their
distinct personalities, they still continue to be contained in Vohu-Manô,
and to be continually produced from whom, their existence being a continuous emanation. Or the grammar may be corrupted, and the real
meaning may be that they *were, thereafter*, to be produced and to emanate
from Vohu-Manô.

They are (*Visp. xxii.*, 4, 5, 6)

The creatures created by the Holy One, the pure, by the all-knowing, understanding Ahura Mazda.

In *Yaçna xxvi.*, 8, 9, 10, they are

the kings, beholding at will, the great, potent, mighty, proceeding from Ahura, who are immortal.

"Beholding at will" is a very absurd rendering of *doithranañm bĕrĕzatañm:* for both words are in the genitive plural. *Doithra* is "eye or ray": and the other word means "high" and "shining." The two simply mean "of" or "having, shining rays."

In the *Farvardin Yasht*, they are

the shining, with efficacious eyes, who are all seven of like mind, all seven of like speech, all seven like-acting. Like is their mind, like also their word, like their actions, like is their Father and Ruler, namely the Creator Ahura Mazda. Of whom one sees the soul of the other, how it thinks on good thoughts, how it thinks on good words, how it thinks on good works, how it thinks on Garo-Nemana. Their ways are shining when they fly hither to the offering-gifts.

To make this number of *seven*, it has sometimes been said that Ahura Mazda himself was one of the Amĕsha-Çpĕntas, and that Çraŏsha afterwards became one. Neither is true. Ahura could not be one of the outflowings from Ahura; and worship does not emanate from the Deity, as an attribute or potency.

The allusion to their "shining ways," or orbits, shows that they were originally luminaries; seven in number, it is also said, and all of one mind, i. e., forming one constellation. No doubt that constellation was the Great Bear, source of the sanctity of *seven* divided by *three* and *four*. Hence their efficacious eyes are spoken of, and their brilliant rays. An Aryan imagination could readily fancy them obedient satellites of the North Star around which they never ceased to revolve, and that as the central point of the sky. The seven Hebraic Archangels had the same origin, for they were unknown until after the Captivity at Babylon, when the Israelitish prophets glorified Kuros as a favored servant of Yehuah.

The expressions referred to are obscure reminiscences of the former worship of the celestial bodies, out of which Zarathustrianism among the Irano-Aryans, and the Vedic faith among the Indo-Aryans, at different periods sprung. The Kabbalah reproduces with exactness the ideas expressed in the passage last quoted. The Sephiroth, like the Amĕsha-Çpĕntas, distinct from each other, are yet one, each higher one containing those below it, and each a manifestation of the Divine Substance. All are contained in Vohu-Manô, which not only *contains* all, but *is* all: as all the Sephiroth are contained in the first Sephirah, *Kether*, the divine all-powerful will.

In the *Farvardin Yasht*, 92, all the Amĕsha-Çpĕntas are said to have like wills with the sun: for the sun also is a manifestation of that light which in its essence is the Deity.   The will of God did not *create* or *make* the light, but caused to appear and be revealed as visible light, so much of the light which is the very substance of the Deity.   "And God said, *'be light; and light is'* ": i. e., he *wills* that somewhat of himself, as light, shall *be*, shall have an existence cognizable by men.

In the *Zamyad Yasht*, the passage that I have cited from the *Farvardin Yasht* is repeated, and it is added,

> (18) which are there the creators and the destroyers of the creatures of Ahura Mazda, their creators and overseers, their protectors and rulers.   They it is (19) who further the world at will [cause the Aryan land to increase in extent and prosperity] so that it does not grow old and die, does not become corrupt and stinking, but ever-living, ever-profiting, a kingdom as one wishes it, that the dead may arise and immortality for the living may come, which gives according to wish furtherance for the world. The worlds which teach purity will be immortal, the Drukhs will disappear at the time.   So soon as it comes to the pure, to slay him and his hundred-fold seed, then is it for dying and fleeing away.

Immediately before this (10, 11, 12) is the same passage, commencing thus:

> Ahura Mazda created the creatures, very good, very fair, very high, very furthering, very lofty, that they might make the world progressive, etc.

The whole of this is a prediction of the final establishment of the Aryan power and Zarathustrian faith, in the country in which the Aryans were then struggling for dominion.   Their power was to increase, not growing old and effete, nor dying nor decaying, but ever-living and ever beneficial, such a kingdom as is prayed for.   "The worlds that teach purity" are the two portions of the Aryan land, in which the true religion is professed; and these would have security of life, the peace and immunity from danger that make life long.   At length, the infidel Drukhs would be expelled or flee from the country.   For, so soon as the true believers were able to overcome and slay the Drukhs and their increase, these would either be killed or would escape from the country.   The immortality for the living, that furthers the world at will, is that greater security of life, which increases the prosperity and wealth of the country.   "That the dead may arise" cannot be accepted literally.   The expression is either figurative, or the translation is incorrect.   The concluding sentence, predicting the slaughter or expulsion of the Toorkhs, is perfectly conclusive as to the meaning of the whole passage; and if any other portion is made to be inconsistent with that, it is wrongly translated. The phrase in question is very probably, in reality, a prediction that the waste places should be made to produce again, or the settlements broken up be renewed, or that the land itself, which seemed dead, should revive.

Bopp, *i.*, 226, gives as the meaning of *Amĕsha*, "unwinking, sleepless," from the Sanskrit, *mish*, to "wink." There are other verbs from which it may be derived, *mî*, to "perish," *mash*, to "kill, hurt," *mas* and *mâ*, to "measure." If *Amĕsha* meant "sleepless," it is an additional proof that the Amĕsha-Çpĕntas were originally stars; and the epithet "sleepless" was peculiarly appropriate to those of the Great Bear, which in northern latitudes never set. The word may mean "imperishable." As *Çpĕnta* is undoubtedly an adjective, *Amĕsha* ought to be a noun, as every other word is, with which *Çpĕnta* is conjoined.

Çpĕnta is habitually rendered by "holy." Haug renders *Çpĕnta-Mainyu* by "white spirit." In Sanskrit, *çveta* and the feminine *çvetni* mean "white." *Sva*, in Sanskrit, means "one's self, own, soul, kinsman, property, wealth"; *svatva*, "self-existence," *svadha*, "spontaneity," and *svanta*, "the mind." As *v* in Sanskrit becomes *p* in Zend, *çva*, "a dog," becoming *çpa*, *svanta* and *çpĕnta* may be the same. Haug derives it from the Sanskrit *çvi*, to "thrive," making it mean "thriving, excellent." The superlative *çpenista* is also found in the *Zend-Avesta*, applied to different Amĕsha-Çpĕntas.

Whatever may be its etymology, it is hardly probable that it has different meanings, in conjunction with different words. We have *Çpĕnta-Mainyu, Çpĕnta-Armaiti, Manthra-Çpĕnta, Amĕsha-Çpĕnta,* and *Çpĕnistâ-Mainyu Mazda,* said of Haurvât and Amĕrĕtât. Now Manthra-Çpĕnta, if Çpĕnta means "excellent," is a particular prayer, excellent, or more excellent than others; and prayers cannot be called *white.* It is perfectly certain that Manthra-Çpĕnta is *all* prayer, prayer as a universal, including all particular prayers; as the unit "humanity" includes all human beings.

It follows that *Çpĕnta-Mainyu* is intellect, the universal; that *Çpĕnta-Armaiti* is the universality of production; and that the *Amĕsha-Çpĕntas,* whatever their name originally meant, were the divine attributes personified as universals.

Sva meaning "self" and "soul," and *svânta,* the "mind"; because the soul or mind is the self, the "me." I think that Çpĕnta is derived from it, and does not mean "holy" or "white." *Çpĕnista* may be equivalent to "very self."

Also, *çev* and *sev* mean to "honor," to "worship"; whence *sevya,* "venerable"; *sevâ,* "worship," "homage"; *sevin,* "honoring"; *sevyatâ,* "rank," "eminence," "state of being honored." *Sap,* the oldest form, means to "worship," whence σεβας, "worship," σεβομαι, to "worship." Benfey thinks that a lost noun *sapas, sapan* meant "worship." And on the whole I incline to think that *Çpĕnta* is from this old verb, and meant "adorable," "worshipful."

Çpĕnta-Mainyu has been considered as a mere appellation of Ahura Mazda. But it is not so. *Mainyu* is from the Sanskrit, *man,* to "think," *manas,* "the mind, intellect"; Zend, *man,* to "think"; *mano* and *manañh,* "mind"; *manas,* "thought, mind." And as *tasyu* is "thief," as "taking," in Sanskrit, and *manâyu,* "the intelligence," as "thinking"; so *mainyu,* in Zend, is "mind, intellect," because it *thinks.*

Çpĕntas-Mainyu is intellect's very self, the self-existent, universal intellect; containing in itself all intellects, as the one universal light with which it co-exists, contains in itself and is, all lights and all rays. It is the Divine Mind, Intellect and Reason, immanent in the Deity and unrevealed in action or manifestation; the unit, containing in itself all the manifold.

Añra or, in the older and rougher form, *anghra* (from the verb *angh,* which we retain in our word "anguish"), means "evil, impure, wicked, malevolent, maleficent": and *añra-* or *angro-mainyus* is the evil mind, as a universal containing in itself all intellectual evil, all evil, wicked and impure thoughts which are uttered in words and become deeds. Realism was the doctrine that genus and species were real things, existing independently of our conceptions and expressions. The Nominalists, on the contrary, held that there is no such thing as reason, intelligence or love, of which the reason, intelligence or love of an individual is a part.

Sensibility, intelligence, reason are *faculties* of the Soul; unity, identity, activity are *attributes* of it. Descartes said,

> We say that in God there are, properly, no modes or qualities, but only attributes,

because in him everything is absolute, involved in the substance and unity of the necessary being. Zarathustra personified certain attributes and potencies of the Deity, as the Hebrews personified the Divine Wisdom, and made them spirits.

But in doing so, he did not separate them from Ahura's self. Of him he thought as Augustine did of God:

> God is not a Spirit as regards substance, and good as regards quality; but both as regards substance. The justice of God is one with his goodness and with his blessedness, and all are one with his spirituality.

Says St. Thomas Aquinas:

> The attributes of God are one with His essential being, and therefore wisdom and virtue are identical in God, because both are in the divine essence.

Though Ahura was light, being and mind, to Zarathustra, yet he was a completely *personal* Deity to him. And the divine mind was, necessarily, to Zarathustra, of the nature of the mind of man. Anthropomorphism, in this sense of the term, is the indispensable condition of all human theology. Kant says:

> We may confidently challenge all natural theology, to name a single distinctive attribute of the Deity, whether denoting intelligence or will, which, apart from anthropomorphism, is anything more than a mere word, to which not the slightest notion can be attached, which can serve to extend our theoretical knowledge.

Also, in the Zarathustrian idea that the human wisdom and force are those of the Deity, we find the doctrine of Hegel, "The human is immediate, present God"; and that of Emerson, "God incarnates himself in man, and evermore goes forth anew to take possession of his world." Strauss says,

> Humanity is the union of the two natures—God becomes man, the infinite manifesting itself in the finite, and the finite spirit remembering its infinitude.

And Marheineke exactly expresses the idea of Zarathustra, in saying,

> Religion is nothing at all but the existence of the Divine Spirit in the human; but an existence which is life, a life which is consciousness, a consciousness which, in its truth, is knowledge. This human knowledge is essentially divine; for it is, first of all, the Divine Spirit's knowledge, and religion in its absoluteness.

True or false, these doctrines are not new; for they are unquestionably the doctrines of the *Zend-Avesta*. And St. Paul repeats them again and again to the Christian Greeks of Asia Minor, as, for example, in the words,

> One God, the Father, of whom are all things, and we in Him; and one Lord Jesus Christ, by whom all things, and we by Him.

And Ahura Mazda was also the essential light, of which all visible light is the outshining; and there are expressions used by St. John, and by the writer of the letter to the Hebrew Christians, which if found in the *Zend-Avesta*, would simply express and repeat, and not more fully and explicitly develop the ideas contained in the very names, Ahura Mazda and Çpĕnta-Mainyus. The words of the Gospel according to St. John,

> In the beginning was the Word, and the Word was with God, and God was the Word,

and those of his first Encyclical Letter,

> the life was manifested, that eternal life, which was with the Father, and was manifested unto us,

are the refrain or echo of a creed pronounced on the Oxus five thousand years before, and first conceived of in regard to the light and flame, immanent in and manifested from the fire.

The original character of the Amĕsha-Çpĕntas is seen in the *Mah-Yasht*, where it is said,

> When I see the moon . . . . then stand the Amĕsha-Çpĕntas, and guard the majesty, and distribute the beams over the land created by Ahura.

And in the *Gâh Rapitan* it is said,

> We praise that assembly and meeting of the Amĕsha-Çpĕntas, which is prepared in the high place of the sky, for the praise and adoration of Zantuma the Chief.

At the end of the *Yasht of the Seven Amshaspands* is a curious old composition, which Haug calls "a short proper spell." I take its meaning to be this:

> May Zarathustra therefore preserve! May the most noble Zarathustra soon destroy the Daevas and their people who occupy the land! Every Drukhs will be slain, every Drukhs will flee away, when he hears these words. Let every Aryan who accepts as his protectors the seven Amĕsha-Çpĕntas, the seven good wise sovereigns, refuse to submit longer to the raidings of the Toorkhish riders, the enemies of Vohu-Manô, and the more especial suppressors of the true worship; for they a hundred hundred times drive away and expel from the land the Mazdayaçnian Law of the Fravashis, supported as they are by the hostile population, that we must of necessity, expel from the land.

In a parenthesis, "the Mazdayaçnian Law which has the body of a horse" is praised. The explanation of this is curious, as illustrating the idiosyncrasy of the Irano-Aryan intellect, the ingenious subtlety of their expressions, and the intricate processes of their fanciful thought. The soul of man is *invested* by a Ahura with its body. The armies of the faithful are a body; as it were, animated by a soul. For *every* body is but an instrument of the soul or intellect which it invests; and all the actions performed by the body are really deeds of the soul or intellect. It is not the army that gains victories, but the soul that uses it to that end. That soul is not the intellect of the general, or *his* will, for these are of *divine* origin, in him as part of the divine potency of Vohu-Manô. The real soul of the general and army is the religion they defend, the Mazdayaçnian Law. This wins victories; and as the Aryan armies consisted chiefly of horsemen, this law and doctrine is said to have had a horse, i. e., the Aryan cavalry, in its body. Such is my interpretation.

Çpĕnta-Mainyu reveals and manifests itself as *Vohu-Manô*, the Divine Wisdom; and is "the First Originated" of the Kabbalah, the doctrine whereof was that from the First Cause or Principle or Origin, there *immediately* emanated only a single originated, which is the instrument and medium as to all subsequent originates, and these are contained in it.

It is said in the *Farvardin Yasht*, that the Fravashis stood on high, when the two spiritual ones created the creatures—the holy spirit and the evil; and in the *Ram Yasht*, "the creatures, both those which Çpĕnta-Mainyus created, and those which Aṅra-Mainyus created," are spoken of. In the *Zamyad Yasht*, the strong Kingly Majesty is praised, in which Çpĕnta-Mainyus and Aṅra-Mainyus viewing themselves, thereinto plunged. From Çpĕnta-Mainyu, it is said, proceeded by emanation, or flowed forth the spiritual being of Vohu-Manô, Asha-Vahista and the fire; and from Aṅra-Mainyus, Ako-Manô and Aêshma with frightful weapons, and Azhi-Dahaka (the snake Dahaka), and Çpityura the cutter-to-pieces of Yima.

In *Fragment* 39, the Fravashis of the pious are said to have their origin from Çpĕnta-Mainyu, from Vohu-Manô. The former is that light, intellect or wisdom, "that *dwelleth* in God," as is said in the *Porta Cœlorum* of

> the first and primitive emanation . . . . which is inherent in himself, the unrevealed intellection and Divine Thought . . . . which, in the oneness of its essence, and without distinction of place and time, contained in itself all other causates.

So is Çpĕnta-Mainyu the *unrevealed* Divine Intellect, thinking, but containing its thoughts within itself.

All these ideas, in regard to emanations and manifestations, were developments of those in regard to fire. The unit, Fire, regarded as containing in itself and being, all fires, as unmanifested, and of course as severed from light and heat, which are its effects or outflowings, is a somewhat, invisible and uncognizable by the senses. It is like the invisible soul, only manifested and revealed by thoughts, words and acts. The visible fire was the very self of Fire, but manifested by determination and limitation, a jet or ray, as it were, from an unseen source or sea of fire, which gave it a distinct and limited being. Its flame, light and heat are all of it, of which the senses can have cognizance; and each of these was an outflow, emanation, manifestation or revealing, of itself; its very self in its entirety remaining unrevealed. The Infinite Light cannot reveal itself in its infinity, but only limitedly, displaying an unsevered portion of itself. Each of these *contains* the light, heat and flame: each *is* the light, heat and flame; for if these are subtracted, no fire remains.

These ideas were readily applied to the Divine Intellect, when it and the primal light took the place of the fire, which then became its outflowing.

Vohu-Manô is literally "the intellect-being" or "existing," i. e., having a positive and distinct existence, manifested and in action. *Vohu* is the Sanskrit *Vasu*, the Greek ουσια; all meaning the condition of existing or living, and "being, existence." He is the Divine Intellect, uttered as the *Logos* or *Word*. In the *Sirozah*, "the understanding created by Mazda" is praised, "the understanding heard with the ears." This is Vohu-Manô, heard in the prayers and hymns. Mazda Ahura, the *Gâthâs* say, rules by Vohu-Manô. I shall very briefly refer to what of most significance is said of this emanation in the Gâthâs.

The worshipper asks Ahura for the entirely pure works of Çpĕnta-Mainyu, the understanding of Vohu-Manô. These are the prayers and hymns. Ahura makes known through Vohu-Manô what measures are best to be adopted. The rule in the Aryan land belongs to Mazda, so far as it prospers to him through Vohu-Manô. Through him Mazda, his *father*, gives prosperity. He came as the first fashioner (the *Demiourgos*), when light revealed itself by the luminaries of the sky. The wise lay hold on Vohu-Manô, him who knows, the Holy Wisdom. He hastens far away from the unbelievers or impious. The good works of Vohu-Manô are intellectual gifts. His fullness is the prosperity that is the consequence of peace, wise councils and good government. Sometimes the "good things" of Vohu-Manô seem to be his prayers and Mañthras.

Ahura Mazda rules through Vohu-Manô; not through his *power* (*Asha-Vahista*) or his *sovereignty* (*Khshahthra Vairya*). His law is not the *enactment* of an arbitrary and omnipotent *will*, but the *conclusions* of his infinite *wisdom*. The victories and extension of the true religion are due to him, to the military skill and judgment which is his, in the general, and to the prayers and Mañthras which are efficient causes and producers of victory. The infidels are friends and creatures of the Daevas, revolted from Vohu-Manô, because they prefer Ako-Manô, Unreason, to him, error to the truth, and are of perverted understanding, neither wise nor reasonable, "removing themselves from the understanding of Ahura Mazda, and from the true faith."

It is to be remembered that the Aryans alone, the true believers, were the "creatures" of Ahura Mazda, and they and their land "the good creation." The unbelievers were, all, the creatures of the Daevas. And St. John expresses a like idea in his first letter, where we read,

Whosoever is born of God doth not commit sin . . . . he cannot sin, for he is born of God. In this the children of God are manifest, and the children of the Devil. Whosoever believeth that Jesus is the Christ, is born of God. We know that we are of God, and the whole world lieth in wickedness.

Vohu-Manô and the other divine emanations (one of them a vĕritable God of arms and battles) are the champions of the Aryans, actually engaging on their side in battle, and even Çraôsha is pictured as a warrior vigorously spearing the infidels. Of course, all this, when composed, was merely figurative; but after a time it came to be accepted as fact. So the Olympian Gods, and even Venus, the Queen of Love, fought on opposite sides in the combats between the Greeks and Troïans, and the Twin Horsemen fought for the Romans, as "the stars in their courses fought against Sisera."

Asha-Vahista is the third Amĕsha-Çpĕnta. *Asha* is said to mean "pure," and *Vahista*, "best." I doubt as to both. There is a Sanskrit verb *vas*, the original form of *ush*, meaning to "shine." From it comes *vasu* "a ray of light," and also "gold, a gem, water," as "shining." *Vahista* I believe to be the Zend equivalent of the superlative of this, and to mean "most brilliant" or "most radiant." From the same Sanskrit verb are *vâsara*, "a day"; *vâsanta*, "vernal"; *vâsu*, a name or epithet of Vishṇu; and *vâsava*, a name of Indra, the Light-God.

Ush means to "burn" (from the light of the fire), and to "shine"; thence, *Ushas*, the Dawn, *usra*, i. e., *vasra*, "a ray of light," and other derivatives. *Asha*, I think, is from the Sanskrit *ash*, to "shine": and *asha*, we know, was identical with the fire.

Asha-Vahista is called the fairest Amĕsha-Çpĕnta, and is named with Airyama-Ishya, "strength," and Çaôka, "the healer," as if these were appellations of him. In the Gâthâs, Asha-Vahista gives long life, and that reward which the Aryans most desire, i. e., liberation. His will and that of Ahura are said to be the same, and he and Ahura to be in most intimate communion. He is coupled with Ahura much oftener than Vohu-Manô is, because the purpose of these hymns was to arouse military ardor, and thereby to conquer the infidels and expel them from the land; and Asha-Vahista, God of weapons forged by means of the fire, out of metal smelted by it from the ore, was God of War. It is into his hand the Drukhs are to be delivered; and the wise chiefs bring help through Asha, i. e., become auxiliaries or captains of Zarathustra, with their armed clansmen.

All human might and power, in war, was deemed to be a part of the Divine Power or Strength, Asha-Vahista, that Divine Strength itself, acting in men. What Ahura, in spiritual way (by inspiration) through the fire and Asha, gives as power for the warriors, as perfection for the intelligent, that Zarathustra prays Mazda to make known to him and his followers, that may learn it with the tongue of his mouth, that he may teach it to all the Aryans. I substitute "power for the warriors" in this passage, for "wisdom for the warriors." Haug and Spiegel alike make *khratu* mean "wisdom, intellect"; but it does not mean that.   It is identical with the Vedic *kratu* and Greek χρατυς, both of which mean "strength, power, empire, victory."

Ahura is "very friendly with the shining Asha," which means, as other passages in which the word "friendly" is used in the translation show, "in intimate connection with, consubstantial with him."   "The precept of Asha," it is said, "is known in the kingdom of Ahura"; and elsewhere "the laudable sayings of Asha" are spoken of.   By both are meant, I think, warlike compositions, addressed to the people, urging them to resist the infidels; religious hymns being the "precepts" and "sayings" of Vohu-Manô.

What Asha-Vahista was, cannot be learned of etymology.   The name was older than the Zarathustrian conception.   A great struggle was in progress, or about to begin, not as Haug and Spiegel think, against spiritual enemies, and to be fought with spiritual weapons, but against the fierce Tâtar riders from the northern steppes, and the native tribes of Bactria.   These, many Aryan chiefs aided, by an ignominious submission; and many of the people paid them tribute.   These Zarathustra denounced.   Ahura Mazda, he cries, has decreed evil fortune to those who by their advice prevent others from serving the true faith and the cause of Aryan freedom and independence; to those who, professing friendship, destroy our herds, and to whom food is dearer than the true faith; and these, as well as those who tamely submitted to be despoiled, he stigmatizes as themselves infidels.

Dr. Haug considers that one chief purpose of Zarathustra was to persuade the people to abandon the occupation of herding cattle, and adopt that of husbandry; and he makes the texts read to suit this notion. Considering the vast importance attached to the cattle of the country, that they are a thousand times spoken of as its chief wealth, that one chief grievance complained of was that the infidel raids prevented the driving of their cattle to distant pastures, and the prominent part played by Geus Urvâ, the soul of the cattle, one wonders that this notion should have suggested itself at all, to any one.   But why wonder at any absurdity that a theory may give birth to, or the human intellect adore?

Whoever was in any way serviceable to the Aryan cause, by devotional services, by arms, or by the cultivation of the soil or the raising of cattle, "finds himself," Zarathustra said, "in the service of Asha and Vohu-Manô." Those who did not, were "despisers of relationship," i. e., disregardful of the ties of blood and kindred.   There is not here any laudation of husbandry at the expense of the herdsman's occupation.   Armies could not be maintained in the field without food, and he who by his labors supplied the soldiery with it, as efficiently assisted to carry on the war, as the soldier that consumed it.

Asha-Vahista is the helper of the other Amĕsha-Çpĕntas. The Divine Power executes what the wisdom decides and the will directs. He "smites" all the sorcerers and Pairikas, issue of Aṅra-Mainyus, through the best of the Maṅthras. He is the great physician who heals with all manner of remedies, and drives away sickness and death, the Daevas, and all manner of mischiefs and evils, physical and moral. Aṅra-Mainyus laments that he will smite these beings; and that the Drukhs will be ruined, perish, flee from the Aryan land, disappear, "go away to the North to the world of death." The Hebrews made the healing of God, Raph-Al, an archangel. In the *Zend-Avesta* it is Asha-Vahista, the strength of God (the Hebrew Archangel Gaburi-Al, Gabriel), that is also the healer; for health is strength, as disease is weakness; and warmth, also, is life, and cold is death. The North is the land of death, because it was considered and is called the Land of Darkness. The fourth Amĕsha-Çpĕnta is *Khshathra Vairya*. The first part of this word means "king" or "sovereign." In the Sanskrit *Kshatra*, from *Kshi*, to "possess, rule," means "Dominion." From it come the Russian "Czar" and the Persian "Shah," as well as the "Tarshatha," "Viceroy," of the Book of Nehemiah. *Khshathra Vairya* means "supreme rule or dominion," and this Amĕsha-Çpĕnta is the Divine Sovereignty and Dominion, which invests also every lawful human ruler. It includes and therefore also means victory. The conquerors alone were kings, in those early days. It is the *Malakoth*, or tenth Sephirah, kingdom or sovereignty, of the Kabbalah.

> *Strength*, which is a weapon against the wicked, and the *Kingdom*, whose creator is Ahura Mazda,

are Asha-Vahista and Khshathra Vairya. The literal meaning of *vairya* is "strong, powerful," from the Sanskrit *vîrya*, "virility, strength, power, heroism, dignity, splendor."

Asha and Khshathra, together with Vohu-Manô, "create good dwellings and pleasantness." To the man

> who through the power of holiness, seeks to increase this nearest world, in which the wicked takes a share [to make prosperous, or enlarge], the country adjacent to the Aryan land, which is in part held by the infidels. Purity [the true faith] is given as a portion, imparted to him by Khshathra, co-operating with Vohu-Manô.

"The man" is Zarathustra. And the passage expresses this profound conviction of the Aryan mind, that to make the land prosperous or annex to it new provinces, were needed not only warlike power of numbers and arms, and the potency of the true faith, but also the divine government and rule, exercised through the will of a single man.

In one passage it is said,

> So will I praise you with laudations, Mazda Ahura, together with Asha, Vohu-Manô and Khshathra, that he may stand on the way of the desiring.

I find the word "desire" in many places, where the original evidently means "endeavoring, working, striving, to attain what is desired." The way of the desiring was, probably, that of progress and advancement by conquest; and to stand on it was to maintain one's self on it, and not be repulsed.

It is added, "I give open offerings in *Gâro-Nĕmâna*." This word came afterwards to mean, and is imagined always to have meant, the celestial home of Ahura Mazda. But he had no local habitation. His "home" was the Aryan land, or wherever else he was worshipped. *Gâro* is "a mountain." The Sanskrit word is *giri*, from the original *gara*, by which it appears that the Zend retained the old form. In the Sclavonic it became *gora*, and in Greek *"ορος*, these also showing the same form as the Zend. *Nĕmâna* meant "worship"; from the Sanskrit *nam*, to "bow to, submit to, bend," whence *namas*, "bowing, adoration." *Gâro-Nĕmâna*, therefore, was a mountain, on which the offerings to the Deity were made, in the time of Zarathustra, in the open air, at early dawn, the people ascending thither to catch the first rays of the coming sun, the body of Ahura Mazda.

A similar destiny awaited the bridge, ford or pass *Chinvat*, where the troops of Zarathustra, rendezvousing or converging to it, fought the decisive battle against the Drukhs. It became the bridge over which the souls (the vitalities) of the dead had to pass.

Khshathra and Vohu-Manô give the Drukhs into the hands of Asha (into the power of the Aryan armies). In the Yaçna, increase is prayed for, in benefits for the body, through Vohu-Manô, Khshathra and Asha, and fulness of good, i. e., abundance: and these potencies "further the world," i. e., make prosperous the Aryan land.

> When [it is asked] will Mazda, Asha, together with Armaiti, come, and Khshathra, the good dwelling with fodder, who will command peace to the rude wicked?

Here Khshathra means Aryan supremacy; and the passage is to be read,

> When will Ahura Mazda, as the Divine Strength come to us, with productiveness, and with supremacy, peaceful and safe homes and food for the cattle—they who will compel the barbarous infidels to be at peace?

In the *Vispered*, Vohu-Khshathra and Khshathra are praised, and the metals. From this and other passages the Parsees call *Shahriver* the lord of metals. But the word here means "arms," because they were forged from metal.

And in the *Sirozah* and *Amshaspands Yasht*, Khshathra and "the charity that feeds the beggar" are praised; showing that it was considered one of the functions of royalty or sovereignty to distribute food among the impoverished of the people.

The original meaning of *kshi* was to "possess." In those patriarchal days, before military leadership gave rule, it was the "possessors" of wealth in herds, and afterwards in lands, who were the rulers. Every such head of a family, clan or tribe, had and maintained a large number of dependents. And this reminds me that, in fixing the penalties for homicide, the highest penalty being for killing a priest, that for killing a rich man was very much larger than that for killing a poor one. This seems to us an outrage upon the first principles of common justice. We can imagine, and need not repeat, the eloquent denunciations of such a rule by modern moralists. But the law added the reason of the disposition,

> For he who kills a rich man [it said] may thereby without knowing it kill many of the poor.

In those days that knew not the manifold blessings of civilization and its multitude of appliances for making the rich grow richer and the poor poorer, the wealth of the rich consisted in lands and herds, and all of it ministered to the needs and comforts of his servants, laborers and dependents, whose number increased, of course, in proportion to his wealth. His prosperity was their comfort and security. They were his armed retainers, too, when necessary, as Abraham's servants were; and they were of his household and his family, the clansmen of the old Aryan chiefs. In this day of immense fortunes made by every manner of gaming and speculation, the gain of the rich, beyond a fair percentum upon their capital, is the loss of the poor; and the laborer is neither of the family nor clan of the capitalist. I leave it to others to compare the modern with the ancient days. Then the rich were the benefactors of the laboring poor, who had an interest in and shared their wealth, which did not consist in that which compels the poorest man to engage in a speculation whenever he buys food for tomorrow's dinner, because tomorrow the same money might, if he waited, buy less or more. The poor depended on the interest more than on the bounty and liberality of the rich, for wealth could not be locked up in securities, but consisted in that which compelled the employment of labor for its preservation and increase. Yet the bounty or munificence that feeds the poor and even the beggar was needed, and it was deemed both a high duty and a prerogative of the ruler to exercise it. It even constituted a portion of that royalty which emanating from the Deity, was vested in the chief or ruler.

Again, the meaning of the word *vairya* was originally, "manliness, heroism." In the original condition of the Aryans, the ruler was one who by his heroism protected his people. As ruler, he was especially and emphatically *protector*, not oppressor or taxer, or devourer of the substance of his people—their protector, guarding and defending them by his heroism, against their enemies: and I conclude with confidence that *Khshathra Vairya* meant, when it was first adopted as a divine name, "Protecting and Heroic Sovereignty."

The fifth Amēsha-Çpēnta is *Çpĕnta-Armaiti*, female. I found it difficult to determine from the text, what divine attribute or potency was intended by her. Spiegel says she is Perfect Wisdom, as well as the Genius of the Earth. Dr. Haug considers her the Genius of Earth. She is Production's Self, the Productive Potency of Ahura manifested, revealed and acting in the material world; what we express by "Mother-Nature."

She gives strength to the body. Through her, Ahura gives strength to men. She is the beneficent daughter of Ahura, and the offerings to Ahura are hers. Through her activity (the labors of husbandry) the Aryan land becomes prosperous.

I must not endeavor to do more as to the last three Amēsha-Çpēntas than endeavor to make you understand what they are and what is said of their functions. In the third *Gâthâ* it is said, according to Spiegel:

> May the corporeal be holy, the vital powers mighty; may the sun be beholding in the kingdom of Armaiti, may they give blessings for works through Vohu-Manô.

The corporeal is the "corporeal world," so often mentioned, the Aryan country and people; and the meaning simply is

> May the Aryan land prosper and its productive power be great: may the sun look warmly upon the realm of production; and may these give abundant harvests, in return for the services rendered to the true faith by those inspired by Vohu-Manô.

Armaiti is the beneficent daughter of Ahura: and the offerings are called hers, because they consisted of food, produced by her. The world is increased through her activity, i. e., the Aryan land becomes prosperous by the labors of husbandry and cattle-raising. She is enthroned there with Asha. With her hands Ahura performs pure deeds; and he gives decision for the combatants by the greatness of Armaiti and Asha. For the labors of the husbandman, supplying food for the armies and people, and extending Aryan settlement, were deemed to be equivalent to acts of devotion, and to be equally the means of winning victories as these or as the strength of armies, which indeed they were. In one passage it is asked how the true faith is extended and propagated; and the answer is, by the bird *Karshipta*. The commentators give no attempt at explanation of this. *Kṛish*, in Sanskrit, means, to "draw furrows, plough": and *Karshû* is "a furrow," *Karshaṇa* "tillage"; *Karshaka* and *Karshin* "a cultivator." Consequently *Karshipta* is "husbandry or agriculture," and it was by it, by the desire for it, for obtaining new lands to cultivate, that the Aryan settlements spread over Asia. The bird *Karshipta* has taken a wide flight since then, over other continents than Asia.

In the fourth *Gâthâ* it is prayed,

> May the good chiefs rule, may bad chiefs not rule over us, with deeds of good wisdom, O Armaiti;

with such a policy and such acts as good sense dictates, by which reference is intended here to the encouragement of husbandry.

In the *Ormuzd Yasht* it is said,

> O Çpĕnta-Armaiti, smite their torments, circumvent their plans, bind their hands, summer and winter smite, restrain the hinderers;

a prayer to her against the infidels, that she will deny them the means of living.

And Zarathustra is made to say,

> I come to you, the eyes of Çpĕnta-Armaiti [the sun and moon, I think], who annihilate what is desert, to hunt the infidels.

And in the *Amshaspands Yasht* and *Sirozah* she is called "skilfulness and liberality, gifted with far-seeing eyes." In the *Vispered* we find "who holds fast Çpĕnta-Armaiti, the Mañthra of the profiting"; which means that they follow husbandry, which is the worship of the laboring man. We still say "*laborare est orare*"; but labor at this day is no more prayer than any other occupation is. The phrase lives, but its meaning died ages ago. In the days of Zarathustra, the labor of the husbandman and herdsman was equivalent to prayer, for the two were equally means and instruments of victory and of Aryan supremacy and the triumph of the true religion.

In the third *Fargard* of the *Vendidad*, Zarathustra asks Ahura Mazda "who fourthly rejoices the earth with the greatest joy?" and is answered, "He who most cultivates the fruits of the field, grass and plants which yield food, or who supplies waterless land with water." And to the question, "What is the increase of the Mazdayaçnian Law?" the answer is, "When one diligently cultivates grain": and it is said "He who cultivates the fruits of the field, he cultivates Purity (the True Faith); he promotes the Máz-dayaçnian Law and extends it abroad." And then these verses follow, metrical, and, Dr. Haug says, showing even a rhyme. The translations of Dr. Haug and Bleeck greatly differ. I follow the former, adding in parentheses some words used by the latter:

> when there is barley, then the Daevas whistle (hiss);
> when barley is threshed (when there are shoots),
> then the Daevas whine (cough);
> when barley is ground (when there are stalks),
> then the Daevas roar (weep);
> when flour is produced (when there are thick ears of corn),
> then the Daevas perish (flee).

By these passages we are able to understand the verse of the _Vispered;_

> He who holds fast Çpĕnta-Armaiti, namely, the Manthra of the Profiting, through whose deeds the worlds of the pure increase.

We learn what "the worlds of the pure" are—the countries of those of the True Faith, Bactria, and probably the valley of the Zer Affshan, or perhaps Margiana. We learn what "the Manthra of the Profiting" is, that it is husbandry; and "the Profiting," the husbandmen. And we learn what is meant by "deeds." And it is by such comparisons of texts that I have arrived at many conclusions, which I have to ask you to take upon trust.

The meaning of the verse is,

> He who devotes himself to husbandry, the worship of the benefactors of the country, by means of whose products the two Aryan countries grow and prosper.

The remaining Amĕsha-Çpĕntas are _Haurvât_ and _Amĕrĕtât_, who are almost always named together, each name being in the dual. Both are feminine, and Bopp thinks they mean "entireness" and "immortality." The same peculiarity, of each of two nouns being in the dual, is found in the _Veda_, in the expressions _mâtara-pitarâu_ and _pitara-mâtara_, literally meaning two of each, mothers and fathers, but in fact merely meaning "parents."

The termination _tât_ and _tâti_ forms denominative abstracts of the feminine gender, like our termination _ness_. _Sarvâtâti_, in the _Veda_, is "allness, entireness, the whole," from _sârva_, "every, all," and Bopp thinks that the Zend _haurva_ is the same as the Sanskrit _sarva_. But it is impossible that any meanation from the Deity could have been styled "entireness."

Spiegel says that _Haurvât_ (or _Haurvatât_) is Lord of the Waters, and _Amĕrĕtât_ of the Trees.

In the *Gâthâ Ustvaiti* we obtain this much of certainty. It is said there by Zarathustra, that when there shall be profound peace, and unbelief shall disappear, and the True Faith shall rule throughout the land, and all the people shall be content under his rule, then Haurvât and Amĕrĕtât will be sovereign; and it is they who promise horses and camels to him who desires to sacrifice to Ahura.

To him who obeys Ahura and extends the true faith to distant regions, it is promised that these shall come, through the deeds of Vohu-Manô; to him who preaches Ahura, with faith and zeal in the Aryan realm they will give continually power and strength.

The worshipper prays for them, "for great friendship, for great delight"; and it is said that if strength and power belong to them, and to the realms of Vohu-Manô and Armaiti, which Asha is asked to increase, then the Ahurian faith and the Aryan people will prosper. In several passages we find Haurvât mentioned as lord, with comfortable homes and the years, and Amĕrĕtât with abundant increase of the cattle, the plenty that blesses the husbandman, and *Gaôkĕrĕna*, which Spiegel says is the white Hom or Haôma, a tree or plant. *Kĕrĕna* is from the Zend *kar*, Sanskrit *kṛi*, to "make, cause, prepare, cultivate, till, etc.," and *gao*, Sanskrit *go*, the original form probably *gau*, means "bull, cow, cattle," and also "earth." Various plants are said in the *Vendidad* to grow round about the one Gao-Kĕrĕna, meaning, I think, all over the one cultivated region. This meaning of the original word is preserved in the Greek γαι, γαια, γαιη, γη, "earth, land"; in the Gothic *gawi* and German *gau*, "country." In the Yaçna, Haurvât and Amĕrĕtât are often praised together with the cattle, the consecrated water, and the sacrifices.

Haurvât, I am satisfied, is "health," "healthfulness"; and *Amĕrĕtât*, "the vital energy or life principle," or, more literally, "undyingness." *Mĕrĕ*, Sanskrit *mṛi*, means to "die": *a* prefixed is our *un-* or *non-*, and *tât* is our suffix *-ness*. The word is as applicable to animals as to men, and does not mean "immortality."

We obtain further information as to the meaning of the Amĕsha-Çpĕntas, from the names of their antagonists. *Aṅra-* or *Aṅgro*-Mainyus is the opposite of *Çpĕnta*-Mainyus. As the first part of the name is from an ancient verb *aṅgh*, originally meaning to "harm, cause pain," still preserved in our words "*anx*ious" and "*ang*uish"; in the Greek 'αγχω, "strangle," 'αχος, "pain, grief," and 'αχνυμαι, "cause pain"; and in the Latin *ango, angere*, "torment, torture, vex," the original form of the name was *Aṅghra-Mainyus*, "harmful, maleficent, a malignant mind." For this reason I have desired to find for *Çpĕnta*, as the opposite of *Aṅghra*, the sense of "beneficent." And it is very probable that it does mean this, and is derived from *çvi*, an old verb, from which we find in the *Rig-Veda*, *açvait*, meaning to "be white, shine," whence ç*vind*, "innocent, harmless." *Âçvâsita* means "blessed," and ç*vasvasîyas*, "fortunate, auspicious, happy." That meaning of ç*vas*, ç*vanta* appears in these words; and what is so beneficent as light?

Six emanations outflowed from Añra-Mainyus, each, and in the same order, the antagonist of an Amĕsha-Çpĕnta. The first is *Akô-Manô*, the opposite of Vohu-Manô. *Ku*, as a prefix has in Sanskrit, the meanings of inferiority, wickedness, etc. *Kutarka* is "a false doctrine"; *ku-dhî*, "a fool"; *ku-mati*, "perversity, error"; *ku-buddhi*, "foolish," and *akô-manô* means "unreason, irrationality, folly."

The next is *Andar*, the opponent of Asha-Vahista. *Andha*, in Sanskrit, is "blind, obstructing the sight"; *andhya*, "blindness"; *andh*, to "make blind, obstruct the light." *Andar*, for *andhar*, is a noun, like *pitar*, *matar*, and it means "the blinder," "one who makes blind." It is the darkness, antagonist of Asha as fire; and falsehood, as the opposite of him as truth, which is the intellectual light.

The next is *Çaurva*, antagonist of Khshathra Vairya. In Sanskrit ç*i* means to "lie down, sleep," and ç*ar*, *sar*, to "be weak." *Urva* means "vital soul, being"; and ç*aurva* is "the spirit of submission, submissiveness, obsequiousness, servility"—the very opposite of the supremacy or superiority of a people or individual.

The next is *Nâonhaiti*, antagonist of *Çpĕnta-Armaiti*. *Âonha* is the Zend form of *âsa*, "he was." *Nâsa*, in Zend *naonha*, is "non-being, loss, destruction." The termination *aiti* gives it the meaning of "causer or creator of sterility or barrenness"; and this means by laying waste and destroying. *Nâonhaiti* is the spirit of únfruitfulness and barrenness, and of waste, devastation and destruction; with direct reference to the Drukhs, offspring of *Añra-Mainyus*, who then caused these evils.

The next is *Taura*, antagonist and opposite of *Haurvâṭ*. *Tṛish*, in Sanskrit, is to "thirst," whence *tarsha*, "thirst," the original root being *tars* or *tarsh*, to "dry up, burn." Hence our word *thirst*; Anglo-Saxon, *thurst*; German, *durst*; Greek, τερσομα, τερσω; Æolic, τερρω, to "dry up, burn"; Latin, *torreo*, with the same meanings; Gothic, *thairsa*. *Taura* means "fever, fever-sickness," in all newly settled countries the most common and fatal of diseases. Caused by malarious miasma, it was naturally considered to emanate from Añra-Mainyus, who is said in Fargard *i.* of the *Vendidad* to have afflicted Hapta-Hindū with irregular fevers.

The last, opposite of *Amĕrĕtâṭ*, is *Zairica*. The Zend *z* often represents the Sanskrit *j*, and *g*, and also *h*. *Jvi*, in compound words, *jar*, in Sanskrit means to "grow old, decay, be destroyed, fade," whence *jaratha*, "old."

I think that *zairika* is from this root, and means "the destroyer": and in this also there is, probably, reference to destruction of life by the infidel enemies of the Aryans.

Çraŏsha, I have already said, was devotion or·worship. Perhaps a more accurate definition is the Devotional Sentiment, the expression whereof is worship. It is identical with the Vedic *Çraddha*, which had the same meaning. It was not an Amĕsha-Çpĕnta: it is not a divine attribute or emanation. But long after the time of Zarathustra, when his philosophical conceptions had ceased to be understood and the divine emanations had become Genii, and Çpĕnta-Mainyu a mere synonym of Ahura Mazda, Çraŏsha was elevated to the dignity of an Amĕsha-Çpĕnta.

Çraŏsha is not named at all in the Gâthâs, except in the first, and does not seem to have been then personified as a Deity. In one place, "the place which belongs to Ahura Mazda" (the land of the Aryans and of the True Faith), the most profitable (fertile and productive), is said to be "shown by Çraŏsha"; i. e., to be acquired by means of worship: and in another, Zarathustra declares that he relies for assistance on the Çraŏsha (worship) of Ahura, as the greatest of all.

The *Çrosh-Yasht* is much later, and in it Çraŏsha is personified as a Deity. The Mañthra is his body. He is therefore the soul of all prayer and of devotional hymns; and he is represented with his weapon uplifted, because the Aryan imaginations, deeming victory due to their faith and devotion, figured that faith or devotion to themselves as a warrior, fighting for them against their infidel oppressors. The same idea produced the legend of the cross that appeared in the sky to the Aryan Constantine, having on it the legend: 'Εν Τούτῳ νίκα. He is sincere, beautiful, victorious, prospers the Aryan land, first among creatures sacrificed to Ahura, binding together the Bareçma, of three, five, seven and nine twigs. He first sang the five Gâthâs. He is a strong and secure place of refuge for men and women against and smites Aeshma (Rapine) with a crushing blow, slays the Drukhs and watches over the faithful when they sleep. The prayer Ahuna-Vairya, the victorious Yaçna Haptanhaiti and all the Yaçna are his weapons. He is lawgiver for the laws: through his power the Amĕsha-Çpĕntas are over the land: four horses bear him, and he smites the Daevas with the axe of a wood-cutter. For even the fuel, felled by the axe, and used for the sacrificial fire, and the axe itself, as auxiliaries and means of the act of worship, were deemed to be part of it and to share its potencies.

All this is very different from the simple and sublime conceptions of Zarathustra; but, after all, these notions are no more *outré*, than those contained in many phrases now in daily use. We represent Faith by a female figure, and see in that, and Fortune with her wheel and blindfolded, and Justice holding aloft her scales, and in such phrases, nothing extravagant or absurd. Milton makes his fallen angels manufacture cannon, powder and balls, and from triple batteries launch the missiles against the ethereal hosts led by the Archangel Michael. Elaborate in its details the stanza:

> Truth, crushed to earth, will rise again,
> The eternal years of God are hers;
> But, Error, wounded, writhes in pain,
> And dies among his worshippers;

and you may rival the adorers of Çraŏsha.

In Fargard 18, Zarathustra asks Ahura, who is the *Çraŏsha-Varēza* of *Çraŏsha*—the *Çraŏsha-Varēza* being a priest to whom were assigned particular functions, and *Varēza* being derived from the Sanskrit *Varivasya*, "worship," or *varhis*, "the sacrificial grass." The answer is, the bird that bears the name of *Parŏdars*, on which evil-speaking men impose the name of *Kahrkâtaç* (the cock), who lifts up his voice on every godly morning dawn, urging men to arise, to pray, and so to destroy the Daevas. *Bushyançta* the Daeva (indolence) urges them to sleep again. Çraŏsha holds a weapon in his hand, against the heads of the Daevas; and this name and many others show that all these were the personifications of mischiefs and vices: which are all the offspring or creatures of Aṅra-Mainyus; and the Drukhs or Drujas are their godless worshippers.

Finally, Çraŏsha originates from Ahura, nourishes the poor, utters blessings. In the *Khordah-Avesta* he is said to watch over the treaties of peace and the compacts with the Drujas. It seems, then, that such treaties were made, and that they had a religious sanctity, reminding us that with the Romans, *religio-jusjurandi* was the sanctity of an oath. How devoutly inclined these ancients were, may be judged of by this passage of the *Khordah-Avesta*, in the *Çrosh-Yasht-Hadokht*:

> Whosoever, O Zarathustra, whether man or woman, utters this prayer, with a devout heart, with words and works of sincere faith, whether at a great river, at a great terror in a dark cloudy night, at the ford of a stream, at the crossings of roads, in the assembly of the faithful, or amid a multitude of Daeva-worshippers at any bad hap, when one fears calamity from evil men, in that day or in that night there will not be seen by him hostile infidels or robbers; and the plague of the predatory bands upon their raids will not reach him.

Ahura created Çraŏsha as an antagonist of Aeshma (Rapine); and he is praised together with the peace that is the fruit of victory. And these and many other passages of the later compositions thus prove that the burthen of the old hymns was the struggle to throw off the yoke of the infidels and expel them from the land.

Two Deities, *Rashnu-râzista* and *Arstât*, are often praised in the later writings. What they are, the commentators do not know. Bopp makes *Rashnu* to mean "justice, righteousness, uprightness, truth." Spiegel says he is the genius of justice. *Râzista*, superlative of *râz*=Sanskrit *râj*, to "excel, shine," means "most royal or most sovereign"—*râj* meaning "king" in Sanskrit; and *râjas*, *rajan*, "sovereign, ruler."

Arstât, Spiegel renders by "probity." Bopp thinks it may mean "invulnerable."

The texts call *Rashnus* "just, merciful and righteous." If the name itself meant these they would not be superadded to it. Mithras gave Rashnus a dwelling-place, and Rashnus, for long friendship, prepared him one. How could this be said of justice, Mithras being the Morning-Star or Light? Why should justice ride on the right hand of Mithras, with the rightest wisdom on the left? Rashnu and Arstât have bodies. The sun is the body of Ahura. What are the bodies of justice and truthfulness? Rashnus is "far-seeing, also," which is said only of luminaries. So he visits the seven Kareshvares, and the constellations Vanant and Tistrya and the Great Bear, and is at the bounds of the Aryan land, at the Sea Vouru-Kasha, on the mountains, at the waters and steppes of Raṅha.

I have been unfortunate if I have not satisfied you that things of this sort cannot have been said by the men who composed these books, of abstractions like justice and truth. If they are, we had better close the books, and speak of them no more.

These Deities were, at the beginning, beyond any question, two luminaries, which, becoming abstract conceptions at a later period, still continued to be associated, in the popular idea, with the bodies of which they were originally the names. It is a curious coincidence that *Tsadôc*, the Phœnician *Sydyk*, "just," was the planet Jupiter. *Rashnu* is probably from the Sanskrit verb *raksh*, to "preserve, guard, govern, tend, protect." The termination *nu* forms adjectives and substantives (Bopp, section 948) and *ksh* in Sanskrit often becomes *sh* in Zend, as in *dashina* for *dakshina*, "right hand," and *tash* for *taksh*, to "fabricate." So that *Rashnu* meant "guardian, protector, warder or sentinel." He was *razista* "most royal," as the Vedic Varuṇa was; and I think he was, like him, the planet Jupiter.

Arch, in Sanskrit, means to "beam, shine"; afterwards it came to mean to "worship, honor." Thence *archi*, "flame," *archis*, "a ray of light." I think that *arch* is the root of *Arstât*. *Raçmi*, also, is "a ray of light," and must have had a root *raç*, to "shine." The resemblance between *Arstât* and the Phœnician *Astarte*, Venus, is curious, but I give it no significance, coming, without it, to the conclusion that *Arstât*, feminine, was originally the Evening-Star, and afterwards the planet Venus, as *Rashnus* was originally the Morning-Star, and afterwards Jupiter. As Goddess of Love, *Arstât* was, of course, the furtherer, promoter and increaser of the Aryan land and people. As planets, they rode, one on one side, one on the other, of the sun, which Mithra had then become. And in their "circles" or circuits the Aryan land was included.

At last, Rashnu became the abstract idea of the Divine Justice, and Arstât of the Divine Truth; the latter being called "the Rightest Wisdom" and the "True-spoken Word." But Rashnu still continued to "find" and to "prepare" a dwelling-place for Mithra; for he continued to be both the protector and the sentinel of the morning.

It is surely a thing worthy to be noted, that the ancient names of these stars, "guide, sentinel, protector," and "radiant one," should at length have come to mean the protecting justice of the Deity, and the effulgent divine truthfulness; and that it was the belief, after the days of Zarathustra, that these would give prosperity, increase and extension to the Aryan domain. But these conceptions may have been, also, of the age of Zarathustra, for we have but a small portion of his teachings in the Gâthâs. There are unmistakable fragments of his instruction incorporated in the later writings. It is not likely that he personified the Divine Justice and Truth, as Rashnu and Arstât, but he no doubt called them by those names, as he called worship Çraôsha; and we may be sure, I think, that the potency of these virtues, to make prosperous and magnify a land, was no new idea, foreign to his teaching.

It is pleasant to know that there was a time once, seven thousand years ago or more, when those of our blood and kin believed, contrary to the modern faith, that nations do not prosper by wrong-doing; nor truly greaten by lies.

A great deal is said in the later poems about a female Goddess, *Ashis Vanuhi*, who is not mentioned in the old Gâthâs, and I was for a long time at a loss to imagine what she could be. And yet it seemed to me that it ought to be possible to determine what was meant by a Deity of whom so much is said, and to whom functions so varied and important are ascribed.

She is daughter of Ahura and Çpēnta-Armaiti, sister of Çraôsha, Rashnus and Mithra. She must therefore be a spiritual being, or some personified attribute or potency of Deity or Nature; and not a luminary. Her sister, also, the Mazdayaçnian Law is; and for this, again, she cannot be a luminary. She is the inseparable companion, who of herself clings close to the instructing; she is in the service of religion; she enters houses, with friendly mind, for long friendship, and brings silver and gold, garments and girdles; she takes the form of a fair young maiden, confirms all the profitable with forward-going understanding (encourages in all the husbandmen the desire to go to new regions), and bestows the heavenly understanding as a gift. She is sweet-smelling, and the house into which she comes, to remain, gives forth fragrance: and she attaches herself to those who cook and bestow much food.

She is grieved on account of those who bear no children, of those who expose them, and of men who will not marry, and consults Ahura whether she shall ascend to the sky or creep close to the earth, on account of it. She goes to the country of the good King, and remains in the midst of it. She unites with the stars of the rain (Tistrya), with the wind, and the Aryan supremacy, all which are like unto her, and makes to thrive the summits of the mountains and recesses of the valleys.

Çpĕnta-Armaiti is the divine power of production, existing as an emanation from him, and *causing* the earth and creatures to produce. Ashis-Vanuhi, her daughter and Ahura's, is this productive capacity of the earth and of living creatures. She is, in other words, Production and Birth. This explains all the texts. She is an inseparable *female* companion, because growth and birth never cease. She clings close to the instructing, and is connected with the service of religion; for she furnishes the meat and grain and milk and haŏma for the sacrifices. She tempts men to seek new fields and pastures. She bestows the spiritual understanding, by bearing a part in the acts of worship.

She takes the form of a fair maiden, which is appropriate to her especial season, the blushing spring, with her rare jewelry of flowers and garnishing of leaves: and she also punishes the Daevas and protects the Aryan homes against them, because she supplies food to the armies: and she is bound with purity, because she is associated with religion by her offerings. She is brightness, for the original word means great prosperity, and she creates that: and majesty, because her supplies are the cause of victory and dominion. And she is "well-created," because she is the manifestation, in act and effort and result, of a potency that emanates from Ahura Mazda.

She is fair and beaming, for production displays itself in beauty and rejoices in the light. She comes hither out of the beams, because the sun's rays cause production by the earth: and her shining "wheel" is the orb of the sun that ministers to her. Çraŏsha is her brother, and the true creed her sister, because she ministers to worship and the rites prescribed by the creed, and these increase production, by protecting the producer who worships; and because all prosperity is the fruit of piety. Rashnu is her brother, because the just alone prosper; and Mithra, because, whether light or sun, he furthers production.

There is much more, but I must refrain. I shall only add a few explanations of names. She drives away the deadly Daeva *Apaŏshô*. *Apa* is a particle of negation, meaning "away from, without." *Oshadhi*, in Sanskrit, means "a plant": and *Apaŏshô*, "barrenness, unproduction." *Çiçti*, *Raçançtat*, *Erĕthĕ* and *Khnoithri* are named in connection with *Ashis*. *Çiçti* means "swelling, increasing, the state preceding production and birth." *Raçançtat* is generation; *Erĕthĕ*, in Sanskrit *Artha*, "desire"; and *Khnoithri*, from the Sanskrit *Khan*, to "dig," whence *Khanitra*, "a spade," is "cultivation," by digging and ploughing.

As to the name of the Goddess herself, *Vanhu*, in Zend, is "wealth, abundance," and *Ashis* means "being, existence, entity." The whole name means "abundance-being," or "the production that creates abundance."

There is a picture of the state of the wealthy men, in the *Ashi-Yasht*, of a very ancient time, but much later than that of Zarathustra. These wealthy Magnates have many dependents and followers, raise abundant crops, keep bounteous tables and dispense food to many retainers. They are rich in horses and chariots, with daggers of tempered metal; and they dwell in well-built houses and are surrounded by comforts and luxuries. Their dwellings are solidly built, and they are always prepared to resist an attack, or to make one, having a large force of retainers and auxiliaries.

Their couches for reclining, or seats, are handsomely made, ornamented, and have rich coverings, and the foot-stools have coverings embroidered with gold. On these seats or couches their beloved wives sit, who are the inmates of their houses, with heels bound (which I do not understand, unless it means wearing sandals, which were tied on the feet), ear-rings pendant, and necklaces of gold, waiting for the lord of the house to come, and anxious to know by what means they can minister to his bodily wants and comfort. And their maidens also sit there, adorned with anklets, with slender waists, fine figures, long toes—beautiful of body, it is said, as those could wish whom they are to marry.

The horses of the men are swift, eager, strongly drawing the chariots, harnessed for the followers of the true doctrine, and bearing along the worshippers mighty in war, who are armed with long, sharp-pointed lances, and flexible arrows, wary when in pursuit of the foe, slayers of them when face to face. Their camels are strong-backed, easily guided by the mere will, move with springy step, and are tractable. And to these wealthy men she brings silver and gold, from other countries, garments and shining girdles.

This indicates clearly enough, that at a very early day, a trade by caravans had sprung up and was carried on, perhaps by the passes of the Hindu Kush, by traders from Kabul and other regions, who exchanged rich goods from the south for the products of the Aryan land, including gold dug from mines spoken of elsewhere, and washed out of the sands of the Oxus. But it is uncertain what region was the chief seat of the Irano-Aryan power, when these Yashts were composed. It is more than probable that they were later than the settlement of Media.

The good *Pârendi* is praised in the later Yaçna. In the *Tistar-Yasht*, she is praised with *Ashis-Vanuhi*. She is invoked in the *Sirozah*, and there, as *Pârendi* with the swift chariot; and in the *Vispered* she is the friendly *Pârendi*, who is rich in friendly thoughts, words and deeds, and makes the bodies light.

Neriosengh makes her the Goddess that presides over hidden treasures. Spiegel says she must be a star. I do not see that. Anquetil's manuscripts call her the Protectress of Mankind. The Sanskrit *l* changes in Zend into *r*, for *l* is wanting in Zend: and the change of *ph* into *p* is a very slight one. *Pârendi* is from the Sanskrit *phal*, to "burst, bear fruit, produce, be fruitful." *Phal* came from the original *spar*, which became *sphar*, and then *sphur*, meaning to "break forth, spring up, flash, shine, sparkle." The *s* was very early dropped in words like this: and I have no doubt that *Pârendi* is from this root, and personified either germination and growth, flowering, or fruit-bearing. She is therefore always and properly named with *Ashis-Vanuhi*.

The *Yazatas* of the *Zend-Avesta* are known to students of the old mythologies in the books of twenty years ago, as the *Izeds*. They were, Guigniaut says, "inferior genii, created by Ormuzd, to shed blessings on the world." Unfortunately for this theory, Ahura Mazda was himself a Yazata. "Each of the Amshaspands has his train of Izeds, who serve him as the Amshaspands themselves serve Ormuzd," he adds. Unfortunately, again, the Amĕsha-Çpĕntas themselves are Yazatas.

He gives the names of twenty-eight Izeds and says that Plutarch knew but twenty-four of them, because he restricted them to those who, with the Amshaspands, presided over the days of the month. Yet he admits that Ormuzd and the Amshaspands are sometimes called Izeds, especially when they preside over the days of the month.

Yaj, in Sanskrit, *yaz* in Zend, means to "pray or praise." From it comes the word *Yaçna* or *Yazânê*, "offering," in Sanskrit, *Yajna*. *Yajata* in Sanskrit, *Yazata* in Zend, means "worthy of honor or worship, adorable, worshipful." In Sanskrit, also, *Yajata* meant an officiating priest at the sacrifice. In the *Qarshet-Yasht* it is said that there are hundreds, thousands, of the heavenly Yazatas; which means that the stars are so called. They spread abroad light, it is there said, portion it out on the land created by Ahura. Fire is the greatest Yazata. So is Mithra, and Vĕrĕthraghna is the best-armed one. In the Vispered they are said to be innumerable.

The word is not used in the Gâthâs, and the later notions in regard to them are not found anywhere in the *Zend-Avesta*. Every thing heavenly and earthly, that is worthy to be praised, is a *Yazata*, the word being merely an adjective, the past participle passive of *yaz*.

Mithra or *Mithras* is more frequently mentioned and better known than any other of the Persian Deities. When the Medians conquered Persia, he had become the sun, and long afterwards his worship was introduced at Rome, during the reign of Trojan, though made known to the Romans, Plutarch says, in the time of Pompey, it being then established in Cilicia, by the pirates whom he broke up and most of whom took refuge there. Afterwards it extended over Greece, and its monuments are found there, and in Switzerland, France and Germany. His mysteries were celebrated at Rome, and human beings were sacrificed to him, a practice prohibited by Hadrian, but revived by Commodus, who himself sacrificed a man to Mithras. He was called *Deus Sol invictus Mithra;* and Archelaüs accused Manes of believing in his divinity and worshipping him.

The principal symbol of his mysteries was a kind of ladder with seven apertures, representing, it was supposed, the spheres of the seven planets, through which souls had to pass descending to unite with bodies, and returning when freed from them. There is no doubt that the Mithriac worship was then utterly variant from the doctrine, worship and symbols of ancient Persia. The mysteries and rites of Mithras were prescribed in the year 378 of our era, and the sacred cave was then opened and destroyed by order of Gracchus the Prætorian Prefect. Eichhorn, in 1815, in a memoir read to the Royal Society of Sciences at Gottingen, showed that Mithras was not the sun, to the Persians, but was taken to be so by the Romans, being really a genius, the constant companion of the sun. Anquetil asserted the same: and the Baron Silvestre de Sacy says that the authorities that seem to confound the sun with Mithra might be reconciled, by admitting that Mihr or Mithra was an Ized who had the charge and direction of the sun, and seemed always to accompany him, having his domicil in the planet Venus. And this would justify what Herodotus says, that Mitra was a female Deity, identical with the Venus-Urania.

Benfey gives to *Mitra*, i. e., *Mid+tra*, also written *Maitra* in the *Veda*, the signification in Sanskrit of "the sun, a friend, an ally." But nothing is more certain than that the Vedic Mitra was the Morning-Star. There are two verbs *mid*, but I do not believe that *Mithra* or *Mitra* came from either. The word is certainly used in the Vendidad in the sense of a contract, bargain or promise; and the *Mithrô-drujas*, "breakers of contracts, alliances or treaties" are denounced there; originally, perhaps, the native tribes, who violated their treaties with the Aryans. *Meth, mith, midh, medh, mid* and *med* are all given by Benfey as at bottom the same; and one of the meanings he gives to *meth* and *medh* is to "associate." Also he gives as a Vedic meaning of *mid*, to "rejoice." Naturally the Morning-Star was considered to be associated or connected with the sun; and as Mithra was called the "associate, companion, friend, or ally" of the sun, the name came afterwards to mean that. Moreover, he *precedes* the sun, and announces or promises his coming, and so may have been called the "promiser," until the word came to mean a promise and a contract or alliance.

By the Persians he was called *Mihr*, and the Yasht devoted to him is the *Mihr-Yasht*. He is not once named in the Gâthâs, although it is not to be doubted that he was adored as the Morning-Star before the Irano-Aryan emigration. At last he became the Deity's Very Self, producing himself in human form. So it has been in all mythologies and religions. If the younger God does not dethrone the elder, he is always magnified into his equal or superior. The Very Deity, the inaccessible, absolute, is too remote from human sympathy and human interests, to satisfy the innate human craving for a divine object of worship that may also be loved, as having these human affections and consequent sympathies for humanity, which, it cannot but sometimes be feared, if not always admitted, the one cannot have who is infinitely beyond the reach of those evils, and free of those duties, that are the only causes of all the human virtues and excellencies, and alone afford the opportunities for their exercise.

Mithra, in the *Zend-Avesta*, possesses wide pastures, and has a thousand ears and ten thousand eyes, and a renowned name. He is called Râma-Qâçtra. *Rama*, in Sanskrit, is "love," and the name of the Deity of Love. *Qâçtra* means "that which shines"; and the whole name, probably, "the light or star of love," or, as *râma* means "beautiful," "the beautiful light or radiance." Spiegel makes it mean the genius who bestows relish for food. The least inquiry would have shown him that it did not mean that.

Mithra, the Sun, and the two eyes of Ahura are invoked together. He is sleepless and vigilant, is within and set over the Aryan regions, is below, before and behind them, and gives protection, joy, profit, healing and victory. Ahura says to Zarathustra, "I created him as worthy of honor and praise as myself." The lords of the regions praise him at the early dawn, when they lead their forces against the hostile squadrons, in the fight in the war for the regions: and the warriors on horseback praise him, asking his aid against the enemy.

As the first heavenly Yazata, he rises over the great mountain range Hara Bĕrĕzaiti, before the sun, and, immortal, with swift steeds, first, with golden form, seizes the fair summits, and then extends over the whole Aryan land, marching into all the Kareshvares, giving glory and victory to those who offer to him. His body is the Manthra, too, and as a warrior he smites the Daevas and Pairikas and gives strength and victory to the regions. He is prayed to for victory, dominion and power, all of which are personified and adored; and thus seems to be invested with the vicegerency under Ahura.

Why? Because he is the visible light, and so the manifestation of the Very Substance, Light, of the Very Deity. Therefore he is said to have been created equal with him, as the Logos, Word or Son is said to be equal to the Father: and therefore it is that the Manthra is his body. But, nevertheless, expressions are retained, that were used when he was only the Morning-Star. His dwelling is broad as the earth, high without limit, broad and affording wide space; and his eight friends sit spying for him on all heights and watch-towers, watching the marches of the infidels, who seek to slay the Aryans. These must have been so many great stars, that rose with the Morning-Star and the dawn, at the time when this Yasht was composed.

Chapter 13 of this Yasht is curiously significant. Mithra says to Ahura Mazda, weeping, with uplifted hands:

> I am the Protector of all creatures, the skilful: I am the Ruler of all creatures, the skilful: yet men do not offer to me by name, as they offer to the other Yazatas.

If they would, he says, he would come at the appointed time of his own life, the shining, the immortal.

So, in the *Tistar-Yasht*, Tistrya, the constellation of rain, probably the three stars in the Belt of Orion, makes the same complaint and offer, and claims to be fit to be praised and worshipped. The result is, that Ahura does offer to Tistrya, giving him the strength he desired.

Which passages clearly show that the worship of Mithra and the stars was either entirely new, or the old worship abolished by Zarathustra, revived, probably against much opposition. It is evident that the new Gods grew into favor by degrees. Either the people remembered them and compelled their recognition, or their worship was adopted from that of the native tribes, with whom the Irano-Aryans intermingled.

> He advances at sunrise, broad as the earth, sweeps both sides of the earth, and envelops all that is between the sky and earth.

And this single passage of the *Mihr-Yasht* is amply sufficient to prove that Mithra was the light, and particularly and especially (I think exclusively), the Day-light. The commentators, on the *Zend-Avesta* and *Veda* alike, do not seem to think that the composers of either used any sort of caution and discrimination in the use of epithets and expressions, or had much care or thought as to their pertinency, congruity, aptness and appropriateness: and therefore not one of them has given to some of the most significant texts their due weight, nor endeavored to reconcile the texts with each other and with their theories as to the meanings of the Deities spoken of; so that they can still complacently say that Indra is the firmament, in the very teeth of texts that make that absolutely impossible. But the truth is that there are, as to almost every Deity, as to every one, of whom much is said, peculiar expressions, not used as to any other, that have a special, peculiar and sometimes logical appropriateness to that Deity alone, which reveal with unmistakable certainty the character of the Deity and identify him or her beyond possibility of mistake, to any one whose eyes are not sealed up by a theory or pre-conception. For example, there are certain expressions that are invariably applied to luminaries only, and others to universals and personifications of potencies. Mithra alone is said to possess broad fields or pastures; and the expressions in the verse last cited are not found anywhere else.

And so the saying ascribed to Ahura, that he created Mithra in all things equal to himself, is not a mere thoughtless one, without special and peculiar meaning. It is, on the contrary, just as definite and precise as a mathematical formula.

What is above equals what is below; the visible is the measure of the invisible,

the Tablet of Emerald of Hermes said.

He thought it not robbery to make himself equal with God,

St. Paul says; and the *Word* is everywhere

"the express image of God."

As light (not as intellect or productiveness or beneficence or power, but in so far as he is light), Ahura manifests and reveals himself as Mithra; and if he were to make himself as light visible in his entirety, that entirety would still be Mithra. Even the words "here" and "there" are not expletives, but always mean the mother-country and the province or new conquest.

And after this revelation of the meaning of Mithra, in the very wantonness of an imagination having no fear of criticism to restrain its luxuriance, or almost as if to mystify the hearer, the reciter of the praises of Mithra furnishes him with a mace, with a hundred knots and edges, before which Aṅra-Mainyus, Aëshma, Bushyançta, and the invisible Daevas, and the Varenian Daevas flee affrighted. His long arms now reach forward, and he subjugates the infidels in Eastern Bactria, making them vassals of the Aryans, and he smites and slays those in Western Bactria, and on the plains of Raṅha, and at the extremities of the Aryan land. Now he wears a helmet of silver and a coat of golden mail, is armed with a dagger, is lord of the clan and a warrior. And the Græco-Aryan sculptor, who carved the statue of Mars or Minerva, cuirassed and helmeted, with shield and spear or sword, or that of Apollo or Diana with the bow, only embodied in marble the kindred Aryan fancies already embodied in verse by the Grecian poets.

Even Ahura Mazda offered to him, on the shining Gâro-Nemâna, from which he rides forth in a golden chariot, of all shapes, with four white horses, their fore-hoofs shod with gold, their hind-hoofs with silver. The commentators have not even noticed the seemingly singular, if not absurd idea that Ahura Mazda *sacrificed* to "the genius that guides the sun." For it is not possible, upon their theories, or in accordance with their notions, to explain this. Is it possible, as I understand the philosophical ideas of the *Zend-Avesta?* It is perfectly and even transparently simple. Each emanation *is* Ahura Mazda manifested. Constantly we are told that he does, what even in the same breath is said to be done by Vohu-Manô, Khshathra or Asha. Vohu-Manô sacrifices and worships, for the words uttered by the worshipper are Vohu-Manô's, and he is the intellect and mind of the priest. Every act of Vohu-Manô is the act of Ahura, and therefore it is Ahura who sacrifices by the priest.

So we read in Spiegel's translation,

When he illumines the body, as the self-illumining moon shines, his countenance shines like the Constellation Tistrya.

This is utter nonsense; but if it means,

The moon is his body, and he shines by it, when revealing him in her light she shines: and visibly revealed as the star or Constellation Tistrya he shines,

the words have some meaning.

I only add that his "mace" or "club," is in the original, *vazra*, in Sanskrit, *vajra*, "hard, forked, a wedge, the thunderbolt of Indra."

We read in Spiegel's translation of "the *air* that works on high," and of "the *bird* that works on high." The original word, rendered by "air," is *vayu*, and as in the *Veda*, it means "the flame," as also does the word rendered by "the bird."

Thus it appears that the Irano-Aryans did not worship the sun, but that in the Fire, the Light and the Flame, Asha, Mithra and Vayu, they adored the invisible God, Ahura Mazda, as revealed and manifested by them. Nor did they worship him thus, as the Light only; but also as the Supreme Will, Power, Beneficence and Intellect. You will find it *said* that he was born in the infinite time, *Zarvan-Akarana.* But it is not anywhere said that *he* was born in the infinite time, nor is this infinite time anywhere a being.   There is not the least foundation for the notion that he and Aṅra-Mainyus were created by the infinite or boundless time.   Anquetil got this notion, and the mistranslation of the passage supposed to state it (in the 19th Fargard of the Vendidad), from his teachers, the Parsee Dustoors. Dr. Haug has clearly shown that the meaning of the passage is, that Çpĕnta-Mainyu created certain potencies in the boundless time.   The only error I find, is, that *Akarana* does not mean "boundless," "endless" or "infinite," but "uncreated," *Kar* and *Kĕrĕ*, in Zend, meaning to "make, create, produce," as *Kṛi*, which is the same word, does in Sanskrit.   As to *Zarvan* or *Zervan*, it is from the Sanskrit *jaraṇa*, "old age," from *jṛî*, to "grow old."   Dr. Haug considers the phrase to mean "at a time unknown or immemorial, or in the beginning."

Ardvîçûra is a particular river, · and at the same time a female Deity, Goddess of rivers, or of waters and irrigation.   She is not named in the Gâthâs, and was probably not adored in the time of Zarathustra.   It is said in the *Farvardin-Yasht*, that she is great and far-renowned, as great as all the other waters that descend swiftly to the Aryan land, flowing down from Hukairya the lofty to the Sea Vouru-Kasha, all flowing across the country, and being poured into the sea, by Ardvîçûra.   She flows with a mighty current, and has a thousand basins, a thousand channels, each forty-days journey long for a man on horseback; and at each canal, it is said, stands a well-built house with a hundred windows, a thousand pillars and ten thousand props; in each house a throne, with pillows.   To these she hastens with the strength of a thousand men.   She is described as a maiden, wearing an out-waving undergarment with many folds, a golden one; as holding the bareçma, a bundle of sacred twigs or sticks, wearing ear-rings and a necklace, her body girdled and breasts beautiful; on' her head a diadem, with a hundred stars, golden, adorned with banners, and wearing garments of beaver-skin, of thirty of the fur-bearing beavers, shining, brilliant, most silver and gold.   Her arms (branches) are fair, very shining, greater than horses.   She drives her chariot along, asking who will praise her and offer to her (which shows that her worship had been recently introduced, and was not generally accepted): and she has four draught-cattle, all white, which torment Daevas and the infidels, sorcerers and Pairikas.   For by affording water for irrigation she enables the husbandmen to cultivate the land, and so to furnish food to maintain the armies and sustain the people.

This singular passage occurs in the *Aban-Yasht*, which is devoted to Ardvîçûra; that the Creator Ahura Mazda, in Airyama-Vaêja, the Aryan land or land of the true believers ("of the pure creation") praised with the haŏma, bareçma, Maṅthra, etc., and prayed Ardvîçûra for a favor, that he might unite himself with Zarathustra, so that he might think, speak and act according to the Mazdayaçnian gospel; and Ardvîçûra "afforded him this favor, him the ever-bringing offerings, giving, offering, him who prays the female-givers for a favor."

In the *Veda*, Agni, the substance of the Devas, and manifested by them, is also the sacrificial fire, and as such, the sacrificer and the messenger and bearer of the oblations to the Devas, his manifestations, i. e., to himself as manifested by them. So it is possible that the Irano-Aryan imagination may have followed to the foregoing conclusion the idea that Vohu-Manô and the Fire (son of Ahura) perform the praise and sacrifice, and that this is done by Ahura, through them. And the meaning would be, though put in this singular form, that Ahura, inspiring Zarathustra, prayed that he would assist the latter in conforming to the Ahurian creed. It was but to carry a doctrine out to its logical consequences.

Several legends are recited in the *Aban-Yasht*, two of which, as brief and curiously illustrative of the processes of Iranian thought, I will repeat.

She ran to help Vifra-navâza, in the form of a beautiful maiden, a very strong one, girt up, fair, with brilliant countenance, noble, clad with shoes beneath her feet (sandals), with a golden diadem on her head. She seized him by the arm. Soon he struggles mighty to the earth created by Ahura, sound, as uninjured as before, to his own dwelling.

So, at the prayer of Vis-taurusha, for a dry ford over the water Vîtañu-haiti, she ran there in the same form, with golden shoes, and

> at the height of the whole ford, made the one waters stand still, and the others flow forward, and so made a dry way across.

These are legends, no doubt, of dangerous passages of rivers by forces of the Aryans, during the wars against the infidels.

Ahura Mazda placed her in charge of the waters, telling her to go hither and thither, from the stars down to the Aryan land, and that the chiefs would sacrifice to her; and warriors pray to her for swift horses and for power that comes from above; the Athravas (priests) for greatness (abundance) for the producers of food, and for victory and the destruction of the enemy (the blow that comes from above).

In a conversation between Zarathustra and her, he asks,

> To whom come thy offerings, when the wicked worshippers of the Daevas offer to thee at day-break?

The Scythians or Tâtars worshipped her, therefore; and her worship may have been adopted by the Aryans, from the native tribes, like the worship of the stars; although it is said in this Yasht that Zarathustra, Kava-

Vîstaçpa (the Gushtasp of Persian legends), and other heroes offered sacrifices to her, and Hvô-gvas (cattle owners).

The character of Ardvîçûra, sometimes river and sometimes Goddess, seems to be the extravagant product of a fantastic imagination; it appearing impossible to conceive of the powers ascribed to her as ever having been coupled, even in the most deranged fancy, with the idea of the Spirit of Water or of a river.

But this is rather apparent than real.

Ahura Mazda [she said to Zarathustra] has created me to be the protector of the whole Aryan land. Through my glory and power are cattle and men.

Ahura created for her the wind, rain, clouds and hail, and so furnished her with water to fertilize the plains. She manifested, therefore, the greatness, the might and the beneficence óf Ahura Mazda, as much as the light did; and she was his instrument and agent to fertilize the fields and to sustain life in animals and men. If a river flowing from the mountains rose to such a height as to overflow the wide alluvial lands that lay along its course, it would stop and delay the march of a reinforcement, and so might cause the loss of a battle. The Spirit of the Water, therefore, might well be invoked, in a poetical composition, originally not at all devotional, to favor and assist the Aryans against the invaders, especially in a country where rivers were numerous, deep and rapid, and a protection against marauders. So an overflow would destroy the growing crops, and sweep away and drown the grazing cattle; and therefore it was natural that the Goddess of the Water should be invoked by the husbandman and the Athravas, with offerings and incense, since the welfare of the whole state depended on its husbandry. Neither could the lands be cultivated without irrigation, and the maintenance of armies depended on the supply of food; and it was natural to ascribe to the River-Goddess the material prosperity of the country, and victory in war; and she might even be figured as engaging hand to hand in the conflict.

And if figured as a maiden, beautiful and well-dressed and decorated with golden ornaments, this is no more than our poets of today imagine and picture, for spring and the moon, or than the ancients did when they figured Cupid as a winged boy armed with the bow and arrows. There is a whole pantheon in Bunyan's *Holy War*, and a gallery of statues of the passions and virtues and vices personified, in Spenser. In all the *Veda* and *Zend-Avesta* there is no bolder personification than Tennyson's of the Old Year, who "frothed his bumpers to the brim," and of whom the poet said, when his eyes were waxing dim,

He was full of joke and jest,
But all his merry quips are o'er.
To see him die, across the waste
His son and heir doth ride posthaste,
But he'll be dead before . . . .
How hard he breathes! . . . .
His face is growing sharp and thin,
Alack! our friend is gone.
Close up his eyes, tie up his chin;
Step from the corpse, and let him in,
That standeth there alone,
And waiteth at the door.

In the Twentieth and Twenty-first Books of the Iliad, the River Xanthus or Scamander takes part, as a God, in the great battle between the Greeks and Troïans—"the watery Godhead, that great flood," "that runs on golden sands"; and, in the words of Chapman, Achilles had slain many more of the men of Troy.

Unless the angry flood
Had took the figure of a man, and in a whirl-pit stood,
Thus speaking to Æacides,

commanding him to desist.

We shall find many of the ancient heroes sacrificing to Ardvîçûra, and by their prayers to her enabled to conquer the infidel chiefs: but these are only interesting as legends of ancient heroes and heroic achievements. Nothing could be less profitable than to trace in detail the degeneration of the ancient, pure and sublime doctrine of Zarathustra into the mass of absurdity which constituted the later religion.

In the next and concluding lecture I will return to the Gâthâs, and shall hope, by a review and explanation of these, and a brief reference to the legendary portions of the *Zend-Avesta*, to convince you of its great value as a record of ancient thought and of primæval history.

LECTURE EIGHT

THE LAST FOUR GÂTHÂS AND LEGENDARY

I propose in this concluding lecture somewhat to acquaint you with the four remaining Gâthâs of Zarathustra, as I understand them. And I deem them eminently worthy to be understood, not only as probably the oldest literary monuments and records of human thought in the world, and as the source and origin of the great philosophical doctrines of the world, but also and far more, because they make known to us a sublime theosophy and purely philosophic faith, believed in and understood by men of our own blood and lineage, at a very remote period, when they dwelt near the cradle of the race, and with the Indo-Aryan branch were beginning that career of conquest which was to make them the Masters of the World—a period heretofore supposed to be far beyond the reach of history, and yet as to which we now know more than we do of the beginnings of Rome.

The second Gâthâ consists of four sections, and is called *Ustvaiti*, from the words *Ustâ ahmâi*, "Hail to him!" with which it begins. Dr. Haug gives a translation of the whole of it in his *Essays;* and in the works from which these Lectures are compiled, I have given, verse by verse, Dr. Bleeck's translation and his, and my own interpretation of each, with comments and explanations. Dr. Haug thinks that, with the exception of five verses only, it contains the sayings of Zarathustra himself, and carries out a certain scheme, the verses being arranged in a certain order, with the intention, on the part of his followers, of presenting a true image of his mission, activity and teaching. It contains, he thinks, in the successive sections, the announcement of his mission, instructions from Ahura about the highest matters of human speculation, the propounding of his new doctrines before an assembly of his countrymen, and verses referring to his own fate, that of the congregation established by him, and those of his most eminent friends and supporters.

I agree with very little of this. In the first Gâthâ, Zarathustra had depicted the wretched condition of the people, announced his commission as commander, and enlarged upon the power of Ahura Mazda and his emanations, and the efficacy of the true faith and of worship, to secure their aid and achieve victory, peace, security, a new country, and glory and dominion.

In the first and second sections of this second Gâthâ, he addresses Ahura asking for power, and the establishment of his rule and government, and the overthrow and expulsion of the invaders.

I follow, for the most part, the translation of Dr. Bleeck from the German of Spiegel and the Guzerat translation, as being in the main a literal rendering of the original, though much of it is, as to the sense, confessedly conjectural. And I shall seldom give any more than my own interpretation, only referring to the two translations when some special reasons require it. And as I cannot give the whole, I shall note by numbers the verses that I quote in each section, that you may know how much, for want of space I am constrained to omit.

Hâ i.

1. Hail to Him who hath in His gift good fortune for each! May Ahura, whose rule is absolute and uncontrolled, create power and strength by the exertion of thy Will! That I may be able to maintain the true religion, give me, O Armaiti, dominion, victory, and the inspiration of Vohu-Manô!

2. May that glory which is the most excellent of all be bestowed on us, by the being who has the fulness of glory. Show thyself forth, O Most Beneficent Intelligence, Mazda! Thou, O source of the true faith, who didst utter forth the excellent thoughts of Vohu-Manô, day after day, desiring thereby to give security of life.

3. May every man attain good fortune who makes known to us the right courses to be followed, to be of benefit to this Aryan land and to our lives; who openly promulgates the faith in the Aryan regions, wherein Ahura abides; the sacrificer, who in wisdom and excellence resembles thee, O Mazda.

These were the coadjutors of Zarathustra, of whom Jamaçpa was the foremost, who traversed the country as missionaries, arousing the people from their lethargic apathy, to make common cause against the Infidels.

4. I conceived of thee, Mazda, as the powerful, as well as beneficent one. For thou with thine own hand preservest the blessing which thou didst create alike for those of the true faith and the infidel oppressors—the heat of thy fire: but endowed by thee with the potency of religious worship, when there came to me energy from Vohu-Manô.

5, 6. I deemed thee to be the Supreme Intelligence, Ahura, when, at the first settlement of the Aryan land, I saw that thou didst cause observances and prayers to produce fruit, of misfortune for the faithless, and prosperity for the true believers. At the final distribution of the country conquered and acquired by thee, by means of thy power, exerted in our behalf, through thy prayers and Mañthras, all those by means of whose exploits and services the domain of the true faith shall have been enlarged in the land, shall, for their loyalty, O Supreme Intelligence, Mazda, share the lands over which thou wilt then reign; and Armaiti will bestow blessing on these, the ministers of the teachings of thy intellect; those whom no one has seduced.

7. I deemed thee to be the Supreme Intelligence, Mazda Ahura, as it came to me through Vohu-Manô, and asked me, "What art thou? of whom art thou the votary?" How shall I, upon thy questioning, teach the revealings of the light, in respect to thy countries and people?

8. Then made Zarathustra this first reply to him: since that which is of vital necessity is utterly to defeat and bring calamity upon the infidels, enable me thus to give occasion for great rejoicing to the faithful Aryans! Since I will use my power

as ruler, to enlighten the people with knowledge, so will I, all my life, adore and worship thee, O Mazda.

9. I deemed thee to be the Supreme Intelligence, Mazda Ahura, when it came to me through Vohu-Manô, asking me "What dost thou desire to know?" The orisons of religious adoration for thy sacrifices, as many as I can receive and recollect.

10. [Bleeck]: Give thou to me perfect Purity, since I desire it for myself, thou who art bound with wisdom! Ask us the questions which thou hast for us, for thy questions are those of the mighty, since to thee the ruler gives strength at will.

[Haug]: Thus mayest thou grant me the truth. Then I shall call myself, if accompanied by the angel of piety, a pious, obedient man. And I will ask in the behalf of both of us, whatever thou mayest be asked: for the king will, as it is only allowed to mighty men, make thee for thy answers a mighty fire.

I assure you, for you might doubt it, that these are really translations of the same verse. As far as I can discern the original, hidden behind the two, it seems to me that Zarathustra continues speaking to Ahura, and Ahura, for himself and Çpênta-Mainyu, replies to him, it being the Divine Intellect that replies, by Vohu-Manô; thus;

"O thou who art one with Çpênta-Armaiti, give thou to me in perfection the true faith, since I ask it for myself." "Ask us," the reply is, "the questions which thou hast for us, for thy questions are those of one invested with power, since to thee Khshathra gives absolute rule."

11. I deemed thee to be the Beneficent, O Mazda, when thy inspiration came to me through Vohu-Manô; when I was first taught, through your prayer [the *Ahuna Vairya*] that by the promulgation of the Ahurian doctrine, through me, among the Aryans the infidel power would be crushed. I will follow that course, which I was thus instructed would secure success.

12. Since thou hast commanded me, "Go especially to those of the Aryan blood," command me not to preach that which will not be heeded, and whereby I may rise in arms before Çraôsha conjoined with victory shall have come to me, who will make your words and prayers be victory for the Aryan armies.

13, 14. I deemed thee to be the Beneficent, Mazda, when thy inspiration came to me through Vohu-Manô that I should teach the people to submit to right government. Give me the gift of security of life, which now none obtain from you, to be bestowed upon the most deserving among the Aryans, who are distinguished in the land which is thy kingdom: and for myself, what a wise man gives his friend, content. What thou, O Khshathra, hast commanded, I will, by the efficacy of the true faith, do, encouraging the religious teachers and all the worshippers who recite thy Manthras.

15. I thought of thee as the Supreme Intellect, Ahura, when it came to me through Vohu-Manô, and imparted to me expressions of thy thoughts comprehensible by the understanding (or, for the understanding to consider). "Prompt decision is best. An Aryan of the true faith should not endeavor to conciliate the infidel, for this is to give thy gifts alike to the unbelievers and to the faithful."

This verse is very obscure. Bleeck reads the latter portion of it, swift thought is the best; a perfect man shall not seek to make a bad one contented, then become all the bad to thee as holy.

It seems to me to mean that every Aryan ought to decide on his course without hesitation, and not endeavor to buy peace by submission. The preceding verses which I have omitted pray for the extension and triumph of the true faith, and for security of life; and here the people are warned that these are not to be obtained except by prompt action and open hostilities.

Verse 16 is a prayer for the prosperity of the Aryan land.

> I, Zarathustra, O Ahura, rejoice in the protection of the divine emanations, and place my reliance in the divine wisdom. May the Aryan people become obedient to the true faith, and the powers of life be strong. May the sun look beneficently upon the realm of Armaiti, and may blessings be bestowed for acts of worship inspired by Vohu-Manô.

Hâ ii.

This section is, for the most part, very difficult to interpret. How widely the translations of Haug and Spiegel differ, I will enable you to judge, by the first verse.

Spiegel reads it:

> That ask I thee, tell me the right, O Ahura, unto the praise of your praise mayest thou, O Mazda, teach me, the friend. Through purity may friendly helpers be our portion, until he shall come to us through Vohu-Manô.

And Haug:

> That I will ask thee, tell it me right, thou living God! whether your friend be willing to recite his own hymn as prayer to my friend, Thou Wise! and whether he should come to us with the good mind, to prepare for us true actions of friendship.

Ahura's friend, he thinks, is Çraôsha; and Zarathustra's, Frashaostra or Vîstaçpa.

It is curious that the two versions neither agree in the meaning of single words, nor in the grammatical construction and connection of the words, nor in the modes and tenses and persons of the verbs.

Each verse of the section commences with the same formula, "This I will ask thee, etc.," Zarathustra now proceeding to ask the questions which he had received permission to put to Ahura. In this verse there seems to be no question, but only a general request for instruction. The meaning seems to be,

> Be pleased, O Mazda, to teach me, your votary, the hymns that belong to your worship. May we, by means of our piety [or, of the true faith], have encouragement and assistance, until through Vohu-Manô worship shall be established among us.

2. In this verse, Spiegel has, "How is the beginning of the best place?" which he considers to be Paradise. Haug has it, "How arose the best present life?" I think the verse means,

> How was the origin of the Aryan mother-land? How is he to succeed who is endeavoring to maintain possession of both? For it is thou, who art, by means of thy true religion, supreme over the infidels, ruler over all, the heavenly, the protector of both Aryan countries, Mazda.

"The best place" I take to be "the Airyana-Vaêjâ of the good creation," of the First Fargard of the Vendidad, the valley of the Zer Affshan; and the other "world" or country, which Zarathustra was endeavoring to hold, to be Bactria, then probably not long colonized, and in which, at any rate, the Aryans were not firmly established, and had been dispossessed of the most fertile portion by the northern Infidels. It is perfectly certain that the "two worlds" always mean the home- or mother-country, and a newly acquired one.

3. That I will ask thee, tell me rightly, Ahura! Who at the beginning was the creator and source of the true faith? Who besides thee made for the sun and stars their path? Who that the moon should increase and wane? These things, Mazda, and others I desire to know.

4. Who upholds the earth and the unsupported, that they fall not? Who the waters and trees? Who has given movement to the winds and clouds? Who, O Mazda, is the creator of Vohu-Manô?

5. Who, beneficent, has made the light as well as the darkness? Who, beneficent, sleep and waking? Who has made the morning-dawns, the noons, the nights, for him who observes the fixed times of worship?

6. Is there doubt as to the answers to these questions? "Does Armaiti, by the labors of the husbandman, extend and amplify the realm of the true faith?" "Do superiority and rule belong to thy children (the Aryans), on account of their loyalty?" "For whom didst thou create the bountiful gift of cattle?"

7. Who created the pre-eminent wisdom, united with dominion? Who, by means of his true religion, the love of father for son [between himself and the believer?]. To know these things, I address myself to thee, above all, divine, beneficent, creator of all things!

8. Thy five-fold precept, O Mazda; the prayer in the words whereof, inspired by Vohu-Manô, thou art petitioned; the true faith, which is to be known by all in the Aryan land—how can my soul, obtaining these excellent favors, rejoice itself with them?

9. How shall I maintain uncorrupted, to effect my purposes, the true religious doctrine, which the lord of the domain of wisdom teaches; loyal dominions and zealous service, O Mazda? Thou who by Asha and Vohu-Manô makest homes happy.

10. As to the doctrine which is of most benefit to man, which continually ameliorates the condition, by the true faith, of the Aryan countries, causing them to prosper with the growth and harvests of Armaiti—that I may have this as mine, I beseech thee for thy beneficence that gives good fortune.

11. How may a part of the favors of Armaiti be bestowed on those to whom, O Mazda, the doctrine of thy religion is imparted? I desire thee to be known, first of all, by them. All the others I will watch, on account of their enmity.

12. Who among the Aryans for whom I pray is devoted to the true faith, and who is irreligious? Is he whom the unbelievers favor himself an infidel? Why is not he to be regarded as an unbeliever, who acting as an infidel might, uses against me, being thereby my enemy, the wealth that comes from thee?

I add Dr. Bleeck's translation of this verse, and Haug's, that you may judge of my interpretation.

> *Bleeck:* Who is pure among those for whom I ask, who wicked? To whom (cleaves) the evil, is he himself the evil? Who to me as a wicked man opposed thy profit as a foe, wherefore is he not the evil whom one takes as such?
>
> *Haug:* Who is the religious man and who the impious, after whom I wish to inquire? With whom of both is the black, and with whom the bright one? Is it not right to consider the impious man who attacks me or thee to be a black one?
>
> 13. How shall we expel the Drukhs from our country, driving them away to where those abide who are the ringleaders of disobedience to thy law; and those who do not ally themselves with the apostle of the true faith, when they recognize them, do not care for that which the soul of the believer prays for?

These latter were not the native tribes, I think, but lukewarm and indifferent Aryans. Dr. Haug has it,

> Those who, full of disobedience, do not respect the truth in keeping it, nor care about the thriving of the good mind.

And the *Drujas*, in his translation, become "destruction," with "destroyers" in parentheses. But in Sanskrit, *dru* means to "run, attack, hurt," and *druh*, to "hurt, an injurer." The Drukhs were not "destruction," but marauding riders. And that they are men and not evil spirits is manifest from the next verse, in which even Dr. Haug's ingenuity cannot conceal it. Spiegel thus translates verse 14:

> How shall I, through purity, get the Drukhs into my power, in order to slay them with the Manthras of thy precept, bring forth a mighty overthrow among the wicked, to the deceivers and godless, that they may not come again?

And Dr. Haug extracts from it this nonsense:

> How shall I deliver the destroyer to the hands of truth, to be annihilated by means of the hymns for thy praise? If thou, wise, communicatest to me an efficacious spell to be applied against the impious man, thus will I destroy every difficulty and every misfortune.

It is of such incoherent, disjointed and paltry babble as this, that all the Gâthâs are composed, as they are translated by Dr. Haug. He considers

them to be religious compositions, and makes such wretched stuff of them
as neither Gods or men can tolerate, his version often producing in the
reader the same uncomfortable feeling that one has who hears publicly
delivered the silly effusions of a premature dotage. Of what possible
interest can these old compositions be to us if their burthen is a kind of
holy war of piety against imaginary evil spirits?

If it be not the key to their interpretation, that they are patriotic appeals
to the chiefs and people, in behalf of the extension of the true faith and of a
combined effort to expel from the Aryan land the unbelievers who possessed
it or marauded in it, then I see no other alternative than to admit that they
are worthless nonsense. Read by that key, I find good sense everywhere:
and this verse to mean:

14. How shall I, by means of thy holy faith, overcome the Drukhs, thereby
to slay them, by means of the hymns which thou hast dictated, and to win a great
victory over the infidels, and over the apostates and atheists, that they may never
again invade the land?

15. That will I ask Thee . . . . Whether thou wilt, by the potency of the
true faith, distinctly determine the issue, giving effect unto that true doctrine,
which it is thyself, O Mazda, that teachest, when the Aryan and infidel armies shall
engage in battle? To which cause and to which army, of the two, wilt thou give the
victory?

16. Who is it that is to be victorious, overthrowing the enemy? Who are to
be so, through thy powerful word? Show unto me a wise ruler for the Aryan people
in both their countries, and let Çraösha come as sustainer, through Vohu-Manô,
unto him whom it may please thee to select.

17. When shall I be endowed with power, emanating from you, for the accomplishment of your will, for which I petition by my prayers; that Haurvaṭ and
Amĕrĕtâṭ may be sovereigns in the land, by the efficacy of this Maṅthra, which is
the utterance of faith?

18. How shall I, by what services of religion, make myself worthy of thy favor?
Shall it be by sacrificing to thee ten male horses and a camel, which Haurvaṭ and
Amĕrĕtâṭ have promised me?

19. What is the present punishment for him who prevents him who deserves
it, from achieving success, by giving no aid to him, the promulgator of the true faith?
What the future punishment will be, I know.

20. Have the Daevas ever been beneficent rulers? Therefore I ask, who will
unite with me in warring against these, by whom the Karapas and Uçikhschas are
enabled to rob us of our cattle, and the Kavas have been so greatly enriched with
booty? Asha will not permit our crops to be given to them in the way of tribute
[i. e., will relieve the people of that burthen].

Spiegel considers the Karapas, Uçikhschas and Kavas to be evil spirits.
What use "evil spirits" would have for the "fodder" of the Aryans, he seems
not to have considered. They were undoubtedly native tribes, enabled
to maraud and plunder, by an alliance with the Drukhs or Toorkhs, who had
invaded the country.

In regard to these names, permit me to say there is good reason for considering them the same. For *t* and *d* are both dentals, as *th* is, and therefore are commonly interchanged. The Sanskrit *duhitri* becomes the Greek δυγατηρ; *dwar*, θυρα; the Zend *dva*, the Gothic *tvai*, the Latin *duo;* our English *two;* and the Zend *dasa* and *dashina*, the Gothic *taihun* and *taihsvo.* The Sanskrit *dhi* becomes the Greek θι; *madhu*, μεθυ, and *dadhami*, τιθημι. The change of Drukh into Toorkh, is therefore simple enough.

Hâ iii.

Having thus enlarged upon the Supremacy, Power, Wisdom and Beneficence of Ahura Mazda, the relations of the Aryans to him as his creatures, the potency of the Amĕsha-Çpĕntas to benefit men, the efficacy of worship, devotion, piety and prayer; and the certainty that to Ahura alone, and to his emanations, could the Aryans look for victory and peace, prosperity and plenty; all which he has endeavored to impress upon the popular mind, in the shape of questions addressed to Mazda, Zarathustra now directly addresses and exhorts the people, for the same great purpose of organizing a powerful and combined movement against the Drukhs and the allied native tribes. He commences thus:

1. Now I will speak unto you. Now give ear unto me! Now hear, ye who are anear and ye who are afar off, that which now necessity demands. It has now been plainly made known to you, that the Amĕsha-Çpĕntas are the authors of all that is good. Irreligious doctrine will not again bring calamity upon the Aryan land. The spirit whose utterances are those of irreligion has chosen that part that shall bring upon him disaster.

2. Now will I make this known: the two intellects were at the beginning of things. Of these two, the beneficent one said to the malevolent one (Çpĕnta-Mainyus to Aṅra-Mainyus), "Neither our thoughts, nor our teachings, nor our understanding, our purposes, our words, nor our works, nor our laws, nor our attributes are in unison."

3. Now will I tell you what to me, first of all in the Aryan land, Ahura Mazda has said: "Whosoever among your people will not obey the commands of this Maṅthra, according to its spirit as well as its letter, upon him what is finally to happen in the land shall bring calamity."

4. Now will I promulgate among you that which in this land is most potent for good, the utterance of the divine truth. Mazda, from whom it came forth, the father of the excellent efficient spirit, is its essence. His daughter is Armaiti, the beneficent, Ahura, the all-knowing, is not to be deceived.

5. Now will I say to you what the most beneficent one has in words imparted to me; a prayer which the people shall recite, the most potential for benefit to the Aryans. Whosoever, therefore, shall pay obedience to me, and gain for me the obedience of others, to him will Haurvaṭ and Amĕrĕtâṭ come, by the action of Vohu-Manô, who is Ahura Mazda.

6. Now I will declare to you what is the most mighty of all things; adoration, with sincere piety, of the Amĕsha-Çpĕntas, who are present. May the most beneficent, divine Ahura hear it, he to whom adoration is due by all who are devoutly loyal. May he, through his divine wisdom, teach me that which is the best.

7. He for the benefits in whose gift all the worshippers offering sacrifices that ever lived have prayed, and those now living do pray; the earnest entreaty of the souls of pious believers is for security of life; for the divine strength, which is a weapon against the infidels; for that superiority and rule which are the creation of Ahura Mazda.

8. Him, Ahura, we will worship with prayers that entitle to blessings, for now it is evident, by what the eyes behold, that he who by the observances and words that are the utterances of Vohu-Manô, knows the true religion, he hath cognition of Ahura Mazda himself. His place of worship, also, we will build on the mountain of adoration.

9. By loyal devotion we will win the favor of him who made prosperity and adversity serviceable to us. May Mazda Ahura make our possessions profitable to us, our cattle, our people; so that through the true faith which is from Vohu-Manô, they make increase with abundant progeny.

10. With him I desire to commune, by means of offerings of the fruits of the earth, to him who is called by us Ahura Mazda. Unto the man who with sincere faith and loyal singleness of heart proclaims him the true God, Haurvaṭ and Amĕrĕtâṭ will give continually increasing might and strength in the Aryan kingdom.

The remaining verses of this section descant upon the efficacy of prayer, the mode of winning the favor of Ahura, and the benefits to arise from it; the eleventh and last being:

11. May contumely be the lot of the Daevas, and through them of men, if they scoff at him; but the contrary fortune to men who revere him! Ahura Mazda is the friend, the brother and the father, of the wise who serve him.

Hâ iv.

Dr. Haug is compelled to permit some of the verses of this section to have a reference to the affairs of this world, and to depict the troubles of Zarathustra and the condition of the country, and the oppressions of its rulers. In this section all doubt as to the meaning of the hymns is caused to disappear, and their purpose becomes too evident to admit of. question. It begins thus:

1. What land shall I commend, whither shall I go to worship, when I have abandoned the struggle for independence, and the free exercise of religious observances? Those do not content me, who in inactivity consult their own pleasure, nor do the unbelieving oppressors of the land. How shall I effect what thou desirest, Mazda Ahura?

2. I know, O Mazda, that I have no ambition; I have little wealth and a slender following. I make my plaint to thee, mayest thou give heed to it, Ahura, and give me that cause for gladness, which a friend gives to a friend—counsel and the spiritual teachings of Vohu-Manô, O Source of Faith?

3. When, O Mazda, will those appear, through whom there will be longer life in the land? those who will march to save from ruin the Aryan land, with full observance of thy precepts, which are the life of that that is the cause of prosperity, and by which comes good fortune through Vohu-Manô? I pray thee, O Ahura, for foreknowledge of this.

Those of whom Zarathustra speaks here are the chiefs whom he expected to join him from other parts of the country, and upon whose co-operation success depended.

The next verse is one of many that conclusively prove the life-purpose of Zarathustra to have been to arouse the Aryan people to unite and organize, under his leadership, to expel the Drukhs from the Aryan country, and to reduce to their former state of submission and dependency the native tribes allied with them. It is thus rendered by Bleeck:

4. They who do purity, these the wicked hinders, the cows from going forward through the districts and regions. He the tyrant, worthy of death by his deeds, he who by resistance to him takes away the rule or the life, O Mazda, he obtains for the cows the granaries of wisdom.

To what use Professor Spiegel and Dr. Bleeck supposed the Aryan cows would put the granaries of wisdom, when these should have been obtained for them, does not appear. Having adopted the notion that Armaiti was the Goddess of Wisdom, they shut their eyes, of course, to anything that was in the way of that notion. Dr. Haug's version is as follows:

The wicked man enjoys the fields of the angel of truth, who is protecting the earth in the district as well as in the province; but by choosing evil instead of good, he cannot succeed in his deeds. Who drives him out of his dominion, or out of his property, thou wise, he is going further on the paths of good intellect.

I interpret the verse thus:

The unbelievers harass those who openly perform their religious duties, and prevent the driving their cattle to be pastured in the districts and distant regions of the Aryan land. Whosoever, O Mazda, by uniting in armed resistance against the tyrants who by their outrages deserve death shall aid in depriving them of power or life, he will obtain for the cattle the granaries of Armaiti.

This and other verses here and there, furnish the key to the interpretation of these old odes; and it seems to me that even one verse, clearly and unmistakably showing, as this certainly does, what were the purposes of Zarathustra and the condition of the country is sufficient to compel the interpretation that I have given them. In the special interpretations of single verses, I must, of course, have fallen into many errors: but I am convinced that the general sense is as I give it.

Wanting this key, Dr. Haug could not translate the hymns otherwise than erroneously. Taking them to be entirely religious, and to have been composed and recited by Zarathustra in order to promulgate his new doctrines, as polemics against the old Aryan fire-worship, whose partizans persecuted him; and as a vindication of his claim to the character of an inspired prophet, Dr. Haug of course found them incoherent and incomprehensible, whenever they could not be made to fit that theory. To him, Zarathustra is wholly priest and prophet, inculcating virtue and devotion, and warring only against evil spirits. He was, in fact, neither priest nor prophet, and he *was* soldier, general and finally king over all the Aryan land.

To Professor Spiegel, also, he was wholly a religious teacher. But his translation conscientiously endeavors to be literal, and I think that we can generally see in it the real meaning through the erroneous one. Of course there are abundant errors and uncertainty in it, which he and Dr. Bleeck frankly admit; and there is a general current of error, in consequence of his conviction that Zarathustra taught the immortality of the soul and a future existence, in the meaning which those phrases now have to us: and certain words are constantly used in the translation, either with no sense or in a wrong sense, in consequence of these and other preconceptions—as, for example, "heavenly," "immortality," "wicked," "world," "purity," "creatures," and "soul."

Words, in those early days, had distinct and definite meanings, that were known to all men. Ever since then, and everywhere, the perverse Aryan race has been sedulously engaged in making the meanings of words vague, nebulous, doubtful, uncertain; and, as far as possible, in divorcing words from ideas. The consequence is that, with us, language has become in large measure, cant and jargon: and that while the world worships symbols and idols, it wrangles about words that represent no ideas, and values most what it understands least. We find, as a general rule, the words employed in the *Veda* and *Zend-Avesta* having always one and the same meaning; and the constant mistranslation of texts into nonsense is chiefly owing to inability to discover the primitive meanings of old words among the swarming and insubordinate derivative meanings.

If we consider, in addition, that the derivation of Zend words is in large measure unknown, and their exact meanings uncertain, and that the translators widely disagree as to punctuation, the order and connection of words, the grammatical construction of sentences, the gender, number and cases of nouns, the modes, tenses, number and person of verbs, and the meanings of the particles, conjunctions and prepositions, no one need wonder that interpretation of the texts is in great part mere conjecture. To meet these difficulties, Dr. Haug has only learning, without judgment, a false theory and idle notions, and great want of common sense.

As to Professor Spiegel and Dr. Bleeck, I shall ask you to judge of their renderings by the next verse, upon which I need not comment:

5. Whoso as ruler gives not to him who brings hurt, skilled from the law, or from the covenants; whoso as a right liver, pure, to the wicked, he is intelligent, he shall speak forth for himself, he is raised, Mazda Ahura, above oppression.

Which I read thus:

Whosoever, being a chief, pays not tribute to the marauding unbelievers, whether in refusing he obeys the precepts of the faith or his obligations as an ally; whosoever, as one of the true faith, living as such, refuses tribute to the infidel, he is of right judgment, and shall speak out boldly for himself, and his boldness will secure him from oppression.

6. The Aryan who does not voluntarily rally to him, unmistakably goes over to the hordes of the Drukhs. For he is an infidel, who gives aid to the infidels, and those are true believers who are allied with the true believers, so long as the law endures that has been from the beginning, O Ahura.

7. Whom has Mazda appointed to be the protector of my comrades, if I should be the victim of the vengeance of the unbelievers? Whom, other than thee, Asha Vahista, and thee Vohu-Manô, by means of the effects outflowing from each of whom the true faith is magnified, and grows? Manifest to me this aid for the Mazdayaçnian Law!

8. Punishment by me may not smite for his shameful course him who pays tribute of the fruits of the earth to the enemies of the true faith; but by continual plundering his means of living will be so destroyed as to compel him to become an exile from the Aryan land, never, for his hostility to Mazda, to leave the land of the unbelievers.

9. Who is the priest that shall first teach me how I may glorify thee, as I desire to do, in my religious observance—thee, Ahura, beneficent and true? Whatsoever truth thou, who art the maker of cattle, hast uttered, that I pray thee to make known unto me through Vohu-Manô.

The tenth verse, as read by Bleeck, is,

What man or what woman, O Mazda Ahura, gives me in this world the best that thou knowest, blessing for purity, the kingdom through Vohu-Manô, and those whom I exhort to your praise, with all these I go forward to the bridge Chinvaṭ.

Dr. Haug's translation is substantially the same, but the conclusion is,

All these I will lead over the bridge of the gatherer [and he adds] to Paradise. [And he says], No one can enter Paradise without having first passed the bridge of the gatherer (called Chinvaṭ), the passing of which can be facilitated to the deceased, by prayers recited for him . . . . [And again]: Between Heaven and Hell is Chinvaṭ Pĕrĕtu, i. e., the bridge of the gatherer, or the bridge of the judge, which the soul of the pious alone can pass, while the wicked fall from it down to Hell.

It became that in the later writings; but it was not that originally. *Chinvat* means, "collecting, arranging, gathering," or "gatherer, collector, hunter"; and *Pĕrĕtu*, "crossing, ford" or "pass."

I think that the meaning of Verse 10 is;

> That Amĕsha-Çpĕnta, male or female [or, literally, that man or woman], who in the Aryan land communicates to me the most precious things that emanate from thee, success as the fruit of piety, dominion through Vohu-Manô, and those whom I exhort to adore you, with all these I will advance to the pass (or ford) of rendezvous.

For the following verses clearly show that this pass or ford was no bridge over Hell, to be crossed by souls, but an actual place to which troops were to march. Thus:

> 11. The Karapas and Karis have allied themselves with the Drukh chiefs [with "empire"], that they may by pillage and rapine bring distress and ruin upon the land, for the Aryan people, and their nature and minds have become hardened. If they come to the pass (or ford) Chinvat, they will be made to find a home always hereafter in the land which is the home of the Drukhs.
>
> 12. When the true faith prevails among the families and races of those who are of the Aryan blood, by means of the teachings of their kinsmen, that true piety which makes the land to prosper through the productive energy of Armaiti, then Ahura Mazda through Vohu-Manô abides with them and rules over them, bestowing happiness.
>
> 13. Whosoever, by efficient service rendered to the Aryan cause as a military leader rejoices the soul of Zarathustra, is worthy of grateful eulogies. To him Ahura Mazda will give high station, and, through Vohu-Manô increase of all the fruits of the earth. Him I regard, on account of his zeal for the true faith, as one devotedly thy adherent, Ahura Mazda.

The next two verses promise that Ahura will rule over the land and make it prosper, when the true faith prevails in it; and that those who aid Zarathustra shall be rewarded. In verse fourteen, Ahura asks,

> Zarathustra, what votary of the true faith has by great deeds of renown proven himself thy friend; or who is it that thou desirest to praise?

And he replies,

> He is that Kavi-Vistâçpa, the heroic soldier. But also, O Mazda Ahura, I commend unto thee in loyal prayers his kinsmen whom he leads.

And in verses fifteen and sixteen he continues to say,

> I commend you, the renowned, who are the descendants of Haêchat-Açpâ, who hold the frontier between the Aryan settlements and the country possessed by the infidels. For the services you render there, eminence is given you, as the foremost among all the Aryan children of Ahura. Thou, Frashaôstra, owner of herds, shalt

take in that region your remuneration [by allotment of part of the country to be conquered], with which also we are content, there to prosper; there, where the divine productiveness and power are enthroned, and the auspicious realms of Vohu-Manô are, and Ahura himself has chosen it, to abide therein.

17. There, where also, through the Magus Jamâçpa, proprietor of herds, litanies in verse only will be recited, and none in prose. Continually he appeals to you by prayers, the offerings of devotion, he who abides between the Aryan settlements and the infidels, ye wise thinkers, Asha and Ahura Mazda.

18. Unto everyone who, in the cause wherein I am engaged, perseveringly does good service, I will give a share of the spoil, which, impoverishing those who have plundered us, I shall acquire by successful leadership. Mazda and Asha, in your worship I will find the accomplishment of my designs. Such is the firm conviction of my understanding and my soul.

In verses eighteen and nineteen Zarathustra declares his intention to despoil the enemy of their lands, and with these to reward his followers. The latter reads,

He who, obeying the dictates of patriotism and duty, thus efficiently aids me, Zarathustra, to compass that which above all things else I have at heart, shall have allotted to him by Mazda and Asha, as a reward, lands in the new country ['the World beyond'], and a share of all the booty that I may acquire. For to thee, Mazda, all the spoil belongs; and so hast thou, perfectly knowing what is to be, given me thy promise.

The third Gâthâ is called *Çpĕnta-Mainyu*.

1. Through Çpĕnta-Mainyu, and through that divine grace that is obtained by acts of devotion, Mazda Ahura has given unto us abundance [or health], and security of life, wealth of chattels and intellectual gifts.

2. Through Çpĕnta-Mainyu, he confers the greatest benefits, that are the issue of prayers uttered aloud, the spoken thoughts of Vohu-Manô. Through the action of Armaiti, he is the author of sacrificial observances, and through his wisdom which is himself, he is the author of the true religion.

3. Thou who art also the beneficent in heaven, hast created cattle, and given them for our sustenance, and hast supplied them with pasturage and comfort, by thy wise providence, taking counsel, O Mazda, with Vohu-Manô.

4. All that is hurtful comes from the maleficent mind; none thereof from the pure beneficent mind, Mazda. Even in small matters, the Aryan strives to do that which the true religion requires, but the unbeliever, even in the most important, does, if he can, that which is pernicious.

It begins by declaring that Ahura has given, or gives, to the Aryans, abundance, security of life, wealth and understanding, through Çpĕnta-Mainyu and the practices of religion; prosperity that is the fruit of the prayers uttered by the mouth of Vohu-Manô. By the hands of Armaiti he performs pure deeds, i. e., by means of her energy and what she causes to

be produced, he maintains the observance of sacrifices. Through his own
wisdom he is the Father of Purity, i. e., as Vohu-Manô, the revealing of the
Divine Intellect, Çpĕnta-Mainyu, he revealed the true faith. Taking
counsel with Vohu-Manô, he created cattle for the Aryans, and pasturage
for them. And then it is said,

> All that is hurtful comes from the maleficent mind (Añra-Mainyus); none thereof
> from the pure and beneficent Mazda. Even in small matters, the Aryan endeavors
> to do that which the true religion requires; but the unbeliever, even in the most
> important, does, if he can that which is pernicious.

The fifth and sixth verses of the first section are peculiarly interesting,
in the inquiry as to the theosophic conceptions of Zarathustra. I read them
thus:

> 5. Give, O Çpĕnta-Mainyu, Mazda Ahura, to those of the true faith, pros-
> perous fortune! The infidels, without thy permission, take for themselves, in part,
> the acquisitions of the Aryans—the unbelievers, who come from the lands where
> Akô-Manô has his home.

> 6. He whom thou didst bring forth [Vohu-Manô], O Çpĕnta-Mainyu, Mazda
> Ahura, making use of the fire [teaching the Aryans to forge weapons by means of it],
> decides the fate of battles between the combatants, through the potency of Armaiti
> and Asha; for Vohu-Manô giveth wisdom to him who asks it by prayer.

You may have noticed that while in the other verses quoted, Ahura
Mazda is said to produce results *through* Çpĕnta-Mainyu, and they are thus
distinguished from each other, here Çpĕnta-Mainyu seems to be but a name
or appellation of Ahura.

The universal belief has been, since the time of Herodotus, that Zarathustra taught the dualism of the Deity, and that Ahura Mazda (known as
Ormuzd) and Añra-Mainyus (as Ahriman) were the good and evil principles,
one of whom created seven Genii and the other seven Devs; and who reign
alternately over the universe. But in the real doctrine of Zarathustra,
Añra-Mainyus is not a power co-equal with Ahura Mazda; nor, on the other
hand is he created by him. He is the opposite of Çpĕnta-Mainyu, the
beneficent divine mind, the hypostasis or person of Ahura afterwards known
as wisdom, and to Philo as the Holy Spirit, the ἅγιον πνευμα, which used
also in the New Testament, is there translated "Holy Ghost." Dr. Haug
has clearly shown that Çpĕnta-Mainyus is not Ahura himself, but a primeval principle in him; and that Ahura Mazda is above both Çpĕnta-Mainyus
and Añra-Mainyus. But beyond this, all that Dr. Haug says on the subject
seems to me clearly erroneous. In the translation of Yaçna 30, these two
minds are called "twins." But it is nowhere said that both issued from
Ahura, nor that he produced Añra-Mainyus. The word rendered "twins"

also means "a pair," and would be properly used to describe two horses harnessed to the same chariot.

Dr. Haug says that Akem-Manô produced non-reality. But how that can be produced or created, it is impossible to conceive. It is the *absence* of reality; and only the *real* exists or is produced. Darkness is merely the absence of the light; and if light had a beginning, darkness *was*, before it.

The problem which Zarathustra endeavored to solve, is insoluble. To suppose a Devil, who was once an angel of light, and rebelled and fell, does not in the least serve as a solution. Proclus states the problem very well, in his *Ten Doubts Concerning Providence*. He says, as Taylor translates, that his fifth subject of inquiry, why, if Providence exists, evil has a place among beings, disturbs the imaginations of many; and he proceeds to consider it. He says:

> The beings which proceed from the causes that owe their existence to Providence, proceed likewise from Providence, if, however, they are produced without Providence co-operating in their existence, we shall make two principles, one of good and the other of evil.

It is useless to repeat his argument. It is that evil is a privation or negation, which, Dr. Mansel says, has been adopted by theologians and philosophers of almost every shade of opinion, and can only be classed among the numerous necessarily fruitless attempts of metaphysicians to explain what is not explainable.

Evil is simply the necessary condition of imperfection; and in creating beings not perfect like himself, indeed, in creating a material world at all, the Deity could not but create or make necessary, the various forms of evil. After all, the question is, whether it was consistent with the infinite goodness of God, to create at all; since he could only create perfection by re-creating or duplicating himself. With all its evils, this is a beneficent creation, though the moth that we crush because it annoys us when we write by the light of the candle that attracts it, may not think so; or the wolf skulking all his life from the hunter and the dogs.

This principle of evil, not co-existent or co-extensive with the Deity, but coming into being with created imperfection, existing only while it exists and where it exists, Zarathustra represented as Añra-Mainyus. He did not speculate upon the subject, nor endeavor to account for the origin of that principle. It is certain that nothing in the *Zend-Avesta* sustains the proposition of Dr. Haug that he regarded this evil spirit as a twin emanation with Çpĕnta-Mainyu, from Ahura Mazda. Nor is it anywhere intimated that he can ever prevail against Ahura Mazda or his emanations. On the contrary it is continually represented that victory over his creations is certain, if the favor of Ahura is gained by adhesion to the truth and by worship and devotion.

Permit me a little further to explain this ancient doctrine of Emanation, nowhere more clearly held than in the Gâthâs. Mackay, in his *Progress of the Intellect*, says:

> Although, through distinctions or personifications, the many aspects or attributes of God might give to him a semblance of plurality, his nature was only *extended*, not divided; each attribute, being an essential part of him, became entitled to represent the entire Godhead; each Emanation was itself the Great Being from which it sprung.

Yamblichus (de Mysteriis, *viii.*, 4) says:

> The Egyptians are far from ascribing all things to physical causes: life and intellect they distinguish from physical being, both in man and in the universe. They place intellect and reason first, as self-existent, and from these they derive the created world. . . . They place pure intellect above and beyond the universe, and another (i. e., mind revealed in the Kosmos) consisting of one continuous mind pervading the universe, and apportioned to all its parts and spheres.

And this is precisely the idea embodied in the Zarathustrian conceptions of Çpĕnta-Mainyus and Vohu-Manô

> that of a Deity both immanent and transcendent; spirit passing into the manifestations of its *anderseyn* (otherwiseness), but not exhausted by so doing.

As Vohu-Manô was the Logos or Word, so Çpĕnta-Mainyu was the Σοφια or *Wisdom*, of later ages. God is said in the Proverbs to have created Wisdom

> the beginning of his ways [the first of his outgoings, outflowings or emanations], for the purpose of his works.

She is, in the language of Philo, the pre-existent Word,

> the brightness [or radiant outshining] of the everlasting light, the unspotted mirror of God's power, and image of his goodness, dwelling alone with God, the spiritual dwelling of the Great King [the literal meaning of *Khshathra Vairya*], the depositary of his thought, and organ of his act,

an emanation before all worlds, God himself as intellect; which manifested as Vohu-Manô, pours itself from above into the souls of men.

Meliton, Bishop of Sardis, about 160 A.D. (in the time of Antoninus Pius), said (*on Faith;* in the *Spicilegium Syriacum* of Rev. Wm. Cureton), of Christ;

He is perfect Reason, the Word of God; who was begotten before the light; who was creator together with the Father; who was the fashioner of man, who was all in all . . . . who in the Law was the Law, ... in the Voice, the Word; among Spirits, Spirit; in the Father, the Son; in God, God; the King forever and ever.

And it is certain that every one of these expressions is to be found in the *Zend-Avesta*.

The first verse of the second section of the third Gâthâ is thus rendered by Bleeck:

When the coming Asha shall smite the Drukhs, when there comes what was announced as delusive, immortality for men and Daevas, then shall thy profitable land increase, O Ahura.

This verse permits no doubt to remain that the Drukhs were mortal enemies, upon whose defeat the Aryan land was to become prosperous. I read it:

When Asha shall defeat and crush the Drukhs, and that shall come to pass, the promise whereof has been derided as delusive, security of life from infidels and Daevas, then, O Ahura, thy fertile land shall be prosperous.

2. Tell me, for it is foreknown to thee, O Ahura, before the two armies reach the pass [or ford], how shall the Aryans there defeat the unbelievers? for that is regarded throughout the Aryan land as a consummation greatly to be desired.

Bleeck has "before that (the man) reaches to the double bridge." The interpretation I give this is of course conjectural. The reply in the next verse is, in substance, that Ahura alone gives victory; and that it must be obtained by worship and prayer and a pious life.

3, 4. By having that wisdom which the best of the teachings are, that the wise Ahura teaches by the true religion. Thou, the beneficent, knowest also the occult meanings. He who is like unto thee, Mazda, by having the wisdom of Vohu-Manô, and who increases in righteousness and performs his religious duties; who conforms to thy law in speech and action, good fortune shall come to him, to the utmost of his desire. At last, the condition of everyone will be according to thy good pleasure.

5. May good rulers and not evil ones rule over us, with wise measures, O Armaiti. During all his life, the true faith is of all things the most beneficial to man. By performance of its duties our cattle are increased and we who are diligent thereby have food.

6. This sincere piety has heretofore given to us the glory of victory, has given us greatness and power, by means of the good will of Vohu-Manô. And also, at the origin of the Aryan land, it caused the growth of vegetation, and of offerings for Mazda.

7. Expel from the land those that pillage it, expel from it those who are our foes, Aryans who were created to be reared by Vohu-Manô, for that possession of piety and virtue, which every man must have, in whom the Divinity abides.

8. How great [general or extensive among the people] is the desire, O Mazda, for thy rule in the land, which, according to thy supreme will, is for me, O Ahura? What shall I, O Asha, living in accordance with the teachings of Vohu-Manô, ask of thee as substantial reward?

9. By what results shall I have certain knowledge, O Mazda and Asha, that you do indeed have control over human affairs, doubts whereof force themselves upon me; or, rather, denials whereof are used to hinder me? Life is hardest to bear, when the divine teachings are set at naught. Show those who have the power to aid me, how they may attain the true faith.

10. When, O Mazda, will the loyal auxiliaries come? When will they expel from our land the vile hordes that infest it? who protect the revolted native tribes in their irreligion [or, in their maraudings], and encourage the wicked rulers of the districts?

11. When, Mazda, will Asha, with Armaiti, come and abide with us? When will Khshathra? When shall we have comfortable homes and pasturage? Who will compel the unbelieving barbarians to cease to harass us? And who will be endowed by Vohu-Manô with the wisdom that shall entitle him to be our leader?

12. Those render effective service in the various districts, who have become well affected through Vohu-Manô, with the religious services that thou, O pure Mazda, hast taught us; these that have been so made by thee to be the adversaries of the—[the rest unintelligible].

Hâ iii.

1. Protect me, O Mazda, so long as those who are of the creation of Anra-Mainyus continue to have rule in the land. I who teach the doctrines of the true religion to those who have been reared in unbelief, have in the fulfilment of duty come hither, among those who are detested by me. Let me, enabled by Vohu-Manô, compass their overthrow.

2. Here, in this region where the unbelievers rule, I am constrained to tarry, for the sake of those Aryans, who, being of the true faith, are yet aiders of the infidels; of the disloyal, whom Çpĕnta-Mainyus visits with calamity; those who do not boldly take that truly wise course for the benefit of their people, nor are inspired in their prayings by Vohu-Manô.

3. To this inducement, O Mazda, is added that of extending the true religion, as profitable for those true to the divine law, and as detrimental to the Drukhs. Therefore I commit myself trustfully to the protection of Vohu-Manô, and proclaim to all the Daevas my allegiance to you.

4. They who, inspired by Akô-Manô, by their talking cause pillaging and slaughter, idle among those who labor, they do not desire the teachings of the true faith, but those of the false, and become the slaves of the Daevas, by accepting their religion.

5. May those, O Mazda, who are in possession of the true faith, by the divine wisdom dwelling in them, enjoy peace and abundance; every one who is devout with the worship for which Armaiti provides; all who are of thy kingdom (obedient to thee), O Ahura.

6. Mazda and Asha, I pray that what shall be firmly determined may be communicated to me from you through the inspiration that flows from you through Vohu-Manô, that we may proclaim it, the true law, yours, O Ahura.

7. May Mazda hear this, in the person of Vohu-Manô! Hear it, Asha! Hear it, thou, Ahura! Who are the well affected? Who are our allies, among the Aryans? Who among them will use in the service of the good cause the wealth bestowed upon him?

It seems that, having already preached resistance to maraudings and refusal to pay tribute, to the people of the Aryan settlements not under the government of Toorkhish chiefs, Zarathustra then went upon the same mission into the settlements over which these invaders ruled. There, he says in the next verse, he was constrained to tarry, on account of the Aryans who were untrue to their faith, by submission to the infidels; and for the purpose of spreading the true faith. He denounces the unbelievers, prays for peace and abundance for the faithful, prays for knowledge of what shall be firmly determined, and asks to know who among the Aryans are well-affected and his allies, and who among them will assist the good cause with his means. Then these verses follow:

8. Thou hast given to Frashaôstra the friendship of Asha [made him powerful]. I pray thee to give him unto me as a captain, and to be for me that whereby thy kingdom shall be benefited; and may we evermore enjoy thy favor!

9. May the laboring men of the Aryans, created by thee to make plenty in the land, heed the teachings of thy law! Let not the words of thy truth be perverted to give rule to the unbelievers! For with observance of the law, good fortune should be inseparably conjoined; and the true faith should crown with success the efforts of the warlike Jamaçpa.

10. That (true faith?), O Mazda, I will foster in the land where thou reignest (or, among thy people); the teachings of Vohu-Manô, and the lives of the true believers. Praise be unto thee for the blessings that flow from wisdom! Let the unfaith of the infidels consume their riches!

11. The disloyal unbelievers (of the native tribes) go to the land where the chiefs of the invaders govern, the oppressors and blasphemers, to provide the slayers with food harmful to us; and there remain residing openly, in the land where the Drukhs abide.

12. What reward wilt thou grant, O Asha, unto Zarathustra, thy worshipper with prayers? What, through Vohu-Manô? to me, Ahura Mazda, who adores you with hymns of praise, striving to accomplish that, the most excellent result, which is desired by thee?

The fourth and last section of the third Gâthâ is devoted to adoration of Ahura Mazda, Vohu-Manô, Asha-Vahista and Khshathra-Vairya, and prayers to them for prosperity, peace, victory and permanent homes for the Aryans. Ahura is worshipped

as conjoined or one with these emanations, that he may favor the enterprise of the liberators. "I adhere to you [Zarathustra says], that I may march to the bridges [fords or passes] where you are worshipped": and he promises true allegiance to the wise divinities, in case he should become supreme ruler.

GÂTHÂ III
Hâ iv.

1. Whose protection shall my mind seek after, and by what means? Who will defend our cattle; and what divinity shall be manifested as my protector, besides Asha and thee, Mazda Ahura, the one desired, the one prayed for, sent by Çpĕnta-Mainyu?

2. How, O Mazda, shall those succeed in obtaining serviceable cattle, who need their work in the Aryan land? Give unto us, in this land, permanent homes, that we may live peacefully therein many years.

3. The true faith is the possession, Mazda, imparted to him by Khshathra conjointly with Vohu-Manô, of every man who, by the power of religious worship, endeavors to better the condition of this hither portion of the Aryan land, in which the unbelievers seize a part by pillage [or exact tribute].

4. Therefore I will worship you with praises, as conjoined with Asha and Vohu-Manô, and Khshathra, that he may assist the enterprise of those who thus endeavor. I will sacrifice on the mountain of adoration.

5. Be graciously pleased, Mazda Ahura, Asha, beneficently to make strong those who promulgate your teachings, with open and mighty assistance, that will give unto us victory.

6. Whatsoever Divinity, O Mazda, utters the words of the Manthra, with prayers of the true faith inspiring Zarathustra, let him speak in words suited to the understanding; and may he teach me the hidden things that are disclosed through Vohu-Manô.

7. I adhere to you, as your ardent votary, that I may march to the bridges (fords or passes) where you are worshipped; to the mighty, Mazda, Asha, together with Vohu-Manô, that you as leaders may assist me to reach them.

8. With hymns that are recited for the sake of abundance, I come unto you, Mazda, with uplifted hands, to you with the pious prayers of the sacrifice; to you with the devout thoughts inspired in the mind by Vohu-Manô.

9. With these Yaçnas I offer you adoration, Mazda, Asha—with the uttered thoughts of Vohu-Manô. When, by reason of my devotion to the true faith, I shall possess supreme power, then will I with all my heart, maintain allegiance to the wise Divinities.

10. I will do that which has been done by others before me, that which appears worthy in thy sight, inspired thereunto by Vohu-Manô; by the light of dawn, at sunrise, at the dawning of the day, in adoration of thee, O Mazda Ahura!

11. I will proclaim thy praise, O Mazda, in words, so long as I, O Asha, have power and skill to do so. And may the creator of the Aryan land grant through Vohu-Manô that which shall conduce to the triumph of those now openly engaged in hostile operations.

The preparation for the struggle, it seems, was now complete. After arousing to action the leaders and people in that part of the country still under the Aryan rule, Zarathustra had gone into that held by the invaders, to arouse the Aryans residing there, and had concerted with Frashaôstra,

Vîstâçpa and Jamaçpa and other chiefs, a combined uprising and attack. His objective-point, the place of concentration of the forces was, it seems, the bridge Chinvaṭ, at which, I think it elsewhere appears, there was an Aryan colony, governed by Jamaçpa, who was both priest and soldier.

As the human mind and intellect were deemed, if Aryan, to be Vohu-Manô, limitedly immanent in each body, so those of the Drukhs were deemed to be "creations," i. e., the issue and progeny of Añra-Mainyus, through Akô-Manô, Unreason. Nowhere, therefore, is the practice of mercy toward them inculcated. There is no such precept anywhere in the *Zend-Avesta* as

> Love your enemies, bless them that curse you, do good to those that hate you, and pray for them that despitefully use you and persecute you.

Nor, if one smote an Aryan on one cheek, was he required to turn to him the other, that he might smite him on that also; nor if a Drukh confiscated the horse of an Aryan, was the true believer required to run after him and persuade him to accept his camel also—maxims so religiously obeyed by all the Christian world as justly to entitle us to special consideration. On the contrary, the Aryan best obeyed the law of Ahura, when he "smote" the Drukhs, and resisted their aggressions; and was least entitled to divine favor when he purchased peace and immunity by tame submission and tribute. For the rest, they had at least the merit of themselves obeying the law which they compelled the conquered to accept. Nor is a barbarous and savage cruelty to women and children and to defenceless prisoners inculcated, or commended as praiseworthy; and it is but fair to say, also, that the reason for "smiting" the infidels is always given. It was not because of their faith or unfaith, but because they were oppressors and "tormentors" of the Aryans. There were no religious wars, or persecutions on account of opinions, among the Aryan nations, for many thousand years. There is certainly no evidence of any in the *Veda* or *Zend-Avesta;* there were none among the Greeks, during all their history, and there were none among the Romans, until Christianity became formidable to paganism.

The Zarathustrian doctrine that the human intellect is the revealing of the divine, has had its echoes in every age, in every school of philosophy, in every creed.

> If any of you lack wisdom [said the Apostle James], let him ask of God, that giveth to all liberally. . . . . Every good gift and every perfect gift is from above, and cometh down from the Father of the lights. Of his own will he begat us with the word of truth.
>
> Holy men of God spake [said Peter], moved by the Holy Spirit.

Bunsen says, in his tenth note to his *Apology of Hippolytus*, that all ancient authorities prove that the third and fourth verses of the prologue of the Gospel according to St. John, were written thus:

> All things were made by him, and without him was not anything made that was made. What was made is life in him, and the life was the light of men.

The present punctuation, he avers, was adopted in order to combat the heresy of the Macedonians towards the end of the fourth century. Thus it has all tradition and ancient authorities against it. And he thinks the internal evidence as great as the external. He says:

> The first words, "In the beginning was the Word," speak of the immanent external existence of the Word as God (as God's thought of himself). Then comes the Demiurgic or world-creating function of the Word, in the beginning of the third verse. It remains, therefore, to speak of the agency of the Word in the created universe. Here the Apostle says, first, that it is the principle of life in the outer world (the infinite factor in Nature); and equally was, originally, the intellectual principle in man (the infinite factor in the mind), enabling man to understand, when born anew, things divine and his own origin.

In considering the problem of the Trinity, in *Hippolytus and His Age, i.*, 81, Bunsen says:

> Religion rests, under whatever form, upon the assumption that divine and human reason are identical, only with the difference between the infinite and the finite. This may be expressed imperfectly, but it must not be negatived. . . . . Negation of the problem being suicidal, let it be well considered that the most absolute form of negation is to declare the problem incompatible with reason.

In the creed of Zarathustra, all prayers, hymns and true words were "Deeds of Vohu-Manô"; and these alone, he taught, could win triumph for the Aryan arms, and royalty for himself.

In this last composition, promulgated when the campaign was on the eve of being opened, Asha is invoked to "instruct with open protection the announcers of the true faith"; i. e., to *provide* (the literal meaning of *instruo*) them with open or declared allies. Having before prayed to Vohu-Manô for wisdom, knowledge of the truth, and military skill and foresight, Zarathustra now prays Khshathra to be with them on the march and direct their movements; for that emanation is leadership as well as royalty, sovereignty and rule. He propitiates Ahura by sacrifices at dawn on the Mountain of Worship; and assures the people that their piety will give them the victory.

This brings us to the fourth Gâthâ called *Vohu-Khshathra;* that of Sovereignty. It was composed and recited after the war of liberation had resulted in success; and it is a song of rejoicing and triumph. The first three verses are:

1, 2, 3. Give us now to cultivate the country that is most productive, the most fertile domain, the undivided, that portion which he who is to make partition is to divide equitably, as donatives: that which was aforetime yours, Mazda Ahura, Asha and Armaiti (was once Aryan land). Give me that to reign over! Let your worship through Vohu-Manô produce its fruit of advantage. Those who rule by means of your aid, Ahura and Asha, with that of the prayers of Vohu-Manô, which thou, Mazda Ahura, first taughtest, now come to you for counsel.

4. That land where the possessor of abundance resides, and where immunity is; where one becomes strong, and where the Divine Productiveness (Armaiti) is; that where Vohu-Manô is, and where thy realms are, O Mazda.

5. For all this, the Aryan laborer of the true faith, with products for the sacrifice, and the priest with prayers, petition Asha (who is mighty and beneficent, and gives to the Aryan people instruction for their guidance) that they may there keep and feed their cattle;

6. Asha, who gives them a better region than the good one possessed before, and grants to the petitioner that for which he asks, and dominion to Ahura Mazda, but will assign nothing by way of requital to those who, among the unbelievers, come professing the true faith, until the final division of the country.

7. O thou who hast produced the cattle, the waters and the plants, grant me security of life and abundance, most beneficent divine Mazda; and authority and power, with wisdom through Çpĕnta-Mainyu.

8. May men, O Mazda, speak publicly thy sayings, that they may become known, as things that work harm to the unbelievers, and safety to those who uphold the true faith! For he makes the Manthra glad, who recites it that it may be learned.

9. The puissance which thou givest to warriors, by means of the red fire and the arms forged by it, that give as a mark of distinction in both Aryan countries, whereby the unbelievers may be vanquished, and victory be with the true believers.

Here there is no obscurity in the text, and it is clear that there is no reference to spiritual "worlds" or to another life; for in "both worlds," in that sense, there are no wars nor warriors, nor forging of "metal" by "the red fire." And also it is to be noted that the infidels are elsewhere spoken of as not having arms like those of the Aryans.

10. Whoso slays me except that, O Mazda, he is an ally of the race of Drukhs, the evil ones who reside in that land. For myself, I ask for the true faith, and that it may prevail in the land to benefit it.

11, 12. What men are friends of the most noble Zarathustra, O Mazda? Who your pious disciple? What is the beneficent wisdom? What true believer has promulgated your doctrine, glorifying Vohu-Manô. These two did not satisfy him, the Vaepayas and the Kevînas, at the bridge of the earth, the most noble Zarathustra, when his forces there assembled.

In the twelfth verse it is said that the Vaepayas and Kevînas did not satisfy Zarathustra, at the bridge of the earth (which I take to mean the mountain-pass) when his forces assembled there. The bridge of the earth is the bridge Chinvaṭ, for we have seen that he had prayed to be enabled to reach that: and those who did not satisfy him were probably two native tribes, or perhaps Aryan bands, that failed to join him.

13. The precepts of the true faith are addressed to the native tribes as well as to the Aryans, when the former, risking their lives at the celebrated bridge Chinvaṭ, earnestly endeavored to attain, by offerings and prayers, to the possession of the true religion.

14. The Karapas are harmful to the Aryan people, molesting them in their peaceful pursuits; but do thou give to our cattle, by means of thy observances and precepts, abundant pasturage; and let those who follow the precepts of the Drukhs, be hereafter driven away, to the land which these inhabit.

The benefits of the true faith are promised to the native tribes who, anxious and disquieted at the pass Chinvaṭ, endeavored to attain it by offerings and prayers; and the Karapas are denounced as troublesome to the Aryans, molesting them in their peaceful pursuits. Ahura is prayed to protect the cattle, and supply them with abundant pasturage, and that those who follow the precepts of the Drukhs (of the native tribes acting with the Drukhs) may be driven away to the home-country of these invaders.

15. The recompense which Zarathustra has already ordained for his warriors, that they should be the first to have lands assigned them in the goodly country wherein Ahura abides, this remuneration shall also be bestowed on you through Vohu-Manô and Asha.

16. Kava-Vîstâçpa (Vîstâçpa the wise) has won for himself a powerful kingdom, by his might in war wherewith the beneficent Ahura Mazda endowed him, by means of the words of Vohu-Manô, with the true faith. May we learn those words!

17. May Frashaôçtra, owner of herds, conquer and possess for me that elevated productive region there; may he loyally cause his highlands to submit to the Ahurian faith. Ahura is mighty: seek his assistance in endeavoring to propagate his religion.

18. Those, O Jamaçpa, who are obedient to the direction of Vohu-Manô, seek by means of the true faith to obtain this might, which is the glory of supreme rule. Give me, Ahura, that whereby thy wishes may be effected.

19. To Maidyomâonhâ, the noble, lands are to be given, for the doctrine which with zeal he taught the Aryan people; to him who by his hymns proclaimed to the children of Mazda the best things of life.

20. This blessing we beseech you to grant us, all ye gracious Deities; true faith, the prayers of Vohu-Manô, in which might is contained; ye, to whom sacrifices are offered, with prayer; ye, who strive to give satisfaction to Mazda.

21. He is the excellent wise man, in knowledge, in teachings and in leadership, to whom Ahura Mazda has given the royal power, as a consequence of obedience to the precepts of religion, and of the true faith through Vohu-Manô. Unto Ahura we pray for his gracious blessings.

22. By means of offerings to whom, expressions of religious faith, good fortune is to me, that Mazda Ahura knows—those that existed of old and still exist. To these I now sacrifice, to each as a Divine Person [the Amĕsha-Çpĕntas], and come near unto them with gratitude.

The fifth and last Gâthâ is called *Vahistoisti*, because it begins with the word *Vahista*. It is short, consisting of a single section of nine verses, two only of which, the last, I care to quote.

V. 1, 1. The most earnest wish of the most noble Zarathustra will be fulfilled, if haply Ahura Mazda shall concede to him this favor, flowing out of the performance of the duties of religion—to-wit, the long continuance of a happy life ["the welfare of the soul forever"; perhaps a permanently peaceful and contented life for the people]. And those who exceed his expectations, as disciples of the good law, with teachings and achievements.

2. May they learn from him, with thoughts, words and words, hymns for Mazda, and prayers for the offerings of religion; Kava-Vîstâçpa, of the blood of Zarathustra and the noble Frashaôstra. They know the ways of truth, the law which Ahura gave to those by whom the land profits.

3. Mayest thou, too, know these, Paouruchiçta, descendant of Haêchat-açpa, noble and worthy of admiration among the daughters of Zarathustra, unto thee, Vohu-Manô and Asha co-operating, Mazda has given one for a husband (or instructor), to have the care of thy education, thou, most noble, wise, and composer of hymns.

4. Thus for him, your father [or husband?], I will be zealous; and I hope that he may give his fathers to be relatives of the workers, the pious ancestors of the devout. May I possess the clear and perfect understanding of Vohu-Manô, created by Mazda to teach the good law always.

5. To you, the maiden to be married, I the bridegroom speak these words. This makes me hopeful. Be conversant hereafter with the places where Vohu-Manô teaches, according to the good law . . . . May one of you clothe the other with the true faith, whereat Vohu-Manô will greatly rejoice.

6. So are both these manifest, ye men and ye women, the way to come away from the Drukhs. Whoso is thankful to me for a benefit, I demand from the Drukhs (saying to them), "Be far away from the body" [do him no bodily harm, or, send his body far from you; or, let his body alone]. May the power of the kingdom of the evil one seize upon those who cut short his breath! May the unbelievers be completely conquered, so as never again to be able to take the lives of Aryans!

7. This shall be your reward for that great work, that the anguish which makes the heart its home, stealing away from the inmost recesses, whereof it has had possession, will go thither to where the lives of the unbelievers are. Strive to attain this great good fortune, and it shall be with you like a friend, until your last breath.

8. Let those who have been faithless flee away, flee away to the unbelieving marauders. May all whom we are to fight, be enfeebled! May he who is the supreme over death, give unto our kindred clans of Aryans good government, and peace and quiet to all, whether Aryans or infidels! May he cause the treacherous to fall by their own snares: and may all this speedily come to pass.

9. Through false religion calamities have come upon our people, and injuries to those who are the apostles of thy faith, who are resolved completely to conquer their unbelieving oppressors. Where is the very self of Ahura, who will drive them away from their abodes and from their predatory raids? May thy rule come, O Ahura, wherewith thou wilt give security and comfort to the pure who live righteously.

This ends the Gâthâs, properly so called. The Yaçna Haptanhaiti is included by Spiegel among them; but it is not a Gâthâ. It is a devotional hymn, in seven parts or chapters, in which Ahura and the Amĕsha-Çpĕntas are praised, with fire, the sun, the earth, women, waters, etc.

The fire is called the son of Ahura "acquainted" with him and with the Amĕsha-Çpĕntas—by which is meant that it is of kin to them, a potency of the same primal energy; and the sun is said to be the body of Ahura, by which is meant that it is that limited form or circular space in which the light, the revealing of Ahura, shines in the sky as the sun.

Fire [it is said to it], son of Ahura Mazda, those are fortunate to whom thou comest in thy power, thou, most beneficent, most worthy of adoration. Come now unto us, enabling us to worship, helping us in this great work! Thou art acquainted with Ahura Mazda, acquainted with the Amĕsha-Çpĕntas; thou that bearest the name Vâzista art the most beneficent of all fires. We draw nigh to thee, O Fire, son of Ahura Mazda, with zealous devotedness and ardent faith, with the ceremonial observances and the prayers and hymns, that are the effluences of Vohu-Manô. We praise thee, Mazda Ahura! We acknowledge ourselves to be thy debtors, with all good thoughts, with all good words, with all good works, we draw nigh unto thee. This thy body, the fairest of all bodies, we invite, Mazda Ahura, the greatest among the great lights, that which men call the sun.

I think I need say no more, nor quote further, to enable you to understand the philosophical and religious doctrine of Zarathustra. This Yaçna is in the same dialect as the Gâthâs, the ancient Bactrian, and was composed during or soon after his reign. And we learn from these verses that the fire and the sun were adored solely as revealings of that Infinite and Perfect Light which was Ahura Mazda, who was also the omnipotent, the beneficent, the creator of all good, of the Aryans and the Aryan land, of the sky and its luminaries; who was also the omnipresent mind or intellect, and the power of production and the life of all living beings.

We learn, also, that the sacrificial fires were lighted, and the sacrifices prepared for, and the invocations uttered, at the coming of daylight. The sun is here invoked to rise, that through him the light of Ahura may be poured upon the earth and illuminate the expanse.

The dawn, *Ushahina*, was adored also, as she was by the name of *Ushas*, by the Indo-Aryans, as also were the constellations, *Tistrya, Vanant, Çatavaêça* and *Haptoiringa*, and *Drvaçpa*, the Twin Horsemen or perhaps *Sirius*—all of them as revealings of the light.

The Emperor Julian expressed the same doctrine, when he said,

> The sun, the greatest God, he has caused to appear out of himself, in all things like himself.

And in the Egyptian dialogue between Pimander and Thoth, the former says,

> I am Pimander, the Thought of the Divine Power . . . . He changed form, and suddenly revealed to me all . . . . all was converted into Light . . . . From this noise went out a Voice: it seemed to me the Voice of the Light, and the Word proceeded out of the Voice of the Light . . . . This Light is *Me*. I am the Intelligence. I am thy God . . . . I am the germ of the Thought, the resplendent Word, the Son of God. Think that what thus sees and perceives in you is the Word of the Master. It is the Thought which is God the Father. They are not at all separated, and their union is Life.

And so Pythagoras taught that God is the universal mind, diffused through all things, the source of all life, the proper and intrinsic cause of all motion, in substance similar to light, and in nature like truth.

So Yehuah spoke the ten commandments to Moses "out of the midst of the fire": He "covereth himself with light, as with a garment"; "His glory," Ezekiel said, "came from the way of the East, and the earth shone with his glory." "His Glory," says Habakkuk, "covered the Heavens, . . . and his brightness was as the light." "And the light," it is said in Daniel, "dwelleth with him."

Cicero held that the reason of man is of divine origin, being implanted in him as an immortal essence by God (*de Leg. i.* 8). Socrates held that in the universal reason there is maintained a correspondence to the reason within us; and that man's reasonable soul derives and has its being from the supreme reason.

Plato held that one idea of God (identical with the Fravashi of Ahura Mazda) was the Supreme Idea, which, as the highest, both is, and contains in itself all others; and that, consequently, God is the unity which in itself comprises the true essence of all things.

I turn now to the legends contained in the later books of the *Zend-Avesta*. We shall find in them historical names, already familiar to us, with others that you have not yet heard, all of them of heroes of the Zarathustrian era.

One of these heroes of the remote past became the expected savior of an uncertain future. In the writings upon the Persian religion much is said about the expected savior *Sosiosch* who is to appear in the future time, and put an end to the reign of Ahriman. Mr. Dunlap says,

The Persians looked for a prophet *Çaôshyanç*, and after him two others, called *Oschedar-bami* and *Oschedar-mâh:* finally (*Messias*) *Sosiosh* will appear.

In *Fargard xix.* of the *Vendidad*, verses 16 to 19, is this passage:

Zarathustra said to Aṅra-Mainyus, ... I will smite the men who were created by the Daevas: I will smite the Naçus whom the Daevas created. I will smite the Pari who are submitted to, until *Çaôshyanç* is born, the victorious, out of the water Kançaôya, from the East region, from the eastern regions.

It is clear enough, from this, that Çaôshyanç was a man, a chief of some tribe in the eastern part of the Aryan country, near or beyond a river called Kançaôya; and who was not to be "born," but simply to come forth or up from his country, or take the field there.

But Spiegel says, in a note to this Fargard:

Çaôshyanç is the future participle of *çu*, to "profit," and denotes the king, the savior, who is expected by the Parsees to come at the end of all things, and accomplish the resurrection, after which he will establish a kingdom full of untroubled happiness.

In *Yacna xxvi.*, 32, 33, we find,

All the good, mighty, holy Fravashis of the true believers we praise, from Gayô-Marathan to Çaôshyanç, the victorious.

And in *Yacna lviii.*, 2, 3, this is repeated, with the addition,

The victory created by Ahura we praise: Çaôshyanç the victorious we praise.

Gayô-Marathan is said by the Parsees to have been the first man. In the *Farvardin Yasht* 87, we find,

The Fravashi of the pious Gayô-Marathan we praise, who first heard the mind of Ahura Mazda, and his commands, from which he [Ahura] created the race of the Aryan regions, the seed of the Aryan regions.

And, *v.*, 98, the Fravashi of the pious Içat Vâçtra, Urvataṭ-Naro and Hvarĕ-Chithra, each called "the Zarathustrian," are praised and afterwards the Fravashi of the Holy Three, the pious. Spiegel says,

the Holy Three are doubtless the three sons of Zarathustra who are to be born hereafter, viz.: Oshedar-bami, Oshedar-mâh, and Çaôshyanç. The first three names in the verse are the sons of Zarathustra, and the progenitors of the three classes, priests, warriors and husbandmen.

All of which is marvelously apocryphal.

In the same Yasht (that of the Fravashis) 110, the Fravashi of the pious (or Aryan) Açtvaṭ-ěrěto is praised, after those of several persons, sons of others named, and therefore men of a former time. And in 128, 129, we find:

the Fravashi of the pious Açtvaṭ-ěrěto we praise, who there will be Çaöshyançi, the victorious by name, and Açtvaṭ-ěrěto by name. He is so helpful that he will save *the whole corporeal world:* he is so high amongst the corporeal, that he, endowed with body and vital powers, will withstand the destroyer of the corporeal, for withstanding the Druja of the race of the two-footed, for withstanding the torment which will overcome the faithful.

That is Bleeck's translation.   Dr. Haug's is,

We worship the guardian angel of Açtvaṭ-ěrěto, who is called the victorious Soshyans. He is called *Soshyans (Sosiosh)* for he *conduces (çâvayat)* to the welfare of the whole animated creation. He is called *Açtvaṭ-ěrěto,* for he is keeping up the animated creation, guarding it against destruction, chiefly against the destruction caused by the two-legged demon-Drukhs, caused by the hatred of who annihilate good things.

The Fravashis are not guardian angels, but the pre-existent spirits of men. Is the Fravashi of Ahura Mazda, *his* guardian angel?   They are the *ideas* of Plato.

The "corporeal world" of Spiegel, Dr. Haug's "animated creation," is always the Aryan country and people. Spiegel says that *Açtvaṭ-ěrěto* means, literally, "uplifted among the corporeal." Haug says that *Açtvaṭ* means "endowed with bodies." It is the present participle of *as,* "to be," from which comes *açti,* "being," and it means "living, existent, being." What *ěrěto* means is entirely uncertain. Probably it is from the Sanskrit *râti,* "war, battle," as *ěrězata,* "silver," in Zend, represents the Sanskrit *rajata;* and means "warrior" or "warlike."

He is so powerful an auxiliary, or so great a champion, that he will liberate the whole Aryan country; and is so eminent among the people, having a strong array of followers, who are active soldiers, that he will resist by arms the ravagers of the land and slayers of the people, the men who are called Drukhs, or the Drukhs who are of the human race, and not mere spirits (of the race of the two-footed).

In the *Zamyad Yasht* 19, is a passage that shows how the Gâthâs were interpreted when that Yasht was composed. It is this,

The powerful royal majesty, which attached itself to (or invested) the victorious Çaöshyançi and the other auxiliary chiefs, that he might make the Aryan land progressive, not growing old, long-lived and not decaying, ever-living, ever-profiting, "a kingdom according to wish"; that the dead may rise, that immortality may come for the living. The lands in which the true faith is inculcated will long continue;

the Drukhs will disappear at the time. As soon as the Aryans become strong
enough to conquer them, they and their multitude of descendants will be in part
slain, and in part will flee from the country.

What is meant by the dead rising? The resurrection of the dead is not a
doctrine of the *Zend-Avesta;* and the passage does not refer to another life,
but to security and length of life in the country, upon the defeat and
expulsion of the Drukhs.

Verse 91 of the same Yasht is,

The strong royal majesty, etc. When Açtvaṭ-ĕrĕto uplifts himself [rises in arms]
from the water Kaṅçuya, an instrument to execute the will of Ahura Mazda, the son
of Viçpa-taurvi who is a minister of the Ahurian religion; which royal majesty the
strong Thraêtaôno was invested with, when the Snake Dahaka was slain; which
the Turanian Fraṅracê was invested with, etc., which Kava-Vîstâçpa was invested
with, when he set the Aryan army face to face against that of the infidels, and drove
these away to the Druja (to Toorkhistan), out of both portions of the Aryan land.

Spiegel explains *Açtvaṭ-ĕrĕto* as the future savior. It is evident that he
was a powerful Aryan, young, energetic, distinguished as a soldier, and the
son of an eminent minister of religion; that the seat of his power was on the
river Kaṅçuya, and that he marched thence with a strong force, to assist
Zarathustra; or that he lived after him and became leader of all the forces.
At all events, he won for himself the title *Çaôshyançṛ,* "Liberator." And in
verse 94, speaking as if of the future, it is said that he exercised a vigilant
supervision over the country, wisely providing for it measures of good
government, and discovering all who were of like faith and nature as the
expelled infidels, restoring to the country abundance and prosperity, and
giving to the people peaceful and secure homes. His followers go forward, it
is said in the next verse, performing good service and winning victories,
attached to the Ahurian faith and uttering no false doctrine. They have
their own tongue, it is said; which I take to mean that they were, in part at
least, natives of the country, who had allied themselves with him, as they
are called his "companions." Before them Rapine, armed and fatally
successful, succumbed; and he destroyed the wicked Drukhs, who came
of a wicked race in the North, the land of darkness.

And the ninety-sixth verse is,

Vohu-Manô will smite Akô-Manô; the truth will smite the falsehood; Haurvâṭ and
Amĕrĕtâṭ subdue hunger and thirst; the evil-doer Aṅra-Mainyu bows himself,
deprived of rule. *Yatha Ahu Vairyo!*

Naturally, this language has been supposed to mean the final destruction
of evil, by means of a redeemer or savior. But we have all the time seen
these divine potencies aiding the Aryans in their struggle against the foreign

invaders, and these represented as assisted and inspired by Anra-Mainyus and the Daevas. That Haurvât and Amĕrĕtât, health and long life, are to subdue hunger and thirst, proves that this world and human life were spoken of. The son of a minister of religion, coming from the neighborhood of a river, was unquestionably a man; and if the recital was not legendary, but a vaticination, it was a man, a soldier and a conqueror who was expected. The truth is, that it is a recital of the past, in the form of a prophecy of the future; for it is certain that Çaŏshyanç came upon the scene before Zarathustra died. Vohu-Manô smote Akô-Manô, and the true faith overcame the false, when the Aryan forces conquered the infidels. When the Drukhs were expelled from the country, Anra-Mainyus fled with them; and hunger and thirst were succeeded by peace and plenty, at the same time.

In the Ormazd Yasht, the followers of Zarathustra march out of their homes, confederacies and regions, against the Varenian Drukhs, who are armed with slings, arrows, knives and clubs, and are called "invisible," because moving by stealth to plunder, or hiding in the recesses of the mountains. In the Amshaspands' Yasht, Zarathustra is told to smite and drive away the Drukhs, who kill his priests and soldiers, until the latter, discouraged and terrified, refuse to serve against them.

Probably this soldiery was as free of restraint as the Toorkhomans themselves have always been. When, Ferrier says, in his *Caravan Journeys*, a Turcoman chief is about to make a foray, he plants a lance, surmounted by his color, into the ground in front of his tent, and a crier invites all good Mussulmen, in the name of the prophet, to join in a raid on the Persian infidels. The Turcoman enjoys most perfect liberty, and only those who choose ride up and strike their lances into the ground near his, in token that they decide to follow his fortunes.

In the latest compositions of the *Zend-Avesta*, certain evil spirits are called Drukhs: but in the earlier ones they are infidels, armed, driven away and overcome by weapons, and forced to retire into the North region from which they came. They are "the godless Daeva-worshippers," incited by Anra-Mainyus, in the nineteenth Fargard, to slay Zarathustra, and defeated by the potency of his prayers. And in the Yasht Khordat, the Aryans smite the Naçu, Hashi, Bashi, Çaêni and Bûji, whom Spiegel thinks evil spirits; but who were clearly infidel tribes, for the heavenly Yazatas defend the Aryans against

> the hosts of many foes, the banners uplifted by many, the men with hostility, the naked dagger, from the foes of the Aryans.

I have already spoken of the historical legend of the emigration led by *Yima*, the son of *Vivanhao*, and of his colonization of an alluvial and irrigated land, as it is recited in the second Fargard of the *Vendidad*.

In the Aban-Yasht, devoted to Ardviçura, the River Goddess, Yima the brilliant, having a numerous people is said to have sacrificed to her on the mountain Hukairya, offering a hundred male horses, a thousand cattle, ten thousand small cattle; and to have prayed that he might be the supreme ruler over all the regions of the Aryan land, over the Daevas and the native infidels, their creatures, over sorcerers and Pairikas, over the Çathras, Kaoyas and Karapanas (native tribes), and that he might win from the Daevas wealth and power, stores of grain and herds, the means of sustenance, and the glory of victory; and all this was granted to him.

In the Gosh-Yasht, Yima Khshaêta offered to Drvaçpa, on the same mountain, the same offering, and she granted his prayer for fat cattle for his people, security of life, freedom from hunger and thirst, old age and premature death, hot wind and cold, for a thousand years.

In the Farvardin-Yasht his Fravashi is praised, for, among other things, preventing the drought that destroys the pasturage: for the grasses had to be raised on the alluvial lands, by means of irrigation; and the system of canals for that purpose had its beginning, at least in Bactria, with him.

Drvaçpa is said by Spiegel to mean "possessing fat horses"; but what is meant by the God or Goddess so named, we have not even a conjecture. It is true that *açpa* means "a horse"; but also *çpa* means "a dog," and *dra*, *dru*, in Sanskrit, to "run," whence *drava*, "running"; and I think it probable that originally *drvaçpa* was Sirius, "the running or hunting dog."

In the Ram-Yasht, Yima offered to Vayu, the Flame, on Hukairya, on a golden throne, on a golden foot-stool, with bareçma and abundant food, and the Flame granted his prayer, that he might be sovereign over the Aryan people, dwelling furthest south of all the Aryans ("the most beholding the sun, of men"), and that he might give his people peace and quiet and other blessings. And in the Ashi-Yasht he offers to Ashis Vanuhi, with the same prayer as in the Gosh-Yasht. We shall find the exploits of the great heroes recited in the same manner.

In the Zamyad-Yasht, the divine sovereignty united itself with Yima, and he reigned long over the seven-regioned land, and won large spoil from the Daevas, and much glory. Under his rule there was exhaustless food in profusion for all, and men and cattle had peace and quiet, and there was neither heat nor cold, old age nor discontent created by the Daevas; all which were the fruits of the entire suppression of the false religion, up to the time when he apostatized and taught false doctrine.

Then the sovereignty left him, flew away from him in the form of a bird, and when he no longer saw it, then he fell affrighted down upon the ground. It was taken possession of by Mithra. He repented and it was again given to him; for it is said that it went from him a second time, and was taken possession of by Thraêtaöna, because he was the most successful of all soldiers, except Zarathustra.

A third time it left him, and the valiant-minded Kĕrĕçâçpa was invested with it, because he was the mightiest among the Aryans, except Zarathustra.

Yima, therefore (the *Yemsheed* of the Persian legends), is a genuine and real Irano-Aryan hero, entitled to be named "the First." When he apostatized the second time, Thraêtaöna succeeded him; and, when the third time, Kĕrĕçâçpa, after which he disappears. He is as historical a person as Alfred the Saxon; and was never deified by the Irano-Aryans, though he became a Deity of the *Veda*. The figurative expressions used in regard to him and to the fertile plain in the vicinity of the site of Balkh (which was a great and populous city in the time of Alexander), gave birth, naturally, to the later myth, that he brought the golden age on earth, and founded a place of delight (like the Greek Elysium and the Semitic Aghdan [Eden], styled the Vara of Yima); and the expression that he was more beholding the sun than other men (or Aryans), because he emigrated further southward, caused it to be said that he was so pure that he could gaze at the sun which blinds other men. So it is that in all religions the figurative and allegorical phrases of their earlier days become inspired traditions and articles of faith essential to salvation, to the generations that come afterward.

Through the hyperbolical expressions used in the second Fargard and elsewhere in the *Zend-Avesta*, it is easy to see the simple historical facts of the ancient legend: and thus the Zendic books, dead to the world for ages, and all memory of their language and its alphabet lost, rescued at last, almost as if by miracle, from the silent custody of the dead past, and of oblivion, unexpectedly explain to us the meaning of a legend in the ancient books of the Indo-Aryans, the venerable *Vedas*, of the history of that separation of the two branches of the same race, which caused the formation, out of the old mother-tongue, of the sister languages, Zend and Sanskrit, and the development and growth of two great systems of religious faith and of philosophy.

And at the same time the recovered books reveal to us the origins of the emanation doctrine of the Hebrew Kabbalah and the later Jewish doctrine; of the Grecian Gnosticism, and the phrases, whether in the same or another sense, of our own religion; as they do those of the doctrines of Pythagoras, Plato and Philo the Alexandrian Jew. Surely it is worth our while to endeavor to understand these most ancient monuments of human thought and Aryan faith.

The next noticeable legend is that of *Thrita*. Fargard *xx.* of the *Vendidad* contains an account of him which is in some respects very curious. Zarathustra inquires of Ahura Mazda who was the first physician, the first of mankind skilled in medicine, the active, successful, able, who defeated sickness and death, and prevented *Vazĕmno-açti*. The Gujerat translation renders this by "smiting scimitar." It is simply fever. The text itself explains it:

> Who kept back *Vazĕmno-açti*, who kept back the heat of the fire from the body of men.

The racking pains of malarial fever could very well be compared to the keen thrusts of a scimitar.

Ahura replies that it was Thrita who did all this: that he desired as a favor from Khshathra-Vairya (the Divine Supremacy, because he had to overpower Añra-Mainyus, the author of all sickness and death) a means to withstand disease, death, pain and fever-heat; and Ahura created all manner of healing plants, "round about the one *Gaŏkĕrĕna*." The Huzvaresh translation explains this as the white *Hom*, of which the Bundehesh says,

> Nearby this tree [namely, *jat-bĕs*] grows the white *Hom* in the source of Ardvisur; whosoever eats of it becomes immortal. It is called the tree *Gokarn*.

According to the *Minokhired*, it grows in the Sea *Var-Kash* (*Vouru-Kasha*), in the most hidden part, and the fish *Kharmahi* moves continually round it, to keep off the frogs and other evil creatures which seek to destroy it.

I venture to think that *Thrita* and the Vedic *Trita Aptya* were the same; and that he was a Ṛishi believed to have been translated to the sky as a star. *Thrita* is called the greatest public benefactor among the *Çamas*. This is supposed to be a family name; but it means simply "healers," from the Sanskrit *çama*, "cure," from *çam*, to "grow calm, be appeased," the causative *pra-çamaya* meaning to "heal."

Gaŏ-kĕrĕna did not mean the white *Hom*. One meaning of the Sanskrit *go*, Zend, *gao*, was "earth, land, ground": and *kara* and *karaṇa* in Sanskrit, *kĕrĕna* in Zend, meant "making, causing, producing." *Gaŏ-kĕrĕna*, therefore, was the productive land or country, over all which grew the medicinal plants. Also *Airyema* comes as healer for the people. This is the prayer so called: and it is elsewhere said that the most eminent and successful practitioners of the healing art were those who healed by prayer and devotion.

In the Farvardin-Yasht, Thrita is said to have been "the spreader of the extended region," by which it appears that by colonization or conquest Thrita had extended the Aryan domain.

In Yaçna *ix.*, we have this: at the time of the morning-dawn came *Haôma* (the *Soma* of the *Veda*) to Zarathustra, as he was making the sacrificial fire and reciting the Gâthâs, and Zarathustra asked him,

Who, O Man, art thou, who appearest to me as the most beautiful among all mankind, endowed with thine own life, majestic, immortal?

And Haôma answered,

I, O Zarathustra, am Haôma the devout, who am exempt from death. Pray to me, thou devout man! Make me ready for food! Praise me with songs of praise, as also the other chiefs have praised me.

Then said Zarathustra,

Praise be to the Haôma! Who first, O Haôma, prepared thee, of all the Aryans? What gifts of the divine beneficence thereby became his share? What wish of his was granted?

So Zarathustra asked, in succession, who were the second, third and fourth of the Aryans, to prepare the Haôma, receiving what gifts and gratification of what wishes. And the answers to these questions are the following legends:

1. That of *Yima*, as already given.

2. That of *Thraëtaonâ*, who smote the serpent Dahaka. *Vivanhao* first prepared the *Haôma*, and a son was born to him, *Yima*.

Athwya next prepared it, and a son was born to him, with a valiant clan, *Thraëtaonâ*.

3. *Thrita*, the greatest benefactor among the *Çamas*, prepared it next, and two sons were born to him, *Urvâkhshya* and *Kërëçâçpa*, the legend of the latter of whom follows:

Thraëtaonâ smote the serpent Dahaka (*Azhi Dahaka*), which had three jaws, three heads, six eyes, a thousand strengths; the very mighty Druj, derived from the Daevas, the wicked oppressor of the Aryans, which Añra-Mainyus brought forth as the mightiest Druj in the Aryan country, for the destruction of the true faith in the land. The Azhi Dahaka was, no doubt, originally a Tâtar or Turanian tribe in the Aryan land, the most numerous and powerful in it, composed of three bands or having three villages or settlements, and able to put a thousand horsemen in the field. Probably the tribe had adopted a serpent as its emblem, and called itself "The Tribe of the Serpent." Or the snake may have been the chief. The "thousand strengths" probably meant that the tribe could put a thousand men in the field. "Three jaws, three heads, six eyes" means but the one thing, that the tribe was composed of three bands, led by three or six subordinate chiefs.

As there are American Indian tribes called Snakes and Crows, and a multitude of chiefs and warriors bearing the names of animals, birds and reptiles.

Of the two sons of Thrita, Urvâkhshya was "a disposer in relation to custom and law," a civil ruler; and Kĕrĕçâçpa, "endued with higher activity," a soldier, "bearer of the Mace Gaeçus." He smote the serpent Çruvara. The legend seems to have little meaning.

4. *Pourushaçpa* next prepared it, and *Zarathustra* was born to him, who deeds are recited.

Zarathustra, it is said, was "created against the Daevas, devoted to the belief in Ahura, the renowned in Airyana-Vaêjo." He was the first to recite the prayer Ahuna-Vairya; and caused the Daevas to hide themselves in the earth, who before then were going about on the earth in the shape of men: and he was the mightiest, strongest, the most active, swiftest, the most victorious among the men created by Ahura. That the Daevas went about as men, means that they were the natives of the country, and that afterwards the word came to mean "evil spirits."

These legends and the Gâthâs together clearly show that Zarathustra was a great soldier, living not very long after Yima, and who had lived in the original Aryan country before coming into Bactria. And also they prove that no schism or hatred was caused among the Aryans by the introduction of the Ahurian faith. Wherever Zarathustra lived, the whole Aryan population was of that faith, and accepted him as their military chief and civil ruler.

These accounts also prove that the two branches did not separate in the Indus country or any other, remote from the original cradle of the race, or long after a first joint movement from that original home. It is clear that the Irano-Aryan emigration under Yima was from the original home itself. It was from a cold and mountainous country; and Zarathustra had resided in the original home.

Nor had the people been so long removed and gone to such a distance, as to have lost their ancient manners and habits. We find in the *Zend-Avesta* no mention of cities or towns. The political system was that of a confederation of clans. The men were chiefly horsemen, and their wealth consisted chiefly in horses, cattle and camels, and in sheep, if these are meant by "small cattle." They were mostly herdsmen, living largely in tents, although Zarathustra encouraged them to build permanent homes; and they drove their cattle to considerable distances, into the steppes probably beyond the Oxus and to the Jaxartes, for fresh pasture.

As to the "two worlds" so often spoken of, they cannot be with certainty identified. In the first Fargard, which undoubtedly contains the ancient traditions, the countries "created" are named in the following order: 1. Airyana-Vaêjo; 2. Gaû, in which Sughda is; and this is undoubtedly Sogdiana, or the valley of the Zer Affshan; 3. Môuru, Merv or Margiana, which is south of the Oxus and southwest of Bactria; 4. Bakhdi or Bactria; 5. Nis-a or Nisai, between Môuru and Bakhdi. Now, if Airyana-Vaêjo was the upper Zer Affshan country, in the vicinity of the present city of Samarcand; Gaû, in which Sughda is, may have been the country lower down that stream, about the present plain of Bokhara, and the great clay plain on the north side of the Oxus, below Balkh, which is even at the present day two hundred miles long by sixty wide, fertile, traversed by many canals of irrigation, and formerly much more extensive, before the sand had been drifted over a large part of the country. If then the next colonization was in Margiana, the emigration to Balkh went up the Oxus from Margiana, and Margiana and Balkh must have been the two worlds. Or they may have been the Bokhara region and Balkh; or eastern and western Bactria. The land of the seven Kareshvares was certainly Bactria, from the mountains westward.

No one has noticed the significance of the phrase that Ahura "created" these countries in succession. He is said to have "created" the Aryan land, when the Aryans *settled* it; and he is never said to have *created* any other countries. The phrase is equivalent, therefore, to saying that these countries were settled in succession by the Aryans.

The *Gosh-Yasht*, addressed to *Drvaçpa* contains several ancient legends, really historical.

The first is that *Paradhata Haôshayañha* sacrificed to her on the top of a high mountain, and prayed to be enabled to smite the Mazanian Daevas, that he might not fear, and they might be forced to bow themselves in terror, and hasten away, terrified, to darkness. His prayer was granted and this Yasht thus preserves the name and memory of one more Aryan hero who defeated the Tâtar horsemen (called *Daevas* because deemed to be inspired by the evil and malignant passions which were originally personified as Daevas), forced them to flee and drove them back to their home in the North.

The *Mazanian* and *Varenian* Daevas are several times mentioned. The former are supposed to have been those supposed to inhabit Mazanderan; the latter, those inhabiting Varena with the four corners, a country named in the first Fargard. They were, no doubt, native names of indigenous tribes. It is possible that *Mazanian* may be from the Sanskrit *magha*, "great, powerful."

It is taken for granted that the Zend word *Daeva* and the Sanskrit *Deva* are the same, and that the Vedic *Devas*, *Gods*, became evil spirits to the Zarathustrians, by the schism created by the promulgation of their new faith.

It is a theory built on very doubtful premises. I have no doubt that *Daeva* is from the Sanskrit verb *dâ*, to "cut, cut off, destroy, bind," the same as *do*, *dya*. The suffix *va* forms appellatives which express the agent, as *açva*, "horse," as "runner." *Daeva*, therefore, means "the destroyer." And several names of individual Daevas mean "death, hurting, wounding, killing," and the like. *Aindra*, twice mentioned as a Daeva, is also supposed to be identical with the Light God *Indra*, and to have in like manner become an evil spirit; but it probably meant "sensuality."

Haôshayañha is called the *Paradhata*, which means "most eminent protector or preserver"; and he is described in the Yasht as "nourisher, bringer of offerings, dispenser, offerer and implorer of the Deities for favors."

In this Yasht it is recounted that *Thraêtaonâ* slew the snake *Dahaka* in Varena, the mightiest Drukh, oppressor of the Aryans, created by Añra-Mainyus, and drove away as a conqueror those who aided him, were in his service, and able-bodied men, forcing them into the most hidden parts of the world, i. e., either into the mountains or into the regions of the North.

In this Yasht, also *Haôma* prays that it may bind the murdering Turanian *Frañraçyâna*, and carry him away bound as a prisoner of King *Huçrava*, and that Kava *Huçrava*, the son of the daughter of *Çyâvarshâna*, the man slain by violence, and *Agraê-ratha*, the son of *Naru*, may slay *Frañraçyâna* behind the water *Chaêchaçta*, the deep, with broad waters.

Also we learn by this Yasht, that Zarathustra "joined himself to" (i. e., secured to be his assistant) the good noble Hutaôça, persuading her to believe in the true faith, and act accordingly. Hutaôça, it seems, was or became the wife of King Vîstâçpa. Like him, Spiegel says, she became converted to the Mazdayaçnian religion. The meaning of the verse is uncertain. Bleeck reads that Zarathustra joined himself to Hutaôça, in order to think the law and speak and act after it. And it is added, "she shall impress the good Mazdayaçnian law from Zarathustra (which therefore she had learned or was to learn from him), in my memory, and then praise, she who shall bestow on me good praise for service." By whom this is said does not appear; and it certainly has no sense unless in the mouth of some one then living, and whom Hutaôça converted or at least instructed. I think it was Vîstâçpa, who is not named at all; and I think so on account of the next passage to be quoted. The meaning seems to me to be she will impress upon my memory the teachings of the true religion, and the hymns of praise, she who will procure me laudations for good service to the Aryan cause.

Zarathustra sacrificed, it is said here, in Airyana-Vaêja, the country of the Aryan race. Vîstâçpa ruled in a remote part of the country, as we know from other passages. There is nothing to induce the belief that he was a native chief, or a Turanian. His *conversion* was his accession to the cause. And there may even have been, at that time, Aryan settlements in Bactria in which the reformed faith had not been accepted, or even preached. Hutaôça may or may not have become Vîstâçpa's wife at the time referred to in this Yasht. Probably she was not, for in the Ram-Yasht Hutaôça with many brothers, offered for the clan of the Naotaras, praying that she might be loved, received with love, in the house of Kavi-Vîstâçpa.

In the Gosh-Yasht we have the legend of the *Běrězaidhi Kava-Vîstâçpa*, beyond the river Daitya, who, offering, prayed that he might put to flight *Asta-Aurva*, the son of *Viçpo-thaurvô-açti*, having a broad helmet, great boldness, a large head, and seven hundred swift camels; that afterwards he might, in battle and pursuit slay the murdering *Oyaônian Arejat-Açpa*, and put to rout and drive away *Darshinika*, the Daeva-worshipper; that he might smite the dark-skinned unbelievers, *Çpinjairista*, the Daeva-worshipper, and reach by skilful movements and marches the regions of *Varedhaka* and *Oyaônya*, and devastate the *Oyaônian* regions with immense slaughter; and his prayer was granted.

Vîstâçpa is the *Gushtasp* of the later Persian legends. In the Aban-Yasht, he is said to have offered to Ardvîçura, behind the water *Frazdânu*, praying that he might slay the malignant infidels invading the country from the land of darkness, and the evil *Arějat-Açpa*, "here in the war of the world," i. e., here, in the struggle for the possession of the Aryan land. *Arějat-Açpa* is the *Ardjaçp*, a Turanian king, of the later legends.

Açpâ-yaôdha Zairivairis, behind the water Daitya (i. e., west of it, and he being an ally of Vîstâçpa), offered to Ardvîçura, praying that he might smite *Pěshô-Chiñha Astô-kâna*, possessed of much craft, and *Arějat-Açpa*, in the wars in the Aryan country. And *Arějat-Açpa* also offered to her, the son of *Vandaěmono*, at the Sea Vouru-Kasha, praying that he might smite *Vîstâçpa* and the *Açpâ-yaôdha Zairivairi* and the Aryan region; but his prayer was not granted.

In the Ashi-Yasht, Zarathustra prays that he may ally himself with Hutaôça, for thinking, speaking and acting the law; and that she might guard him the Mazdayaçnian Law in the heart, and afterwards praise, and afford him good praise for the work.

In the Farvardin-Yasht is this singular passage in regard to Vîstâçpa, the pious. He, the mighty, it is said, whose body is the Mañthra (a phrase

elsewhere applied to other men, and meaning that he composed hymns), ·
who as an ally and helper submitted to the Mazdayaçnian Law; who has
mighty weapons, the Ahurian, who with a strong force of armed men, by his
conquests enables the Ahurian faith to extend into other regions,

> who brought forth the firm-placed, bound, from the Hunus, and made it sitting in
> the midst, high-working, teaching, pure, the nourisher and beloved of the cow and of
> fodder.

As to this compare the Zamyad-Yasht, where it is said that the Divine
Sovereignty attached itself to him, for thinking, speaking and fulfilling the
Law, and driving away the Daevas. He opened for the extension of the
true faith a broad way, and became its champion and defender; and he

> brought out the same, the fast-placed, chained by the Hunus, teaching, and made it
> sitting in the middle, high, uplifted, pure, abundance and beloved of meat and
> fodder,

when he smote those from the northern regions, of the false religion, Peshana
the Daevayaçnian, and the wicked Arĕjat-Açpa and the other infidel allies,
the Oyaŏnians. The meaning seems to be that the practice of the true
religion had been suppressed in the country, by the Hunus, and was
restored and established by Vîstâçpa, when he conquered and expelled the
infidels, and even carried the war, by long and difficult marches, into their
own country.

We find in the Khordah-Avesta a blessing addressed by Zarathustra
himself to Vîstâçpa, wishing him long life and good fortune, and that he
might be victorious, distinguished and powerful, like Jâmâçpa, Thraêtaŏna,
Kava-Uç, Aŏsnara, Takmo-Urupa, Yima, Kĕrĕçâçpa, Urvaksha, Çyâvarshâna and Vifra-navâza, and without sickness and death, like Kava-Huçrava.

In the Aban-Yasht, Zarathustra prays to be enabled to effect an alliance
with Vîstâçpa, son of Aurvât-Açpa, that he might think, speak and act
according to the law. They were therefore co-temporaries; and though
the blessing attributed to Zarathustra is clearly not genuine, yet it shows
that, at the very ancient time when it *was* composed, the various heroes
named in it had lived or were co-temporaries of Zarathustra.

Thraëtaonâ is the *Feridoun* of Iranian or Persian legend, slayer of the
infamous tyrant *Zohak*, on the Alborj or more properly on the mountain of
Demavend, to the south of the Caspian. He was of the Athwyanian clan,
and said in the first Fargard of the *Vendidad* to have lived in Varena with
the four corners, the fourteenth country created; while Kĕrĕçâçpa is said
in the same to have lived in Vaekĕreta, in which Duzhaka is situated. Now
the snake Dahaka, in the Aban-Yasht, desired or attempted to depopulate

the seven Kareshvares, though he was slain in Varena. Haug thinks that Varena was Ghilan. Lassen looks for it in Kabul; Roth seeks it in the southeast part of the Aryan territories. The Parsee traditions place it in Taberistan, and the Huzvaresh translation makes it a mountain there. The historian of Taberistan makes Feridoun to have been born in the village Werek of Taberistan, and another tradition makes him to have dwelt in Gosh.

Vaêkereta, the seventh country created, in which the Pairika Khnathaiti lived, who attached herself to Kěrěçâçpa, is said by Haug to be certainly Segestan: while Spiegel makes it Kabul. Thraêtaonâ and Kěrěçâçpa were, according to Zarathustra's blessing of Vîstâçpâ, either co-temporaries of the two latter, or lived before them; and Zarathustra is more than once said to have sacrificed in Airyana-Vaêja. Kabul, south of the Hindu Kush, may have been the "other world" or new Aryan country, beyond the pass Chinvaṭ: but how could Thraêtaonâ have lived in the fourteenth country settled by the Aryans? The Varenian Daevas are continually spoken of, and these texts as to places cannot be reconciled unless there was some part of the Aryan land called Varena, in the time of Zarathustra. But it is useless to speculate on that; for when these later legends appeared, the ancient heroes had become mythical persons whose real homes were no doubt unknown.

The tract of arable land on which Yima settled his colony, is termed his *Vara*, and it is represented as a square. In Sanskrit, *varaṇa* means "an inclosure raised on a mound of earth, a causeway, a bridge": also, "surrounding, screening, covering." It is from *vri, vrî*, meaning, among other things, to "surround," and of which *vâraṇiya* is the future participle passive. *Varena* meant "the enclosed or encompassed space," and it was probably, or rather certainly, "enclosed" by the great main canals of irrigation. This was "Varena with the four corners." The only question is, where was this? I think it was the plain of Balkh.

Kěrěçâçpa is said in the Aban-Yasht, to have resided beyond Vara-Pishininha, *supposed* to be the modern Pishin or Pishing, in eastern Sejestan. But he slew Gandarewa on the shore of the Sea Vouru-Kasha, which must have been the Caspian.

The Vara-Pishininha was another body of alluvial and irrigated land, lying on the lower Oxus, towards its mouth.

Raghâ is the twelfth country created; and yet in Yaçna it is said that there was no local ruler over the whole of Raghâ, but the chiefs of tribes were under the immediate government of Zarathustra, it being a province, remote from the mother-country. And Raghâ is supposed to have been Media, Raghu being the name of a well-known town in Media, mentioned by Darius in the inscription of Bisutun, and by Isidor Charac, who calls it "the greatest of all the Median cities, near Mount Caspius; from which the Caspian gates have their names."

Kava-Uç was chief ruler over all regions; and Huçrava, behind the Vara Chaêchaçta was the valiant uniter of the Aryan regions into one kingdom, destroying the long rule of darkness. The strong Fuça expelled from the country he governed, the unbelieving *traders*, slaying the *Aurva Hunava* in Vaêshaka, at the gate (or pass) *Khshathro-Çaŏka*, the uppermost in Kanha. He fought against the Turanians, who are named as a hostile tribe, in several passages, and in the Farvardin-Yasht with the Çanians, Cairimians and Dahians.

Thraêtaonâ summoned to his assistance *Vifra-Navaza*, who marched three days and nights, toward his own country, the Aryan land, to join him. At the morning-dawn, the melting of the dawn, of the third night, he crossed with difficulty a deep stream, that was the boundary of his native land; for he is represented as praying to Ardviçura for aid, to enable him to reach the Aryan land, his original home. She ran to him in the shape of a maiden, seized him by the arm, and he struggled through to the Aryan shore, uninjured.

So she made a dry crossing of a great stream for *Vis-taurusha*, the descendant of *Naotairya*, at the water *Vîtanuhaiti*, the waters standing like a wall above, and flowing away below. *Vifra-Navaza* called for help from the water *Ranha;* and elsewhere the steppes of *Ranha* are spoken of. It is supposed that these are the plains on the Jaxartes; but it is quite as likely that they are the desert plains of Margiana. *Arĕjat-Açpa*, whom Vîstâçpa slew, offered at the Sea Vouru-Kasha.

Furthermore, when the divine sovereignty left Yima, it went to Thraêtaonâ, and the next time to Kĕrĕçâçpa; and as both these heroes reigned in his stead, the Aryan settlements must have constituted one kingdom, if they resided in places remote from him: and it may very well be that the Aryan colonists had, in the time of Zarathustra, settled Kabul, in the valley of the Helmund, and Media south of the Caspian.

A few additional remarks must conclude these necessarily imperfect lectures.

The separation of the Indo- and Irano-Aryan branches of the race, however and wherever it occurred, must have taken place at a very remote period, long before the composition of the Vedic hymns or the Gâthâs of Zarathustra. For it is certain that in his time the Zend and Sanskrit had become very different languages—partly by the slow process of change, and partly by intermixture with the tongues of the native tribes; and the two families of the race had few names of Deities in common.

It is now impossible to determine which of the two languages most resembled the ancient tongue from which each was developed. We find in

Zend, Greek and Welsh; *h* for *s* in Sanskrit, Latin and Erse; and Dr. Donaldson thinks, independently of this, that Greek, in one element at least, and Welsh, are younger than Latin, Sanskrit and Erse, respectively, and that Zend is younger than Sanskrit, or belongs, at least in one element, to the High Iranian class. In some cases, the older forms are found in the Zend; and it is certain that many of the original roots are lost in the Sanskrit, and that meanings are often assigned to one root which originally belonged to different roots. An exhaustive comparison of all the derivative languages is a task reserved for some great scholar.

It is evident that the Vedic and Ahurían faiths were formed, almost entirely, after, and probably very long after, the separation. Of the pre-existent faith, very little is retained by both. Each has the same philosophic ideas, which may be deemed essentially Aryan, of emanation of subsistences from substance; each essentially the same mode of personifying attributes and qualities; each those ideas of manifestation and self-limitation, of divine creation and action by intermediates, which afterwards received more formal expression in Plato's idea of the Logos, in the doctrines of Philo as to the same, and in the Sephirothic personifications of the Kabbalah. That Hakemah, the Divine Wisdom, *is* the Very Deity, manifested *as* Wisdom, in one aspect, and, as it were, through one aperture; and that the Logos was with God, contained in God, and himself God, are applications and developments of the Avestic notions in regard to the Amësha-Çpëntas, and the Vedic tenets as to the manifestations of Agni and Indra.

It is doubtful whether more than one Deity, by the same name, embodying the same conception, meaning the same thing, was common to the two faiths.

Mitra, in the ante-Vedic age, and *Mithra* in the ante-Zarathustrian period, were undoubtedly one and the same Deity, the Morning-Star. In the *Veda*, *Mitra* is Venus: in the *Zend-Avesta*, *Mithra* continues to be the Morning-Star, or becomes the Light.

Vayu is the flame, in both faiths, and of course an effluence of the fire in each. Asha-Vahista was more than the spirit of fire; and is not identical with Agni. Ushahina, in the *Avesta*, and Ushas, in the *Veda*, are the same thing, the Dawn; but the conceptions embodied in the two are not identical.

The Avestic Haöma is the Vedic Soma; and as to this plant and its juice, the notions of the two creeds are so very much alike that they must have been a part of a previous common creed, held by the ancestors of both races. Both had the same ideas as to the efficacy of praise and prayer; the Mantras of the one and the Manthras of the other were alike sacred and divine; praise and prayer with one were Brahmanaspati and Bṛihaspati, and with the other, Manthra-Çpënta; and devotion or worship was the Çraddha of one and the Çraösha of the other.

A fragment included in the Khordah-Avesta (*xxxvii.* 21) will perhaps give you a more complete appreciation of the Aryan idea of prayer and of its efficacy, than you can otherwise obtain. I condense it somewhat by omissions of unessential phrases, but otherwise give it according to the translation of Bleeck:

> Zarathustra asked Ahura Mazda; Ahura Mazda, heavenly, holiest, creator of the corporeal world, pure! Wherein alone is thy word, which expresses all good, all that springs from purity?
>
> Him answered Ahura Mazda, the prayer *Ashem*, O Zarathustra.
>
> Whoso utters the prayer Ashem with believing mind, from the memory, he praises me, Ahura Mazda; the water, earth, cattle and plants, and all good things created by Mazda which have a pure origin.
>
> For this speech the right-spoken, O Zarathustra, when it is spoken, the prayer *Ahuna-Vairya*, the uttered, is strength and victoriousness for the pure soul and the law.
>
> For it, the mere prayer Ashem, is worth, O holy Zarathustra, as a *khshnaôthra* of the pure [repeated at a sacrifice by the faithful], a hundred prayers at sleeping, a thousand flesh meals, ten thousand head of small cattle, all that is come from bodies to incorporeality [that is, all that, consumed by the sacrificial fire, becomes invisible].
>
> What is that prayer Ashem-Vohû which in greatness, goodness and beauty is worth as much as ten other prayers Ashem-Vohû?
>
> Him answered Ahura Mazda: that which a man eating prays with purity for Haurvaṭ and Amĕrĕtâṭ, praising good thoughts, words and works, putting away all evil thoughts, words and works.
>
> What is that one prayer Ashem-Vohû, which in greatness, goodness and beauty is worth a hundred other prayers Ashem-Vohû?
>
> Him answered Ahura Mazda: that, O pure Zarathustra, which a man, after having eaten of the prepared Haôma, prays with purity, praising good thoughts, words and works, putting away evil thoughts, words and works.
>
> [Then it is asked what one is worth a thousand, and what one, ten thousand other prayers Ashem-Vohû. The first is that which one stretched out for sleep prays with purity: the other, that which a man waking from sleep prays with purity, lifting himself up; in each case praising good thoughts, words and works and putting away the evil.]
>
> Which is the one prayer Ashem-Vohû, which in greatness, goodness and beauty, is worth as much as the whole Kareshvare Oaniratha, with cattle, chariots and men?
>
> Him answered Ahura Mazda: that one, O pure Zarathustra, which a man at the latter end of his life prays with purity, praising, etc.
>
> Which is the one prayer Ashem-Vohû, which in greatness, goodness and beauty is worth all that is between heaven and earth, and this earth, those lights, and all good things created by Mazda, that have a pure origin?
>
> Him answered Ahura Mazda: that one, O pure Zarathustra, when one renounces all evil thoughts, words and works.

I must conclude these quotations with portions of another fragment of the Khordah-Avesta, and of the nineteenth Fargard of the *Vendidad*, in regard to the fate of the *soul*, not the *spirit*, the *Psuchē* or *vital soul*, not the *Pneuma, spirit* or *intellectual soul*, of the dead.

. Zarathustra asked Ahura Mazda: when a pious man dies, where does his soul abide, that night?

Answered Ahura Mazda: near his head it seats itself, reciting the Gâthâ Ustavaiti, praying happiness for itself: "Happiness be to the man who conduces to the happiness of each! May Ahura Mazda create, ruling after his wish!" On this night the soul sees as much joyfulness as the whole living world [i. e., all living souls] possesses.

Where does the soul abide during the second night? Then answered Ahura Mazda: near his head it seats itself, etc. (as in the former verse).

Where does his soul abide during the third night? Then answered Ahura Mazda: [as before].

When the lapse of the third night turns itself to light, then the soul of the pious man goes forward, recollecting itself at the perfume of plants. A wind blows to meet it from the mid-day regions, a sweet-scented one, more sweet-scented than the other winds.

In it there comes to meet him his own rule of life and conduct, in the figure of a maiden, beautiful, well-grown, slender, with full bosom and admirable body, with bright face, of the age of fifteen, as fair in her growth as the fairest of women.

Then to her speaks the soul of the pure man asking: what maiden art thou whom I see here as the most beautiful of all maidens?

Then replies to him his own law: I am, O Youth, thy good thoughts, words and works, thy good law, the own law of thine own body.

Thou hast made the pleasant yet more pleasant to me, the fair yet fairer, the desirable yet more desirable, that sitting in a high place, sitting in a yet higher place, in these, Humata, Hûkta, Hvarsta. Afterward men praise me, and ask Ahura Mazda, praised long ago.

The soul of the pious man goes the first step, and arrives in Humata; takes the second and arrives at Hûkta; the third, and arrives at Hvarsta; the fourth, and arrives at the eternal lights [stars].

To it speaks a pious one, deceased before, asking it; how art thou, O pious deceased, come away from the fleshly dwellings, from the earthly possessions, from the corporeal world, hither, to the invisible; from the perishable world hither to the imperishable, has it happened to thee, to whom belong felicity?

Then speaks Ahura Mazda, ask not him whom thou askest; he is come on the fearful, terrible, trembling way, the separation of body and soul.

Bring him hither of the food, of the full fatness, that is the food for a youth who thinks, speaks and does good, who is devoted to the good law after death, that is the food for the woman who especially thinks good, speaks good, does good, the following, obedient, pure, after death.

The same questions are asked as to the soul of the impious man. Three nights it runs about near the head of the corpse, while it utters the prayer *Kemanm*. In this night it sees as much displeasing, as the whole living world. Then it goes to the impure place, recollecting itself continually by the stench. To it comes a wind from the north region, an evil-smelling one. He meets a most ugly and hateful maiden, his own evil thoughts, words and deeds. His fourth step brings him to the darkness without beginning. Here a formerly deceased wicked one addresses him, asking when he came away from the Drukhs: and Añra-Mainyus forbids asking him, and directs that he be fed on food that is poison and mixed with poison, the proper food for a sinful youth or harlot.

In the nineteenth Fargard we find this:

Creator, where are those tribunes, where do they assemble, at which a man of the corporeal world gives account for his soul?

Then answered Ahura Mazda: after the man is dead, the wicked evil-knowing Daevas work.

In the third night, after the coming and lighting of the dawn;

And when the victorious Mithra with lucent radiance stands upon the summits of the mountains, and the brilliant sun rises,

Then the Daeva called Vizaresho leads the souls bound, the sinful-living, of the wicked Daeva-worshipping men.

To the ways which were created by time comes he who is godless and he who is holy.

To the bridge Chinvaṭ, the created by Ahura Mazda, where they interrogate the consciousness and the soul regarding the conduct practised in the corporeal world.

Thither comes the beautiful, well-created, swift and well-formed, accompanied by a dog [or, I think, by his own holiness or purity of life].

It leads away the souls of the pious above the Harabĕrĕzaiti: over the bridge Chinvaṭ it brings the host of the Heavenly Yazatas.

Vohu-Manô arises from his golden throne:

Vohu-Manô speaks: How hast thou, O pious, come hither?

From the perishable world to the imperishable world?

The pious souls go contented, to the golden thrones of Ahura Mazda, of the Amĕsha-Çpĕntas; to Garo-Nemâna, the dwelling of Ahura Mazda, the dwelling of the Amĕsha-Çpĕntas, the dwelling of the other pious. .

These fancies, that had their origin at a period long subsequent to the age of Zarathustra, are curious and interesting; but their principal interest consists in the fact, which they show, that as in India so in Iran, the immortality expected was the translation of the vital soul to the sky, there to shine as a star. It ascends above the huge snow-summits of Harabĕrĕzaiti and passing through Humâna, Hûkta and Hvarsta, reaches the eternal luminaries and dwells among them there, fed by the light which ascends from the sacrifices.

Humana is probably from the Sanskrit *Sûma*, "water, sky"; and means the cloud-region; *Hûkta*, from *Sûka* "air, wind"; and *Hvarsta*, from *Svar*. In Zend, *hvare*, "the sun, splendor," whence *Svaru*, "sunshine." The three words undoubtedly mean the three divisions of the expanse between the earth and the stars, the three steps of Vishṇu.

ARYAN NOTIONS OF PHILO JUDÆUS

This world is a younger Son of God, inasmuch as it is perceptible by the external senses; for the only Son he speaks of as older than the world, is Idea, and this is not perceptible by the intellect; but having thought the other worthy of the rights of primogeniture, he has decided that it shall remain with him; therefore this younger Son, perceptible by the external senses being set in motion, has caused the nature of Time to shine forth and to become conspicuous, so that there is nothing future to God, who has the very boundaries of Time subject to him; for their life is not Time; but the beautiful model of Time, Eternity; and in Eternity nothing is past and nothing is future, but everything is present only.—*Philo: On the Unchangeableness of God, vi.*

God distributes his benefits, not like a vender selling his wares at a high price, but is inclined to make presents of everything, pouring forth the inexhaustible fountains of his graces, and never desiring any return; for he has no need of anything, nor is there any created being competent to give him a suitable gift in return.—*On Cain and His Birth, xxxiv.*

Those who have studied philosophy in a sincere and pure spirit, have derived as the greatest good arising from their knowledge, the absence of any inclination to change with the changes of affairs, and the disposition, with all immovable firmness and sure stability, to labor at everything which it becomes them to pursue.—*On the Unchangeableness of God, v.*

For, in real truth, the wise man is the king of those who are foolish, since he knows what he ought and what he ought not to do; and the temperate man is the king of the intemperate, as he has attained a knowledge not careless or inaccurate, of what relates to choice and avoidance. Also the brave man is king over the cowardly inasmuch as he has thoroughly learned what he ought to endure, and what he ought not. So, too, the just man is king of the unjust, as he is possessed of the knowledge of undeviating impartiality as to what is to be distributed. And the holy man is king over the unholy, as he is possessed with the most just and excellent notions of God.—*On the Change of Scripture Names, xxxviii.*

The wise man alone is a ruler and a king, and virtue is the only irresponsible authority and sovereignty.—*On Dreams Being Sent from God, xxxvii.*

For in real truth, the wise man is the foremost man in the human race, being what a pilot is on a ship, a governor in a city, a general in war, the soul in the body, or the mind in the soul; or, again, what the heaven is in the world, and what God is in heaven . . . . A man according to the law, as some persons think, but, as my argument has shown, one who is himself the unwritten law and justice of God.—*On Abraham, xlvi.*

We must therefore have recourse to allegory, which is a favorite with men capable of seeing through it; for the Sacred Oracles most evidently conduct us towards and instigate us to the pursuit of it. For they say that in the Paradise there were plants in no respect similar to those which exist among us; but they speak of trees of life, trees of immortality, trees of knowledge, of comprehension, of understanding; trees of the knowledge of good and evil. Now these cannot have been trees of the ground, but must indisputably have been plants of a rational soil, which was a road to travel along, leading to virtue, and having for its end, life and immortality; and another road leading to vice, having for its end the loss of life, and immortality; that is to say, death.—*About the Planting of Noah, ix.*

Investigating the allegories of their Natural philosophy, since they look upon their literal expressions as symbols of some secret meaning of Nature, intended to be conveyed in these figurative expressions.—(Philo speaking of the Therepeutæ): *On a Contemplative Life, iii.*

These explanations of the Sacred Scriptures are delivered by mystic expressions in allegories, for the whole of the law appears to these men to resemble a living animal, and its express commandments seem to be the body, and the invisible meaning concealed under and lying beneath the plain words resembles the soul, in which the rational soul begins most excellently to contemplate what belongs to itself, as in a mirror, beholding in the very words the exceeding beauty of the sentiments, and unfolding and explaining the symbols, and bringing the secret meaning naked to the light, to all who are able by the light of a slight intimation to perceive what is unseen by what is visible.—*Id., x.*

Then Moses entered into the Tabernacle, leading his brother by the hand (and it was the eighth and last day of the festival, for the seven previous days had been devoted to the initiation of the Hierophants), he now initiated both him and his nephews.—*On the Life of Moses, xviii.*

Now the true magical art, being a science of discernment, which contemplates and beholds the books of Nature, with a more acute and distinct perception than is common, and appearing as such to be a dignified and desirable branch of knowledge, is studied, not merely by private individuals, but even by kings, and the very greatest of kings, and especially by the Persian monarchs, to such a degree, that among that people no one can possibly succeed to the kingdom, if he has not been previously initiated into the Mysteries of the Magi.—*On Special Laws, iv.*

It is not lawful to divulge the Sacred Mysteries to the uninitiated until they are purified by a perfect purification: for the man who is not initiated, or who is of moderate capacity, being unable either to hear or to see that Nature which is incorporeal and appreciable only by the intellect, being deceived by the visible sight, will blame what ought not to be blamed.

Now, to divulge Sacred Mysteries to uninitiated people, is the act of one who violates the laws of the privileges that belong to the priesthood.

It is absurd that there should be a law in cities that it is not lawful to divulge Sacred Mysteries to the uninitiated, but that one may speak of the true rites and ceremonies which lead to piety and holiness, to ears full of folly. All men must not partake of all things, nor of all discourses; above all, of such as are sacred: for those that desire to be admitted to a participation in such things, ought to have many qualifications beforehand.—*Fragment in Eusebius.*

The inmost part of the Temple, the very Holy of Holies itself, into which once in the year, the High Priest enters, on the day called the Great Fast, to offer incense, and on no other day, being then about, in accordance with our natural law, also to offer up prayers for a fertile and ample supply of blessings, and for peace to all mankind, and of any one else, I will not say of the Jews, but even of the priests, and those not of the lowest order, but even those who are in the rank next to the first, should go in there, either with him or after him, or even if the Very High Priest himself should enter in thither on two days in the year, or three or four times on the same day, he is subjected to inevitable death for his impiety, so great are the precautions taken by our lawgiver, with respect to the Holy of Holies, as he determined to preserve it alone inaccessible to and untouched by any human being.—*On the Virtues and Office of Ambassadors, xxxix.*

The statement that the Paradise was in the East, is a proof of what has been here said. For folly is a thing of darkness and setting, and which brings on the night; but wisdom is a most brilliant thing, radiant all around, and in the truest sense of the word rising (*oriens*). And as the sun, when it rises, fills the whole circle of the heaven with its light, so, in the same manner, when the beams of virtue shine forth, they make the whole place occupied by the mind full of pure light.—*About the Planting of Noah, x.*

The candelabrum was placed on the southern side of the Tabernacle, since by it the Maker intimates, in a figurative manner, the motions of the stars which give light: for the sun and the moon and the other stars, being all at a great distance from the northern parts of the universe, make all their revolutions in the south. And from this candlestick there proceeded six branches, three on each side, projecting from the candlestick in the center, so as in all to complete the number of seven; and in all the seven there were seven candles and seven lights, being symbols of those seven stars which are called planets by those who are versed in physics; for the sun, like the candlestick, being placed in the middle of the other six, in the fourth place, gives light to the three planets which are above him, and to those of equal number, which are below him, adapting to circumstances the musical and truly divine instrument.—*On the Life of Moses, ix.*

Among numbers, seven is the virgin number, the Nature which has no mother, that which is most nearly related to the unit, the foundation of all numbers; the idea of the planets, just as the unit is of the immovable sphere; for of the unit and the number seven consists the incorporeal heaven, the model of the visible heaven . . . . For all these reasons and more besides, the number seven is honored. But there is no one cause on account of which it has received its precedence so completely as because it is by means of it that the Creator and Father of the Universe is most especially made manifest; for the mind beholds God in this as in a mirror, acting and creating the world, and managing the whole universe.—*On the Ten Commandments, xxi.*

The greatest feast is assigned to the number 50, the most holy and natural of numbers, being compounded of the power of the right-angled triangle, which is the principle of the origination and condition of the whole. —*On a Contemplative Life, viii.*

We will not act the part of Hierophant or expounder of Sacred Mysteries to those who are afflicted with the incurable disease of pride of language and quibbling expressions, and juggling tricks of manners, and who measure sanctity and holiness by no other standard.—*On Cain and His Birth, xii.*

Now I bid ye, initiated men, who are purified as to your ears, to receive these things as Mysteries which are really sacred, in your inmost souls; and reveal them not to any one who is of the number of the uninitiated, but guard them as a sacred treasure, laying them up in your own hearts, not in a store-house in which are gold and silver, perishable substances, but in that treasure-house in which the most excellent of all the possessions in the world does lie, the knowledge, namely, of the Great First Cause, and of virtue, and, in the third place, of the generation of them both. And if ever you meet with any one who has been properly initiated, cling to that man affectionately, and adhere to him, that if he has learnt any more recent mystery, he may not conceal it from you, before you have learned to comprehend it thoroughly. For I myself, having been initiated in the great Mysteries by Moses, the friend of God, nevertheless, when subsequently I beheld Jeremiah the Prophet, and learned that he was not only initiated into the Sacred Mysteries, but was also a competent Hierophant, or Expounder of them, did not hesitate to become his pupil.—*Id., xiv.*

Thus also Moses, ... begins to worship God, and having entered into the darkness, that invisible country, remains there, practising the most Sacred Mysteries; and he becomes, not merely an initiated man, but also a Hierophant of Mysteries, and a Teacher of divine things, which he will explain to those whose ears are purified; therefore the divine spirit is always by him, conducting him in every right way.—*On the Giants, xii.*

Those who have received a fortunate disposition, and an education in all respects blameless, finding the path of life which proceeds in this direction plain and straight, take truth with them as the companion of their journey; by which they are initiated in the true Mysteries relating to the living God, and therefore they never attribute any of the properties of created beings to him.—*On the Unchangeableness of God, xiii.*

Therefore, also, Moses will be summoned upwards, the steward and guardian of the Sacred Mysteries of the Living God.—*About the Planting of Noah, vi.*

Drive away, therefore, drive away, O ye who have been initiated in, and who are the Hierophants of, the Sacred Mysteries; drive away, I say, the souls which are mixed and in a confused crowd, and brought together promiscuously from all quarters, those unpurified and still polluted souls, which have their ears not closed, and their tongues unrestrained, and which bear about all the instruments of their misery ready prepared, etc. —*On Fugitives, xvi.*

And wisdom is the court and palace of the all-governing and only absolute and independent king. Accordingly this is his abode, discernible only by the intellect; but the world is perceptible by the external senses; since Moses made the curtains of such things as are symbols of the four elements; for they were made of fine flax, and of hyacinthine color, and of purple and of scarlet—four numbers, as I have said before. Now the fine flax is an emblem of the earth, for the flax grows out of the earth; and the hyacinthine color is a symbol of the air, for it is black by nature; purple, again, is a symbol of the water, for the cause of this dye is derived from the sea, being the shell-fish of the same name [Gr. 'η πορφυρα], and scarlet is a symbol of fire, for it most nearly resembles a flame.—*On Seeking Instruction. xxi.*

THE LOGOS

The most universal of all things is God: and in the second place, the Word of God. But other things have an existence only in word, but in deed they are at times equivalent to that which has no existence.—*Philo: On the Allegories of the Sacred Laws, xxi.*

Now, passing on from these particular buildings, consider the greatest house or city, namely, this world, for you will find that God is the cause of it, by whom it is made. That the materials are the four elements of which it is composed; that the instrument is the Word of God, by means of which it was made; and the object of the building you will find to be the display of the goodness of the Creator.—*On Cain and His Birth, xxxv.*

God, while he spake the Word, did at the same moment create: nor did he allow anything to come between the Word and the deed; and if one may advance a doctrine which is very nearly true, his word is his deed.—*On the Sacrifice of Abel and Cain, xviii.*

It follows, therefore, since the soul of man has been fashioned in accordance with the Archetypal Word of the Great Cause of all things, that his body also, having been raised up to the purest portion of the universe, the heaven, must extend its vision, in order that, by a comparison with what is visible, it may attain to an accurate comprehension of what is invisible. —*About the Planting of Noah, v.*

I have also heard of one of the companions of Moses having uttered such a saying as this, "Behold! a man whose name is The East." A very novel appellation, indeed, if you consider it as spoken of a man who is compounded of body and soul; but if you look upon it as applied to that incorporeal being who in no respect differs from the divine image, you will then agree that the name of The East has been given to him with great felicity. For the Father of the Universe has caused him to spring up as the eldest son, whom, in another passage, he calls the first-born; and he who is thus born, imitating the ways of his Father, has formed such and such species, looking to his archetypal patterns.—*On the Confusion of Languages, xiv.*

His image, the most sacred Word; and next to that, the most perfect work of all the things perceptible by the outward senses, namely, the World. For to philosophize is nothing else but to desire to see these things correctly. —*Id., xx.*

And even if there be not as yet any one who is worthy to be called a Son of God, nevertheless let him labor earnestly to be adorned according to his first-born Word, the eldest of his angels, as the Great Archangel of many names; for he is called the authority and the name of God, and the Word, and man according to God's image, and he who sees Israel . . . . For even if we are not yet fit to be called the sons of God, still we may deserve to be called the children of his eternal image, of his most sacred Word; for the image of God is his most ancient (first uttered) Word.—*Id., xxviii.*

And the Father who created the universe has given to his Archangelic and most ancient Word a pre-eminent prerogative, to stand near both and between the created and the Creator. And this same Word is continually a suppliant to the immortal God, on behalf of the mortal race, which is exposed to affliction and misery; and is also the ambassador, sent by the Ruler of all to the subject race. And the Word rejoices in the gift, and, exulting in it, announces it and boasts of it, saying, "And I stood in the midst, between the Lord and you"; neither being uncreated as God, nor yet created as you, but being in the middle between these two extremities, like a hostage, as it were, to both parties.—*On Who Is the Heir of Divine Things, xlii.*

For the divisions into two equal parts which have been mentioned become six in number, since three animals were divided (from three), so that the Word which divided them made up the number seven, dividing the two triads, and establishing itself between them. And a thing very like this appears to me to be very clearly shown in the matter of the candelabrum that was sacred; for that also was made having six branches, three on each side, and the main candlestick itself in the middle made the seventh, dividing and separating the two triads . . . . For the unit, being one and single and pure, begat the number seven, which had no mother, but is born of itself alone.

Concerning the candelabrum . . . . from its branches respectively three arms project on each side of it, each the same in all respects as the others, and having on their upper extremities lamps like nuts, in the shape of flowers supporting the lights, the seventh flower being fashioned on the top of the candelabrum, of solid gold, and the flowers having seven places of gold on the upper part, to hold the lights; so that in many accounts it has been believed to be so fashioned because the number six is divided into two triads by the Word, which makes the seventh, and is between them . . . .

The sacred candelabrum and the seven lights upon it are an imitation of the journeying of the seven planets through the heavens . . . . Brilliant beyond them all is he who is the central light of the seven, the sun . . . . There is an equal number of planets below him and above him. Those above him are Saturn, Jupiter and Mars; then comes the Sun himself, and next to him Mercury, Venus and the Moon, which last is close to our atmosphere. The Creator, therefore, wishing that there should be a model, on earth among us, of the seven-lighted sphere, as it exists in the heavens, ordained the making of this exquisite work, the candelabrum. And its likeness to the soul is often pointed out also; for the soul is divisible into three parts, and each of the parts, as has been already pointed out, is divided into two more. And thus there being six divisions, the sacred and divine Word, the divider of them all, naturally makes up the number seven. —*On Who Is the Heir of Divine Things, xlv.*

Therefore the two natures are indivisible; the nature, I mean, of the reasoning power in us, and of the Divine Word above us; but though they are themselves indivisible, they divide an innumerable multitude of other things. For it is the Divine Word, which divided and distributed everything in Nature; and it is our own mind which divides everything and everybody which it comprehends, into an infinity of parts, by the exertion in an infinite manner of its intellect; and which, in fact, never ceases distinguishing . . . . So that the two things which thus resemble each other, the mind within us and that above us, being without parts and indivisible, can still potently divide and distinguish all existing things.—*Id., xlviii.*

This difficult and scarcely explicable perplexity we may escape, if we adopt the esoteric and allegorical explanation, that accords with natural philosophy. For we say that the High Priest is not a man, but is the Word of God . . . . God being his Father, who is also the Father of all things, and Wisdom being his mother, by means of whom the Universe came to be created . . . .

And the most ancient Word of the living God is clothed with the world as with a garment, for it has put on earthiness and water and air and fire, and the things that proceed from those elements. But the particular soul is clothed with the body, and the mind of the wise man is clothed with the virtues . . . . The Word of the living God being the bond of everything, holds all things together, and binds all the parts, and prevents them from being loosened or separated.—*On Fugitives, xx.*

We must now proceed to mention what these cities are, and why they are six in number. Perhaps we may say that the most ancient and the strong-est, and the most excellent metropolis, for I may not call it merely a city, is the divine Word, to flee whereto first is the most advantageous course of all. But the other five, being, as it were, colonies of that one, are the potencies of him who utters the Word; the chief of which is His Creative Power, by the exercise whereof the Creator made the world with a Word. The second is His Royal Power, by the exercise of which he has made laws to govern what he has created. The third is His Merciful Power, exercising which, 'the Creator pities and shows mercy towards his own work: the fourth is His Legislative Power, by which he prohibits what ought not to be done.

The images of the cities of command and prohibition are the laws in the ark; that of the Merciful Potency of God is the covering of the ark, and he calls it the Mercy-Seat. The images of the Creative Potency and of the Royal Power are the winged Cherubim that are upon it. But the Divine Word, which is above these does not come into any visible appearance, inasmuch as it is not like unto any of the things that are cognizable by the external senses, but is itself an image of God, the most ancient of all the objects of intellect of the whole world, and that which is nearest unto the only truly existing God, without any separation or distance being interposed between them . . . . So that the Word is, as it were, the charioteer of the Potencies, and he who utters it is the rider, who directs the charioteer how to proceed with a view to the proper guidance of the universe.—*On Fugitives, xviii, xix.*

His Word, which is his interpreter, will teach me.—*On the Change of Scripture Names, iii.*

When he has arrived at the external sense, he is represented no longer as meeting God, but only the Divine Word, as his grandfather Abraham, the model of wisdom, did.—*On Dreams Being Sent from God, xii.*

He has shown the similitude of the soul (to God), in another passage . . . .
But the likeness of the sun he only indicates by symbols. And it is easy
otherwise, by means of argument, to perceive this, since God is the first
light . . . . and not only the light, but he is the archetypal pattern of
every other light, or rather, he is more ancient and higher than even the
archetypal model, though he is spoken of as the model; for the real model
was his own most perfect Word, the light, and he, himself, is like to no
created thing.—*Id., xiii.*

When he speaks of the sun, he means the Divine Word, the model of
that sun which moves about through the heavens . . . . For the Word of
God, when it reaches to our earthly constitution, assists and protects those
who are akin to virtue, or whose inclinations lead them to virtue, so that it
provides them with a complete refuge and salvation, but upon their enemies
it sends irremediable overthrow and destruction.—*Id., xv.*

There are, as it seems, two temples belonging to God; one being this
world, in which the High Priest is the divine Word, his own First-born Son.
The other is the rational soul, the priest of which is the real true man.
—*Id., xxxvii.*

All immutability and stableness and the abiding forever in the same
place, unchangeably and immovably, is first of all seen in the living God,
and next in the Word of the living God, which he has called his Covenant.
—*Id., xxxv.*

And the Divine Word, like a river, flows forth from wisdom as from a
spring, to irrigate and make fruitful the celestial and heavenly shoots and
plants of such souls as love virtue, as if they were a paradise, and this sacred
Word is divided into four beginnings, by which I mean it is patterned out
into four virtues.—*Id., xxxvii.*

The Divine Word is full of the streams of wisdom, and has no part of
itself empty or desolate, or rather, as someone has said, which is diffused
everywhere over the universe, and is raised up on high, on account of the
continued and incessant rapidity of that ever-flowing spring.—*Id., xxxviii.*

Now, the image of God is the Word, by which all the world was
made.—*On Monarchy, v.*

For it was indispensable that the man who was consecrated to the
Father of the world, should have as a Paraclete, his Son, the being most
perfect in all virtue, to procure forgiveness of sins, and a supply of unlimited blessings.—*On the Life of Moses, xiv.*

Moses has not spoken of the rational soul as it resembled in its kind any
created thing, but he has called it the Image of the Divine and Invisible God,
looking upon it to be a glorious and carefully wrought image, the seal of God,
the character of which is the everlasting Word.—*On the World, iii.*

"For," says he, "I will speak to you from above the Mercy-Seat, in the midst, between the two Cherubims": that he might show that the Most Ancient Powers [the first emanations] of the God that is Existence are equal, that is to say, his beneficent and his chastising Power [Khased or Gedulah, Benignity, and Geburah, Severity; the fourth and fifth Sephiroth of the Kabbalah], being separated from each other by the separating Logos. —*On Who Is the Heir of Divine Things, xxiv.*

When the soul is shone upon by God as if at noonday, and when it is wholly and entirely filled with that light which is appreciable only by the intellect, and by being wholly surrounded with its brilliancy is free from all shadow or darkness, it then perceives a three-fold image of one subject, one image of the living God, and others of the other two, as if they were shadows irradiated by it. The one in the middle is the Father of the universe, who in the sacred writings is called by his proper name, "*I AM THAT I AM*": and the beings on either side are those most ancient Powers which are always close to the living God, one of which is called His Creative Power, and the other His Regal Power.

And the Creative Power is God; for it is by this that he made and arranged the universe, and the Regal Power is the Lord; for it is fitting that · the Creator should lord it over and govern the creature. Therefore the middle person of the three, being attended by each of his Powers as by body-guards, presents to the mind endowed with the faculty of sight, a vision at one time of one being, and at another time of three.—*On Abraham, xxiv.*

The fact of having been created implies a liability to destruction, even though the thing created may be made immortal by the providence of the Creator; and there was a time once when it had no existence, but it is impiety to say that there was a previous time when God did not exist, and that he was born at some time, and that he does not endure forever.—*On the Ten Commandments, xii.*

That everlasting and invisible Being who can be comprehended, appreciated, by the mind alone; who is not only the God of all Gods, whether appreciable only by the intellect, or visible to the outward senses, but is also the Creator of them all.—*On Monarchy, ii.*

There is another meaning figuratively concealed under the enigmatical expressions, and the words employed are visible symbols of what is invisible and uncertain.—*On Animals Fit for Sacrifice, v.*

Some are verbal symbols of things appreciable only by the intellect, and the mystical meaning which is concealed beneath them must be investigated by those who are eager for truth, in accordance with the rules of allegory. —*On Those Who Offer Sacrifice, v.*

Why then does he use the expression, "in the image of God I made man," as if he were speaking of that of some other God, and not of having made him in the likeness of himself? This expression is used with great beauty and wisdom. For it was impossible that anything mortal should be made in the likeness of the Most High God, the Father of the universe, but it could only be made in the likeness of the Second God, who is the Word of the other; for it was fitting that the rational type in the soul of man should receive the impression of the Word of God, since the God below the Word is superior to all and every rational Nature; and it is not lawful for any created thing to be made like the God who is above reason, and who is endowed with a most excellent and special form belonging to himself alone. —*Fragment: Eusebius Præp. Evan. B. viii, Ch. 13.*

The eye of the living God does not need any other light, to enable him to perceive things, but being himself Archetypal Light, he pours forth innumerable rays, not one of which is capable of being comprehended by the outward sense, but they are all only intelligible to the intellect; in consequence of which God alone uses them, who is only comprehensible to the intellect, and nothing that has any portion in creation uses them at all; for that which has been created is perceptible to the outward senses, but that Nature which is only susceptible to the intellect cannot be comprehended by the outward sense.—*On Cain and His Birth, xxviii.*

The light perceptible by the outward senses is a created light: and even before the creation, God saw, using himself as light.—*On the Unchangeableness of God, xii.*

As the sun, when he has arisen, hides the stars, pouring forth his own light altogether over our light, so also when the beams of the Light-giving God, immingled as they are, and entirely pure, and visible at the greatest distance, shone upon the eye of the soul, being comprehensible only by the intellect, then the eye of the soul can see nothing else.—*On Drunkenness, xi.*

When you hear it said that God has been seen by man, you must consider that this is said without any reference to that light which is perceptible by the external senses, for it is natural that that which is appreciable only by the intellect should be presented to the intellect alone, and the fountain of the purest Light is God; so that, when God appears to the soul, he pours forth his beams without any shadow, and beaming with the most radiant brilliancy.—*On the Change of Scripture Names, i.*

The divine Light, which is in no respect different from knowledge, which opens the eye of the soul . . . . It is owing to Wisdom, that what is wise is contemplated; but not only is Wisdom *like* Light, the instrument of seeing; but it also beholds itself. This, in God, is the Light which is the archetypal model of the sun, and the sun itself is only its image and copy: and he who shows all things is the only all-knowing being, God.—*On the Migration of Abraham, viii.*

Under the symbol of the sun, he intimates our mind; for what reasoning is in us, that the sun is in the world.   Since each of them gives light; the one casting a light which is perceptible by the external senses, to shine upon the universe; and the other shedding their beams, discernible only by the intellect, by means of our apprehensions, upon ourselves . . . . When the divine Light shines, the human Light sets; and when the divine Light sets, this other rises and shines . . . . for the mind that is in us is expelled at the incoming of the divine Spirit, but is restored to its former habitation, when that Spirit departs; for it is contrary to holy law for what is mortal to dwell with what is immortal.—*On Who Is the Heir of Divine Things, liii.*

He to whom all things are known, who illuminates the universe by the most brilliant of all lights, himself.—*On Fugitives, xxiv.*

Those who seemed to philosophize in the most excellent manner, said that from the world and from its several parts, and from the powers which existed in those parts, we formed our notions of the Creator and Cause of the world . . . . They, then, who draw their conclusions in this manner, perceive God in his shadow, arriving at a due comprehension of the artist through his works.

There is also a more perfect and more highly purified kind, which has been initiated into the great Mysteries, and which does not distinguish the Cause from the things created, as it would distinguish an abiding body from a shadow; but which, having emerged from all created objects, receives a clear and manifest notion of the Great Uncreated, so that it comprehends him through himself, and comprehends his shadow, too, so as to understand what it is, and his reason, too, and this Universal World . . . . For the images which are presented to the sight in executed things are subject to dissolution; but those which are presented in the One Uncreated may last forever, being durable, eternal and unchangeable.—*On the Allegories of the Sacred Laws, xxxii., xxxiii.*

At all events, he will now penetrate into "the darkness where God was." That is to say, unto these unapproachable and invisible conceptions which are formed of the living God.   For the Great Cause of all things does not exist in time, nor at all in place, but is superior to both time and place; for, having made all created things in subjection to Himself, He is surrounded by (included in) nothing, but is superior to everything.   And being superior to, and also external to, the World that he has made, he nevertheless fills the whole world with himself; for, having by his own power extended it to its utmost limit, he has connected every portion with another portion, ac-

When therefore the soul that loves God seeks to know what the one living God is, according to his essence, it is entering upon an obscure and dark subject of investigation, from which the greatest benefit that arises to it is, to comprehend that God, as to his essence, is utterly incomprehensible to any being; and also to be aware that he is invisible. And it appears to me that the Great Hierophant (Moses) had attained to the comprehension of the most important points in this investigation, before be commenced it, when he entreated God to become the exhibitor and expounder of his own Nature to him; for he says, "Show me thyself." Showing very plainly by this expression that no created being is competent by himself to learn the Nature of God in his essence.—*On the Posterity of Cain, v.*

For as long as the pure rays of wisdom, shine forth in the soul, by means of which the wise man sees God and his powers, no one of those who bring false news ever enters into the Reason, but all such are kept at a distance, outside of the sacred threshold.—*On the Unchangeableness of God, i.*

The holy writing here indicates that it is the true God that is meant, by the use of the article, the expression being, "I am 'O Θεος *The* God": but when the word is used incorrectly, it is put without the article, the expression being, "He who was seen by thee in the place," not of *the* God (τοῦ Θεοῦ) but simply "of God" (Θεοῦ), and what he here calls God, is his most ancient Word . . . . In other passages, the sacred historian, when he considered whether there really was any name belonging to the living God, showed that he knew that there was none properly belonging to him, but that whatever appellation any one may give him, will be an abuse of terms; for Al Khi is not of a Nature to be *described*, but only to *be*.—*On Dreams Being Sent from God, xxxix.*

As those who are not able to look upon the sun itself, look upon the reflected rays of the sun as the sun itself, and upon the halo around the moon as if it were the moon itself; so also do those who are unable to bear the sight of God, look upon his image, his angel Logos, as himself.—*Id., xli.*

Do not, however, think that the living God, he who is truly living, is ever seen so as to be comprehended by any human being; for we have no power in ourselves to see anything by which we may be able to conceive any adequate notion of him . . . . and what wonder is there, if the living God is beyond the reach of the comprehension of man, when even the mind that is in each of us, is unintelligible and unknown to us? Who has ever beheld the essence of the soul?—*On the Change of Scripture Names, ii.*

God, as apprehending beforehand, as a God could not but do, that there could not exist a good imitation without a good model, and that of the things perceptible to the external senses nothing could be faultless that was not fashioned with reference to some archetypal idea conceived by the intellect, when he had determined to create this visible world, previously formed that one which is perceptible only by the intellect, in order that so using an incorporeal model formed as far as possible on the image of God, He might then make this corporeal world, a younger likeness of the elder creation, which should embrace as many different genera perceptible to the external senses, as the other world contains of those which are visible only to the intellect.—*On the Creation of the World, iv.*

And if any one were to desire to use more undisguised terms, he would not call the world, which is perceptible only to the intellect, any thing else but the Reason of God, already occupied in the creation of the world; for neither is a city, while only perceptible to the intellect, any thing else but the reason of the architect, who is already designing to build one perceptible to the external senses, on the model of that which is so only to the intellect. —*Id., vi.*

And the invisible divine Reason, perceptible only by intellect, he calls the Image of God. And the image of this image is that light, perceptible only by the intellect, which is the image of the divine Reason, which has explained its generation . . . . If anyone were to call it Universal Light, he would not be very wrong, since it is from it that the sun and the moon and all the other planets and fixed stars derive their one light, in proportion as each has power given to it; that unmingled and pure light being obscured when it begins to change, according to the change from that which is perceptible by the intellect only, to that which is perceptible by the external senses.—*Id., viii.*

God is not as man, but neither is he as heaven, nor as the world; for these species are endued with distinctive qualities, and they come under the perception of the outward senses. But he is not even comprehensible by the intellect, except merely as to his essence; for his existence, indeed, is a fact which we do comprehend concerning him, but beyond the fact of his existence, we can comprehend nothing.—*On the Unchangeableness of God, xiii.*

· For God is not as man, but the reason why we at times represent him as such, for the sake of instruction, is because we are unable to advance out of ourselves, but derive our apprehension of the uncreated God from the circumstances with which we are surrounded.—*On the Confusion of Languages, xxi.*

It was quite consistent with reason, that no proper name could with propriety be assigned to him who is in Very Truth the living God. . . . . To the prophet . . . . who asks what answer he is to give to those who question him as to the name of him who has sent him, he says, "*Ahih asar Ahih*" (I am that which I am): which is equivalent to saying, "It is my nature to Be, not to be described by name": but in order that the human race may not be wholly without any appellation to give to the Most Excelling of All

Existences I allow you to use the word *Jod He Vav He* as a name, the *Ihuh Alohim* of three natures, of instruction and of holiness and of the practice of virtue; of which Abraham and Isaac and Jacob are recorded as the symbols. For this, he says, is the everlasting name . . . . and the sacred oracle which is delivered as from the mouth of the Ruler of the universe, speaks of the proper name of God never having been revealed to any one . . . . and indeed the living God (Al Khi) is so completely indescribable, that even those powers which minister unto him do not announce his proper name to us . . . . He does not tell him his peculiar and proper name, for, he says, it is enough for thee to be informed of the ordinary words that endeavor to give an idea of me. But as for names which are the symbols of created things, do not seek to find *them* among immortal natures.

Therefore do not doubt, either, whether that which is more ancient than any existing thing (the senior seniorum, of the Adra Raba), when his Very Logos is not mentionable by us, by his proper name. So that we must understand that the expression "IHUH was seen by Abraham" has not the meaning that the Cause of all things shone forth and became visible (for what human mind has capacity to contain the magnitude of his revealment?). but that some one of the potencies that are about him, viz., his Regal Potency, became an object of the sight; for the appellation, Lord, belongs to authority and sovereignty. (The Regal Potency is the tenth Emanation of the Kabbalah, Malakoth, Regnum.)—*On the Change of Scripture Names, ii., iii.*

The third law is one about the Name of the Lord, not about that name which has not yet reached his creatures; for that name is ineffable; but about the Name which is constantly applied to him as displayed in his powers; for it is commanded that we shall not take his Name in vain.—*On Who Is the Heir of Divine Things, xxxv.*

It told me that in the one living and true God there were two supreme and primary potencies, Goodness and Authority; and that by his Goodness he had created every thing, and by his Authority he governed all that he had created; and that the third thing which was between the two, and had the effect of bringing them together, was Reason, for that it was owing to Reason that God was both a Ruler and Good.—*On the Cherubim, &c. ix.*

The living God, who is superior to the Good, and more simple than the One, and more ancient than the Unit.—*On a Contemplative Life, i.*

God, being one being, has two Supreme Powers, of the greatest import-ance. By means of these Powers, the incorporeal world, appreciable only by the intellect, was put together, which is the archetypal model of this world which is visible to us, being formed in such a manner as to be percep-tible to our invisible conceptions just as the other is to our eyes.—*On the World, i.*

I, consisting of soul and body, and appearing to have a mind, and reason, and outward sense, find that not one of all these things is my own property. For where was my body before my birth? and where will it go, when I am departed? And what becomes of the differences of age of that being which at present appears to exist? Where is now the infant? where the child? where the boy? where the youth just arriving at the age of puberty? where the young man? where is he now, whose beard is just budding, the vigorous and perfect man? Whence came the soul, and whither will it go? and how long will it remain with us? and what is its essence, or what may we speak of as such? Moreover, when did we acquire it? Was it before our birth? But then we ourselves did not exist. Shall we have it after our death? But then *we* shall not exist, we, who are now a combination of distinctive qualities in combination with our bodies; but rather we shall then be hastening to a regeneration, becoming in combination with incorporeal beings; and now, when we are alive, we are governed rather than governing, and we are understood ourselves, rather than understanding anything else; for our soul understands us, without being understood by us, and it imposes commands upon us which we are necessitated to obey, as servants are compelled to obey a mistress; and whenever it chooses to abandon us and to depart to the Ruler of all things, it will depart, leaving our house destitute of life. And even if we attempt to compel it to remain, it will disappear; for its nature is composed of unsubstantial parts, such as afford no handle to the body.—*Of Cain and His Birth, xxxii.*

INDEX

Abraham, date of... 1
Açvinau..151–158
Açvinau, heliacal rising of....................................... 8
Açvins—Twin Horsemen.. 6
Aeshma.. 255
Affront.. 45
Agni...74, 81–91
Agni was fire.. 73
Agriculture equal to worship and devotion......................... 19
Ahriman... 284
Ahura Mazda...231–244
Ahura Mazda contains in himself Infinite Wisdom................... 77
Ahura Mazda is our God... 203
Akem-Manô... 285
Akô-Manô.. 253
Aldebarân.. 6
Alexander the Great.. 16
Alexander the Great, date of..................................... 200
Amĕrĕtât..251–252
Amĕsha-Çpĕntas...235–237
Ancestors, our Aryan, were not barbarians......................... 2
Ancient and modern languages, relationship of..................... 47
Ancient Aryans, belief in efficacy of prayer by.................... 27
Ancient Aryans, gambling denounced among......................... 28
Ancient Aryans, medicine and surgery among....................... 27
Andar.. 253
Animosity... 46
Anquetil du Perron..195–196
Añra... 239
Añra-Mainyus... 234
Apaôshô.. 259
Arabs—Semitics.. 2
Aral, Sea of... 1
Ardeshir Babegan... 194
Ardvîçûra..266–267,312
Ardvîçûra, Irano-Aryan River Goddess............................. 15
Arstât..256–257
Ârya, dates of... 1
Aryaman..130–135
Aryan civilization, original seat of............................... 19
Aryan countries only ones created by Ahura Mazda.................. 3
Aryan language, mother of.. 1
Aryan languages...34–70
Aryan languages not related to Turanian or Semitic................ 3
Aryan languages, the various..................................... 49
Aryan laws.. 25
Aryan race, chronology of.. 1
Aryan race, origin of.. 14

Aryans, ancestors of Greeks and Romans.................................... 1
Aryans, ancient, nature and life of.. 23
Aryans, Indo- and Irano-.. 2
Aryans, previous writers on.. 2
Aryans, primitive, choice of supreme chief.................................. 13
Aryans, we are descendants of.. 1
Aryans were white... 1
Asgard.. 197
Asha-Vahista...209, 244–246
Ashis-Vanuhi.. 257
Atharva-Veda.. 46
Avesta and Zend.. 193
Azhi Dahaka.. 305

Bactrian language older than the Vedic Sanskrit............................. 192
Balkh..18, 311
Behistun.. 6
Behistun, Rawlinson's translation.. 196
Bhaga.. 145
Bible, the, and the Zend-Avesta.. 225
Bokhara..16–17
Bolor Tagh Mountains.. 4
Brahmaṇaspati.. 99
Bridge of the Gatherer..281–282
Bṛihaspati 99
Burnouf.. 196

Cabul, west of the Punjab... 22
Canaanites were Semitics.. 2
Candor.. 45
Çaöshyanç.. 300
Caspian Sea, area of.. 22
Castor and Pollux...6, 7, 151–158
Çaurva... 253
Chaldeans—Semitics 2
Charity and liberality inculcated 26
Chinese and Egyptians are Turanians...................................... 2
Chinvaṭ, the Bridge..281–282, 294
Christianity is Aryan.. 69
Comparative period of Vedas.. 39
Çpĕnta... 238
Çpĕnta-Armaiti...249–250
Çpĕnta-Mainyu...239–242, 283–286
Çraddhâ...99, 210
Çraddhâ and Çrăosha... 313
Çraŏsha...210, 254–255
Creation by God.. 291
Creation of countries, order of... 4
Creed, each, the development of an original creed.......................... 21
Cyrus—Kuros... 33

Daeva and Deva.. 308
Dahaka.. 308
Dasyus, the native tribes.. 18
Deities of the Veda..71–105
Deities of the Veda were mere names... 74
Deity, our conception of the Aryan.. 69
Drukhs...217, 287, 301
Dualism of the Deity.. 284
du Perron's Zend-Avesta... 198
Dyu, the Sky... 43

Egyptians and Chinese not Aryans nor Semitics, but Turanians.................... 2
English words, examples of ancient meanings of.............................45–46
Equinoxes, precession of... 157
Eternity of existence is self-existence....................................... 76
Exodus from Egypt, date of.. 35
"Ex Oriente Lux"... 229

Family relations, words for...50–52
Few Deities are common to Veda and Zend..................................... 19

Ganges.. 175
Garô-Nemâna, the "mountain of worship"...................................42, 247
Gâthâs..203–209
Gâthâs, authorship of.. 204
Gâthâs composed in Bactria.. 9
Gâthâs, divisions of..204–205
Gâthâs, Fargards and Vendidad.. 3
Gâthâs older than Vedas... 6
Gâthâs, oldest part of the Zend.. 192
Gâthâs, translations of...206–208
Genesis, Book of... 55
Gêus Urvâ...212–213
God, and the Word (Logos)...321–322
Gods, identity of...202–203
Grammar, comparative, Bopp.. 50
Gushtasp.. 268

Haôma... 308
Haôma exhilarated the Gods... 73
Haôma first offered by Yima.. 12
Hapta Hendu—Punjab.. 4
Harkness, Professor William... 8
Haug, Professor... 196
Haurvât..251–252
Hebrews learned their religion at Babylon.................................... 76
Hebrews are Semitics... 2
Hindûs in the Punjab 4,000 years before our era............................. 21
Homer, date of.. 150
Human intellect and divine.. 291
Hutaôça...308–309
Huzvaresh, the.. 192

Idiot.. 45
Immortality of the soul learned by the Hebrews at Babylon...................... 76
Indo- and Irano- separation... 197
Indo-Aryans, life of.. 24
Indo-Aryans, occupations of... 29
Indo-Aryans of Punjab did not amalgamate with native tribes.................... 42
Indra...92–102
Indra, the Light.. 103
Indus country, seven rivers of... 22
Indus—Hydaspes.. 4
Irano-Aryans, life of.. 24
Irano-Aryans, where first settled.. 11
Izeds.. 260

Just... 46

Kabbalah, the..96–97
Kabul... 311
Karshipta... 250
Kĕrĕçâçpa.. 13
Khshathra Vairya...246–248

Lake Aral, sources of... 15
Language, our, derived from Aryans.. 1
Language, our, derived from one original Aryan language......................... 34
Lectures, authorship of these... 2
Lectures, scope of these.. 2
Legislation and laws... 30
Libel.. 45
Logos, the... 78

Maruts...121–123
Maruts were the winds... 73
Mazanian Daevas... 307
Medes... 191
Meliton...286–287
"Melting Pot" was written before Zangwill was born............................69–70
Menes, date of.. 1
Migration, first Aryan, 10000 B.C... 5
Migration of Aryans to Europe... 14
Migration, the Celtic earlier than the Gothic and Sclavic....................... 36
Migrations, later, caused composite languages................................... 41
Migrations opposed by aboriginal races.. 41
Migrations proven by philology.. 5
Mithra...261–263
Mitra..130–135
Muir, Dr.. 196

Nâonhaiti... 253
Nâsatyas.. 145
Nervous... 45
Nimrod, date of... 1
Nuisance.. 45

Orientalists, some.. 2
Oxus River...14–16

Pârendi.. 260
Parjanya...164–165
Paropamisus.. 1
Pehlevi 192
Philo Judæus, Aryan notions of 317–332
Philology proves migrations... 5
Phœnicians are Semitics... 2
Physicians and surgeons, Irano-Aryan....................................... 27
Planets and stars, adoration of..149–158
Plato's date..8–9, 200
Prajâpati.. 182
Prayer and its efficacy... 314
Pre-Aryan races.. 48
Priçni... 149
Primitive language from which Zend and Sanskrit were formed.................. 13
Prithivi... 107
Punjab (a Persian word meaning "five waters") is a plain.................... 21
Punjab invaded by Alexander the Great 937 B.C.............................. 22
Punjab is between 30° and 35° N. Lat....................................... 21
Punjab is 400 miles from north to south and 350 miles from east to west 21
Purusha Sûkta...175–181
Pushan..135–140

Raghâ...311–312
Rashnu..256–257
Rask, Professor.. 196
Reason, man's, of divine origin... 297
Regard.. 45
Religion, basis of.. 292
Respect... 45
Respectable 45
Ribhus..161–164
Rig-Veda, age of...3, 5
Rig-Veda, when compiled... 6
Right... 46
Rishis were sages or poets... 43
Rudra...147–149

Samarkand... 16
Sanskrit and Zend.. 5
Sanskrit and Zend formed from one original language........................ 21
Sanskrit not the mother of Zend.. 197
Saramâ..78, 166–172
Saranyû...123–124
Sarasvatî, the River-Goddess of the Veda..........................15, 172–174
Savitri...141–145
Semitic races not our ancestors.. 2
Semitic words all derived from triliteral roots.............................. 2

Seven, sanctity of the number 39
Sogdiana.. 1
Soma...159–162
Soma exhilarated the Gods 73
Sophist... 46
Soul, abode of, after death...315–316
Soul and spirit, the... 314
Spiegel, Professor.. 196
Spiegel, Professor, translation of Zend... 199
Spirit, abode of, after death...315–316
Spirit and soul, the... 314
Sûrya was the Sun.. .73

Tales and fables...66–67
Taura... 253
Thraêtaöna...13, 310
Thrita...303–306
Tistrya... 263
Toorkhistan... 1, 4
Toorkhistan northwest of Punjab... 22
Tvashṭri...120–123
Twin Horsemen..151–158

Umbrage.. 45
Universe created.. 292
Upper Oxus climate... 11
Ushas..127–139
Ushas was the Dawn... 73
Ustvaiti.. 270

Vahistoisti Gâthâ.. 295
Vaiçvânara..86–87
Vajata...260–261
Valley of Cashmere in Punjab... 21
Vara.. 311
Varenian Daevas... 307
Varuṇa...130–135
Vâta.. 164
Vayu...116–119
Veda, the...34–70
Veda and Zend-Avesta... 198
Veda and Zend-Avesta, few Deities are common to.................................. 20
Vedas..18–33
Vedas, date shown by astronomy... 6
Vedas, comparative period of... 39
Vedas compiled 1200 B.C.. 35
Vedas composed between 4500 and 5000 B.C... 7
Vedas, date... 200
Vedas, difficult of translation.. 44
Vedic and Ahurian faiths.. 313
Vedic Deities..147–164

Vedic faith and worship very ancient.. 19
Vedic hymns composed by the ancient Rishis.................................. 22
Vedic hymns composed in Punjab... 40
Vedic hymns, date of... 200
Vedic hymns, when composed.. 30
Vedic hymns, where composed... 18
Vendidad.. 192
Vendidad, second Fargard of... 9
Vendidad, Fargards, and Gâthâs... 3
Vernal equinox... 156
Vishṇu..106–116
Vishṇu and Indra..112–115
Vishṇu, three steps of...108–109
Vispered, the.. 192
Vistâçpa...309–310
Vistâçpa-Gushtasp.. 32
Vohu-Manô..209, 241–242
Vouru-kasha... 311

Westergaard... 196
Wits.. 46
Words, derivations of Aryan.. 2
Words, comparative philology of..50–62
Words, vitality of... 48

Yama deified.. 14
Yama, first mortal to die.. 14
Yashts, the... 192
Yima...10, 12, 13, 301–303, 305
Yima (as Yama)...13, 14
Yima the oldest historical name of our race................................. 13
Yima never deified... 14
Yima, settlement of.. 11
Yima, son of Vivanhao.. 13
Yima-Yemshid.. 9
Yima's "Circle"... 23
Yumna... 175

Zairica...253–254
Zamyad-Yasht.. 310
Zangwill's "Melting Pot".. 69
Zarathustra, a soldier and king.. 10
Zarathustra became monarch..23–24
Zarathustra composed the Gâthâs... 193
Zarathustra, date of..8–9, 200
Zarathustra, doctrine of..191–229, 296
Zarathustrians not Fire-Worshippers....................................... 203
Zend alphabet of Semitic origin... 195
Zend and Sanskrit are sister languages.................................... 303
Zend and Sanskrit languages, separation of................................312–313
Zend-Avesta... 3

Zend-Avesta, age of.. 3
Zend-Avesta and the Bible.. 219
Zend-Avesta, Bactrian.. 5
Zend-Avesta became a dead language.. 6
Zend-Avesta-English dictionary, none.. 198
Zend-Avesta grammar, none.. 198
Zend-Avesta older than Sanskrit... 6
Zend-Avesta older than the Veda.. 201
Zend-Avesta preserved through Sanskrit.. 194
Zend-Avesta written from right to left.. 192
Zend-Avesta, written text of, age of.. 194

Lightning Source UK Ltd.
Milton Keynes UK
UKHW022124151222
414018UK00006B/20